MW00618768

Developing a Schoolwide Framework
to Prevent and Manage
Learning and Behavior Problems

Also Available

Managing Challenging Behaviors in Schools:
Research-Based Strategies That Work

Kathleen Lynne Lane, Holly Mariah Menzies,
Allison L. Bruhn, and Mary Crnobori

Supporting Behavior for School Success:
A Step-by-Step Guide to Key Strategies

Kathleen Lynne Lane, Holly Mariah Menzies,
Robin Parks Ennis, and Wendy Peia Oakes

Systematic Screenings of Behavior to Support Instruction:
From Preschool to High School

Kathleen Lynne Lane, Holly Mariah Menzies,
Wendy Peia Oakes, and Jemma Robertson Kalberg

Developing a Schoolwide Framework to Prevent and Manage Learning and Behavior Problems

SECOND EDITION

Kathleen Lynne Lane
Holly Mariah Menzies
Wendy Peia Oakes
Jemma Robertson Kalberg

THE GUILFORD PRESS
New York   London

Copyright © 2020 The Guilford Press
A Division of Guilford Publications, Inc.
370 Seventh Avenue, Suite 1200, New York, NY 10001
www.guilford.com

All rights reserved

Except as noted, no part of this book may be reproduced, translated, stored in a retrieval system, or transmitted, in any form or by any means, electronic, mechanical, photocopying, microfilming, recording, or otherwise, without written permission from the publisher.

Printed in the United States of America

This book is printed on acid-free paper.

Last digit is print number: 9   8   7   6   5   4   3   2   1

LIMITED DUPLICATION LICENSE

These materials are intended for use only by qualified professionals.

The publisher grants to individual purchasers of this book nonassignable permission to reproduce all materials for which photocopying permission is specifically granted in a footnote. This license is limited to you, the individual purchaser, for personal use or use with students. This license does not grant the right to reproduce these materials for resale, redistribution, electronic display, or any other purposes (including but not limited to books, pamphlets, articles, video- or audiotapes, blogs, file-sharing sites, Internet or intranet sites, and handouts or slides for lectures, workshops, or webinars, whether or not a fee is charged). Permission to reproduce these materials for these and any other purposes must be obtained in writing from the Permissions Department of Guilford Publications.

Library of Congress Cataloging-in-Publication Data

Names: Lane, Kathleen L., author.
Title: Developing a schoolwide framework to prevent and manage learning and behavior problems /
    Kathleen Lynne Lane, Holly Mariah Menzies, Wendy Peia Oakes, Jemma Robertson Kalberg.
Other titles: Developing schoolwide programs to prevent and manage problem behaviors
Description: Second Edition. | New York : The Guilford Press, [2020] | First edition: 2009. |
    Includes bibliographical references and index.
Identifiers: LCCN 2019019779| ISBN 9781462541737 (paperback : acid-free paper) |
    ISBN 9781462541744 (hardcover : acid-free paper)
Subjects: LCSH: Problem children—Education—United States. | Behavior disorders in children—
    United States—Prevention. | Problem children—Behavior modification—United States. | School
    improvement programs—United States.
Classification: LCC LC4802 .L36 2019 | DDC 371.93—dc23
LC record available at *https://lccn.loc.gov/2019019779*

To the people who continue to inspire me:

> *To my family—I am thankful you are each pursuing what makes you happy.*

>> *Katie, I admire your passion for special education and commitment to fitness.*

>> *Nathan, I admire your passion for statistics and love of college teaching.*

>> *Craig, I admire your passion for supporting people in buying homes at each stage of their lives and your commitment to our family.*

>> *. . . Thanks to each of you for staying close and keeping our family a priority through the years and across the miles. I love everything about you—100%.*

> *To my father, Charles James Fanning II—thank you for giving me enough.*

> *To my grandfather, Dr. William Paul Frank—I miss you every day.*

> *To my professors, colleagues, project directors, research assistants, administrators, teachers, staff, parents, and students—thank you for teaching me through all the years.*

Constantly humbled,

—K. L. L.

To my brother, Scott, one of the most talented special education teachers I know; my sister-in-law, Eva, an amazing teacher of children and adults alike; and my daughter, Lucia, who has proven to be gifted and capable right from the start of her career as an educator.

—H. M. M.

To the students who challenged me most: thank you for everything you taught me.

To the new teachers going out into the field each year: thank you for your commitment to making a positive difference in the lives of young children and their families.

To Dan, Abby, and Katie: thank you for your constant support and for being a champion for teachers and children in your own ways.

—W. P. O.

To Maisie, Lachlan, and Aulay for putting up with an overcommitted mom.

To Leif for moving me halfway across the world in the name of adventure.

To GG for being my sunshine.

—J. R. K.

About the Authors

Kathleen Lynne Lane, PhD, BCBA-D, is Professor in the Department of Special Education and Interim Associate Vice Chancellor for Research at the University of Kansas. She worked as a classroom teacher of general and special education students for 5 years. Dr. Lane's research interests focus on designing, implementing, and evaluating comprehensive, integrated, three-tiered (Ci3T) models of prevention. She is President Elect of the Division for Research of the Council for Exceptional Children. Dr. Lane is coeditor of *Remedial and Special Education* and the *Journal of Positive Behavior Interventions* and has published over 190 refereed journal articles. She is coauthor of books including *Supporting Behavior for School Success: A Step-by-Step Guide to Key Strategies*; *Systematic Screenings of Behavior to Support Instruction: From Preschool to High School*; and *Managing Challenging Behaviors in Schools: Research-Based Strategies That Work*.

Holly Mariah Menzies, PhD, is Professor in the Charter College of Education at California State University, Los Angeles. She worked as both a general educator and special educator for over 10 years. Dr. Menzies has provided staff development in the areas of assessment, language arts, and schoolwide positive behavior support. Her scholarly interests include inclusive education and the role of reform in curricular practices. Dr. Menzies is coauthor (with Kathleen Lynne Lane and associates) of *Supporting Behavior for School Success: A Step-by-Step Guide to Key Strategies*; *Systematic Screenings of Behavior to Support Instruction: From Preschool to High School*; and *Managing Challenging Behaviors in Schools: Research-Based Strategies That Work*.

Wendy Peia Oakes, PhD, is Associate Professor in the Mary Lou Fulton Teachers College at Arizona State University. She worked as a special educator for 13 years. Dr. Oakes's work focuses on practices that improve educational access and outcomes for young children with and at risk for emotional and behavioral disorders, including the use of Ci3T models of prevention.

She serves as an associate editor of *Behavioral Disorders* and *Remedial and Special Education,* and as coeditor of an annual special issue of *Education and Treatment of Children.* Dr. Oakes is coauthor (with Kathleen Lynne Lane and associates) of *Supporting Behavior for School Success: A Step-by-Step Guide to Key Strategies* and *Systematic Screenings of Behavior to Support Instruction: From Preschool to High School.*

Jemma Robertson Kalberg, MEd, BCBA, is a Board Certified Behavior Analyst living in Cape Town, South Africa. She formerly conducted research on supporting students who were at risk for and identified with emotional and behavioral disorders, and was involved in designing, implementing, and evaluating schoolwide positive behavior support plans with academic, behavioral, and social components. In the context of schoolwide positive behavioral supports, Ms. Kalberg focused her efforts on using schoolwide screeners to identify students who were nonresponsive to the primary prevention model. She is coauthor (with Kathleen Lynne Lane and associates) of *Systematic Screenings of Behavior to Support Instruction: From Preschool to High School.*

Acknowledgments

We extend our sincere thanks to those gentle giants who set the foundation of our field and have shaped our thinking, the district leaders and educators who collaborated on this inquiry, the project directors and research assistants who participated in this work, our university officials who have supported our inquiry, and the personal and professional relationships that provided the foundation for this book. We have been conducting tiered interventions since 1996, and we hope this book will help shape the thinking of the next generation of educators and researchers.

We would especially like to thank Robert Rutherford for the invitation to write the first edition of this book and Rochelle Serwator for inviting this second edition. We thank Steven Driscoll and Allison Bruhn for their feedback and support during the initial writing process during the first edition and Mark Buckman for his feedback and support as we crafted this second edition.

In this edition, we have featured a few select contributions from our district partners. We thank them for sharing their lessons learned and acknowledge the thousands of other contributions made through the years by a host of talented professionals. To all of you—including those who prefer to work behind the scenes (K. H.)—it continues to be an honor to collaborate and learn with you.

With respect,
Kathleen, Holly, Wendy, and Jemma

Contents

Purchasers of this book can download and print copies of the reproducible figures
at *www.guilford.com/lane-forms* for personal use or use with students
(see copyright page for details).

PART I

An Introduction to Comprehensive, Integrated, Three-Tiered Models of Prevention

Since the first edition of this book was published in 2009, the use of schoolwide tiered systems of support is now widely recognized as an effective approach to improving students' educational outcomes. In this book, we explain how to design, implement, and evaluate a comprehensive, integrated, three-tiered model of prevention (Ci3T). Ci3T is a tiered model that addresses academic, behavior, and social–emotional domains of learning for a comprehensive approach to student learning and school improvement (Lane, Oakes, & Menzies, 2014).

In Chapter 1, *Preventing and Managing Learning and Behavior Challenges in Our Schools: A Comprehensive, Integrated Approach,* we discuss the importance of meeting students' multiple needs in an integrated model, with attention to academic, behavioral, and social–emotional skills sets. We explore how educators and policymakers have shifted from reactive to proactive approaches and their commitment to tiered systems of support. Then we provide a description of and rationale for Ci3T.

In Chapter 2, *A Look at Evidence Surrounding Tiered Systems,* we continue the conversation about Ci3T, providing an overview of the evidence regarding tiered systems. In this new chapter, we provide updated evidence for the effectiveness of tiered models focusing on the building blocks of Ci3T: academic (performance in reading and math), behavioral (positive behavioral interventions and supports [PBIS]), and social (social–emotional learning) domains. Then, we introduce lessons learned regarding low-intensity, teacher-delivered supports (e.g., instructional choice, opportunities to respond). We provide examples of the research on these strategies conducted within tiered systems and connect readers with recent reviews of the literature examining the methodological rigor of the studies. Next, we provide illustrations of Tier 2 and Tier 3 inquiry conducted within a Ci3T model and other tiered models of prevention, demonstrating the impact of academic, behavioral, and social supports. We share lessons learned about how teachers fare during systems change efforts as they design and implement tiered systems such as the Ci3T model. We conclude with lessons learned regarding professional learning needs with respect to comprehensive and integrated practices such as those in the Ci3T model of prevention.

CHAPTER 1

Preventing and Managing Learning and Behavior Challenges in Our Schools

A COMPREHENSIVE, INTEGRATED APPROACH

A Formidable Task

Since the first edition of this book was published in 2009, the use of schoolwide tiered systems of support is now widely recognized as an effective and responsive approach to improving students' educational outcomes. There is extensive evidence documenting how a systems approach to addressing students' multiple needs can be successfully implemented (McIntosh & Goodman, 2016). Districts across the country, including those in states such as Washington, Oregon, California, Colorado, Kansas, Missouri, Maryland, Pennsylvania, Vermont, and Florida, to name a few, have worked with researchers to investigate a wide range of issues related to schoolwide systems (Eagle, Dowd-Eagle, Snyder, & Holtzman, 2015; Lane et al., 2017). Researchers and practitioners have partnered to explore issues as diverse as how the levels of student risk shift in schools that use schoolwide systems (Lane, 2017), the role of culturally relevant practices in schoolwide positive behavioral support (Bal, Thorius, & Kozleski, 2012), and the use of data by school teams in sustaining implementation (Andreou, McIntosh, Rash, & Kahn, 2015). In addition, these partnerships have studied stakeholders' views of and participation in tiered models. This work has included not only faculty and staff members' experiences but also those of administrators (Lane, Carter, Jenkins, Magill, & Germer, 2015) and families (Weist, Garbacz, Lane, & Kincaid, 2017).

These and other lines of inquiry by practitioner–researcher partnerships have refined the design and implementation of what are now called tiered models of prevention. While substantial gains have been made as a result of these shared efforts, we believe there are still several challenges. One challenge is that students face many conditions *outside* of school that can negatively affect their ability to succeed if not provided with additional support while *in* school. We understand a teacher's primary responsibility is to ensure academic success, but we also know academic success is influenced by social–emotional well-being and meeting behavioral expectations in a range of school settings (Corcoran, Cheung, Kim, & Xie, 2018; Horner & Sugai, 2015; Leerkes, Paradise, O'Brien, Calkins, & Lange, 2008; Substance Abuse and Mental Health Services Administration [*www.samhsa.gov*]).

Addressing students' nonacademic needs (e.g., soft skills; Watson, 2015) poses significant challenges for teachers and other school personnel who may not have the training, resources, confidence, and/or time in the instructional day to do so. However, a tiered systems approach provides a structure for supporting school personnel in fostering the development of the whole child. With new understandings of how adverse childhood experiences (ACEs) (Hughes et al., 2017; Manyema, Norris, & Richter, 2018; McKelvey, McKelvey, Mesman, Whiteside-Mansell, & Bradley, 2018; Purewal Boparai et al., 2018) and mental health impact students' academic development, we can design tiered systems to support students who need more than academic attention.

Another challenge is helping teachers move from reactive to proactive classroom management and discipline systems. This requires not only a change in method but also a shift in thinking. Using proactive approaches such as positive behavioral interventions and supports (PBIS; an instructive approach to teaching expected behavior) and high-engagement teaching strategies while reducing reliance on punishment-based measures takes time and sustained effort to show results (Horner, Ward, et al., 2019). Yet, in the long term, proactive approaches deliver exponential benefits as positive, productive relationships are built between adults and students (Bernstein-Yamashiro & Noam, 2013).

Teachers have many demands on their time and often work under difficult conditions. As such, district and site leadership are crucial in providing the time, professional development, and clear commitment to implementing tiered models with proactive methods if teachers are to embrace new practices successfully (George, Cox, Minch, & Sandomierski, 2018).

In this book, we explain how to design, implement, and assess a comprehensive, integrated, three-tiered (Ci3T) model of prevention. The Ci3T model offers a system to address academic, behavioral, and social–emotional domains for a comprehensive approach to student support and school improvement (Lane, Oakes, & Menzies, 2014).

Supporting Students' Multiple Needs

From the late 1970s through the early 2000s, the research community looked carefully at the relation between academic performance and student behavior (Hinshaw, 1982). Some studies documented how student behavior improved when academic performance was strengthened, while others demonstrated it is possible to improve academic outcomes by first improving behavior (DiGangi, Maag, & Rutherford, 1991; Nelson, Benner, Lane, & Smith, 2004; Stewart, Martella, Marchand-Martella, & Benner, 2005). Some researchers argued it is necessary to intervene in both areas, while others noted how variables such as hyperactivity and inattention negatively affect student performance (Hinshaw, 1982). Now there is a consensus that regardless of the directionality of the relation between academic and behavioral performance patterns, the most important issue is meeting students' multiple needs—including social–emotional skills sets, which have long been overlooked. In fact, Michael Yudin (2014), former U.S. Assistant Secretary for Special Education and Rehabilitative Services, emphasized how educators must be committed to addressing students' behavioral and social–emotional needs if they hope to improve educational outcomes for underperforming students. He emphasized it is often students with the greatest challenges in these areas who miss the most instruction. We have wholeheartedly embraced these priorities since the late 1990s, consistently noting the importance of meeting students' multiple needs: academic, behavioral, and social–emotional (Lane, 1999; Lane & Menzies, 2002; Nelson et al., 2004).

A Look at Academic Performance

As we look at students' academic performance, few would disagree that reading is a critical skill that holds the key to unlocking other learning (Foorman, Francis, Shaywitz, Shaywitz, & Fletcher, 1997; D. Fuchs, Fuchs, & Compton, 2012; Lyon, 1996). Yet many students continue to struggle with reading skills: phonemic awareness, phonics, vocabulary, fluency, and reading comprehension. The National Assessment of Educational Progress (NAEP; National Center for Education Statistics [NCES], 2018) indicated the national percentage of students at or above the proficient level was only 35% for both fourth and eighth graders. It is not just students attending general education that are struggling. This same report suggested that very little progress has been made to improve the reading skills of students with disabilities who receive services as part of the Individuals with Disabilities Education Improvement Act (IDEIA; 2004). A recent Supreme Court case, *Endrew F. v. Douglas County School District* (2015), ruled that school districts have a responsibility to offer services to students with disabilities that ensure adequate academic progress. This is in contrast to an earlier court case, *Board of Education v. Rowley* (1982), which set a lower standard—a minimum floor of opportunity. *Rowley* required districts to provide adequate resources so that students could access education, not necessarily make meaningful educational gains. Clearly, the latest ruling will have significant consequences for districts as they decide whether their current services for students with disabilities are robust enough to meet the new standard.

Academic achievement in the United States in other core content areas is also lower than desired. For example, according to the NAEP report (NCES, 2015, 2018), average proficiency in math and science is not higher than 40% in fourth, eighth, or 12th grades (and as low as 22% average proficiency in 12th-grade science). Statistics on performance in writing are even more dismal with average proficiency in fourth, eighth, or 12th grades at about 28% (NCES, 2015). These scores are reflected in U.S. performance on the Program for International Student Assessment (PISA), which is administered every 3 years (NCES, 2015). There has been no improvement over the past two decades in math, reading, or science, and the United States ranks lower than many other economically developed countries.

Collectively, despite our very best efforts, there is work to be done to improve students' academic performance in the core content areas. To achieve this goal, we must acknowledge how students' behavioral strengths and challenges, as well as their social–emotional well-being, impact their instructional experience.

A Look at Behavioral Performance

If we were to take a picture of schools in the United States, we would see that approximately 12% of school-age youth have moderate-to-severe emotional or behavioral disorders (EBD), which includes externalizing (e.g., acting out, noncompliance) and/or internalizing (e.g., shy, anxious, socially withdrawn) behaviors (Forness, Freeman, Paparella, Kauffman, & Walker, 2012). If we include all students experiencing mild-to-severe EBD, the percentage increases to 20%. For many, these point-prevalence statistics are surprising. In the past, educators often believed students with behavior challenges did not belong in the general education community, but this is far from true. With a priority placed on inclusive programming, and the fact that less than 1% of students are served in special education in the category of emotional disturbance means most students with or at risk for EBD will be educated in the general education setting. Therefore, administrators and teachers must be prepared to meet the multiple needs of students with and at risk for EBD, whether or not they are identified for special education services.

As teachers know, students with EBD experience a host of challenges. While most often noticed for behavioral deficits and excesses, students with EBD also have academic difficulties (e.g., reading, writing, mathematics; Greenbaum et al., 1996; Landrum, Tankersley, & Kauffman, 2003; Lane, Barton-Arwood, Rogers, & Robertson, 2007; Mattison, Hooper, & Glassberg, 2002; Reid, Gonzalez, Nordness, Trout, & Epstein, 2004; Wagner & Davis, 2006). Landrum and colleagues (2003, p. 148) noted students with EBD "experience less school success than any other subgroup of students with or without disabilities." Even when students receive special education services for emotional disturbance (ED), their academic skills sets tend to remain stable over time: They typically do not improve (Lane, 2004; Mattison et al., 2002) and may even deteriorate (Nelson et al., 2004).

In the absence of effective interventions, life is challenging for these students. Furthermore, the wide range of terms used by various professionals who address their needs, for example, the mental health, research, and educational communities, often complicate the challenges (Kauffman, 2004, 2005). Consider *antisocial behavior*, which is a general term referring to the opposite of prosocial behavior; it describes a range of behaviors that each professional community refers to using different terminology. Generally, instead of positive, cooperative, and helpful, a student with antisocial behavior is one who is negative, hostile, and aggressive in his or her interactions across a range of settings (Walker, Ramsey, & Gresham, 2004). The term *antisocial behavior* refers to persistent violations of normative rules and expected behaviors (Simcha-Fagan, Langner, Gersten, & Eisenberg, 1975). Students with antisocial behavior patterns pose challenges to teachers, parents, and peers.

In turn, the psychiatric community uses terms such as *oppositional defiant disorder, conduct disorder,* and *antisocial personality disorder* (American Psychiatric Association, 2000). Antisocial behavior is a broader term than *antisocial personality disorder,* as specified in the *Diagnostic and Statistical Manual of Mental Disorders* (4th ed., text revision [DSM-IV-TR]; American Psychiatric Association, 2000). The term *antisocial personality disorder* is used by the mental health community to refer to adults with extreme patterns of highly aggressive, delinquent behaviors (Lane, Kalberg, Parks, & Carter, 2008). The research community uses terms such as *internalizing* (overcontrolled: anxious, somatic complaints, and depression) and *externalizing* (undercontrolled: delinquency [law-breaking behaviors] and aggression; Achenbach, 1991). Finally, the educational community uses the terms *emotional disturbance* (ED) and *social maladjustment*. This wide range of terminology makes it difficult to identify and support students and conduct research, and inhibits effective communication between educators and mental health professionals (Lane, 2004; Lane, Gresham, & O'Shaughnessy, 2002).

One way of ameliorating these challenges is to ensure educators have an understanding of the social–emotional needs of learners. Moving forward, we use the more global term EBD to refer to the behavioral patterns of students who experience these challenges in our educational systems.

A Look at Social–Emotional Performance

In addition to the behavioral challenges facing many students, there are broader concerns in terms of social competencies. Students with and at risk for EBD struggle interpersonally with peers and adults (e.g., Walker, Irvin, Noell, & Singer, 1992). They demonstrate high levels of aggression toward people, property, and even themselves (e.g., high-risk behaviors such as drug and alcohol abuse; Walker et al., 2004). Socially, these students struggle to interpret social situations accurately, often misinterpreting neutral social interactions as hostile (e.g., being bumped by another student while standing in the lunch line; Crick, Grotpeter, & Bigbee, 2002). During playground time, elementary school-age students with EBD demonstrate more than twice the amount of negative-aggressive behavior than do typical students (Walker, Hops, & Greenwood, 1993) even though prosocial behavior interactions tend to be comparable.

Students are unlikely to "outgrow" these social challenges without intervention. Data from the Special Education Elementary Longitudinal Study–2 (SEELS-2) and National Longitudinal Transition Study–2 (NLTS-2) indicate students with EBD continue to struggle well after they leave PreK–12 settings. For example, adults with EBD are often unemployed or underemployed, battle substance abuse, struggle interpersonally (e.g., high rates of divorce), and frequently require mental health services (e.g., Newman et al., 2011; Wagner & Davis, 2006). As a society, we simply cannot afford to ignore the academic, behavioral, and social needs of students with EBD (Lane, Royer, & Oakes, in press). Their challenges make their own lives difficult, and the impact of their behavioral manifestations make life challenging for their families, educational systems, peers, and society as a whole (Kauffman, 2004). In the most extreme cases, the impact on society is seen by shocking and tragic instances of violence in our nation's schools that have untold costs emotionally, socially, and financially (Kauffman, 2005; Lane, 2017). Although many general educators did not imagine they would have to address issues such as violence and antisocial behavior, these facts of life must be addressed by our school systems (Walker et al., 2004).

This is particularly true given the number of students who have experienced trauma. There is extensive evidence showing trauma has a severe negative impact on children, and affects not only their academic performance in school but also is correlated with negative outcomes later in life (Leerkes et al., 2008; McKelvey et al., 2018; Substance Abuse and Mental Health Services Administration [*www.samhsa.gov*]). These traumas, called adverse childhood events (ACEs), are events such as child abuse and neglect or living in families experiencing domestic violence, incarceration, mental illness, and/or substance abuse. ACEs also include family separations such as divorce. Schools have become more aware of how these events affect a child's academic performance and mental health. When schools have systems in place to address these issues, they can reduce the effects of trauma.

A Shift in Focus: Tiered Systems of Support

Fortunately, in attempting to meet students' academic, behavior, and social–emotional needs, there has been a shift away from approaching this important task as a within-child challenge where each child is treated reactively once levels of concern rise to the school's notice. Across the United States, federal, state, and local education agency leaders have moved toward the design, implementation, and evaluation of integrated systems to address all students' multiple needs proactively (Lane, Menzies, Oakes, Zorigian, & Germer, 2014; McIntosh & Goodman, 2016; Yudin, 2014). Tiered system of supports were first introduced to the educational community by Hill Walker and colleagues in 1996 in the *Journal of Emotional and Behavioral Disorders*. In their seminal article, the authors illustrated how an integrated model of universal, selected, and indicated interventions could be organized to achieve primary (Tier 1), secondary (Tier 2), and tertiary (Tier 3) prevention responses to improve outcomes in schools. This work served as the foundation for the PBIS (Sugai & Horner, 2009) model referenced in the federal special education legislation (IDEIA, 2004), currently implemented in more than 26,000 schools across the United States. This logic is evident in other tiered systems such as response to intervention (RTI; focused primarily on addressing students' academic outcomes; D. Fuchs et al., 2012), multi-tiered systems of support (MTSS; focused on addressing students' academic and behavioral outcomes; McIntosh & Goodman, 2016), the interconnected systems framework (ISF; focused on addressing students' behavioral and social–emotional outcomes; Barrett, Eber, & Weist, 2013), as well as Ci3T (focused on addressing students' academic, behavioral, and social outcomes). The Ci3T model is a systems approach for addressing students' academic, behavioral, and social needs in one coordinated model (Lane & Menzies, 2002; Lane, Oakes, Cantwell, & Royer, 2018).

Initial developmental work for Ci3T began in 1996, inspired by Hill Walker's work as presented in Walker, Colvin, and Ramsey (1995) and Walker and colleagues (1996). Thanks to a forward-thinking, solutions-based principal committed to addressing the challenges at her school site, initial development and testing of Ci3T began in one elementary school on the West Coast. With this university partnership, lessons were learned about primary prevention (Lane & Menzies, 2002, 2005), secondary prevention supporting reading (Lane, Wehby et al., 2002) and social skills (Lane, Wehby, et al., 2003), and tertiary prevention for students with intensive intervention needs (Lane, Menzies, Munton, Von Duering, & English, 2005). As part of our inquiry involving school systems from coast to coast, the model has been tested and continues to be refined in partnership with district partners (Lane, 2017).

The Ci3T model blends the principles of RTI and PBIS, and includes a commitment to students' social–emotional needs with validated programs such as Positive Action (Flay, Allred, & Ordway, 2001). Ci3T features a comprehensive, integrated, data-driven prevention model, using data-informed professional learning for faculty and staff, and data-informed decision making to support instruction for students. Specifically, Ci3T includes structures for monitoring systems-level data such as treatment integrity (Is it happening?) and social validity (Are people comfortable with the goals, procedures, and intended outcomes?), as well as student-level data (e.g., academic and behavior screenings, attendance, and office disciplinary referrals, to name a few) to determine effectiveness in meeting systems/school goals and to inform instruction for students. Schools implementing a Ci3T model collect and monitor implementation data (treatment integrity and social validity) in fall and spring of each year. These data are shared with faculty and staff to inform ongoing professional learning. At the student level, multiple sources of data are collected and analyzed on a regular schedule to determine how students are performing academically, behaviorally, and socially over time. For example, the Ci3T model uses academic and behavior screening data collected in fall, winter, and spring to (1) examine overall student performance over time within and across school years and (2) determine individual students for whom primary (Tier 1) prevention efforts are insufficient, then connecting these students to appropriate evidence-based strategies and practices at Tier 2 or Tier 3 (Cook & Tankersley, 2013). As such, two hallmark characteristics of Ci3T are using data to make decisions about professional development offerings for adults (data-informed professional learning featuring high-quality, ongoing, practice-based professional learning opportunities including coaching) and adapting instruction for students (data-informed instruction), with an emphasis on using systematic screening data (Briesch, Chafouleas, & Chaffee, 2018; Lane, Menzies, Ennis, & Oakes, 2018; Lane & Walker, 2015; Oakes, Lane, Cox, & Messenger, 2014). Many districts establish a district-level Ci3T leadership team, and each school site has a Ci3T Leadership Team. Each team includes a district coach (a point we discuss more fully in Chapter 3), who serves as a conduit for communication between district leaders and faculty and staff.

During the past two decades, our research team has had the privilege of collaborating and learning with more than 100 schools in four regions in the United States to design, implement, and evaluate the Ci3T model as an integrated framework addressing academic, behavioral, and social learning domains. In the next section, we provide an overview of Ci3T, including a brief description of each level of prevention.

Ci3T Models of Prevention

Given the number of students with academic, behavioral, and social–emotional challenges, it is critical educators build effective, efficient systems to facilitate collaborative practice among general and special educators (Ervin, Schaughency, Goodman, McGlinchey, & Matthews, 2006; Gage, Sugai, Lewis, & Brzozowy, 2015). Ci3T provides one such model to select and establish procedures for implementing evidence-based strategies, practices, and programs at each level of prevention (Cook, Smith, & Tankersley, 2012). As with many tiered systems, the supports at each level of prevention increase in intensity, providing focused interventions for students according their specific needs (see Figure 1.1). This systematic approach embraces the data-informed processes we mentioned earlier to identify and support students. We briefly describe each level of prevention below.

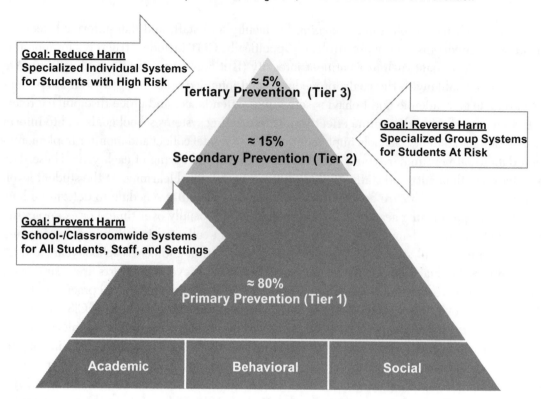

FIGURE 1.1. The comprehensive, integrated, three-tiered (Ci3T) model of prevention (Lane, Kalberg, & Menzies, 2009). From Lane, Oakes, and Menzies (2014). Reprinted by permission of Taylor & Francis (*www.tandfonline.com*).

Primary (Tier 1) Prevention for All

Primary prevention plans are designed to prevent harm from occurring. Just as parents may decide to have their children vaccinated to decrease the likelihood of getting the flu, primary prevention plans are constructed to prevent certain undesirable academic, behavioral, and social–emotional outcomes (e.g., academic failure, school violence, bullying). All students enrolled in a school are eligible for participation in primary (Tier 1) prevention efforts just by virtue of showing up; there are no referral, screening, or eligibility determinations to be made (Lane, Robertson, & Graham-Bailey, 2006). Primary (Tier 1) prevention includes validated curricular programs such as literacy, violence prevention, conflict resolution, anti-bullying programs, or schoolwide social skills.

In a Ci3T model, primary (Tier 1) prevention efforts include three building blocks or domains: academic, behavior, and social–emotional domains that include evidence-based strategies, practices, and programs. When designing their Ci3T model, Ci3T Leadership Teams work with district leaders to build a schoolwide positive behavioral interventions and supports (SWPBIS) plan using the Schoolwide Expectations Survey for Specific School Settings (SESSS; Lane, Oakes, & Menzies, 2010) data to identify those behaviors critical for student success in each setting. These expectations are taught to all stakeholders, including students, who are also given opportunities to practice and receive reinforcement for meeting these expectations. Ci3T Leadership Teams also identify and adopt validated academic and social skills or social–emotional learning curricula, and then define roles and responsibilities for ensuring these curricula are implemented with integrity. Furthermore, decisions are made so that other priorities within these domains are implemented as planned (e.g., teachers using research-based, low-intensity supports such instructional choice and active supervision to increase productive engagement and minimize disruption). As part of primary prevention efforts, procedures are defined for teaching, reinforcing, and monitoring implementation. There is an intentional effort to integrate supports across domains. Formal structures to detect and assist students for whom Tier 1 efforts are insufficient are put into place (Lane, Menzies, Ennis, & Bezdek, 2013). We discuss these more fully in the chapters that follow.

In brief, primary prevention efforts are developed to support a large number of students with generally low levels of risk. An anticipated 80% of students are likely to respond to this level of support (Gresham, Sugai, Horner, McInerney, & Quinn, 1998; Sugai & Horner, 2006). Then, multiple data sources are analyzed to inform professional learning objectives and identify students who require more targeted levels of support: secondary and tertiary prevention efforts.

Secondary (Tier 2) Prevention for Some

Students identified as nonresponsive to the primary (Tier 1) prevention plan are connected with relevant secondary prevention efforts (strategies, practices, and programs) according to their individual needs. In some instances, students are connected directly with tertiary supports—particularly those students exposed to multiple risk factors. In terms of Tier 2 supports, students with similar academic, behavioral, and social concerns are provided focused interventions to address their acquisition (can't do), fluency (trouble doing), or performance (won't do) deficits (Gresham & Elliott, 2008, 2017). Examples of low-intensity supports include small-group instruction in anger management, social skills, or reading comprehension strategies. Or they may include programs such as check-in/check-out (Hawken, O'Neil, & MacLeod, 2011) or strategies such as self-monitoring (Ennis, Lane, & Oakes, 2018). The goal of each is to reverse harm by teaching functional skills and adjusting levels of reinforcement (Severson & Walker, 2002).

Approximately 10–15% of the student body is apt to require secondary (Tier 2) prevention. For each Tier 2 support, information is collected to determine: (1) whether the support is taking place as planned (integrity); (2) stakeholders' views about the goals, procedures, and intended outcomes (social validity); and (3) how students are responding. If evidence suggests students are not responding despite interventions being implemented as designed, then a new secondary support or a more intensive tertiary prevention is considered.

Tertiary (Tier 3) Prevention for a Few

Tertiary (Tier 3) prevention, the most intensive level of support, is reserved for students for whom primary or secondary efforts are insufficient or those who are exposed to several risk factors (e.g., impoverished living conditions; parents with mental health or addiction problems; chaotic family environments). In short, Tier 3 is for students with the most intensive intervention needs (see also National Center on Intensive Interventions [NCII]; *http://intensiveintervention.org*). Examples of tertiary prevention efforts include function-based interventions (Umbreit, Ferro, Liaupsin, & Lane, 2007), multisystemic therapy (MST; Henggeler, 1998), cognitive-behavioral therapy (Joyce-Beaulieu, & Sulkowski, 2015), and highly intensive academic interventions. The goal of this level of support is to reduce harm by addressing the severe, multiple difficulties facing these students.

Approximately 5–7% of the student body may require this intensive level of support. Potentially, schools have the ability to be a strong, positive host setting for coordinating the specialized supports some students will need.

A Commitment to Comprehensive, Integrated Systems

In the last few years, there has been a clear commitment from U.S. education policymakers in this area. We have seen the call to action made by Michael Yudin (2014) to prioritize students' behavior and social needs in the same way we prioritize students' academic needs. In both 2017 and 2018, the Institute of Education Sciences (IES) issued a request for applications from researchers to examine the implementation of tiered systems of support focused on an integrated approach to meet the academic, social–emotional, and behavioral needs of all learners. Dedicating funding to tiered systems addressing all domains that support student learning acknowledges the importance of this work. There have been similar calls to action made by forward-thinking state leaders such as Randy Watson (Commissioner of Education in Kansas), who issued a call for Kansas schools to prioritize students' "soft skills" to ensure that when they graduate they are ready to be globally competitive in the workplace.

As longtime general and special educators, we are heartened to see priority placed on empowering general *and* special education communities to work collaboratively to meet the multiple needs of students experiencing learning and behavioral challenges (Ervin et al., 2006; Gage et al., 2015). These models offer resource-efficient approaches to prevent learning and social–behavioral challenges from occurring, and the ability to respond effectively when they do (Lane & Walker, 2015). The Ci3T model provides an integrated approach comprised of evidence-based practices for supporting the academic, behavioral, and social development of all students. Instead of waiting for problems to occur, then responding with a series of increasingly harsh consequences, schools are developing tiered models of support that subscribe to a proactive, instructional approach to academic, behavioral, and social performance (Lane, Robertson, & Graham-Bailey, 2006). Faculty and staff members participate in focused, sustained professional learning opportunities to detect and respond to student needs and to develop inclusive systems that provide a context for student success.

Purpose

To empower educators to effectively and efficiently serve an increasingly diverse group of students, coupled with the increased demand for academic accountability while maintaining positive, productive learning environments, we offer this second edition of *Developing a*

Schoolwide Framework to Prevent and Manage Learning and Behavior Problems. We hope this text will be an easy-to-use tool for administrators, educators, reading specialists, behavior specialists, school psychologists, and researchers alike to better serve all students, including those with and at risk for learning and behavioral challenges.

Specifically, this book is a research-based, practical guide for designing, implementing, and evaluating primary prevention programs to (1) prevent the development of learning and behavior challenges in our schools and (2) identify and support students who may need more assistance beyond Tier 1 efforts to thrive (Lane, 2007, 2017). To this end, we describe Ci3T models of prevention, designed to feature primary prevention efforts that contain academic, behavioral, and social components to meet students' multiple needs. Below you will find a brief description of the remaining chapters.

Chapter 2, *A Look at Evidence Surrounding Tiered Systems,* provides an overview of the evidence regarding tiered systems. In this new chapter, we begin by providing updated evidence for the effectiveness of tiered models focusing on evidence for the building blocks of Ci3T: academics (performance in reading and math), behavior (PBIS), and social (social–emotional learning) domains. Then, we introduce lessons learned regarding low-intensity, teacher-delivered supports (e.g., instructional choice, increased opportunities to respond). We provide examples of how these interventions have been conducted within tiered systems and connect readers with recent reviews of the literature examining the methodological rigor of the studies. Next, we provide illustrations of Tier 2 and Tier 3 inquiry conducted within a Ci3T model and other tiered models of prevention, demonstrating the impact of academic, behavioral, and social supports. Then, we share lessons learned about how teachers fare during systems change efforts as they design and implement tiered systems such as the Ci3T model. We conclude with lessons learned regarding professional learning needs with respect to comprehensive and integrated practices such as those in the Ci3T model of prevention.

Chapter 3, *Designing and Implementing a Ci3T Model: Building a Primary Prevention Plan,* provides an updated, step-by-step approach for designing and implementing a comprehensive primary prevention model containing academic, behavioral, and social–emotional components. More specifically, the chapter illustrates one method of constructing primary plans that has been used across the PreK–12 continuum (Lane, Kalberg, Bruhn, Mahoney, & Driscoll, 2008; Lane & Menzies, 2003, 2005; Lane, Wehby, Robertson, & Rogers, 2007; Robertson & Lane, 2007). We describe a team-based process for designing Tier 1 elements of the Ci3T model.

Chapter 4, *Examining Tier 1 Efforts: Monitoring Treatment Integrity and Social Validity,* provides guidance to determine whether the plan has been put in place as designed (treatment integrity), as well as how to solicit stakeholders' views of the goals, procedures, and intended outcomes (social validity). In this new chapter, we define both components, explain their importance, introduce methods for measuring each, and provide tips regarding logistical considerations.

Chapter 5, *Determining How Well Ci3T Is Meeting the Goals: Procedures for Monitoring Overall Student Performance,* focuses on student performance in tiered systems. We review the use of academic and behavior screening tools to determine how students are responding to Tier 1 efforts. We discuss the importance of systematic screening, introduce an overview of existing tools and procedures, and provide recommendations for conducting screenings.

Finally, we provide illustrations of how to analyze multiple sources of data in tandem to examine student performance.

Chapter 6, *Empowering Teachers with Low-Intensity, Teacher-Delivered Strategies* (a new chapter in the second edition), provides an overview of research-based, low-intensity supports teachers can use to increase engagement and decrease disruption. We begin by discussing practical methods for using data to inform decision making regarding how and when to refine the use of low-intensity, teacher-delivered supports. Then we introduce seven low-intensity, teacher-delivered strategies that can be used across the tiers.

Chapter 7, *Supporting Students Who Require More Than Primary Prevention Efforts: Tier 2 and Tier 3*, provides guidance for establishing transparency of secondary and tertiary supports. We offer illustrations of how students respond at the elementary, middle, and high school levels. We also provide recommendations for structuring Tier 2 and Tier 3 interventions using schoolwide data, implementing these interventions during the school day using existing resources, monitoring student progress, and determining when the extra support is no longer required. The illustrations feature academic, behavioral, and social domains, with an emphasis on integrating them.

Chapter 8, *Understanding Implementation Science: Responsible Implementation of System Change Efforts* (another new chapter in this second edition), focuses on respectful, responsible inquiry, and situating this important work within an implementation sciences framework. This chapter provides a detailed discussion of professional learning, with concrete illustrations of how to provide a range of high-quality professional learning offerings. We close with recommendations for getting started in designing, implementing, and evaluating Ci3T models of prevention by providing concrete information that addresses logistical issues.

In summary, this second edition of *Developing a Schoolwide Framework to Prevent and Manage Learning and Behavior Problems* provides the foundational knowledge, tools, and procedures necessary to design, implement, and evaluate Ci3T models developed to honor students' multiple needs. In addition, it illustrates how to use schoolwide data to monitor how students respond to global intervention efforts and determine who may need more than Tier 1 efforts have to offer. This book is designed for use by administrators, general and special educators, behavior specialists, school psychologists, positive behavior support or discipline teams, building leadership teams, and researchers. Throughout the book, we address concerns and recommendations from practitioners who have implemented Ci3T models from preschool through high school. In selected chapters you will find lessons learned from district partners, as well as resources to support you in moving forward in designing, implementing, and evaluating Ci3T models of prevention.

CHAPTER 2

A Look at Evidence Surrounding Tiered Systems

As detailed in Chapter 1, at the base of any tiered system of support is a primary (Tier 1) plan for all students. You may have previously heard the terms *universal, Tier 1, schoolwide,* or *primary prevention.* Not surprisingly, the first tiered framework—response to intervention (RTI)—focused on the academic learning domain. Not long after the introduction of RTI, Hill Walker introduced the concept of tiered systems focused on students' behavioral needs to the educational community (Walker et al., 1996)—the beginning of positive behavior interventions and support (PBIS) (Sugai & Horner, 2002).

To date, more than 26,000 schools in the United States have designed and implemented PBIS. As part of the PBIS approach, a school-site team develops a primary plan with input from the faculty. In brief, designing a PBIS model involves establishing common expectations so students know what is expected behaviorally and socially to be successful at a particular school. Once expectations are established, school personnel teach them to all students in the building using a variety of direct and indirect tools such as lessons, videos, precorrection, behavior specific praise, and explicit modeling of the expectations. Then students are given opportunities to practice and receive reinforcement for demonstrating the desired behaviors. Students who demonstrate these schoolwide expectations may receive reinforcement from any adult in the building—teachers, paraprofessionals, administrators, office staff, cafeteria employees, custodians, substitute teachers, and volunteers. Thus, all students participate in this schoolwide primary prevention. There is no screening or referral process to determine eligibility. Just like measles, mumps, and rubella vaccinations—everyone gets them!

It is important to note PBIS is a framework, not a curriculum (Scott & Caron, 2005). The PBIS model specifies progressively more intensive and individualized supports based on the students' needs. The advantage of a framework, as opposed to a specific curriculum, is a school-site leadership team can choose programs, identify strategies, and select interventions for each level of prevention that best addresses the needs of the student body and school context.

While the field of PBIS was developing, there was a parallel interest in meeting students' social–emotional needs, with this approach often involving curricula designed and tested to develop students' "soft skills" (Collaborative for Academic, Social, and Emotional Learning [CASEL], 2019; Watson, 2015). There are several stand-alone primary (Tier 1) prevention programs that address very specific behavioral and social needs, such as violence prevention, bullying prevention, drug abuse prevention, social skills, and conflict resolution programs (see Table 2.1 for example programs). Yet not all programs provide additional graduated support, which means that they do not include targeted or intensive support for students who require more than the primary prevention efforts. For example, if office discipline referral (ODR) or bullying referral data indicate bullying is a key problem on campus, then the team may want to consider incorporating a research-based schoolwide bullying prevention program such as the Second Step's Bullying Prevention Unit (previously Steps to Respect; grades K–5; Committee for Children, 2013) or Olweus Bullying Prevention Program (OBPP; Olweus et al., 2007) into their primary (Tier 1) prevention plan. Adopting a PBIS framework alone may not prompt schools to adopt a validated social–emotional curriculum. It is possible, however, for a school to adopt a validated primary prevention program, as a complement to their schoolwide PBIS model, to address a specific need of students at the school.

This book focuses on developing a comprehensive, integrated, three-tiered (Ci3T) prevention model that addresses academic, behavioral, *and* social–emotional needs beginning at Tier 1 to prevent the development of learning and behavioral challenges, as well as provide *additional* support for students with existing challenges (e.g., emotional and behavioral disorders [EBD]), given that they struggle in all three areas of development. Specifically, we focus on how to (1) construct comprehensive, integrated primary plans; (2) empower teachers with low-intensity, proactive strategies to facilitate instruction; and (3) use multiple sources of data to monitor student progress and detect students who require more intensive supports in the form of secondary (Tier 2) or tertiary (Tier 3) interventions that address acquisition, fluency, and performance deficits in academic, behavioral, and social domains.

In the first edition of this book, we described several treatment–outcome studies that illustrated how schoolwide programs that include a behavioral component influenced student behavioral as well as academic outcomes. For example, at that time, a systematic review of the literature by Lane, Kalberg, and Edwards (2008) identified 19 studies of primary prevention efforts that involved a behavioral component at the elementary level published between 1997 and 2007. Except for the studies that employed single-case designs that took place in specific school settings such as playgrounds and hallways (e.g., Colvin, Sugai, Good, & Lee, 1997; Lewis, Powers, Kelk, & Newcomer, 2002; Lewis, Sugai, & Colvin, 1998), most studies used quasi-experimental, correlational, or descriptive designs to evaluate how well the interventions worked (Mills & Gay, 2019). Findings were encouraging as the studies reported positive changes in student outcomes. For example, researchers reported improvements in hallway (Leedy, Bates, & Safran, 2004; Lewis et al., 1998), playground (Lewis et al., 1998; Lewis et al., 2002), and transition (e.g., Colvin et al., 1997) behaviors. Several other studies reported decreases in ODRs (e.g., Bell, Coleman, Anderson, Whelan, & Wilder, 2000; Ervin et al., 2006; George, White, & Schlaffer, 2007; McCurdy, Mannella, & Eldridge, 2003; Nelson, 1996; Nelson, Martella, & Galand, 1998; Nelson, Martella, & Marchand-Martella, 2002; Scott & Barrett, 2004; Sprague et al., 2001; Todd, Haugen, Anderson, & Spriggs, 2002) and suspensions (Bell et al., 2000; George et al., 2007; Netzel & Eber, 2003; Scott, 2001; Scott & Barrett, 2004). By decreasing problem behaviors and improving the atmosphere or climate in a school, educators can increase instructional time and ultimately improve students' academic performance—a goal of all educators. We provided examples of primary prevention efforts in elementary schools to illustrate how these programs can influence overall performance in school, as well as hallway (e.g., Colvin, Kameenui, & Sugai, 1993) and recess (e.g., Lewis, Colvin, & Sugai, 2000) behavior. We also showed how primary prevention programs implemented at the elementary level can target academic, behavioral, and social performance (e.g., Lane & Menzies, 2002; Nelson et al., 1998). This three-pronged focus is important to keep in mind given academic and behavioral objectives are not separate goals—they interact to influence each other (Hinshaw, 1982; Lane & Wehby, 2002).

In addition, we provided evidence of successful implementation at the middle and high school levels. A review of how schoolwide interventions with primary-level efforts targeting behavioral concerns, conducted in secondary schools between 1990 and 1996, found only 14 studies, some of which focused on SWPBIS. These studies revealed decreases in ODRs (Lohrmann-O'Rourke et al., 2000; Metzler, Biglan, Rusby, & Sprague, 2001; Taylor-Greene et al., 1997; Taylor-Greene & Kartub, 2000), decreases in the level of physical and verbal aggression (Metzler et al., 2001), decreases in detentions (Luiselli, Putnam, & Sutherland, 2002), decreases in hallway noise during lunchtime (Kartub, Taylor-Green, March, & Horner, 2000), and increases in the proportion of students who reported receiving praise or rewards (Metzler et al., 2001). In fact, the prototype for what is now called SWPBIS was actually developed in middle schools (Gottfredson, Gottfredson, & Hybl, 1993; Mayer, Butterworth, Nafpaktitis, & Sulzer-Azaroff, 1983).

Since the first edition of this book, the field has continued to advance and priorities have shifted to learning how to meet students' multiple needs in an integrated fashion (What Works Clearinghouse, 2008). Studies conducted in the last 10 years have provided additional evidence for core components of the Ci3T model. In this chapter, we begin by providing updated evidence for the effectiveness of tiered models focusing on evidence for the building blocks of Ci3T: academics (performance in reading and math), behavior (PBIS), and social (social–emotional learning) domains. Then we introduce lessons learned regarding low-intensity, teacher-delivered supports such as instructional choice, increased opportunities to respond, behavior-specific praise, precorrection, active supervision, instructional feedback, and high-probability request sequences. We provide examples of how these interventions have been conducted within tiered systems and connect readers with recent reviews of the literature examining the methodological rigor of the studies. Next, we provide illustrations of Tier 2 and Tier 3 inquiries conducted within a Ci3T model and other tiered models of prevention, demonstrating the impact of academic, behavioral, and social supports provided at Tier 2, as well as functional assessment-based interventions and other academic intervention provided as a Tier 3 support for students with intensive intervention needs. We then share lessons learned about how teachers fare during systems change efforts as they design and implement tiered systems such as the Ci3T model, including a rich discussion on teachers' perceptions during initial implementation. We conclude with lessons learned regarding professional learning needs with respect to comprehensive and integrated practices such as in the Ci3T model of prevention.

(text resumes on page 22)

TABLE 2.1. Primary Prevention Social Skills Programs

Name	Description	Representative supporting research	Target group	Cost/contact info
Connect with Kids (Connect with Kids Network)	Connect with Kids is a video- and story-based program that addresses core character values. Lessons are designed to "promote positive social action and improved community culture." This program can be used as a supplement to existing programs or as a stand-alone program. Schools adopting this program access the curriculum materials through a customized website. Schools work with the developers to customize their website and select the units and lessons. Parent engagement and professional development programs are available.	Page, B., & D'Agostino, A. (2005). *Connect with Kids: 2004–2005 study results for Kansas and Missouri.* Available from Compass Consulting Group, LLC, 5726 Fayetteville Road, Suite 203, Durham, NC 27713.	Grades 3–12	Full descriptions, example products, and stories of their engagement are available at *www.connectwithkids.com;* Connect with Kids Network, Inc., 6285 Barfield Road, 2nd Floor, Atlanta, GA 30328; *assistance@cwknetwork.com;* 888-598-KIDS (5437). Contact Connect with Kids for pricing.
Incredible Years™ Series (Webster-Stratton)	There are programs available for parents, teachers, and students. The parent programs help parents promote their children's social competence. Skills covered include helping children learn and play with others, using praise and incentives effectively, setting limits, and handling misbehavior. The teacher program is designed to increase the use of effective classroom management practices. Skills covered include use of attention, praise and encouragement, and incentives; proactive teaching strategies; management of inappropriate classroom behaviors; building positive relationships with students; and teaching empathy, social skills, and problem solving in the classroom. The Dinosaur curriculum is for students. Skills include development of emotional literacy, empathy or perspective taking, friendship skills, anger management, and interpersonal problem solving. The classwide program is designed to be taught two to three times per week (20- to 30-minute lessons) by the	Drugli, M. B., Larsson, B., Fossum, S., & Morch, W. T. (2010). Five- to six-year outcome and its prediction for children with ODD/CD treated with parent training. *Journal of Child Psychology and Psychiatry, 51*(5), 559–566. Webster-Stratton, C. H., Reid, M. J., & Beauchaine, T. (2011). Combining parent and child training for young children with ADHD. *Journal of Clinical Child and Adolescent Psychology, 40*(2), 191–203. Webster-Stratton, C., Reid, M. J., & Stoolmiller, M. (2008). Preventing conduct problems and improving school readiness: An evaluation of the Incredible Years Teacher and Child Training Program in high risk schools. *Journal of Child Psychology and Psychiatry, 49*(5), 471–488.	Ages 2–8	Program descriptions and pricing available at *www.incredibleyears.com.* Prices range by program and package selected: parent and teacher programs are under $2,000. The Incredible Years, 1411 8th Avenue West, Seattle, WA 98119; *incredibleyears@incredibleyears.com;* 206-285-7565.

Program	Description	References	Grade level	Cost/Contact
	classroom teacher. Programs are available for Tier 2 and Tier 3 intervention. Tools are included for monitoring treatment integrity (self-report).			
Lions Quest, Skills for Adolescence (Lions Club International Foundation)	Lessons address students' self-awareness, social awareness, relationship skills, and responsible decision making. The purpose of the program is to build a caring, participatory, and well-managed learning environment. Lessons include activities for cooperative learning and reflection (pair-share, group work, discussions, peer teaching, problem-solving scenarios, and group reflection). The high school curriculum addresses workplace skills and two service-learning projects to foster civic responsibility. For middle school, there are 108 lessons for use over 3 years. The program suggests ways to integrate lesson content into academics and to make the program culturally relevant to diverse students. Planned use for responding at Tier 2 and Tier 3.	Eisen, M., Zellman, G. L., & Murray, D. M. (2003). Evaluating the Lions-Quest "Skills for Adolescence" drug education program: Second-year behavior outcomes. *Addictive Behaviors, 28*(5), 883–897. Malmin, G. (2007). *It Is My Choice (Lions Quest) evaluation part 5 of the report: The impact on the behavior of the students.* Unpublished evaluation report.	Middle school; high school	*https://www.lions-quest.org* Middle School Teacher's Curriculum kit is $150 for each grade level. High school Teacher's Curriculum Kit is $150. Student journals are $5 each or $120 for a class set of 30.
Positive Action® (Allred)	Positive Action lessons address self-management, social skills, character development, mental health, goal setting and goals attainment. Units address the "Self Circle" of Thoughts–Actions–Feelings (positive thoughts lead to positive actions lead to positive feelings), and physical, intellectual, social, and emotional areas. Additional supplemental programs include Bullying Prevention, Family, Drug Use Prevention, Conflict Resolution, School Climate, and Community. There are 140, 15-minute lessons for grades K–6, 82, 15- to 20-minute lessons for grades 7 and 8. Counselor kits are also available. Spanish kits are available for grades K–4, 7–8, and Conflict Resolution.	Bavarian, N., Lewis, K. M., Acock, A., DuBois, D. L., Yan, Z., Vuchinich, S., . . . Flay, B. R. (2016). Effects of a school-based social–emotional and character development program on health behaviors: A matched-pair, cluster-randomized controlled trial. *Journal of Primary Prevention, 37*(1), 87–105. Oakes, W. P., Lane, K. L., Cox, M., Magrane, A., Jenkins, A., & Hankins, K. (2012). Tier 2 supports to improve motivation and performance of elementary students with behavioral challenges and poor work completion. *Education and Treatment of Children, 35,* 547–584.	PreK–12	Full descriptions and pricing available from *www.positiveaction.net*. Elementary Classroom Kits $400; Middle School Kits $450; High School Kits $525; Bullying Prevention Kit $250. Positive Action, Inc. 264 4th Avenue South, Twin Falls, ID 83301; 208-733-1328; 800-345-2974 (U.S. Toll-Free); 208-733-1590 (Fax); *info@positiveaction.net*.

TABLE 2.1. *(continued)*

Name	Description	Representative supporting research	Target group	Cost/contact info
Promoting Alternative Thinking Strategies® (PATHS; Kusche & Greenberg, 1994)	PATHS is intended to improve student behavior, reduce classroom disruption, and increase academic engagement and achievement. The program focuses on peaceful conflict resolution, handling emotions, empathy, and responsible decision making. Integration with academic areas. There are 40–52 lessons that include suggestions for engaging families and ways to generalize skills into academic curricula. Tools included for monitoring treatment integrity (self-report and observations) and student behavioral outcomes.	Conduct Problems Prevention Research Group. (2010). The effects of a multiyear randomized clinical trial of a universal social–emotional learning program: The role of student and school characteristics. *Journal of Consulting and Clinical Psychology, 78,* 156–168. Riggs, N. R., Greenberg, M. T., Kusche, C. A., & Pentz, M. A. (2006). The mediational role of neurocognition in the behavioral outcomes of a social–emotional prevention program in elementary school students: Effects of the PATHS Curriculum. *Prevention Science, 7,* 91–102.	PreK–6	Classroom Kits range from $489 to $519 (based on ordering one kit). Counselor's package for PreK–6 is $3,509. Discounted pricing when ordering multiple copies. Full details at *https://shop. channing-bete.com/onlinestore/ store.html?cid=134563.* Channing Bete Company, One Community Place, South Deerfield, MA 01373-0200; 877-896-8532; *custsvcs@channing-bete.com; www.channing-bete. com/prevention-programs/paths/ paths.html.*
Responding in Peaceful and Positive Ways (RIPP; Meyer, Farrell, Northup, Kung, & Plybon, 2000)	RIPP is a universal violence prevention program designed especially for middle school students. The curriculum develops students' social and cognitive skills so that they can utilize nonviolent conflict resolution and positive communication. There is a different focus for each year to meet the identified development needs of middle school students. Weekly lessons are taught by a prevention facilitator.	Farrell, A. D., Valois, R. F., Meyer, A. L., & Tidwell, R. P. (2003). Impact of the RIPP Violence Prevention Program on rural middle school students. *Journal of Primary Prevention, 24*(2), 143–167. Farrell, A. D., Meyer, A. L., Sullivan, T. N., & Kung, E. M. (2003). Evaluation of the Responding in Peaceful and Positive	Middle school	Manual available on Amazon for approximately $50 ($160 hardback)

| Second Step (Committee for Children) | Second Step: A Violence Prevention Program (SSVP) teaches social and emotional skills for violence prevention. Skills focus on four main areas: empathy, emotional management, friendship skills, and problem solving. Additional units and materials are available, including an additional component for young children to support transition to kindergarten; a bullying prevention unit for grades K–5; a child protection unit to train adults in how to "recognize, respond to, and report abuse"; and a mindfulness program.

The curriculum is designed to offer multiple practice opportunities, home communication (in Spanish and English), and connections to apply skills in academic activities.

There are 22–28 weeks of lessons for each grade.

Tools included for monitoring treatment integrity (self-report and observations) and student behavioral outcomes. | Ways (RIPP) seventh grade violence prevention curriculum. *Journal of Child and Family Studies, 12,* 101–120.

Espelage, D. L., Polanin, J. R., & Rose, C. A. (2015). Social–emotional learning program to reduce bullying, fighting, and victimization among middle school students with disabilities. *Remedial and Special Education, 36,* 299–311.

Low, S., Cook, C. R., Smolkowski, K., & Buntain-Ricklefs, J. (2015). Promoting social–emotional competence: An evaluation of the elementary version of Second Step. *Journal of School Psychology, 53,* 463–477.

Upshur, C. C., Heyman, M., Wenz-Gross, M. (2017). Efficacy trial of the Second Step Early Learning (SSEL) curriculum: Preliminary outcomes. *Journal of Applied Developmental Psychology, 50,* 15–25. | Preschool–8 | Full descriptions and pricing available from *www.secondstep. org.*

Grade-level kits range from $209 (Bully Prevention and Child Protection) to $459 (SEL program Early Learning–Grade 5). The Middle School SEL program is available by site licenses and range from $199 (one grade, 1 year) to $7,999 (grades 6–8, 5 years).

Materials include a teacher's guide, lesson plans, posters, academic integration activities, formative knowledge assessments, etc.

Committee for Children, 2815 Second Avenue, Suite 400, Seattle, WA 98121; 800-634-4449, ext. 1; *support@ secondstep.org.* |

Note. See *https://casel.org* for additional information about the programs in this table. See *https://casel.org/guide/programs* for preschool and elementary and *https://casel.org/middle-and-high-school-edition-casel-guide* for middle school and high school program reviews. See also *www.blueprintsprograms.org* and *https://ies.ed.gov/ncee/wwc/FWW.* We do not endorse any specific curriculum or program. We encourage Ci3T Leadership Teams and District Leaders to review current evidence to inform their decision making.\

Evidence for the Effectiveness of Tiered Models: Tier 1 Efforts

Academic Performance in Reading and Mathematics

Schools have traditionally used a schoolwide curriculum for reading in the form of a textbook series adoption. However, a tiered approach to reading instruction, or RTI, was novel because it incorporated additional elements to ensure effective instruction, as well as systematically identify students who might be at risk for reading failure. These included (1) a validated core reading curriculum, (2) universal screening to identify students at risk, (3) use of evidence-based practices to provide intensive instruction for those who needed it, and (4) progress monitoring to evaluate whether the additional instruction was having a positive impact (Johnson, Mellard, Fuchs, & McKnight, 2006).

The National Association of State Directors of Special Education (NASDSE) released a policy document (Batsche et al., 2006) to guide districts in navigating the challenges of adopting the new model, as it required districts to think differently about student assessment and teachers' professional development. NASDSE emphasized the new focus on process, looking at how students were performing and providing additional support rather than on identification of low performance solely for referral to special education services. In addition, RTI would offer support to students at risk for reading failure, not just those who qualified for special education. Importantly, the new model provided districts another method of identifying students with specific learning disabilities. RTI offered an earlier opportunity for intervention (rather than waiting for students to fall so far behind that special education services may have been warranted), which was likely to result in better academic outcomes for students (D. Fuchs & Fuchs, 2017; L. Fuchs & Fuchs, 2007).

As schools and districts have put RTI into place over the past two decades, a considerable body of research documents best practices. For example, schools (or districts) should create a multiyear plan clearly specifying the elements to be developed and how they will be integrated into a school's current procedures (McDougal, Graney, Wright, & Ardoin, 2010). These include building knowledge and support for the RTI model, creating a blueprint for professional learning, and identifying needed resources (e.g., curricula, assessment measures, personnel). Also, strong leadership is essential in the adoption of any new systems-level practice, particularly one with the complexity of RTI (McIntosh et al., 2014).

In addition to the preliminary work of planning for implementation, there are several technical considerations. Deciding on the core instructional program and ensuring teachers' expertise in delivering it is essential. Researchers have emphasized that without a strong Tier 1 program there will be errors in identifying students who need additional or more intensive intervention (D. Fuchs, Fuchs, & Vaughn, 2014). While core programs should be *validated*, which means experimental or quasi-experimental studies demonstrate the curriculum is effective for the intended population because of the difficulties of conducting this type of research, most programs are research *derived*. A research-derived program comprises evidenced-based strategies; that is, each part of the curriculum has been proven to work, even though the entire model has not been empirically tested.

When identifying students who will receive Tier 2 and Tier 3 services, school or district leadership teams must decide what constitutes insufficient academic progress (both the level and trend of performance and the amount of time at that level without growth), which instruments will be used to measure performance, and how interventions will be chosen and delivered (Denton, 2012; L. Fuchs, 2003). As in Tier 1, professional expertise is paramount. At each step, it must be clear that lack of student progress is not due to poor instruction (e.g., low-levels of Tier 1 implementation) or an inappropriate curriculum or intervention, or lack of access to the curriculum (e.g., low attendance, exclusion by in-school or out-of-school suspensions).

The RTI model has been extended to mathematics because of the support it can offer to struggling students (Gersten & Newman-Gonchar, 2011). In most states, passing high-stakes tests in mathematics is required for a high school diploma. This has brought awareness of the additional academic assistance many students need to graduate high school. RTI in math is a way to deliver this support systematically. The main features of the RTI model in math also include a research-based core program, universal screening, intervention for students who are at risk, and progress monitoring. Due to the nature of the subject matter, the specifics will differ, such as screening measures and how intervention is delivered. Yet equally important for RTI in math is teacher expertise, clear procedures, valid measures, and fidelity of implementation (Lembke, Hampton, & Byers, 2012). The success of the model depends on the integrity of each element working reliably and effectively.

Although the entire RTI model has yet to be empirically validated (D. Fuchs & Fuchs, 2017), there is considerable research to validate interventions used in Tiers 2 and 3 for both reading and mathematics (Gersten, 2016; Wanzek et al., 2018). There is optimism that as researchers work out methodological issues and districts improve implementation, it will be possible to document its overall effectiveness. RTI offers the possibility of reducing the over-representation of minority students and English learners in special education while meeting the needs of culturally and linguistically diverse students (Montalvo, Combes, & Kea, 2014). It may even provide intervention early enough to reduce or ameliorate the occurrence of learning disabilities (Fletcher & Vaughn, 2009). RTI is also a move away from a deficit perspective of student achievement and demands that schools examine their practices to ensure all students are provided with equitable access to high-quality instruction and adequate opportunities to learn.

Schoolwide Positive Behavior Interventions and Supports

In education research, a randomized controlled trial (RCT) is considered the "gold standard" for determining whether an intervention is effective, but due to the nature of working within authentic school contexts, it can be difficult to conduct this type of research. An RCT requires random assignment to treatment and control conditions, which means that each school, classroom, or student (depending on the unit of analysis) has an equal and independent chance of being placed in these conditions. By design, people do not get to choose their condition (e.g., "I want to participate in the treatment condition"); the assignment is random. Because administrators, teachers, and parents may have strong feelings about being part of an intervention study or equally strong feelings about *not* being part of the study, it can be hard to find districts willing to participate in such research trials. However, Bradshaw and her colleagues

(Bradshaw, Mitchell, & Leaf, 2010; Bradshaw & Pas, 2011; Bradshaw, Reinke, Brown, Bevans, & Leaf, 2008) conducted a wide-scale RCT that examined the effect of schoolwide PBIS on student suspensions, ODRs, and academic achievement (Bradshaw et al., 2010).

Thirty-seven elementary schools in a single urban district volunteered to participate in the study. Twenty-one schools were randomly assigned to the PBIS condition and 16 were assigned as comparison sites. Each school in the PBIS condition put together leadership teams of 6–10 members who attended a 2-day summer training led by Dr. George Sugai, a highly respected researcher and the developer of SWPBIS. After learning how to design and implement a SWPBIS model, the teams led two additional trainings for their school sites. In addition, school-site staff attended two training events led by Dr. Sugai. Each school was assigned a coach who attended special trainings to prepare for his or her role of providing on-site technical assistance with SWPBIS.

After implementation, the researchers looked at the pattern of ODRs, suspensions, and academic achievement over a 4-year period. Both ODRs and suspensions were significantly lower over time at the participating schools demonstrating SWPBIS made a difference in these outcomes. However, although achievement scores showed a rise in the treatment schools, it was not a statistically significant difference. Researchers noted that a change in procedure for state testing may have affected academic outcomes.

In addition to examining student outcomes, researchers looked at how PBIS affected a school's organizational health, which comprises the following five elements

1. Institutional integrity (the school's ability to cope successfully with destructive outside forces; teachers are protected from unreasonable community and parental demands)
2. Staff affiliation (warm and friendly interactions, positive feelings about colleagues, commitment to students, trust and confidence among the staff, and sense of accomplishment)
3. Academic emphasis (students are cooperative in the classroom, respectful of other students who get good grades, and are driven to improve their skills)
4. Collegial leadership (the principal is friendly, supportive, open, egalitarian, and neither directive nor restrictive)
5. Resource influence (the principal's ability to lobby for resources for the school and positively influence the allocation of district resources).

These elements are directly quoted (Bradshaw, Koth, Bevans, Ialongo, & Leaf, 2008, p. 466) and reformatted to enhance readability.

Researchers administered the Organizational Health Inventory for Elementary Schools (OHI-E; Hoy, 2003) annually over 4 years. Respondents answered 37 items measuring the construct of organizational health. Survey results showed treatment schools had significantly higher average OHI-E scores than comparison schools, and higher scores on two of the individual items, resource influence and staff affiliation. This suggests that as schools implemented PBIS, they changed the culture of the school itself as teachers and staff altered how they interacted with students.

Social–Emotional Learning

CASEL defines *social–emotional learning* (SEL) as a "process through which children and adults understand and manage emotions, set and achieve positive goals, feel and show empathy for others, establish and maintain positive relationships, and make responsible decisions" (CASEL, 2019). Schools have adopted SEL programs because it is now widely understood how integral these skills are to students' educational success. Both behavioral and academic achievement are influenced by students' emotional maturity, mental health, and ability to get along with others.

There is strong evidence SEL programs can improve academic performance, increase prosocial behavior, and reduce internalizing and conduct problems (Durlak, Weissberg, Dymnicki, Taylor, & Schellinger, 2011). These programs cover a wide range of skills development, including social skills, self-regulation, awareness of one's own and others' feelings, and decision making (Lawson, McKenzie, Becker, Selby, & Hoover, 2018). Durlak and colleagues (2011) conducted a meta-analysis examining the impact of various Tier 1 SEL programs delivered to over 270,000 students. They were interested in determining whether SEL programs taught by regular school personnel would result in positive outcomes, especially when offered as a schoolwide or Tier 1 intervention. Studies reported in the meta-analysis included elementary, middle, and high schools, were located in a variety of geographic locations, and situated in urban, suburban, and rural areas. On average, programs offered 40 lessons and were primarily taught by the regular classroom teacher. Results showed that when compared to control groups, students had a significant improvement in test scores and grades, SEL skills, attitude, and positive social behaviors. They also had fewer conduct problems and lower levels of emotional distress.

These findings were echoed by January, Casey, and Paulson (2011), who conducted a meta-analysis of 28 classroomwide social skills interventions. While the meta-analysis did not examine schoolwide results, it did investigate the effects of social skills lessons taught to the entire class (rather than as a Tier 2 or Tier 3 intervention to a small group or individual students at risk). All studies included comparison to a control group to determine whether students demonstrated an increase in prosocial skills as a result of the social skills program. Researchers found there was an overall positive effect for social skills training, although it was small. However, they identified several modifiers, which showed the conditions under which the effect was much stronger. These included the grade students were in, the duration of the social skills program, and the type of instructional delivery used.

First, students in preschool and kindergarten showed larger gains, pointing out the importance of beginning early with attention to students' social and emotional needs. Second, longer programs had increased positive outcomes on overall social competence. Finally, social skills programs involving higher student engagement and using active learning or role playing were more effective than passive programs. Findings strongly suggested that when used as part of a comprehensive, schoolwide plan, SEL curricula are likely to have a positive impact on student outcomes.

Ci3T: One Unified System

As we discussed in Chapter 1, the Ci3T model of prevention may benefit a range of students, including those with and at risk for EBD. Students with EBD include a large and diverse group struggling with externalizing (e.g., aggression, defiance) and/or internalizing (e.g., anxious, withdrawn, somatic complaints) behaviors that often negatively affect their learning, as well as that of their classmates (Skibbe, Phillips, Day, Brophy-Herb, & Conner, 2012). Prevalence rates indicate 12–20% of school-age youth demonstrate mild-to-severe EBD (Forness et al., 2012; Merikangas et al., 2010), but less than 1% of students are typically served by special education under the category of "emotional disturbance" (ED; IDEA, 2004); most of these students are served exclusively by the general education community. Thus, addressing the complex learning needs of all students is the shared responsibility of the general and special education communities. The Ci3T model creates a collaborative, integrated context for general and special educators to work together to meet the academic, behavioral, and social needs of all students, including those at risk for learning and behavioral difficulties and receiving special education services. This model creates an opportunity for equitable access to supports, with formal structures (e.g., academic and behavior screenings; Tier 2 interventions) to detect and assist students for whom Tier 1 efforts are insufficient (Lane, Menzies, Ennis, & Oakes, 2015).

Ci3T supports shifts in thinking and practice with the provision of ongoing professional learning for school-site Ci3T Leadership Teams, district leaders, and all school faculty and staff (see Lessons Learned 2.1). For example, all general and special education teachers learn about data-informed decision making and engage in data-informed professional learning, creating a highly collaborative and data-rich environment. The goal is to continue to shift away from the refer–test–place model of identifying individuals with learning and behavioral differences and move toward prevention-minded, schoolwide standard operating practices. These practices involve examining data at school and student levels. First, schoolwide practices are examined (e.g., treatment integrity and social validity of Tier 1 practices) followed by student-level data. Specifically, systematic screening data are examined alongside data collected as part of regular school practices to connect students (e.g., those with intensive intervention needs, including both students at risk for learning and behavior challenges and students currently receiving special education services) with additional evidence-based practices at Tiers

---

LESSONS LEARNED 2.1. Bridging Theory to Practice

The Ci3T planning process has been a powerful professional learning tool for our district. Teams engage in deep reflection around critical aspects of educational programming. Grounded in research, the Ci3T model provides clarity and accountability to the practices we expect from all of our stakeholders. Our blueprints bridge the theory–practice gap as we integrate new knowledge in systemic ways. The iterative nature of the Ci3T model encourages a continuous improvement mind-set that allows us to respond to both internal and external pressures.

Ann Matthews, EdD
Executive Director of Teaching and Learning

2 and 3 according to their individual needs. This model is designed to address two primary goals: (1) facilitate stronger partnerships and collaboration between special education and general education teachers and (2) assist school leaders (e.g., Ci3T Leadership Team members, administrators) to improve outcomes for all students—including those with and at risk for disabilities—by empowering general education teachers with the knowledge, skills sets, and confidence to implement not only evidence-based practices across all three tiers with integrity but also strategies, practices, and programs specified in students' individualized education programs (IEPs). Collaboration affords general and special educators an understanding of the full range of students' educational experiences and a common language to fully connect learning (e.g., social skills taught in a resource setting use the same or similar language and will be those reinforced in the general education classroom), avoiding potential disjointedness between students' general and special education experiences. The goal is to create a general education context in which students with and at risk for disabilities can successfully apply and generalize new learning and skills in a receptive, positive, and productive environment. To continue to develop their knowledge and skills sets, Ci3T Leadership Teams (which include the principal, two general education teachers, one special education team, a district coach, and one other professional, such as the school psychologist, and a parent) meet monthly on site and also attend five professional learning sessions during implementation. With direction from their district leadership team, school-site Ci3T Leadership Teams collaborate and provide direction and support for all faculty and staff at the school site (e.g., provide guidance on how to examine data during grade-level team meetings; implement district-developed structures to connect students to more intensive supports and monitor students' movement between tiers).

Ci3T: A Broadening of Multi-Tiered Systems of Supports

A Ci3T model of prevention is one framework for a unified system to address students' academic, behavioral, and social needs (Lane, Oakes, Cantwell, & Royer, 2016; McIntosh & Goodman, 2016; Yudin, 2014). Historically, there has been a progression of tiered systems: RTI (D. Fuchs et al., 2012), PBIS (Horner & Sugai, 2015), multi-tiered systems of supports (MTSS; emphasizing academic and behavioral domains often in a coordinated framework adopted over time), interconnected system framework (ISF; Weist, Lever, Bradshaw, & Owens, 2014; emphasizing behavioral and mental health domains), and Ci3T. Ci3T can be described as a broadening of MTSS, expanded to include principles of both RTI and PBIS, coupled with the implementation of a validated program to address social–emotional learning (SEL) (e.g., Positive Action; Flay et al., 2001). Ci3T provides one comprehensive, integrated, data-informed prevention model enabling general educators, special educators, administrators, families, and students to collaborate using system- and student-level data to inform practices and attain educational goals.

In our work with schools, Ci3T models are designed as part of a year-long training process, then the full Ci3T model is implemented (academic, behavioral, and social components) using their Ci3T Implementation Manual as a guide. During the design year, Ci3T Leadership Teams draft the blueprints with multiple points of full faculty and staff input (see Building Your Ci3T Model at *www.ci3t.org/building*) using the manualized training process (see interactive e-book: Lane, Oakes, Cantwell, & Royer, 2018). At the end of the Ci3T professional learning series, they have a fully developed Ci3T model (Tiers 1, 2, and 3 academic, behavioral, and social skills components) ready to be implemented the following academic year (e.g., Lane & Menzies, 2003).

Our inquiry focuses on the design, implementation, and evaluation of this model. For example, in one of the earliest studies, Lane and Menzies (2002) conducted a study to determine the degree to which a tiered program with academic and behavioral components influenced the reading and behavioral performance of elementary students attending a school with a high at-risk population. The school, located in the Western United States, served students in preschool through grade 6, with 78% of the students receiving free or reduced-price lunches, and a 64% transiency rate. The behavioral component included (1) posting rules, consequences, and rewards; (2) delivering consequences and rewards per the plan; (3) teaching the behavioral expectations to all students; (4) interacting positively with students, consistently and frequently; (5) responding effectively to students who demonstrate problematic behaviors; and (6) assisting students who demonstrate problematic behaviors. Students participated in the district literacy plan and the schoolwide behavior plan (SBP). Professional learning for teachers to implement the SBP included an initial 3-hour training followed by three 1-hour trainings during the year. The district literacy plan included whole-group, small-group, and individual instruction as part of a district-developed balanced literacy program. The teacher-developed lesson plans adhered to the district standards, and a literacy coach provided ongoing training and in-class demonstrations during the academic year. A number of outcome measures were administered to monitor student responses to the plan: district multiple measures in reading (DMR), curriculum-based measures in reading (CBM-R), state achievement tests (Stanford Achievement Test–9 [SAT-9]), the Student Risk Screening Scale (SRSS; Drummond, 1994), negative narrative comments recorded in school records (Walker, Block-Pedego, Todis, & Severson, 1991), absenteeism, and special education enrollment. Results indicated that regardless of behavioral risk status (low, moderate, or high), as measured by the SRSS, students improved on all academic outcomes (DMR, CBM-R, and SAT-9).

Later, Lane, Kalberg, Bruhn, Mahoney, and Driscoll (2008) examined issues of treatment integrity, systematic screening, and reinforcement at two rural elementary schools in the southeastern United States. In this study, schools implemented a comprehensive, integrated framework attending to academic, behavioral (SWPBIS), and social (Character Under Construction) domains of learning. Authors reported three methods for monitoring treatment integrity (e.g., teacher self-reports and direct observations). Results showed treatment integrity varied according to rater and the method of measurement, indicating the importance of assessing treatment integrity from various points of view. Systematic behavior screening scores showed increases in the percentage of students scoring in the low-risk category after 1 year of implementation. Results also suggested the rates of reinforcement varied between schools. Authors illustrated methods for using systematic screening data to examine overall level of risk in a school and connect students to more intensive intervention needs.

We wish to note we introduced the term *Ci3T* in the previous decade (approximately 2011), but the framework has been applied since the late 1990s, consisting of all three components (academic, behavioral, and social) addressed in an integrated fashion across the tiers.

PBIS is at the heart of the model, but Ci3T is broader than RTI, PBIS, or MTSS, as it also includes social–emotional learning at the base (Tier 1 for all students). We introduced the term *Ci3T* to emphasize the model addresses academic, behavioral, and social–emotional learning domains in a comprehensive, integrated prevention framework. Feedback from researchers and practitioners indicated we needed to clarify the distinction (e.g., How is Ci3T different from PBIS? MTSS?).

Distinguishing Features of Ci3T

In considering how the Ci3T model is unique compared to other tiered systems of support, we offer the following distinctions.

- A data-informed approach to building the expectation matrix (i.e., using the Schoolwide Expectations Survey for Specific Settings [SESSS; Lane, Oakes, & Menzies, 2010]), to support building the behavioral (PBIS) component during the initial training year. Rather than relying solely on what the Ci3T Leadership Team views to be a priority, Ci3T involves securing *all* adult input for developing the expectation matrix—an important teaching tool.

- Selection and adoption of a validated curriculum taught at Tier 1 schoolwide to address students' social and emotional needs (broadening of integrated RTI/PBIS seen in some MTSS models). This is important for students with exceptionalities as they are learning these skills in the general education context with their peers to level the playing field. These same skills can be addressed more intensively for students with Tier 2 and 3 needs. In this way, the Ci3T model supports school environments in programming for generalization of social skills interventions conducted at Tier 2 and 3 (and other skills areas) for students with exceptionalities.

- A high priority on empowering faculty and staff with research-based, low-intensity supports in an integrated fashion to increase engagement and minimize challenging behaviors for all students. These refined skills sets are critical for supporting inclusive contexts for students receiving special education services.

- Data-informed decision making for students *and* data-informed professional learning for adults (using faculty and staff feedback on social validity and treatment integrity measures) collected in fall and spring each year. It is simply not sufficient to build any blueprint, then hope it works. Ci3T moves away from the "train and hope" method, and toward a build, teach, examine, refine model.

The comprehensive, integrated nature of the Ci3T model creates a common language between general and special education communities, students, parents, and administrators. Each Ci3T Implementation Manual supports transparency, communication, and equal access to more intensive intervention efforts according to individual needs (see Lessons Learned 2.2). In the sections that follow, we provide lessons learned regarding teacher-delivered, low-intensity supports; Tier 2 and 3 interventions, teachers' views and emotional well-being; as well as professional learning needs.

LESSONS LEARNED 2.2. Benefits of Transparency

Using the Ci3T framework has made a difference in our district. Our teachers and staff members enjoy the transparency of the Ci3T framework. Using staff input in planning and during implementation, leadership teams create Ci3T plans that are relevant and effective. Filled with well-researched supports and strategies, our Ci3T plans have increased the capacity of our staff to effectively meet the academic, social–emotional, and behavioral needs of our students.

Stacey Kramer
Consulting Teacher

Teacher-Delivered Low-Intensity Supports

In Chapter 6 you will read about several teacher-delivered, low-intensity supports such as behavior-specific praise, precorrection, active supervision, opportunities to respond, instructional choice, instructional feedback, and high-probability requests (Freeman, 2018; Lane, Menzies, et al., 2015). Ideally, all educators use these strategies regularly as part of Tier 1 efforts, weaving them throughout instruction (Lane, Oakes, Buckman, & Lane, 2018). Teachers would develop integrated lessons plans, choosing the strategies that help students achieve lesson outcomes. They would embed the strategies in various stages of the instructional process (see *ci3t.org/implementation* for a lesson plan template; see also Figure 2.1 [Oakes, Lane, Lane, & Buckman, 2019]). For example, teachers may offer students choices of a starter activity, providing one of three journal prompts to activate prior knowledge before a social studies lesson on the Civil War. The teacher may do a 15-minute check for understanding, offering a high rate of briskly paced opportunities to respond to basic facts learned over the previous weeks. The teacher may open the independent practice section of the lesson with precorrection, referring to the expectation matrix to remind students how they will show respect and responsibility when drafting their argument for the class debate to be held the following week. Finally, the teacher may engage in active supervision while students move into the independent practice component of a lesson as they later transition from fifth period to lunch.

In addition to using low-intensity strategies in an integrated fashion within lessons and throughout the school day, these same strategies can be used as a Tier 2 support for students who may require more targeted assistance. For example, Lane, Royer, Messenger, and colleagues (2015) incorporated instructional choice into classwide writing instruction delivered by a classroom teacher in an inclusive first-grade classroom. They compared the effectiveness of two types of instructional choice: across task (students given choices of doing different tasks at the same time: "Your choice today is to choose the order in which you complete today's activities or where you would like to work") and within task (students working on the same tasks, but given options of how they wanted to accomplished that task: "You can use a mechanical pencil or markers"). In this study, the teacher looked at academic and behavior screening data collected as part of regular school practices to determine which students needed more intensive support. The participants were two students—Neal and Tina—who scored in the moderate- to high-risk range on the SRSS (Drummond, 1994) and who scored in the progressing- to limited-progress range on report card grades in writing and independent work. Neal

Topic			Active Supervision	Behavior-Specific Praise	High-*P* Request Sequence	Instructional Choice	Instructional Feedback	Opportunities to Respond	Precorrection
Standards									
Core Lesson Elements	**Tier 1 (for All)**	**Equitable Access and Inclusion**							
Academic Objective(s)		Differentiated Objectives							
Social Skills Objective(s)		Differentiated Objectives							
Behavioral Expectation(s)		Individually Targeted Expectations							
Materials and Technology		Adaptive or Assistive Technologies / Instructional Choices							
Opening Activity (independent)		Instructional Choices							
Introduction 1. Activate prior knowledge 2. Rationale/purpose 3. Lesson vocabulary									
Practice Sequence 1. Modeling 2. Guided practice 3. Independent practice		Reteaching, Additional Instruction							
Closing Activity 1. Review/assessment 2. Connection to future learning		Differentiation (Content/Process)							

(continued)

FIGURE 2.1. Ci3T: Integrated Lesson Plan template. Available at *www.ci3t.org.*

From Oakes, Lane, Lane, and Buckman (2019). Reprinted by permission in *Developing a Schoolwide Framework to Prevent and Manage Learning and Behavior Problems, Second Edition* by Kathleen Lynne Lane, Holly Mariah Menzies, Wendy Peia Oakes, and Jemma Robertson Kalberg (The Guilford Press, 2020). Permission to photocopy this material is granted to purchasers of this book for personal use or use with students (see copyright page for details). Purchasers can download additional copies of this material (see the box at the end of the table of contents).

Teacher Reflection Implementation: 0 = *not at all*, 1 = *limited*, 2 = *partial*, 3 = *full*						
Active Supervision (AS)	Behavior-Specific Praise (BSP)	High-P Request Sequence (HPRS)	Instructional Choice (IC)	Instructional Feedback (IF)	Opportunities to Respond (OTR)	Precorrection (PC)
0 1 2 3	0 1 2 3	0 1 2 3	0 1 2 3	0 1 2 3	0 1 2 3	0 1 2 3
Met individual student plan for academic, social skill, and behavioral supports.						0 1 2 3
What went well?						
What did not go as expected?						
What would I change in the future?						

FIGURE 2.1. *(continued)*

received special education services under the category of autism, and Tina was a typically developing student who received the Tier 2 reading intervention in the classroom at the beginning of the study and later received a Tier 3 reading intervention (Reading Recovery, a daily one-to-one intervention) because Tier 2 supports were insufficient. This study took place in a large, suburban, public elementary school in the midwestern United States. One teacher, who was responsible for teaching all content-area instruction, taught this first-grade class. Students who qualified for special education services participated a continuum of services, with many students receiving services in the general education classroom and some receiving support in a resource room.

During the baseline condition, the teacher led a whole-group, mini-lesson to teach a concept. Most days, students sat on the carpet during this time. When the mini-lesson was done, teachers explained the tasks they would do for the rest of their writing time, and students returned to their desks to work on these items. During the intervention phase, an A–B–A–B alternating treatment withdrawal design was used to compare how well across-task and within-task approaches worked to increase engagement and minimize disruption during the writing block. Results indicated the intervention was implemented with a high level of treatment integrity. A functional relation was evident between choice conditions and increases in academic engaged time and decreases in disruptive behavior for Tina. Neal showed improvement; however, the intervention was not as effective for him. When both choice conditions were reintroduced, academic engagement increased from initial baseline levels (which were initially below 60%) to close to 80% engagement. Despite the modest gains for Neal, his social validity data suggested he enjoyed the intervention. There was less variability in his daily engagement, which likely facilitated his learning opportunities (as well as the learning experiences of others).

In another study, Messenger and colleagues (2017) examined how increasing students' opportunities to respond (OTR) influenced active student responding and accuracy during mathematics. Building on the work of Todd Haydon, they compared choral and mixed responding (with mixed responding including 70% choral and 30% individual). In this study, both fourth-grade girls (Jackie and Meg) had internalizing behaviors as determined by the Student Risk Screening Scale for Internalizing and Externalizing (SRSS-IE; Drummond, 1994; Lane & Menzies, 2009), challenges working independently according to report card data, passing grades in math instruction (to ensure challenges were not related to acquisition deficits or "can't do" problems), and parent and student permission.

The intervention took place over 16 days (8 days for choral responding and 8 days for mixed responding). The teacher put the 16 dates into a container, then randomly selected 8 days to be the choral responding date. Then, for both conditions, the general education teachers completed a four-step sequence as follows:

1. Presented a question to the class using an Elmo machine (placing a $4'' \times 6''$ card with a question to be projected on the whiteboard) and noting whether it would be for the whole class or an individual student to respond.
2. Cued the students verbally "5–4–3–2–1" to offer wait time (e.g., holding up five fingers and counting down with five fingers and using words).
3. Offered feedback as to whether the answer was correct (e.g., "That is correct," or "That is not correct. The correct answer is _____").
4. Offered another question and began the next learning trial.

Results suggested the general education teacher was able to implement both choral and mixed OTR conditions as planned. Neither choral nor mixed responding was better than the other. One student (Jackie) was highly accurate but responded less than 75% of the time (a little less than hoped for). The other student (Meg) showed a high level of active student responding, with less than 80% accuracy. Over the course of this study, Meg was referred to and qualified for special education services under the specific learning disability category in the areas of math calculation and problem solving. Social validity was assessed to determine what Jackie and Meg thought about this experience and the three adults involved in the intervention and data collection. With the exception of the administrative interns' scores, everyone's social validity data indicated the intervention met (or exceeded) their initial expectations.

In addition to choice and OTR, a range of other Tier 2 and Tier 3 supports have been tested within tiered systems. In the next section, we illustrate a few of the lessons learned at Tiers 2 and 3 within Ci3T models of prevention.

Tier 2 and Tier 3 Supports

Important lessons have been learned about how to meet students' needs when they need more than primary prevention efforts have to offer.

Tier 2: Supporting First-Grade Students with Literacy and Behavioral Challenges

In one of the first Tier 2 academic interventions conducted within a Ci3T model, Lane, Wehby, Menzies, and colleagues (2002) conducted a supplemental early literacy program for first-grade students identified by their teachers as having behavioral challenges and as not making adequate progress with a Tier 1 efforts alone. Students were invited to participate in this extra literacy instruction if they met two criteria. First, students had to be rated by their teachers as at high risk (scores 9–21) on the SRSS in winter. Second, students had to be identified by their teachers as being in the lowest third of their class in terms of early literacy skills.

The intervention was conducted in a general education classroom during the course of the regular school day. After securing parents' permission, seven students were assigned randomly to one of two intervention groups (Group 1: $n = 4$; Group 2: $n = 3$) and evaluated using a multiple baseline design. The school literacy leader, a doctoral candidate, conducted both intervention groups in a general education classroom. Thirty lessons 30 minutes in length were held 3–4 days per week over a 9-week period. Although students showed initial variability in their decoding skills and behavior in the classroom, all students showed improved word attack skills and decreased levels of disruptive behavior in the classroom following the completion of the intervention. Improved early literacy skills were associated with lasting decreases in disruptive classroom behavior, which has also been observed in other academic interventions in relation to students with EBD (Falk & Wehby, 2001; Wehby, Falk, Barton-Arwood, Lane, & Cooley, 2003).

Tier 2: Supporting Second-Grade Students with Writing and Behavioral Challenges

In another study, Lane, Harris, and colleagues (2011) conducted an RCT of self-regulated strategy development (SRSD) for writing with second-grade students with writing and behavioral difficulties. Specifically, the goal was to see whether a Tier 2 intervention focused on improving writing skills would also result in improved academic engagement and behavior. This study took place in five inclusive elementary schools implementing a Ci3T model of prevention that included academic, behavioral (PBIS), and social (Positive Action) components.

Students were invited to participate in this study if they had challenges in writing according to the Test of Written Language–3 (TOWL-3; Hammill & Larsen, 1996) but could write at least one complete sentence, and behavior challenges as measured by the SRSS or the Systematic Screening for Behavior Disorders (SSBD; Walker & Severson, 1992). Across the five schools, 44 students (32 boys, 12 girls) participated.

After securing teacher and parent permission as well as student assent, students were randomly assigned to experimental (SRSD) or control (business as usual) conditions. Students with the SRSD experimental condition received Tier 2 support that included learning strategies for writing opinion essays and stories in addition to regular classroom writing instruction. Students in the control condition received only the regular classroom writing instruction. Intervention sessions were led by 11 graduate students who received 12 hours of training to learn how to lead SRSD lessons. Lessons were conducted three to four times each week in 30-minute sessions outside of the general education classrooms, with students requiring between nine and 13 lessons to master each writing genre.

Results indicated students who received SRSD instruction made greater improvements in writing quality and compositional elements for both opinion essays and stories than students in the control condition. Also, students in the experimental condition made greater improvements in academic engagement when writing their opinion essays in their general education classroom setting. The intervention was implemented with a high degree of fidelity, and students' social validity data suggested the intervention met their expectations.

Tier 2: Supporting Students with Social Skills Challenges

Building on the work of Lane, Wehyby, Menzies, and colleagues (2003), Common, Buckman, and colleagues (2019) conducted a study with second- and third-grade elementary student in four schools in which Ci3T was in place. As part of an Institute of Education Sciences (IES)–funded partnership grant, principals, counselors, and university partners examined the usability and feasibility of two commercially available programs: *Social Skills Improvement System—Intervention Guide* (SSiS-IG) and *Positive Action Counselor's Kit* (PACK), both of which were designed to teach and reinforce social skills associated with success within and beyond the school setting.

This study involved 10 second-grade and 14 third-grade students who were invited to participate based on fall 2016 scores on the Student Risk Screening Scale–Internalizing and Externalizing (SRSS-IE; Drummond, 1994; Lane & Menzies, 2009). In addition to scoring in the moderate- or high-risk range on the SRSS-IE, students had to have two or fewer absences during the first 3 months of school to ensure that they had regular access to Tier 1 supports before providing them with Tier 2 interventions.

After securing permissions from adults (counselors, teachers, parents) and students, students were randomly assigned to either the SSiS-IG or PACK intervention groups. Counselors at each school taught two groups (one for each curriculum) with 25- to 30-minute lessons taking place 2 days a week in general. The content of each social skills group was constructed based on students' acquisition deficits (e.g., skills that did not occur but were important to the teacher), identified by the Social Skills Improvement System—Rating Scale (SSiS-RS; Gresham & Elliott, 2008). To support generalization of skills taught in small-group sessions and to make transparent what took place in these counselor-led lessons, counselors sent emails to each student's teacher describing the lesson objectives and social skills topics (see Elliott & Gresham, 2008a, 2008b). This way, teachers were aware of what was taught and could acknowledge students for using the skills learned beyond the intervention session.

This study focused on practical considerations and includes a detailed description of how to determine which students might need Tier 2 supports in social skills. In addition, it provided a rich illustration of how to construct social skills content relevant to each student and implement lessons with fidelity during the regular school day in light of the multiple constraints faced by teachers and others (e.g., scheduling, ensuring core instruction is not missed). Furthermore, this study showed how it is possible to attend to practicalities, while still conducting a rigorous study that allows people to determine the extent to which the interventions were in place (treatment integrity); how those involved with day-to-day activities felt about the goals, procedures, and outcomes (social validity); and how it impacted student performance (e.g., learning and using new skills).

Tier 2: Check-In/Check-Out to Support Middle School Students

Check-in/check-out (Crone, Hawken, & Horner, 2010) is an individualized program designed to facilitate home–school communication and to connect students to caring adults in the school setting (Drevon, Hison, Wyse, & Rigney, 2019). It can be used when a student is having academic difficulties, is not completing class or homework, has emotional challenges, or is struggling with any issue that could be ameliorated with adult attention and support. It is also an effective intervention for students who have organizational or attentional difficulties, or low motivation.

The intervention consists of a student meeting with an adult mentor at the beginning of the school day (it can be a teacher, psychologist, administrator, or any other suitable school personnel) to pick up a personalized goal sheet and words of encouragement. Throughout the day, teachers use the goal sheet as a communication tool and write notes that the student's parents will review at home that evening. Before leaving school at the end of the day, the student meets again with the mentor. When the student returns the following morning to check-in, he or she returns the goal sheet that has been signed by a parent or guardian.

Studies show the effectiveness of this relatively simple intervention. For example, Lane, Capizzi, Fisher, and Ennis (2012) conducted a study of the efficacy of a check-in/check out behavior education program (BEP; Hawken, MacLeod, & Rawlings, 2007) with four middle school students. The eighth-grade boys attended a fully inclusive school in the Southeastern United States in their third year of implementing Ci3T. Students were identified for the Tier 2 intervention based on the following criteria: scored in the moderate- or high-risk category on the SRSS or had low levels of work completion and teacher-indicated poor classroom behavior. One student also received special education services under the category of other health impaired (OHI) at the time of the study. The mentor was a male, a paraprofessional, and an athletic coach.

After teachers, parents and students gave permission for participation, research assistants (interns pursuing Board Certified Behavior Analyst [BCBA] certification) conducted functional behavioral assessments (FBAs) using direct and indirect assessment methods (Umbreit et al., 2007). Target behaviors were operationally defined (e.g., incomplete work, off task, disrespect) and, using the FBA data, the functions of the behavior(s) were hypothesized to be access to attention and escape from difficult tasks for all four students. A changing criterion design was used to evaluate the Tier 2 intervention. The goal criterion for the daily progress report points (referred to as *cooperation* or *compliance*) was increased when the previous goal was met for 3 consecutive days, until students met an 85% criterion. There was a modest functional relation between the BEP intervention and changes in student behavior for three of the students, although maintenance effects were limited. The intervention was implemented with adequate treatment fidelity ($M = 93\%$) using two approaches: observing the check-in and check-out sessions, and evaluating the completeness of the daily progress reports. Teachers and students rated the intervention as mostly favorable.

Tier 3: Functional Assessment-Based Interventions for Students with Intensive Intervention Needs

There is a substantial evidence based for the use of functional assessment-based interventions (FABIs; Umbreit et al., 2007), with potentially positive effects on school engagement and problem behavior for students with and at risk for EBD (What Works Clearinghouse, 2008). FABIs have been used as Tier 3 interventions by schools implementing Ci3T models to improve academic engagement during writing at the elementary level and to improve on-task behavior at the high school level. FABIs are intensive, individualized interventions conducted by a team of school personnel with expertise in behavioral principles and applied behavior analytic (ABA) techniques. Due to the intensity of supports and resources needed, school personnel often implement FABIs for students with the most intensive need.

The two studies we present here were conducted by graduate research assistants who were interns in a BCBA program at a local university. They supported schools implementing Ci3T models by designing and implementing Tier 3 efforts. They worked in teams to conduct an FBA; hypothesize the function of the students' problem behavior; and develop an intervention with antecedent adjustments, shifts in reinforcement, and extinction procedures to promote the use of the identified replacement behavior (Umbreit et al., 2007). The examples address students' academic and behavioral needs using FABIs.

In the first example, Aitken and colleagues (2011) conducted an FABI as a Tier 3 intervention for a school in their first year of implementing Ci3T. Four interns worked with a local elementary teacher to support the academic and behavioral needs of one third-grade student with off-task behavior during writing assignments. The student was identified as needing Tier 3 support according to teacher-reported academic needs and a SRSS high-risk category score. After teacher, guardian, and student gave permission, the interns conducted the FBA using direct (antecedent–behavior–consequences observations) and indirect measures (teacher and parent interviews, rating scales). Off task was identified as the students' target behavior. The FBA data were summarized in the Function Matrix and a hypothesis statement formed. The student was off task during independent work time to access positive reinforcement (teacher attention) and negative reinforcement (avoiding writing activities). Therefore, an intervention was designed to increase the student's academic engaged time. To determine the appropriate intervention method, the functional-based intervention decision model was used to determine (1) whether the student was capable of doing the replacement behavior and (2) whether antecedent conditions in the classroom represented best practices for this study. It was determined the student, Caleb, could not perform the required writing task necessary to be academically engaged (the replacement behavior) and that the antecedent conditions were not optimal for Caleb. Therefore, the decision was made to teach the needed academic skills and adjust the antecedent conditions necessary to set the stage for Caleb to be engaged (a combination of Method 1: Teach the Replacement Behavior and Method 2: Improve the Environment).

Next, an intervention was developed with ARE components: antecedent (A), teach the needed skills and set the stage for them to be used; reinforcement (R), shift to ensure the new behaviors worked well for the student in getting his needs met, and; extinction (E), of the undesirable target behavior. The intervention tactics included teaching a writing strategy; using a self-monitoring checklist; providing behavior specific praise, using the school reinforcement systems (e.g., earning tickets) and the ability to earn computer time for work completion; and using a nonverbal gesture to redirect the student when needed. The teacher implemented the intervention with adequate treatment integrity. Data showed an increase in treatment integrity during the second intervention phase. A withdrawal design (A–B–B′–A–B′) was used to evaluate the effectiveness of the intervention for the student. Results indicated a functional relation between the intervention and an increase in the student's academic engaged time. The student also improved his writing in terms of word count and functional story elements. Social validity was high for the teacher and student. Authors demonstrated an effective intervention addressing academic and behavioral needs in one Tier 3 intervention.

In another example at the high school level, Majeika, Walder, Hubbard, Steeb, and Ferris (2011) conducted an FABI to assist a school implementing Ci3T. Interns worked with two local high school teachers, an English teacher and special education teacher, to address the academic and behavioral needs of one 11th-grade student receiving special education under the category of OHI and with attention-deficit/hyperactivity disorder (ADHD). The student was identified as being in need of Tier 3 support, with a grade point average below 2.75, 24 ODRs earned in the previous school year, and a high-risk score on the SRSS spring time point. After teacher, parent, and student gave permission, the interns conducted the FBA using direct (antecedent–behavior–consequences observations) and indirect measures (teacher and parent interviews, rating scales). The teachers agreed being off task was an appropriate target behavior. The team summarized FBA data using the Function Matrix and made a hypothesis statement. The student was off task during instruction to access positive reinforcement (teacher and peer attention) and negative reinforcement (avoiding assigned academic activities). Therefore, an intervention was designed to increase the student's on-task behavior during instruction. Working through the functional-based intervention decision model (Umbriet et al., 2007), it was determined the student was capable of engaging in the target behavior, but there were environmental conditions that could be enhanced to improve his engagement. Therefore, an intervention was designed in accordance with Method 2: Improve the Environment. The intervention included antecedent adjustments, shifts in reinforcement of the desired behavior, and extinction.

The intervention included a behavior contract, a self-monitoring checklist, instruction for accessing attention; contingent behavior-specific praise, daily and weekly awards, access to the schoolwide reinforcement system; and brief redirections and praise to other students who are on task. The teacher implemented the intervention with low levels of overall treatment integrity. However, data showed high implementation of antecedent components (e.g., behavior contact, self-monitoring). A withdrawal design (A–B–A–B) indicated a functional relation between the intervention and the student's on-task behavior; in other words, the student's on-task behavior improved as a result of the changes the teacher made. Social validity was high for the teacher and moderate and stable from pre- to postintervention for the high school student. This study demonstrated the effective implementation of a Tier 3 support for a high school study in a cotaught inclusive class.

Teacher Efficacy and Perceptions

Another important, emerging body of evidence is examining how teachers fare in tiered systems. When thinking about the logic behind tiered systems, one might say this shift toward a systems-level approach involves empowering teachers who then empower students (Lane, 2017). As such, it is wise to also consider how implementing the plan impacts teachers' experiences (e.g., teacher self-efficacy, burnout; Oakes, Lane, Jenkins, & Booker, 2013; Ross & Horner, 2007; Ross, Romer, & Horner, 2011).

Teachers' Sense of Efficacy

As schools implement a Ci3T model, which may provide benefits related to improved school climate similar to PBIS (Bradshaw et al., 2010), there may be promise in supporting teachers' sense of efficacy in addressing the multiple educational needs of students. *Self-efficacy* refers to the belief that one is capable of effecting change (Bandura, 1993). Specifically, *teacher self-efficacy* can be defined as teachers' beliefs about their ability to yield desired student outcomes (Tschannen-Moran & Woolfolk Hoy, 2001). Teachers' beliefs influence their instructional choices and persistence. Teachers who report lower levels of teaching self-efficacy also have higher levels of burnout (Brouwers & Tomic, 2000), which is the outcome of long periods of feeling ineffective. With higher levels of burnout, teachers may become discouraged about teaching, surrender to chaotic classroom environments (Chang, 2009) or increase the use of exclusionary practices (Brunsting, Sreckovic, & Lane, 2014).

Inquiry related to efficacy and indicators of burnout in relation to working in tiered systems is important. To date, three studies have examined these constructs within the context of three-tiered models of prevention (Oakes et al., 2013; Ross & Horner, 2007; Ross, Romer, & Horner, 2011). Ross and Horner (2007) conducted a study with four schools implementing PBIS and found a statistically significant, positive relation between the level of integrity of PBIS and teacher efficacy (higher implementation, higher sense of teacher efficacy)—but not for teacher burnout. Ross and colleagues' (2011) findings indicate a significant relation between level of implementation and teacher efficacy and burnout with a larger sample. Teachers at schools with high fidelity had significantly higher levels of efficacy and lower levels of burnout relative to teachers working in schools with lower levels of PBIS implementation. In other words, teachers in schools using PBIS effectively were more likely to feel positive about their teaching and less likely to feel burned out.

To extend this work, Oakes and colleagues (2013) examined teacher efficacy and burnout for middle school teachers in their first year of Ci3T implementation. Participating teachers completed the Teachers' Sense of Efficacy Scale 24-Item Long Form (TSES; Tschannen-Moran & Woolfolk Hoy, 2001) and the Maslach Burnout Inventory (MBI; Maslach, Jackson, & Leiter, 1996) at the end of the school year. In schools implementing Ci3T, teachers generally had lower levels of burnout relative to national norms, yet higher levels of emotional exhaustion. Additional inquiry is needed to examine teachers' sense of efficacy in schools implementing Ci3T models of prevention and the relation between efficacy, treatment integrity, social validity, and student outcomes.

Clearly there are still other questions that need to be addressed. Examples of next steps may include exploring the following questions:

- To what extent do teachers view the Ci3T plans as socially valid before their first year of implementation?
- To what extent do teachers in schools implementing Ci3T models report feelings of burnout and efficacy?
- To what degree do teachers' feelings of self-efficacy and burnout shift over time during implementation?
- What is the relation between teachers' reported levels of self-efficacy, burnout, social validity, and treatment integrity of their school's Ci3T plans?
- To what extent do stakeholders' initial views of the Ci3T plan at the end of training (as measured by the Primary Intervention Rating Scale; Lane, Kalberg, et al., 2009) predict treatment integrity over time?

Our team looks forward to answering these questions in the years ahead with current and future district partners. We encourage other team to explore these and other questions as well.

Teachers' Perspectives on Tiered Models

In addition to exploring how teachers fare in tiered systems, other inquiry is taking place to learn from teachers' experiences and ultimately use this information to inform professional learning and subsequent inquiry. A recent study examining the efficacy of Ci3T (Menzies et al., 2019) identified several issues important to teachers when implementing a tiered system of support. One essential element in adopting Ci3T was strong administrative leadership. Without it, new programs are unlikely to be valued or sustained. Another area of enduring concern for teachers is adequate time for planning, collaboration, and training. Finally, teachers noted the difficulty in moving from a reactive to a proactive approach to managing student behavior. Each of these areas requires intentional thought and support from school and district administrators, and how they are handled will greatly affect the success a school has with implementing a tiered model.

Leadership

A principal's leadership is instrumental to an initiative's success. It is the principal who rallies teachers and staff members to use their time and energy to pursue the reform or new practice. They signal the importance of the endeavor (Dolph, 2017). Principals have discretion over how resources and teacher time are allocated. They also prioritize school and district goals. Without a principal's leadership to focus attention on district and school goals, there is unlikely to be a cohesive effort to reach them (Lohrmann, Forman, Martin, & Palmieri, 2008). In a national sample of school personnel, Mathews, McIntosh, Frank, and May (2014) found administrator support was rated as one of the most important factors in sustaining schoolwide PBIS.

Time

The need to allocate time for professional learning and collaborating with colleagues is a constant theme in the literature on reform. Teachers feel there is little time available to work on their everyday responsibilities, and even less time for new initiatives (Merritt, 2016). There is evidence that when teachers spend time collaborating over data, schoolwide systems are likely to be have better outcomes (Andreou et al., 2015; McIntosh et al., 2018), and since tiered systems are premised on strong collaboration among all stakeholders in the school community, time is a primary resource and must be managed judiciously.

Behavior and Classroom Management

The switch from a reactive to a proactive model of behavior management is a monumental change in practice for many teachers. It requires attention to technical concerns such as professional learning, as well as a change in a school's culture about student discipline. A Ci3T model uses a host of techniques to shape the environment so student misbehavior is prevented rather than addressed after the fact (although consequences, too, are an integral part of a Tier 1 plan). These include a focus on ABA principles, as well as careful attention to instructional practices that promote active student engagement. Historically, schools have defaulted to punishment strategies (e.g., time-out, suspension, expulsion, shaming, reprimands) that create a culture of exclusion. Teachers need access to training that explains the harm of punishment-based discipline to understand why it may seem work in the short term but results in serious negative outcomes in the long term (Pierce & Cheney, 2017). Teachers would also benefit from more information about the relation between engaging instruction and student behavior. Since Kounin's work in the 1970s (e.g., Kounin, 1977) and Brophy and Good's research (1986), we have been aware of how teachers' instructional choices and classroom management practices impact student achievement and behavior, but student behavior is still frequently characterized as a within-child phenomenon, without giving enough weight to the ability of teachers to arrange the environment to minimize behavioral issues.

Teachers report being underprepared by their preservice training on using classroom management strategies (Cooper et al., 2018). There are also structural elements of schools that can exacerbate behavior problems, such as too many students in a class and limited space. High-stakes accountability policies (Thangarajathi & Joel, 2010; von der Embse, Sandilos, Pendergast, & Mankin, 2016) may also reduce teachers' tolerance for misbehavior because of the pressure they feel to deliver academic instruction. In addition to structural and resource barriers, teachers' opinions about punishment are influenced by societal beliefs (Stearns & Stearns, 2017). Some teachers sincerely believe punishment to be an appropriate response that will teach students how to navigate the "real" world in the future.

Summary

Teachers' perceptions about the barriers and facilitators to reform are interrelated. Good leadership is attentive to managing time and allocating resources such as training. It is also the job of leadership to help teachers move away from old practices and adopt new ones, which, in turn, is dependent on adequate planning time and professional development. Sensitivity to teachers' perceptions is critical to successful reform, as teachers are highly aware of the difficulties that impede change.

Data-Informed Professional Learning

In addition to considering how teachers fare in tiered systems, it is important to explore professional development needs to address issues of sustainability (McIntosh, Martinez, Ty, & McClain, 2013). In a statewide survey of administrators' perspectives on Ci3T, Lane and colleagues (2015) gathered information from 365 site-level administrators to (1) learn about the degree to which schools across the state were implementing components of Ci3T and (2) determine professional development and resources needs to support implementation. Most administrators reported that Tier 1 features were implemented with a high level of integrity, with the exception of instruction in schoolwide behavioral expectations. Not surprisingly, results indicated that Tier 1 implementation was greater in elementary schools compared to middle and high schools. Administrators reported Tier 2 and Tier 3 behavioral and social supports were implemented to a lesser degree than were academic supports. The majority of administrators reported high-fidelity implementation of the 15 research-based educational practices and supports examined. There was a positive relation between administrators' ratings of currently implemented practices and the desire for support for all educational practices and interventions, with the exception of increasing behavior-specific praise. When asked to provide input on potential venues for professional development and learning, in-district, during-school workshops and practices guides were rated most favorably by administrators.

As part of a recent IES-funded partnership grant, one district used a modified version of this survey to assess current levels of implementation and determine next steps for professional learning. The survey was given to faculty and staff after 3 years of Ci3T implementation in the elementary schools and 2 years of implementation in middle and high schools. Summary reports were shared with each school's Ci3T Leadership Team depicting its school's results, as well as summary information at each school level (e.g., for all elementary school, for all middle schools, and for all high schools). The district Ci3T Leadership Team used this information to inform the content and avenues for professional learning in the following year. This is but one illustration of the data-informed approach to professional learning characterized by Ci3T models of prevention.

Summary

Research conducted by Lane, Menzies, Oakes, Kalberg, and colleagues over the last 20 years has yielded a series of descriptive, experimental, and psychometric studies of this model. However, an important next step is to conduct an RCT of the full model. Similar to the progression of inquiry for PBIS (which also began with descriptive inquiry, then RCTs), an RCT is viewed as the "gold standard" for determining the impact of Ci3T when implemented with integrity.

In the meantime, in the work conducted to date, we have learned several important lessons with our district partners (e.g., see Lessons Learned 2.3 and 2.4), some of which include the following:

- When examining school-site averages of social validity ratings during the Ci3T professional learning series (training year), faculty and staff who rate the plan as more socially valid

LESSONS LEARNED 2.3. Fostering Positive Relationships

The Ci3T model is a powerful tool for fostering the important relationships that make a classroom a successful environment for learning. I have witnessed teachers utilize Ci3T's common sense and compassionate student management techniques to transform their classrooms into environments in which all students feel valued. It is in these types of environments that academic and social growth are most prominent.

Bill DeWitt
Vice Principal/Athletic Director

LESSONS LEARNED 2.4. Empowering Ci3T Leadership Teams and Serving Students

Using the Ci3T process to design plans of prevention has had a transformative effect on each of our participating schools. The work begins as a way for schools to organize the amazing things they are already doing, so that everyone involved—faculty, staff, students, and community—all know who they are and how they do business. Then, because the process is grounded in research-based, effective practices, the work, quite naturally, also becomes a positive catalyst for teams to analyze and reconsider some of those practices, reflecting on why and how adjustments should be made. In other words, the nature of the process empowers teams to create truly informed and responsive plans that will best serve the needs of their student population.

Therese Brink Edgecomb
Professional Development Coordinator

prior to implementation are more likely to implement Ci3T with integrity than faculty and staff who view the plan as less socially valid (Lane, Kalberg, Bruhn, et al., 2009).

- Schools implementing their Ci3T plan—inclusive of academic, behavioral, and social components—with high integrity show decreases in the overall level of behavioral risk for students (evidenced in descriptive studies; e.g., Lane, Kalberg, Bruhn, Mahoney, et al., 2008; Lane, Menzies, Oakes, & Kalberg, 2012). To be clear, these studies involved all components of Ci3T implementation, including academic, behavior, and social skills exemplifying the broadening of MTSS offered by Ci3T. For example, in Lane, Kalberg, Bruhn, and colleagues (2008), the social skills component included Character Under Construction, the program adopted by the district. Other programs have included Positive Action, Connect with Kids, Social Skills Improvement System, and so on.

- Student behavior screening scores predict academic performance across the K–12 continuum (e.g., reading measures, grade point average [GPA], course failures) in addition to performance on social and behavioral measures (e.g., ODRs, suspensions, self-control skills; e.g., Ennis, Lane, & Oakes, 2012; Lane, Kalberg, Parks, & Carter, 2008; Lane et al., 2013; Oakes et al., 2010). Many of these screening studies were conducted in schools implementing Ci3T.

- Findings from experimental studies at Tier 2 (group and single case designs) offer evidence how academic interventions, such as SRSD for writing, have resulted in improved written expression and increased academic engagement when implemented within the context of Ci3T models (e.g., Lane, Harris, et al., 2011). Again, these schools were implementing the full Ci3T model. Other experimental studies have also been conducted (e.g., Oakes et al., 2012).

- Several single-case design Tier 3 studies have shown FABIs implemented in schools with Ci3T models resulted in improved behaviors—including academic engagement—for students experiencing the most intensive challenges (e.g., Cox, Griffin, Hall, Oakes, & Lane, 2011; Germer et al., 2011). In the methods sections of many of these articles, you will find treatment integrity data on procedures for teaching, reinforcing, and monitoring at Tier 1 to ensure that the reader understood Tier 1 practices were in place.

- An initial study by Oakes and colleagues (2013) showed teachers working in Ci3T schools generally had higher levels of self-efficacy and lower levels of burnout relative to national norms.

- A recent qualitative study identified several areas for additional professional learning opportunities—including information on the detriment of punishment and underlying ABA principles—as Ci3T is an application of ABA at scale (Menzies et al., 2019). As part of our IES Researcher Partnership grant, we also learned that strong school and district leadership are essential to shifting school practices, and teachers want and require ongoing professional development in a variety of modes to better understand behavioral principles and proactive practices (Menzies et al., 2019).

Although not yet published, schools are sustaining Ci3T. For example, also in our IES partnership grant, despite four superintendents in the last 6 years, the partner district is still implementing Ci3T districtwide. For example, see Figure 2.2 for a graph of treatment integrity data from one of our partner elementary schools.

This collective evidence suggests Ci3T models of prevention show promising outcomes for systems and students, yet an RCT is necessary at this time. Ultimately, RCTs are needed to establish the evidence base for the full model, and our team is poised to conduct such inquiry. In the meantime, when designing primary prevention plans, we encourage you to build a strong, defensible plan that allows you to draw accurate conclusions about whether primary prevention is achieving the desired outcomes (Cook & Cook, 2013; Council for Exceptional Children [CEC], 2014; Gersten, Fuchs, et al., 2005; Horner et al., 2005). Specifically, we recommend the following:

1. Design a Ci3T model based on the needs of your school.
2. Describe clearly both your school's characteristics and the plan so others can replicate what you have done and make accurate decisions about the circumstances under which your program "worked."
3. Include a range of outcome measures that are reliable, valid, and sensitive to change.
4. Include a method for monitoring the degree to which the plan is implemented as designed (referred to as *treatment integrity*; Gresham, 1989; Lane & Beebe-Frankenberger, 2004, see Chapter 4) and the consumers' opinions about the plan's

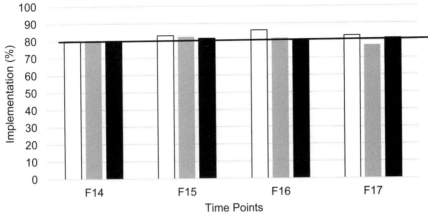

FIGURE 2.2. Treatment integrity data using multiple perspectives. Ci3T TI, comprehensive, integrated, three-tiered model of prevention: treatment integrity; TSR, teacher self-report; DO, direct observation. Horizontal line indicates goal of 80%.

goals, procedures, and outcomes (referred to as *social validity*; Kazdin, 1977; Lane & Beebe-Frankenberger, 2004; Wolf, 1978).

5. Employ an experimental design that allows you to draw accurate conclusions about how the Ci3T plan influenced student behavior, using caution not to draw causal conclusions if the design did not include a true experimental test.

6. Use data analysis procedures appropriate to the design.

The Ci3T plan should provide very clear guidelines and procedures for identifying students who require more intensive intervention that can be provided within the context of secondary and tertiary levels of prevention (Walker, Forness, & Lane, 2014).

As a practitioner, adhering to core quality indicators will allow you to create and implement a primary prevention program that is well documented and defensible, should the need arise. Furthermore, by designing a well-defined primary (Tier 1) plan that is more comprehensive because it includes an academic emphasis in addition to the behavioral and social domains, you are more apt to (1) meet the instructional goals you set for your school as the instructional leader and (2) inform broad-scale changes and targeted interventions for students with additional needs, as mandated by the Every Student Succeeds Act (ESSA; 2015) and the IDEA (2004). As a researcher, including core quality indicators will allow valid inferences to be drawn about the internal and external validity of your study and enable others to determine whether the practices employed are truly evidence-based (CEC, 2014).

PART II

Overview of the Ci3T Implementation Manual

The Ci3T Implementation Manual comprises the following blueprints developed over the course of the yearlong professional learning series (see *ci3t.org,* Building your Ci3T Model):

- Ci3T Blueprint A Primary (Tier 1) Plan
- Ci3T Blueprint B Reactive Plan
- Ci3T Blueprint C Expectation Matrix
- Ci3T Blueprint D Assessment Schedule
- Ci3T Blueprint E Secondary (Tier 2) Intervention Grid
- Ci3T Blueprint F Tertiary (Tier 3) Intervention Grid

The building process begins with constructing the primary (Tier 1) prevention plan that includes Ci3T Blueprints A–F.

In Chapter 3, *Designing and Implementing a Ci3T Model: Building a Primary Prevention Plan,* we explain the rationale for using a Ci3T model and the process Ci3T Leadership Teams use to begin their primary (Tier 1) prevention efforts. The focus of the first step is to define the mission, purpose, roles, and responsibilities of students, faculty and staff, parents, and administrators in academic, behavioral, and social domains. As part of Tier 1 efforts, Ci3T Leadership Teams develop a reactive plan to provide guidance on how to respond when challenging behavior occurs, as well as expectations for specific settings to facilitate school success. After establishing these roles and responsibilities, we focus on procedures for teaching and reinforcing all stakeholders. Then, in

Chapter 4, *Examining Tier 1 Efforts: Monitoring Treatment Integrity and Social Validity,* we focus on establishing procedures for monitoring implementation. This includes assessing the degree to which Tier 1 plans are put in place as planned (treatment integrity); stakeholders' views about the goals, procedures, and outcomes (social validity); and student performance, which involves the use of systematic screening to detect the first signs of concern. As part of this process, Ci3T Leadership Teams build an assessment schedule to make transparent all information collected at the program level and for all students in a building.

CHAPTER 3

Designing and Implementing
a Ci3T Model

BUILDING A PRIMARY PREVENTION PLAN

Our goal in this book is to help you design, implement, and evaluate a comprehensive, integrated, three-tiered (Ci3T) model to prevent the development of learning and behavioral challenges and to provide additional support for students who struggle academically, behaviorally, and socially. Specifically, this chapter focuses on a method of constructing primary plans that has been used across the K–12 continuum (Lane, Oakes, & Menzies, 2014). The process we illustrate is a data-informed, team-based approach for developing a framework that is closely tied to the model introduced by Sugai and Horner (2002, 2006), with positive behavior interventions and supports (PBIS) at the center of the model. However, Ci3T is broader in scope, in that it includes (1) an academic emphasis, (2) a data-based process for constructing expectations, and (3) the adoption of a validated social–emotional curriculum to meet district- or school-identified priorities. In addition, during implementation, Ci3T features use not only data to inform instruction for students but also data to inform professional learning (topics and venues) for those responsible for implementation (e.g., teachers, paraprofessional, related service providers, administrators). As we discussed in Chapter 1, Ci3T includes an explicit commitment to meeting students' academic, behavior, and social–emotional needs in one comprehensive, integrated continuum of supports. Like other tiered systems, this model includes primary (Tier 1), secondary (Tier 2), and tertiary (Tier 3) levels of prevention (see Figure 3.1).

In this chapter, we provide an overview of a step-by-step, team-based approach for designing and implementing a primary prevention model that integrates academic, behavioral, and social components, based on the work of Lane, Menzies, Kalberg, and colleagues (Lane, Kalberg, Bruhn, et al., 2009; Lane & Menzies, 2002, 2005; Lane, Wehby, et al., 2007; Robertson & Lane, 2007). We begin by discussing district-level considerations—how to involve district leaders to establish priorities around systems change. Next, we provide a detailed description of how to use a team-based approach, with input from faculty, staff, parents, and students to

Ci3T Professional Learning Series

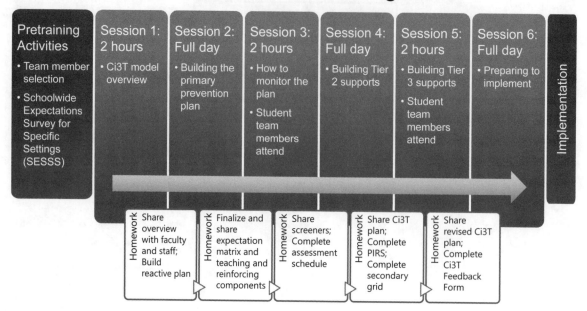

FIGURE 3.1. Ci3T training graphic. From Lane, Oakes, Cantwell, and Royer (2016). Copyright © 2016 the authors. Reprinted by permission. Available at *www.ci3t.org*.

construct a context-sensitive, customized primary (Tier 1) prevention plan that addresses the core values held by the school community. Then we explain specific procedures for implementing the primary (Tier 1) prevention efforts at the school site, namely, procedures for teaching and reinforcing the desired expectations to all stakeholders (e.g., students, faculty and staff, as well as parents and community members). We provide suggestions on how to "kick-off" or launch primary (Tier 1) efforts, as well as how to continue teaching and reinforcing expectations throughout the school year. We end the chapter with a brief summary of the content and a preview of the next steps: monitoring student progress. In Chapter 4, we discuss procedures for monitoring implementation. This is critical because knowing whether the model has been implemented as designed provides information to determine whether it works. If your school does not see positive changes in student outcomes, monitoring implementation lets you know if it is because the plan is not being followed. If it is being followed and the desired changes have not occurred, then the plan needs to be adjusted.

A Team-Based Process for Training and Developing the Model: A Focus on the Schoolwide System

Determine the Need for Systems Change: District-Level Considerations

In our experience with installing Ci3T districtwide, we have found it is important to establish a district-level leadership team. Lessons learned from Kent McIntosh and colleagues have taught the field the importance of strong district support. When a district has a critical mass of schools participating in schoolwide initiatives at the same time, sustained implementation several years later is more likely (McIntosh et al., 2018). This may be due to the training and support a district can provide as schools adopt the new practices. In particular, schools that have strong implementation fidelity during the first year and use a team-based approach to examine data for decision making are the most successful. Both of these elements require professional development and coaching as schools become comfortable with the new approach. For example, school personnel must learn how to create systems for collecting data and how to systematically analyze and disseminate it in a manageable and meaningful way. Schools also require assistance with how to conduct efficient meetings in which they take action on the data to meet goals and establish new priorities. Districts can be instrumental in expanding a school's capacity to successfully adopt and implement a reform.

Many of our district partners have developed Ci3T District Master Implementation Manuals featuring elements to be consistent across school levels (e.g., across all elementary, middle, and high schools), as well as some elements to be consistent across the entire district. For example, if a district has adopted validated reading curricula such as Reading Street (Pearson Education, 2013) and AIMSweb (Pearson Education, 2015a) as the benchmarking systems for reading and mathematics, these would be specified in the Ci3T District Master Implementation Manual for elementary schools. This ensures all elementary students have access to the same instruction and screenings districtwide, and it supports equitable access to tiered preventions. Similarly, if the district adopted Connect With Kids (Connect With Kids Network, 2017) for middle and high schools, the curriculum would be detailed in the manual (sometimes referred to as district non-negotiables or certainties).

At the onset of the building process, issues of sustainability and continuous improvement (Fixsen, Blasé, Metz, & Van Dyke, 2013) must be considered. Increasing district capacity to not only design but also implement and evaluate is critical. District leaders provide communication to all stakeholders about the adoption of a Ci3T model. Districts consider a long-term plan for dedicating resources and developing the capacity of school personnel to meet students' multiple needs (Horner, Sugai, & Fixsen, 2017). For example, resources are dedicated for data systems and structures such as academic and behavior screening, treatment integrity, and social validity measures. As well, investments are planned for selecting and purchasing evidence-based academic and social skills curricula and materials for tiered interventions, and related professional learning. Ongoing professional learning is needed so that selected curricula and interventions are implemented with fidelity and educators feel adequately prepared to achieve the desired student outcome. To address sustainability, district leaders may appoint personnel with time dedicated to Ci3T efforts rather than just tacking these responsibilities on to existing duties. As such, we encourage districts to identify Ci3T Trainers and Ci3T Coaches to facilitate the goals of installation and continuous improvement. For example, Ci3T Trainers provide regular professional learning for Ci3T Leadership Teams as they launch and continue to implement their Ci3T plan in the first 2 years. Experienced Trainers predict the content needed by teams as they implement in the first year, such as conducting systematic screening, collecting and analyzing data, and developing leadership structures. Furthermore, principals and Ci3T Leadership Teams change over time, so Ci3T Coaches support consistency over time. Ci3T Coaches keep teams current with new research, ensure alignment with all district initiatives and board policies, and support the review of data for continuous high-fidelity implementation.

District plans for rolling out Ci3T must be carefully constructed, with attention to resources—personnel, time, and financial considerations. For example, some districts begin with early adopters and allow principal leaders to self-select who will be trained in the first cohort. Others districts have developed installation plans that train all elementary schools first, then all secondary schools. Others have organized their installations plans by feeder patterns (e.g., training the elementary, middle, and high schools that students begin and "flow through" to graduation).

In other circumstances, Ci3T does not begin as a district initiative (see Lessons Learned 3.1). Instead, one or more schools' leadership teams may wish to develop a Ci3T model. In these instances, it is important to secure district support to ensure that district leaders are supportive of this direction because the Ci3T Leadership Teams will need professional learning and resources (e.g., implementing a social skills curriculum, data collection systems, and increasing use of low-intensity strategies) to assist with the design process and implementation efforts.

Begin at the School Site

After determining the district's role in the process, the next step is a meeting with the full faculty and staff to establish a Ci3T Leadership Team to work through the design process (see Figure 3.1 for the Ci3T Professional Learning Training Series; Lane, Oakes, Cantwell, & Royer, 2016, 2018). Once established and ready, it is the role of the Ci3T Leadership team to provide an overview of the Ci3T model, with an emphasis on the importance of developing a comprehensive primary plan. During a 1-hour faculty meeting, the Ci3T Leadership Team should introduce the rationale for developing a primary (Tier 1) prevention plan that meets

LESSONS LEARNED 3.1. A Success with Professional Learning

Ci3T began as a grassroots movement at two of our elementary schools and has grown to include all of our elementary schools and our middle school. Because of this, our District Leadership Team has had the task of playing catch-up in determining how best to provide support and guidance. We have had the most success when we have responded to genuine needs and have built in an iterative process with feedback loops, much like the work done within the schools as they develop their plans. The benefits of this process have been most clear in how we have provided a layered approach to our professional learning opportunities. Whether we are going into schools directly to make presentations, providing un-conference sessions for discussion, building quick mini-sessions for fly-by training, displaying posters of amazing Ci3T work throughout our district, creating editable slide shows for leaders to use with their staff members, or inviting our in-house leaders and the KU Ci3T team to present specific topics, we are constantly checking back in with our teams and listening to individuals with regard to what is needed next to support our schools.

Therese Brink Edgecomb
Professional development coordinator

the schools' unique needs (academically, behaviorally, and socially) and cultural values and is aligned with district and board priorities (e.g., equity, excellence, and engagement). We are not suggesting schools do "one more thing" by adopting a Ci3T model. Instead of working "harder," we want to help schools work "smarter" (Sugai & Horner, 2006) by developing a three-tiered model that streamlines delivery of academic, behavioral, and social–emotional supports. The Ci3T plan should include the district and school's already established goals for improvement, and use the supports and expectations currently in place (e.g., elements noted in the Ci3T District Master Implementation Manual; see Lessons Learned 3.2). This latter point of emphasis is particularly important because of what we call "hit and run" research and/ or professional development. Many teachers have attended professional development sessions that recommend a new strategy or curriculum, only to find that 6 months, 1 year, or 2 years later, the district recommends or mandates *another* new strategy or curriculum to address the same issue. However, Ci3T—like PBIS—is not a curriculum. It is a model based on the needs and resources of the district and school, and it changes as the district and school change. Thus, it is comparable to a constitution—a living document that accommodates and allows for change at the end of each academic year.

The next step is to explain the training activities that occur in Year 1 and to have the school form a Ci3T Leadership Team (discussed below). It is the team's job to explain how a Ci3T model may improve the school's ability to meet the needs of all students, with a particular emphasis on better supporting students with, or at risk for, learning and behavior problems. The Ci3T Leadership Team members plan how they will communicate with the full faculty and staff each month during regularly scheduled faculty meetings to provide updates, engage in conversation, and allow for input to inform the design process. During these meetings, faculty and staff learn more about the potential benefits and receive an overview of how to design, implement, and evaluate their Ci3T model. As part of the Ci3T data-informed design process, all faculty and staff complete three surveys: (1) the Schoolwide Expectations Survey for Specific Settings (SESSS; Lane, Oakes, & Menzies, 2010), (2) the Primary Intervention Rating Scale (PIRS; Lane, Kalberg, Bruhn, et al., 2009; Lane, Robertson, & Wehby, 2002), and (3) the Ci3T Model of Prevention Feedback Form (Lane, 2002). The SESSS is completed by faculty and staff before beginning the Ci3T Professional Learning Series to identify specific skills to support success in specific school settings (details to follow).

After Session 4, faculty and staff review the Ci3T Blueprints A–D plan drafted by their Ci3T Leadership Team during the training series and provide feedback by completing a social

---

LESSONS LEARNED 3.2. A Comprehensive Framework

As a building principal and now district leader, Ci3T provides us the first real comprehensive framework that includes everything our schools do, from a global perspective to day-to-day operational beliefs. It's a system that provides focus, philosophy, and a cycle of monitoring and data review that truly informs our practice.

Jennifer Bessolo, EdD
Curriculum Director

validity survey (Lane, Kalberg, Bruhn, et al., 2009) to determine faculty and staff members' opinions about the goals, procedures, and potential outcomes of the primary (Tier 1) plan (see Figure 3.1). Some Ci3T Leadership Teams solicit parental and student feedback by randomly selecting parents and their children to complete a similar social validity survey. We strongly advise collecting input from multiple stakeholders. For schools and districts with the resources to seek and incorporate parent and student feedback, it is useful information for the building process. Information gleaned from the PIRS is used to inform revisions by the team during Session 5 and determine specific areas for professional learning in the months ahead (e.g., additional learning opportunities on low-intensity supports to increase engagement and decrease disruption, the difference between bribery and reinforcement, and how to develop integrated lesson plans). Following Session 5, faculty and staff provide a final point of feedback on the fully drafted Ci3T plan, Blueprints A–F, using the Ci3T Feedback Form. To this end, faculty and staff receive the revised Ci3T Blueprints A–F along with a brief explanation about (1) what people appreciated, (2) what has been changed based on input, and (3) areas for ongoing professional learning in the months ahead. When installing Ci3T in a school-initiated endeavor, faculty and staff often vote on whether they would like to implement the Ci3T plan during the next year (see Lane, Oakes, Cantwell, & Royer, 2018). If more than a simple majority of the faculty and staff agree to offer their input on the building process, then this is enough of a critical mass to move forward with training activities. Faculty and staff who indicate they do not wish to implement the plan may be asked to sign a "no sabotage" clause, which means that although they are not in favor of the plan, they are willing to refrain from saying anything derogatory about it. However, when Ci3T is a district initiative, "voting" on the plan may not be necessary. When district leaders decide to adopt Ci3T, the structure becomes the accepted way of doing business to meet students' multiple needs. In essence, Ci3T becomes similar to a constitution for the district and each school, serving as the structure for housing all district initiatives to meet school board goals.

Establish a District-Level Leadership Team

When Ci3T is a district-level vision, it is important to establish a District-Level Leadership Team, which typically includes the superintendent, associate superintendents, and directors of student services, teaching and learning, curriculum and instruction, assessment, and instructional technology. In some districts, the full cabinet focuses on learning about Ci3T and makes key decisions regarding K–12 commonalities and/or school-level commonalities. For example, district leaders typically make decisions about which reading curriculum will be adopted at the elementary level, as well as which social–emotional curriculum will be adopted at the elementary, middle, and high school levels. They apply board policies for the adoption of a new curriculum. They also lead decisions regarding the selection and adoption of academic and behavior screening tools and provide oversight for the development of the data collection systems (see Lessons Learned 3.3). District leaders communicate with all stakeholders about the new practices. Procedure or policy manuals are updated. District leaders also may engage in research partnerships with university researchers to examine outcomes related to implementation of Ci3T (Lane, 2017; see Lessons Learned 3.4).

LESSONS LEARNED 3.3. Strong District-Level Leadership

Focusing on a comprehensive approach (Ci3T) at the district level has resulted in systems that support staff members to ensure that every student is set up for success in Ferguson–Florissant School District (FFSD).

- A systematic districtwide behavioral screening process has made completing and interpreting the behavior screening more efficient. As a result, by October of every year, building teams know what every student in every classroom needs and can respond quicker to ensure behavioral success. This work included publishing a district behavioral assessment schedule integrated with the district academic assessment schedule.
- A districtwide focus on providing every teacher in every classroom professional learning on four research-based low-intensity classroom strategies (precorrection, behavior-specific praise, active supervision, and opportunities to respond) has provided tools for educators to implement a proactive, positive classroom environment in the FFSD, providing the structure for all children to have a successful learning experience.

Joseph Davis
Ferguson–Florissant Superintendent of Schools

LESSONS LEARNED 3.4. Practitioner–University Partnerships

The Ci3T models of prevention have provided a systemic framework for how our school supports students' academic, social–emotional, and behavioral needs. We went from being a school that reacted to student behavior to one that teaches behavior just as we teach the core content areas. Dr. Lane and her team of experts have equipped our staff with the skills necessary to work with students in a positive and proactive manner. Our school climate has improved dramatically, in that we recognize students for their behavioral contributions and use adverse behaviors as opportunities to teach and improve students' overall skills set.

Martha Cassidy
Elementary School Principal

Establish a School-Site Team: Ci3T Leadership Team

After the decision is made to move forward with Ci3T, a Ci3T Leadership Team is selected at each school to design a comprehensive plan that includes schoolwide, classroom, nonclassroom, and individual systems (Sugai & Horner, 2002) based on resources available at the school. Clearly, establishing a committed and diverse team is an important step in this process. When we work with schools, we recommend that teams include a minimum of one administrator, two general education teachers, one special education teacher, one other adult from the school site (e.g., counselor, school psychologist), one to two parents, and one to two students (who are sons or daughters of the parent team members). Schools may also select a staff member to be included on the team (e.g., paraprofessional). In this case, resources to compensate that person for his or her time will need to be planned for in advance. In addition, the team includes a district coach, the Ci3T Coach, to support implementation. In some of our partnerships, this has been an instructional coach or behavior specialist. Ideally, the administrator should be the principal. If not, it is imperative the administrator be someone with decision-making authority. We have seen instances in which an administrative designee has been asked to serve as the administrator in this process, only to later have his or her decisions overturned by the principal. Such an occurrence can be disheartening to not only the administrative designee but also the Ci3T Leadership Team as a whole.

When selecting Ci3T Leadership Team members, it is important to ensure all groups of teachers have a voice in the planning process. Therefore, we recommend recruiting at least one teacher who serves students with special needs. At the elementary level, we recommend at least one teacher from the primary and upper elementary grades. For middle and high schools, we advocate representation from the different departments to ensure adequate representation from faculty and staff. When selecting parents and students, we strongly suggest choosing people who will return the following year. Parental involvement can be a tremendous asset not only in the planning process but also when it comes time to implement the plan.

If you are conducting a Ci3T Professional Learning Series as part of a research project, obtain separate consents and assents for the following Ci3T Leadership Team members: (1) a team consent form for adult members of the Ci3T Leadership Team (teachers and parents), (2) a parental consent form for the student Ci3T Leadership Team members, and (3) a child assent form for the student team members. If you are collecting data as part of a research study, you will need approval from both the district and the university with whom you are partners. In our early work, the information collected as part of research partnerships was confidential (which means information is collected with people's names, but people's individual responses are not know by the district; information is shared without their names and in an aggregated fashion). In more recent years, as districts have developed their own Ci3T Trainers and Coaches and data collection systems, data collected as part of the Ci3T Professional Learning Series are not confidential (which means information is collected with names and individual responses *are* known by the district). Decisions about confidentiality should be discussed and clearly communicated whether this work is part of a research collaboration or solely a district or school effort. As an important reminder: *Confidential* means the identity of the person providing information is known by district (or others collecting the information) but not shared. Sometimes the term *confidential* is confused with the term *anonymous,* with the latter meaning the identity of the person providing information is not known (and therefore cannot be shared). To be clear, information needs to be collected in such a way that the identity of the person providing information is known, so that the various types of information collected can be connected and ultimately used to shape instructional experiences for students and professional learning for adults.

The Ci3T Leadership Team should be a reasonable size. This is a delicate balance between having enough people on the team to participate in the planning process, which includes reading key works, having solutions-based conversations, and coming to consensus on drafts of plans to share with faculty and staff. Yet the team should not be so large that these tasks become overwhelming and unmanageable. Often, schools have leadership teams, equity teams, PBIS teams, and so on. The Ci3T Leadership Team takes on the responsibility of meeting students' academic, behavioral, and social needs, so we recommend combining these various teams into one effective, representative team. By *combining* we do not suggest having one very large team, but instead selecting representation from current teams to serve in this leadership capacity. Then there may be subcommittees to addresses specific needs. The subcommittees are led by a member of the Ci3T Leadership Team who acts as the liaison and supports alignment between efforts.

As part of this planning process, the Ci3T Leadership Team members commit to the following activities that are beyond the regular school program responsibilities. First, the team members agree to participate in three full-day trainings (for all adult members) and three 2-hour sessions held after school. The sequence alternates between 2-hour sessions and full-day sessions (see Figure 3.1). We recommend student team members not attend the full-day trainings to avoid missing instructional time and instead only attend Sessions 3 and 5. However, all Ci3T team members participate in the afterschool trainings. Between each session, the Ci3T Leadership Team meets to continue the conversation and develop the Ci3T plan. In addition, the Ci3T Leadership Team meet with faculty and staff to involve them in the conversations and to seek more formal input according to the training model (see *ci3t.org/building* to build your Ci3T model tab). Second, Ci3T Leadership Team members, with the help of those conducting the training, agree to design and give a presentation to their entire school staff (including *everyone*—teachers, paraprofessionals, administrators, office staff, cafeteria staff, and custodians) to introduce the proposed Ci3T plan. Third, if resources allow, team members agree to participate in a 20- to 30-minute interview to share their thoughts about the plan—referred to as a *social validity interview*. Fourth, the Ci3T Leadership Team members agree to complete the Ci3T Knowledge, Confidence, and Use (Ci3T KCU; Lane & Oakes, 2010) rating scale (approximately 20 minutes) before and after the training to determine what has been learned during the training process. This information can be collected electronically using a reputable platform such as Qualtrics (*www.qualtrics.com*) or Panorama (*www.panoramaed.com*) or paper and pencil. This information is used to identify how Ci3T Leadership Team members' knowledge, confidence, and perceived utility of concepts and components of Ci3T change over time. Fifth, Ci3T Leadership Team members, teachers, and some randomly selected parents and their students (approximately 100 of each, depending on the school size) share their opinions about the Ci3T plan. A copy of the Ci3T plan and a rating scale (the PIRS; discussed in Chapter 4), is distributed electronically to each person who was asked to evaluate the proposed primary prevention plan (approximately 15 minutes).

In selecting the Ci3T Leadership Team members, not all members need to be enthusiastic, early-adopter type people. The goal is to have representation from all major groups or constituencies in the school. Now that you have selected your Ci3T Leadership Team members, it is time to begin the planning process.

Develop a Data-Based Action Plan

At the onset of the training, it is essential to achieve clarity on priorities (Lane, Oakes, Cantwell, & Royer, 2016). Ci3T Leadership Teams are asked to engage in constructive conversations around three questions: (1) "What are our district priorities for improvement?"; (2) "What are our school priorities for improvement?"; and (3) "What are individual teacher priorities (formally and informally)?" This initial round of conversations sets the stage for determining the "Why?"—"Why does my district or school want to move forward with Ci3T?"; "What are the main objectives for participating in the training series?"; "What do the faculty and staff members value in terms of student behavior?" In this section, we clarify these questions and explain how we collect information to help answer them.

Determine Priorities

Ci3T Leadership Teams should leverage existing data available from their schools to help determine their main concerns. Schools collect a substantial amount of data in the form of (1) academic performance scores on standardized measures; (2) academic performance scores on curriculum-based measures; (3) office discipline referrals; (4) suspension and expulsion records; (5) referrals to the prereferral intervention team, special education, mental health team, and alternative learning centers; and (6) absentee and tardiness records. Some schools even conduct systematic screening procedures (discussed in Chapter 5) to identify students for whom primary prevention efforts are insufficient to address their academic and/or behavioral needs. Still other schools conduct self-assessments or surveys to collect information from teacher, parent, and/or student perspectives as to how the school is functioning.

It is wonderful that school personnel have become more concerned with addressing instructional and behavioral programming from a data-driven perspective. But, too often, it is assumed that the collection of data means the use of data when schools often do not have a structure in place for regularly examining their data to determine what is and is not working in their building. One of the goals in this training should be to help Ci3T Leadership Teams find reasonable, efficient systems for viewing their data on a monthly basis to inform practice. During the first training session, we suggest Ci3T Leadership Teams review their current data (e.g., items 1–6) to identify concerns and priorities (see Box 3.1).

Establish Objectives

Once priorities are established, clarify the main objectives for the training series. The goals are to develop (1) a mission statement; (2) a purpose statement; (3) clear expectations for students' performance in all key instructional settings; (4) primary (Tier 1) prevention efforts including roles and responsibilities for all stakeholders (students, faculty and staff, parents, as well as administrators) in academic, behavioral, and social domains; (5) procedures for teaching and reinforcing Tier 1 elements in an integrated manners; (6) procedures for monitoring implementation, securing feedback, and using data to inform instruction; (7) secondary (Tier 2) prevention supports; and (8) tertiary (Tier 3) prevention supports.

We think it is important to clarify what the training *will* and *will not* address, just to make sure that the participants' and trainers' expectations are aligned. Also, we emphasize that the training process is designed to develop a Ci3T plan customized for the community it serves, so it should be context specific. The goal is not to introduce a one-size-fits-all "canned" program.

Design Expectations for Students' Success

Finally, we encourage faculty and staff to formally determine what they value in terms of student behavior (Kerr & Zigmond, 1986; Lane, Givner, & Pierson, 2004; Lane, Pierson, &

BOX 3.1. Examples of Concerns Identified Using Schoolwide Data	
Data Source	**Concerns and Priorities Identified**
Office discipline referrals (ODRs)	• 80% of ODRs were given to boys during the fall semester. • 60% of the ODRs occur in the hallways. • During the 2020–2021 academic year, the rate of ODRs per instructional day increased by 50% during Spring semester compared to the Fall semester.
Behavioral Screeners: Student Risk Screening Scale—Internalizing and Externalizing (SRSS-IE; Drummond, 1994; Lane & Menzies, 2009)	• In the Fall, 25% of students fall in the moderate-risk category, and 10% fall in the high-risk category on the Externalizing scale. • In the Fall, 30% of students fall in the moderate-risk category, and 12% fall in the high-risk category on the Internalizing scale. • In Winter, there is an increase in students at elevated risk (moderate or high) on the Externalizing scale.
Report cards	• 10% of students received failing grades in more than one class. • 5% of failing grades are due to class tardies.
Attendance	• 75% of students have been late to school more than 3 times per month. • 95% of high school seniors have 3 or more tardies each month.
Curriculum-based measurement (CBM) Reading and Math	• 18% of elementary students scored below grade level on the fall fluency benchmark. • On the Fall math benchmark, 27% of students scored below grade level on computation.
American College Test (ACT)/Scholastic Aptitude Test (SAT)/Preliminary Scholastic Aptitude Test (PSAT) scores	• 20% of sophomores did not take the PSAT test. • 60% of students received scores below state average on the ACT test.
Writing Assessment	• 25% of sixth graders are performing below the 25th percentile. • 30% of students are at or above grade level according to a writing assessment.
Bullying Referrals	• The number of bullying referrals related to social media has increased from the previous year, on a month-to-month comparison. • Bullying referrals show a slight increase from December to March.

Givner, 2004; Lane, Wehby, & Cooley, 2006; Walker & Rankin, 1983). In other words, which student behaviors are essential for success?

Rather than trying to arrive at the desired expectations and specific student behaviors through committee discussion, the team can administer a formal survey—the SESSS (Lane, Oakes, & Menzies, 2010)—designed to allow faculty and staff to identify behaviors critical for student success at their particular school. The SESSS is completed by all faculty and staff employed at a given school. Each person provides information on the importance of a range of expectations for seven school settings: classroom, hallway, cafeteria, playground, restroom, bus, and arrival/dismissal. Importance is rated using a 3-point Likert-type scale: 0 = *not important for success in this setting*, 1 = *important for success in this setting*, and 2 = *critical for success in this setting*. Scores for each item are aggregated and reported to show the number and percentage of faculty and staff members who rate the behavior as critical for success. The Ci3T Leadership Team uses SESSS data to develop the first draft of the schoolwide expectation matrix or to revise an existing expectation matrix. The goal is to establish the behavioral expectations likely to be reinforced by the majority of adults in the building (see additional detail in Lane, Oakes, Jenkins, Menzies, & Kalberg, 2014; Lane et al., 2019). This step is *very* important because it is essential that students receive more attention (and other types of reinforcement) for demonstrating the desired behaviors (e.g., arriving to class on time) than they previously received for demonstrating less desirable behaviors (e.g., arriving to class 5 minutes after the bell rings).

Once information is collected regarding district and school priorities, the main objectives for participating in the training series, and faculty and staff members' views on behaviors essential for success, it is time to construct the schoolwide plan. Ideally, this information would be collected prior to developing the plan to ensure that it addresses key concerns and incorporates the core values shared by the faculty and staff. In the next section, we describe this process.

The Ci3T Implementation Manual comprises several blueprints that are developed over the course of the professional learning series (see *ci3t.org*, Building Your Ci3T Model):

- Ci3T Blueprint A Primary (Tier 1) Plan
- Ci3T Blueprint B Reactive Plan
- Ci3T Blueprint C Expectation Matrix
- Ci3T Blueprint D Assessment Schedule
- Ci3T Blueprint E Secondary (Tier 2) Intervention Grid
- Ci3T Blueprint F Tertiary (Tier 3) Intervention Grid

The building process begins with constructing the Tier 1 elements, which includes Ci3T Blueprints A–F. In this chapter, we explain the process by which Ci3T leadership teams begin considering primary (Tier 1) prevention components. The focus of the first step is to define the mission, purpose, roles and responsibilities of students, faculty and staff, parents, and administrators in academic, behavioral, and social domains. As part of Tier 1 efforts, Ci3T Leadership Teams develop a reactive plan to both provide explicit guidance on how to respond when challenging behavior occurs and establish specific expectations for specific settings to facilitate school success. After discussing roles and responsibilities for the primary plan, we focus on procedures for teaching and reinforcing all stakeholders.

Constructing the Primary (Tier 1) Prevention Plan

There are many different approaches to developing primary plans, and these may include a range of components. In general, they focus on improving systems-related objectives, one at a time, by developing an action plan. Action plans include (1) a 2- to 3-year time frame for design, implementation, and evaluation (Fixsen et al., 2013; Fixsen, Blase, Naoom, & Wallace, 2009); (2) faculty and staff commitments; (3) specific activities that lead to measurable outcomes; (4) professional learning activities; (5) measurable outcomes; and (6) required resources and supports (Sugai & Horner, 2002).

Although many schools are eager to begin with tertiary (Tier 3) prevention efforts for students with the most intensive needs, Ci3T Leadership Teams should begin by implementing and refining their primary (Tier 1) prevention plan. By designing and implementing a solid base program, it is possible to prevent problems from occurring, thereby reducing the proportion of students who require secondary and tertiary levels of prevention (Severson & Walker, 2002; Walker et al., 2014).

In developing the primary (Tier 1) prevention plan, the connection between academic and behavioral performance is facilitated by constructing a schoolwide plan that includes procedures for teaching expectations in the behavioral, social, and academic domains in an integrated fashion (see Boxes 3.2 and 3.3). Embedding skills that promote academic performance into the primary prevention efforts provide a framework for unifying the features of schoolwide and classroom settings.

When developing the academic and social domains of the program, teachers and administrators select curricula that are culturally sensitive, developmentally appropriate, and evidence-based (meaning that studies have been conducted to make sure that it "works" for students with similar characteristics or at least provides a promising approach to that end; CEC, 2014; What Works Clearinghouse, 2011). In other words, avoid incorporating curricula or strategies that you might have heard about at an inservice (no matter how inspiring!) unless the validity of the curriculum or strategy is well documented. Using current standards, optimal decisions are those focused on adopting, installing, and providing professional learning about evidence-based practices (Cook, Tankersley, & Landrum, 2013): strategies, practices, and programs with sufficient evidence to suggest that when implemented as intended, they are likely to yield the desired changes in student performance.

In the next section, we describe the components of a primary (Tier 1) prevention plan and illustrate the following: (1) mission statement (see Box 3.4); (2) purpose statement; (3) expectation matrix (see Boxes 3.5 and 3.6); (4) student, teacher, parent, and administrator roles and responsibilities in academic, behavioral, and social domains; (5) procedures for teaching; (6) procedures for reinforcing; and (7) procedures for monitoring integrity, social validity, and student performance. In addition, we explain how ongoing professional learning and resource needs can be addressed at the onset of implementation and throughout the many years ahead. See Boxes 3.2 and 3.3 for illustrations of three-tiered models designed for an elementary schools and high schools, respectively.

Mission Statement

First, a mission statement is designed to provide direction and focus. Specifically, a *mission statement* is a clear, succinct declaration to help guide the school. It typically contains socially meaningful concepts, goals, and ambitions ("Make Time to Evaluate," 2018). For example, in Box 3.2, Orange Elementary School's mission is to "provide a safe, inclusive learning environment for students, families, and school personnel to engage in experiences to develop students as knowledgeable, skillful, and caring citizens." A mission statement is worded positively; focuses on the relation between academic and behavioral outcomes; and involves all adults (faculty, staff, administrators, etc.), the entire student body, and all key settings. In our work, we have encouraged parent and student participation in the development of the mission statement, purpose statement, and expectations (the latter two are described below). The intent is to enhance home–school partnerships and increase the likelihood that students will be acknowledged and reinforced with verbal praise both in home and school settings.

(text resumes on page 72)

BOX 3.2. Elementary School Primary Prevention (Tier 1) Plan

Orange Elementary School's Primary Intervention Plan

Mission Statement	The mission of Orange Elementary School is to provide a safe, inclusive learning environment for students, families, and school personnel to engage in experiences to develop students as knowledgeable, skillful, and caring citizens.
Purpose Statement	All of the Orange Elementary community, including administrators, faculty, staff, families, and students, will work together to ensure the academic, behavioral, and social needs of all student are served.
Schoolwide Expectations	Show respect. Be responsible. Give best effort. *see Expectation Matrix

Area I: Academic Responsibilities	Area II: Behavior Responsibilities	Area III: Social Skills Responsibilities
Students	**Students**	**Students**

• Arrive on time and stay all day
• Participate in class activities
• Complete all work to the best of their ability
• Be prepared with all materials
• Communicate with school personnel and families
• Persist in the face of challenge and ask for help when needed
• Participate in:
  ○ 60 minutes of math instruction (*Saxon Math,* Houghton Mifflin Harcourt)
  ○ 120 minutes (90 minutes reading, 30 minutes writing) of English language arts instruction (*Reading Street Common Core,* Pearson Education)
	• Meet schoolwide expectations stated in the **Expectation Matrix**
	• Take responsibility for own actions and their effect on others
	• Tell an adult about any unsafe behaviors
	• Ask an adult for help or tell an adult when there is an unsafe situation
	• Use self-management and decision-making skills and strategies learned during lessons on the expectations and *Social Skills Improvement System* (SSiS) *Social–Emotional Learning* (SEL) *Edition Classwide Intervention Program* (CIP; Pearson Education)
		• Meet schoolwide expectations stated in the **Expectation Matrix**
		• Actively participate in weekly *SSiS SEL Edition CIP* social skills lessons
		• Use social skills at school, at home, and in the community to make responsible decisions, develop positive relationships, and productively manage their social interactions
		• Participate in bullying prevention lessons and resolve conflicts peacefully using *Stop, Walk, and Talk* (Office of Special Education Programs Technical Assistance Center on Positive Behavioral Interventions and Supports; *pbis.org*)

Faculty and Staff	**Faculty and Staff**	**Faculty and Staff**

• Plan, provide, and assess instruction with fidelity according to district and state standards
  ○ Mathematics: 60 minutes of instruction (*Saxon Math,* Houghton Mifflin Harcourt)
  ○ English language arts: 120 minutes (90 minutes reading, 30 minutes writing) of (*Reading Street Common Core,* Pearson Education)
• Provide engaging lessons, maximizing instructional time with starter and closing activities
• Plan the integration of academic objectives, PBIS expectations, and social skills
• Use proactive, evidence-based strategies to support engagement:
  ○ Active supervision
  ○ Precorrection
  ○ Instructional choice
  ○ Instructional feedback
  ○ Increased opportunities to respond
  ○ Behavior-specific praise
  ○ High-probability request sequences
	• Implement Positive Behavioral Interventions and Supports (PBIS) with fidelity
	• Foster a safe environment for all students
	• Display, teach, and model schoolwide expectations
	• Provide behavior-specific praise and use the school reinforcement system (intermittently) to recognize students who display schoolwide expectations
	• Follow the reactive (consequence-based) discipline plan consistently when infractions of expectations occur
	• Use a positive response to initial behavioral concerns:
	  ○ Praise students who are demonstrating expectations
	  ○ Reteach expectations
	  ○ Redirect students as needed
	  ○ Allow student time to respond to the redirection and reengage
	  ○ Recognize changed behavior
		• Plan, provide, and assess social skills instruction with fidelity
		• Teach the social skills curriculum according to school schedule: *SSiS SEL Edition CIP* (one new unit weekly, 20–30 minutes, teacher led, counselor supported through rotating schedule or as needed)
		• Model social skills
		• Integrated social skills throughout daily instruction and interactions
		• Provide praise and reinforcement to students who demonstrate social skills
		• Teach and support the bullying prevention program *Stop, Walk, and Talk* according to school schedule (weekly lessons of 20–50 minutes and daily integration of concepts)
		• Engage in productive collaborations with colleagues and parents
		• Seek ways to engage parents in school activities
		• Maintain positive communication with students' families

(continued)

BOX 3.2. *(continued)*

Area I: Academic Responsibilities	Area II: Behavior Responsibilities	Area III: Social Skills Responsibilities
Faculty and Staff	**Faculty and Staff**	**Faculty and Staff**
• Differentiate instruction according to student needs • Support students who miss instruction • Engage in positive and respectful interactions • Provide varied, meaningful, and appropriate practice opportunities • Conduct assessments according to the school or district assessment plan • Report data in a timely way • Use data to inform instructional decisions and to ensure students' access to appropriate Tiered Interventions • Seek professional learning to continue to develop knowledge and skills for high fidelity instruction and assessment • Communicate about student progress with families	• Conduct assessments (e.g., behavior screenings) and complete data collection procedures (e.g., ODRs, attendance) according to the school or district assessment plan • Report data in a timely way • Use data to inform instructional decisions and to ensure students' access to appropriate Tiered Interventions • Communicate student progress with families	• Use data to inform instructional decisions and to ensure students' access to appropriate Tiered Interventions
Parents	**Parents**	**Parents**
• Make learning and school attendance a priority • Provide a place, materials, and assistance to complete homework • Follow attendance policies • Communicate with school regularly • Encourage their child to give their best effort • Attend school events when possible • Attend parent–teacher conferences, contact the teacher to schedule an alternative time if needed	• Know, understand and support school expectations • Post **Expectation Matrix** at home • Communicate with teachers and administrators • Review and support proactive and reactive disciplinary plans	• Support social skills program • Support antibullying program • Work with teachers to support their child at school and with homework • Ask their child about the social skills and bullying prevention lessons learned each week
Administrators	**Administrators**	**Administrators**
• Provide faculty and staff with materials to facilitate instruction • Facilitate access to professional learning of all curriculum, low-intensity strategies, and other Tier 1 components (e.g., deescalation) • Work with district leaders regarding efficient data management tools and ensure school personnel have training and access to needed data • Develop positive relationships with all stakeholders • Provide fair, timely, and productive feedback on teacher evaluations • Learn about community strengths and develop relationships with community stakeholders	• Implement the reactive plan with fidelity and communicate with parents and teachers regarding disciplinary actions (as appropriate) • Collect and monitor behavior screening data three times per year • Ensure all students are screened within the screening assessment window • Support teachers implementation of tiered interventions (e.g., resources for materials, time, scheduling, space) • Reinforce students and school personnel meeting expectations • Develop relationships with students and families	• Provide a master schedule that allows time for social skills instruction • Support staff in implementing the social skills and bullying prevention programs consistently • Model social skills • Collect and track data on implementation of the social skills and bully prevention program • Provide for professional learning for all school personnel to implement the two programs • Maintain positive communication with student and families • Listen to family and school personnel concerns and respond in an appropriate and timely way

(continued)

BOX 3.2. *(continued)*		
Area I: Academic Responsibilities	**Area II: Behavior Responsibilities**	**Area III: Social Skills Responsibilities**
Administrators	**Administrators**	**Administrators**
• Support parent teacher collaborations (e.g., provide resources as needed for parent conferences outside of the scheduled window)		

Procedures for Teaching

Faculty and Staff: Ci3T Leadership Teams and District Leaders will teach procedures to faculty and staff by

- Providing the Ci3T Implementation Manual (paper copy or electronic access) and regularly using the manual in faculty and staff meetings and professional learning offerings
- Providing Expectation posters and **Expectations Matrix**
- Providing a copy of the school mission statement and purpose for each classroom and shared spaces
- Providing Ci3T bookmarks (substitute teachers, bus drivers and aides, related service providers, cafeteria staff, office and instructional staff)
- Offering professional learning to support Tier 1, Tier 2, and Tier 3 components
- Offering district- and school-led professional learning and coaching support for curriculum, strategies, low-intensity strategies, assessment tools, data management systems
- Providing regular updates at faculty meetings of Ci3T activities and data summaries from monthly Ci3T Leadership Team meetings
- Sending regular (weekly) communications through email and announcements (PBIS tips, social skills lesson, successes)

Students: Ci3T Leadership Teams will collaborate with faculty and staff to teach procedures to students by

- Conducting expectation lessons for each school setting at the beginning of the year, after all major breaks, and as indicated by ODR data
- Leading students in the first days of school on a "schoolwide expectations tour"
- Giving each student a Ci3T school T-shirt and teaching students the expectation chant on the first day of school
- Allowing students to watch daily announcements, including Ci3T instructional videos
- Making regular announcements regarding Tier 1 elements
- Providing behavior-specific praise (stating how the student met the expectation), intermittently paired with schoolwide tickets
- Participating in monthly schoolwide drawings
- Allowing students to visit the school Ci3T store at the scheduled time (and scheduling a time for students who are absent)
- Planning for integrated lessons with social skills and behavior expectation objectives students will need for academic engagement

Parent/Community: Ci3T Leadership Teams and District Leaders will teach procedures to parents and community members by

- Sending home family letters and supporting Ci3T materials
- Providing Ci3T family brochure and bookmarks
- Conducting Ci3T updates at back to school night presentations
- Having a Ci3T booth at all family events to share information, answer questions, and sign up families for other events
- Maintaining up-to-date information on the school website (e.g., family events calendar, instructional schedule for *SSiS SEL Edition CIP* curriculum)

Procedures for Reinforcing

Faculty and Staff: Ci3T Leadership Teams and District Leaders will provide reinforcement to faculty and staff by

- Providing administrator (school and district) written notes of recognition and appreciation
- Hosting celebration/potluck/Parent Teacher Student Organization (PTSO)–catered lunch after schoolwide data collection windows (target goals met for 100% of students to be screened; 90% or more faculty and staff participate in treatment fidelity and social validity surveys)
- Providing school spirit wear drawings (teacher recognized who gave the winning student ticket drawn)
- Recognizing high fidelity implementation and participation on the school or district website, newsletter, and in announcements

(continued)

BOX 3.2. *(continued)*

Procedures for Reinforcing *(continued)*

Students: Ci3T Leadership Teams will collaborate with faculty and staff to provide reinforcement to students by

- Providing behavior-specific praise to students demonstrating expectations
- Intermittently providing a Ci3T ticket with the behavior-specific praise
- Taking photos and nominations for the "You Caught Me" Wall (upon entering school building; the wall contains pictures of student displaying expectations)
- Allowing students to participate in Ci3T drawings (prizes from reinforcer menu for staff, parents, and students)
- Allowing students to attend Ci3T assemblies
- Participating in and allowing students to select the "Lunch with a favorite staff" reinforcer option
- Allowing students to redeem "Lunch with a peer" and "Special seating during lunch" reinforcer options
- Mailing home "You Caught Me," "Look at My Progress," and "I Helped a Friend" postcards
- Posting the reinforcer menu in the classroom and shared locations (hallways, office, cafeteria, gym, library, flexible learning spaces)
- Posting student-made Ci3T posters in the classrooms and shared locations
- Conducting random surprise drawings (as items are donated or opportunities are available)
- Providing leadership opportunities as a reinforcer for students to "purchase" with tickets (e.g., teacher helper, office assistant, new student ambassador)

Parent/Community: Ci3T Leadership Teams and District Leaders will provide reinforcement to parents and community members by

- Mailing postcards home of their child's recognition: "You Caught Me," "Look at My Progress," "I Helped a Friend"
- Giving families attending parent conferences or school events a Ci3T ticket for their child to use
- Offering a free family photography session
- Providing recognition on the school or district website, newsletter, and in announcements
- Providing window signs expressing appreciate of support for community partners (made by students)
- Offering a free yearbook ad or website shout out for community supporters

Procedures for Monitoring

	Academic:	Behavior:	Social Skills:
Student Measures	• Curriculum-based measures (CBMs) • Progress reports • Writing assessments • Report card • State assessments	• Office discipline referrals (ODRs) • Behavior Screenings: Student Risk Screening Scale for Internalizing and Externalizing (SRSS-IE) • Attendance • Nurse visits	• ODRs • Counseling referrals • Bullying referrals • Mental health referrals • Social Skills Improvement System Social–Emotional Learning Edition (SSiS SEL)
	Social Validity:	**Treatment Integrity:**	**Program Goals:**
Program Measures (school-level)	• Primary Intervention Rating Scale (PIRS; Lane, Robertson, & Wehby, 2002) • Monthly surveys (brief) to parents regarding the *SSiS SEL CIP* lessons	• Tiered Fidelity Inventory (TFI; Algozzine et al., 2014; available from *www.pbisapps.org*) • Ci3T Treatment Integrity Teacher Self-Report (Ci3T TI: TSR) • Ci3T Treatment Integrity Direct Observations (Ci3T TI: DO) • Curricula fidelity data (walk throughs, self-report checklists, log of social skills lessons taught)	Year 1 implementation: 1. Meet or exceed criteria on program fidelity measures 2. Screen all students in reading, math, and behavior three times (fall, winter, spring); complete IEP progress data when academic screening is not appropriate 3. 80% or more of students reading on grade level by spring screening 4. 80% or more of students meeting math computation benchmarks by spring screening

Note. We do not endorse any specific curriculum, program, or assessment tool. We encourage Ci3T Leadership Teams and District Leaders to review current evidence to inform their decision making.

BOX 3.3. High School Ci3T Primary Intervention Plan

Contra Costa High School's Ci3T Primary (Tier 1) Intervention Plan

Mission Statement	The mission of Contra Costa High School is to provide a safe and productive learning environment that allows students to develop as lifelong learners and engage as responsible global citizens.
Purpose Statement	All of the Contra Costa community will work together to design and implement a variety of programs to support the specific academic, behavioral, and social needs of all students.
Schoolwide Expectations	• Be Respectful • Be Responsible • Be Engaged *see Expectation Matrix

Area I: Academic Responsibilities	Area II: Behavior Responsibilities	Area III: Social Skills Responsibilities
Students	**Students**	**Students**
• Arrive and leave school on time • Participate in all classroom activities • Produce their best work • Persist until all work is completed • Be prepared for class each day with all materials • Seek support when needed	• Meet schoolwide expectations stated in the **Expectation Matrix** • Participate in the positive behavioral interventions and supports (PBIS; see *pbis.org*) program • Know the reactive and proactive components of the behavior plan	• Actively engage in the *Lions Quest* Lessons (Lions Club International) in monthly social skills lessons • Apply lessons learned from *Lions Quest* in daily interactions at school and in the community
Faculty and Staff	**Faculty and Staff**	**Faculty and Staff**

• Provide engaging lessons, linked to the district standards
• Differentiate instruction
• Include starter and closing activities as part of each lesson plan
• Plan for the social skills and behavioral objectives needed for students to be successful in the academic lesson
• Use proactive evidence-based, low-intensity strategies to support active student engagement:
  o Active supervision
  o Behavior specific praise
  o Instructional choice
  o Instructional feedback
  o Opportunities to respond
• Support students who miss instruction
• Engage in positive interactions with all adults and students
• Create clear routines within the classroom
• Communicate with parents about students' successes and concerns
• Conduct assessments according to the school **Assessment Schedule**
• Use data to monitor student performance
• Keep class information and grades updated in the online management system
	• Implement the PBIS component with fidelity
	• Display posters of schoolwide expectations
	• Model schoolwide expectations
	• Teach schoolwide expectations
	• Use clear and consistent classroom procedures
	• Provide behavior-specific praise and intermittently use the schoolwide reinforcement system to acknowledge or students who display schoolwide expectations
	• Follow the reactive plan consistently when infractions of expectations occur; begin with an instructional approach:
	  o Show empathy
	  o Redirect the student
	  o Reteach the expectation
	  o Reinforce student when they later use the expected behaviors
	• Foster a safe environment for all students
	• Complete assessments according to the **Assessment Schedule**
	• Communicate with parents about students successes and concerns
		• Teach weekly *Lions Quest* social skills curriculum lessons according to the school curriculum map (monthly lesson during block schedule—30 minutes)
		• Complete treatment integrity tracker to monitor students' access to the social skills curriculum
		• Model the social skills taught in the Lions Quest curriculum
		• Provide behavior-specific praise and intermittently use the schoolwide reinforcement system for students who demonstrate social skills taught
		• Communicate with parents about students' successes and concerns

(continued)

BOX 3.3. *(continued)*

Area I: Academic Responsibilities	Area II: Behavior Responsibilities	Area III: Social Skills Responsibilities
Parents	**Parents**	**Parents**
• Provide a place, materials, and assistance to completed homework • Read communications from the school • Check websites for announcements • Follow attendance policies and monitor student attendance • Check their child's online grade and course information • Communicate with the school • Encourage students to give their best effort • Schedule appointments for the child outside of the school day	• Are familiar with schoolwide expectations • Communicate with teachers and administrators • Review and support proactive and reactive disciplinary components, share any concerns and ask questions when needed • Work in collaboration with school personnel if disciplinary issues arise	• Support student in participating in *Lions Quest* social skills program • Support students in problem solving by discussing issues at home in a positive manner • Communicate with teachers and administrators
Administrators	**Administrators**	**Administrators**
• Ensure accurate collection and reporting of data to the Ci3T Leadership Team and teachers for instructional decision making • Provide faculty and staff with materials to facilitate instruction • Facilitate and support professional learning to support implementation of Tier 1 efforts • Conduct walk-throughs and provide formative, constructive, and timely feedback • Conduct evaluations with fidelity and provide feedback in respectful ways • Review data to ensure students have equitable access to Tier 2 and Tier 3 interventions • Provide professional learning for implementation of Tier 2 and 3 supports and interventions with fidelity	• Implement the proactive and reactive behavioral components of the schoolwide plan consistently and with fidelity • Implement the PBIS component with fidelity • Model and promote schoolwide expectations • Be an active member of the Ci3T Leadership Team • Review data to ensure students have equitable access to Tier 2 and Tier 3 interventions • Support the provision of funding to support the PBIS plan • Monitor treatment integrity and social validity of the Ci3T plan • Communicate the importance of participation in the full monitoring plan • Recognize faculty and staff as they shift practices to be consistent with the Ci3T plan	• Implement social skills consistently • Review data to ensure students have equitable access to Tier 2 and 3 interventions • Create opportunities or students to be civically engaged through community partnerships • Monitor data regarding students' access to the *Lions Quest* curriculum • Collect and review student and faculty feedback on the social skills curriculum with the Ci3T Leadership Team • Manage the school schedule to ensure adequate time for *Lions Quest* lessons • Facilitate access to professional learning to implement *Lions Quest* with fidelity

Procedures for Teaching

Faculty and Staff: Ci3T Leadership Teams and District Leaders teach procedures to faculty and staff by

• Providing the Ci3T Implementation Manual and regularly using the manual in faculty and staff meetings and professional learning offerings.
• Sending weekly emails to faculty and staff, prompting PBIS tips, social skills lessons, assessment time lines, and sharing successes
• Providing announcements and facilitating discussions during faculty meetings
• Offering professional learning to support Tier 1, Tier 2, and Tier 3 components
• Conducting onboarding meetings for new faculty and staff
• Providing Ci3T bookmarks (substitute teachers, bus drivers and aides, related service providers, cafeteria staff, office and instructional staff)
• Offering district- and school-led professional learning (curriculum, strategies, assessment tools, data management systems)
• Providing updates on activities and data summaries monthly from the Ci3T Leadership Team

(continued)

BOX 3.3. *(continued)*

Students: Ci3T Leadership Teams collaborate with faculty and staff to teach procedures to students by

- Posting Ci3T expectation posters and using them as an instructional tool for teaching expectations
- Making regular announcements regarding Tier 1 elements
- Conducting an assembly on the first day of school to launch the year
- Participating in regularly scheduled lessons on the expectations for each setting
- Providing behavior-specific praise (stating how the student met the expectation), intermittently paired with schoolwide tickets
- Participating in monthly schoolwide drawings
- Listening to morning and afternoon announcements
- Participating actively in weekly social skills lessons
- Watching student-made videos about expectations and social skills and engagement activities

Parents and Community: Ci3T Leadership Teams and District Leaders teach procedures to parents and community members by

- Providing Ci3T parent brochure and bookmarks
- Writing family letters about school activities
- Conducting Ci3T updates at presentations on back-to-school night
- Scheduling and encouraging attendance at school-sponsored family and community events (communicating needs for scheduling)
- Maintaining up-to-date information on the school website (e.g., instructional schedule for the *Lions Quest* curriculum)

Procedures for Reinforcing

Faculty and Staff: Ci3T Leadership Teams and District Leaders provide reinforcement to faculty and staff by

- Providing administrator (school and district) written notes of recognition and appreciation
- Offering preferred parking in the Ci3T school parking spot for teachers with high-fidelity implementation
- Hosting celebration/potluck/PTSO-catered lunch after schoolwide data collection windows (target goals met for 100% of students to be screened; 90% or more faculty and staff participate in treatment fidelity and social validity surveys)
- Providing school spirit wear (e.g., t-shirt) drawings to recognize the teacher who gave the winning student ticket drawn
- Recognizing high-fidelity implementation and participation on the school or district website, newsletter, and in announcements
- Offering coupons to wear jeans to school
- Partnering with PTSO to offer recognition (e.g., gift cards, a coffee delivered to their room)

Students: Ci3T Leadership Teams collaborate with faculty and staff members to provide reinforcement to students by:

- Providing verbal praise paired with a PBIS ticket (Contra Costa Cash!), when staff observe students displaying schoolwide expectations
- Offering one-on-one time with adults (e.g., help with work, post–high school planning)
- Conducting drawings (prizes from reinforcement menu for staff, parents, and students)
- Having lunch with favorite staff or more time in favorite class (e.g., extra time to work on creative projects)
- Conducting random surprise drawings (as items are donated or opportunities available)
- Appearing or starring in the monthly PBIS videos
- Serving in a student leadership role (e.g., peer tutor, ambassador)
- Accepting Contra Costa Cash! for school fees and sporting events

Parents and Community: Ci3T Leadership Teams and District Leaders provide reinforcement to parents and community members by

- Offering preferred parking for school events
- Sending postcards home
- Providing window signs for community supporters
- Giving families attending parent conferences or school events Contra Costa Cash! for their child to use
- Providing recognition on the school or district website, newsletter, and in announcements
- Offering a free senior portrait, graduation, or family photography session
- Providing VIP seating at graduation
- Offering a free yearbook ad for community supporters
- Selecting and recognizing a Ci3T business partner of the month (window sign, recognition on the school/district website, school announcements)

(continued)

	BOX 3.3. *(continued)*		
	Procedures for Monitoring		
Student Measures	**Academic:** • Grade point average (GPA) • Quarterly grades • Writing Assessment • ACT/SAT Scores (Pre-ACT and PSAT) • State assessments • Credit accrual • Percentage of students enrolled in advanced placement classes • Graduation rates	**Behavior:** • Office discipline referrals (ODRs) • ODR outcomes: in-school and out-of-school suspensions • Student Risk Screening Scale – Internalizing and Externalizing (SRSS-IE; Drummond 1994; Lane & Menzies, 2009) • Attendance	**Social Skills:** • ODRs • Counseling referrals • Mental health referrals • Bullying referrals • SRSS-IE (Drummond 1994; Lane & Menzies, 2009)
Program Measures (school-level)	**Social Validity:** • Primary Intervention Rating Scale (PIRS; Lane, Robertson, & Wehby, 2002) • Weekly student surveys of the *Lions Quest* lesson	**Treatment Integrity (TI):** • Schoolwide Evaluation Tool (SET; Sugai, Lewis-Palmer, Todd, & Horner, 2005) • Ci3T TI: Teacher Self-Report (completed by all faculty and staff members) • Ci3T TI: Direct Observation by Ci3T school or district observers (completed for a random sample of staff) • Monthly student surveys (e.g., knowledge of expectations, access to Contra Costa Cash!, feedback from adults, interest in current reinforcers, additional ideas for reinforcement)	**Program Goals:** • Decreased problem behaviors as measured by ODRs and SRSS-IE risk scores (a goal of 80% of students with low risk; reduce ODRs by 20%) • Improved attendance as measured by unexcused tardies and absences (goal is 95% of students with fewer than 7 absences). • Improved academic outcomes as measured by GPA (goal is increase of students with 2.5 or higher GPA by 10%)

Note. We do not endorse any specific curriculum, program, or assessment tool. We encourage Ci3T Leadership Teams and District Leaders to review current evidence to inform their decision making.

BOX 3.4. Sample Mission Statements	
School	**Mission**
Roosevelt Elementary School	Roosevelt Elementary School, in a collaborative effort with families, students, and community partners, seeks to cultivate the unique potential and ability of each student by providing a positive, productive, and safe environment that addresses academic, behavioral, and social–emotional needs of all learners.
Mountain Vista Middle School	The Mountain Vista Middle School community is committed to providing an intellectually engaging and safe environment in which students learn to become responsible global citizens and self-determined individuals.
North High School	North High School provides a safe, positive, civic-minded educational community coupled with rich learning experiences that promote a common respect and understanding. We advocate for our students as we help them reach our high expectations so that they will be well prepared for future learning and employment experiences, as well as engaged actively in a democratic society.

BOX 3.5. Expectation Matrix: Orange Elementary School

Settings

	Classroom	Hallway	Cafeteria	Playground	Bathroom	Bus
Show Respect	• Follow directions • Use kind words and actions • Be encouraging and helpful to others • Cooperate with others • Use an inside voice	• Use a quiet voice • Walk on the right side • Keep hands to yourself • Use kind words	• Use an inside voice • Use manners • Listen to and follow adult requests	• Respect other people's personal space • Follow the rules of the game • Be kind to others • Resolve conflict peacefully	• Use the restroom, then return to class • Stay in your own bathroom stall • Minimize chatting	• Use kind words towards others • Listen to and follow the bus driver's rules • Talk quietly with others
Be Responsible	• Arrive to class on time • Remain in school for the whole day • Bring your required materials • Use time wisely • Respond appropriately to conflict • Follow the dress code	• You're your hands to yourself • Walk in the hallway • Stay in line with your class	• Make your choices quickly • Eat your own food • Remain in established area • Clean up after yourself	• Play approved games • Use equipment appropriately • Return equipment when you are done • Line up when the bell rings	• Flush toilet • Throw away any trash properly • Report any problems to your teacher	• Listen to and follow the bus driver's rules • Remain in your seat after you enter the bus • Use self-control • Be alert and watch for your stop
Give Best Effort	• Participate in class activities • Complete work with best effort • Try first, then ask for help politely	• Walk quietly • Walk directly to next location	• Use your table manners • Use an inside voice • Make healthy choices	• Include others in your activities • Be active • Respond to conflict appropriately	• Keep bathroom tidy • Wash hands with soap • Use an inside voice	• Listen to and follow the bus driver's rules • Keep your hands and feet to yourself

Note. Items selected using the SESSS Report. Items rated as *critical to success* by a majority (e.g., 75–100%) of faculty and staff members.

BOX 3.6. Sample Expectation Matrix: Middle and High School Levels

Settings

	Classroom	Hallway	Cafeteria	Bathroom	Bus
Be Respectful	• Follow the dress code • Listen to and follow directions • Use kind words toward others; avoid gossip • Use classroom supplies and books appropriately	• Use a quiet voice • Walk on the right side of the hallway • Keep hands to yourself • Use appropriate ways to show affection to others	• Know your order when walking through lunch line • Have money ready • Stay in assigned locations • Share lunch tables with others	• Give others privacy • Keep surfaces and walls free of graffiti • Minimize chatting • Keep water in the sink	• Be ready when bus arrives • Carry on all personal belongings needed
Be Responsible	• Be in assigned location before the tardy bell • Bring all necessary materials to class • Make up work when absent • Participate in all activities • Complete all assignments to the best of your ability	• Keep your hands to yourself • Use appropriate ways to show affection to others • Walk in the hallway • Keep the hallways clean	• Share lunch tables with others • Follow directions first time asked • Clean up area • Recycle	• Report any problems to a school employee • Return to class promptly • Have a pass when necessary	• Share seating on the bus • Listen to and follow the bus driver's directions the first time given • Speak in a quiet inside voice • Remain seated after entering the bus
Be Engaged	• Keep desk area clean • Tell the truth • Participate in all class activities • Give your best effort	• Pay attention to where you are going • Help others when needed • Report unsafe conditions	• Keep lunch tables clean • Pick up any trash • Help others who may be unfamiliar with the cafeteria • Include others	• Keep the bathroom clean • Throw away any trash properly • Avoid using your cell phone	• Keep the bus clean • Remove all personal belongings • Be alert and prepared for emergency situations

Note. Items selected using the SESSS Report in addition to collective experience of the CI3T Leadership Team. Items faculty and staff (e.g., 75–100%) rated on the SESSS as *critical to success* are considered for inclusion.

Purpose Statement

Next, the Ci3T Leadership Team generates a statement as to the purpose of designing and installing a Ci3T model. This is done to clarify to all parties—administrators, faculty, staff, parents, community members, and students—how the proposed plan aligns with the school's mission statement. For example, Orange Elementary School's purpose statement in Box 3.2 reflects the spirit of its mission statement while adding specificity: "All of the Orange Elementary community, including administrators, faculty, staff, families, and students, will work together to ensure the academic, behavioral, and social needs of all student are served."

Expectation Matrix

When constructing the expectation matrix, team members first identify the common areas in their school, such as classrooms, cafeteria, hallways, playground or outdoor areas, bus loading and unloading areas, and bathrooms. Once these are identified, the next major goal is to establish three to five expectations that will be operationalized across these key common areas (see *pbis.org* for additional details).

Then the team reviews data from the SESSS survey to see which behaviors are most critical to their faculty and staff. On *ci3t.org*, you will find resources to support you in completing the SESSS and summarizing the data received swiftly and in a visually accessible way (see Figure 3.2 and *www.ci3t.org/measures*). In Figure 3.3, you will find an image of part of a report reviewed by Ci3T Leadership Teams. The report begins by reviewing response rates to determine whether a sufficient number of faculty and staff provided information for the summarized data to be representative of the full faculty and staff (check current guidelines for desired response rates; *https://nces.ed.gov/statprog/2002/std2_2.asp* [National Center for Education Statistics, 2002]). Then, teams examine item-level data.

Specifically, we advise that Ci3T Leadership Teams highlight items rated by more than 75% of respondents as critical for success (see Figures 3.2 and 3.3). For example, the top panel of Figure 3.3 indicates that 93.75% of respondents rated *follows directions* as a 2 (critical for success in this setting). This item would be highlighted as a critically important skill. They focus next on items rated by 50–75% of the faculty as critical for success. For example, the top panel of Figure 3.3 indicates that 54.55% of respondents rated *share lunch tables with others* (item 4 in the cafeteria setting) as a 2. This item would be highlighted in a different color to note a priority—but not necessarily a top priority. Ci3T Leadership teams discusses these high-priority behavioral expectations to develop the expectation matrix that will become the teaching tools for their school.

In addition, they consider other expectations that might be specific to their respective buildings to inform the development of the expectation matrix. This information from faculty and staff is used to determine general themes to build the three to five schoolwide expectations mentioned previously. For example, if several items focus on self-control or cooperation, the Ci3T Leadership Team may select *respect, responsibility,* and *best effort* (see Box 3.5).

Next, the specific items prioritized by the majority of faculty and staff (as previously described) are placed in the appropriate "boxes" or "cells" in the expectation matrix. For example, in Box 3.5 you will see the following statement in the Respect: Classroom intersection: (1) *follow directions* (item 1, rated a 2 by 93.75% of faculty and staff who responded, see

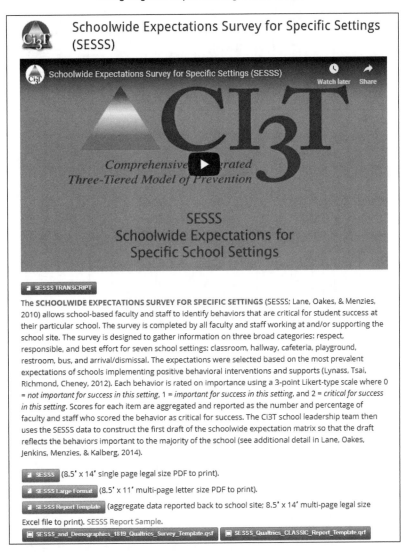

FIGURE 3.2. Schoolwide Expectations Survey for Specific Settings—Website Access. From Comprehensive, Integrated Three-Tiered Model of Prevention Research Project. Available at *www.ci3t.org/measures*. Reprinted by permission.

top panel of Figure 3.3); (2) *use kind words and actions* (item 2, rated a 2 by 72.92% of faculty and staff who responded); (3) *control your temper* (item 3, rated a 2 by 81.25% of faculty and staff who responded); and (4) *cooperate with others* (item 4, rated a 2 by 85.42% of faculty and staff who responded). Items *use an inside voice* and *follow the dress code* were not included in the matrix because those items were not rated by the majority of faculty and staff as critical for success in this setting. Taken collectively, these entries indicate students are considered respectful in the classroom if they perform these four behaviors. If a school's results were those illustrated in the bottom panel of Figure 3.3, the items *use an inside voice* and *follow the dress code* would be included in the expectation matrix because those were prioritized as critical for success by the majority of faculty and staff at that school.

(text resumes on page 76)

Directions: For each item in the identified setting, please indicate how important each behavior is for students to be successful at school in the specific setting. Circle the number to the right of each item indicating your opinion regarding importance.

Key: How Important?	
0 =	Not Important for success in this setting
1 =	Important for success in this setting
2 =	Critical for success in this setting

N = number of responses rating the skill as critical (rated a 2). % are based on the number of respondents who completed that item

School: Ben Franklin Middle School
County: Independence
Number Completed: *N* = 55 (61.11%)

Settings

Respect	Classroom	*N*	%	Hallway	*N*	%	Cafeteria	*N*	%	Playground	*N*	%	Restroom	*N*	%	Bus	*N*	%	Arrival/Dismissal	*N*	%
	APPLICABLE? 44 (88.00%)			APPLICABLE? 42 (91.30%)			APPLICABLE? 36 (78.26%)			APPLICABLE? 4 (8.51%)			APPLICABLE? 33 (73.33%)			APPLICABLE? 14 (29.17%)			APPLICABLE? 27 (67.50%)		
	Follow directions	45	93.75	No talking	3	5.88	Use an inside voice	18	40.91	Respect other people's personal space	5	62.50	Stay in your own stall	34	85.00	Use kind words toward the bus driver and others	15	71.43	Respond immediately when teacher/adult calls	26	63.41
	Use kind words and actions	35	72.92	Walk on the right side	1	2.04	Use manners	17	38.64	Follow the rules of the game	2	25.00	Take care of your own business	35	87.50	Listen to and follow the bus driver's rules	21	100.00	Raise your hand for help	18	43.90
	Control your temper	39	81.25	Keep hands to yourself	32	62.75	Listen to and follow adult requests	35	79.55	Respond immediately when teacher/adult calls	2	25.00	Give others privacy and remain in own stall	35	87.50	Share seating on the bus	14	66.67	Maintain dress code	13	31.71
	Cooperate with others	41	85.42	Use a quiet voice	13	25.49	Share lunch tables with others	24	54.55	Be kind to peers while playing games	4	50.00	Minimize chatting	6	15.00	Speak in a quiet voice	12	57.14	Control temper in conflict situations	36	87.80
	Use an inside voice	16	33.33	Stay calm and controlled in conflict with adults and peers	41	80.39	Follow directions the first time asked	25	56.82				Keep water in the sink	21	52.50	Remain seated after entering the bus	20	95.24			
	Follow the dress code	12	25.00	Avoid gossip and use kind words	30	60.00	Keep food on your plate	23	52.27				Knock before entering	13	32.50	Stay clear of roadway	21	100.00			

FIGURE 3.3A. Schoolwide Expectations Survey for Specific Settings—Report Options. Image of SESSS Report if using the paper version of the measure. Scores for the number and percentage of people who rated each setting as applicable and each item as *critical for success in this setting* are hand entered by the data leader of the Ci3T Leadership Team. SESSS measures, hand-entry report template, and sample report available from *www.ci3t.org/measures*.

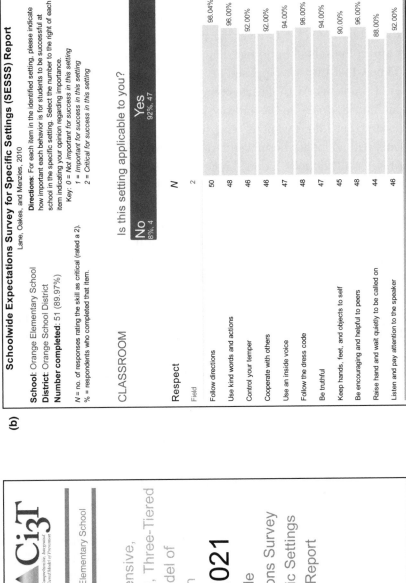

Schoolwide Expectations Survey for Specific Settings (SESSS) Report

Lane, Oakes, and Menzies, 2010

School: Orange Elementary School
District: Orange School District
Number completed: 51 (89.97%)

Directions: For each item in the identified setting, please indicate how important each behavior is for students to be successful at school in the specific setting. Select the number to the right of each item indicating your opinion regarding importance.

Key: 0 = *Not important for success in this setting*
1 = *Important for success in this setting*
2 = *Critical for success in this setting*

N = no. of responses rating the skill as critical (rated a 2).
% = respondents who completed that item.

(b)

CLASSROOM	Is this setting applicable to you?		
	No 8%, 4	**Yes** 92%, 47	
Respect		**N**	
Field		2	
Follow directions		50	98.04%
Use kind words and actions		48	96.00%
Control your temper		46	92.00%
Cooperate with others		46	92.00%
Use an inside voice		47	94.00%
Follow the dress code		48	96.00%
Be truthful		47	94.00%
Keep hands, feet, and objects to self		45	90.00%
Be encouraging and helpful to peers		48	96.00%
Raise hand and wait quietly to be called on		44	88.00%
Listen and pay attention to the speaker		46	92.00%

(a)

FIGURE 3.3B. Image of (a) SESSS Report cover for either version of the measure and (b) one setting (classroom) of the SESSS Report if using an online survey version of the measure. Scores for the number and percentage of people who rated each setting as applicable and each item as *critical for success in this setting* are generated by the survey system. The data leader on the Ci3T Leadership Team can export the data and generate the report to share with the team and then faculty and staff. From *Comprehensive, Integrated Three-Tiered Model of Prevention Research Project*. SESSS measures and sample report are available from *www.ci3t.org/measures*. Reprinted by permission.

One goal of an expectation matrix is to level the playing field for all students. Now, no matter where students are in the school building, they know what is expected of them. This eliminates the "I didn't know that I wasn't supposed to . . ." or "No one ever told me that I was supposed to . . ." types of problems. With clearly communicated and taught expectations, if students decide to use an "outside voice" in the hallway, it is most likely a performance problem ("I can do what you're asking, but I don't want to"; Gresham & Elliott, 2008; Gresham, Elliott, & Kettler, 2010). Students will no longer be in a situation in which they do not have or know the expected skills, that is, a skills deficit ("I don't know how to or what to do"). This is important because performance deficits and skills deficits require different types of intervention supports. Performance deficits require changes in reinforcement rates to motivate students to want to meet the expectations, whereas skills deficits require explicit instruction to make sure that students know how to do the expected task or behavior (Gresham & Elliott, 2008). Keep in mind that students need regular instruction and multiple opportunities to learn the expectations. The primary (Tier 1) prevention plan contains specific responsibilities for teachers and parents to make sure the environment, and the adults' behavior, sets the stage for the desired student behaviors to occur. Students will be able to access reinforcement from adults when they engage in these behaviors that have been determined to be critical for success by the majority of faculty and staff. The plan also contains strategies for teaching all stakeholders these expectations, as well as other roles and responsibilities, then how to reinforce them for meeting these roles and responsibilities.

Stakeholders' Roles and Responsibilities in Academic, Behavioral, and Social Domains

In addition to establishing these expectations to facilitate student success in key areas, the primary (Tier 1) plan explicitly states student, faculty, parent, and administrator roles and responsibilities in academic, behavioral, and social domains.

For example, faculty and staff responsibilities are stated explicitly for the three areas constituting the primary (Tier 1) plan: academics, behavior, and social skills. To illustrate, in Box 3.2, as part of the academic component of the primary plan, faculty and staff are expected to (1) use the district-adopted curriculum for teaching reading and mathematics (note the specificity included to ensure students' access to high-quality core instruction); (2) provide engaging lessons linked to the district and state standards; (3) differentiate instruction; (4) use research-based, low-intensity, teacher-delivered supports during instruction (e.g., increase students' opportunities to respond, active supervision); (5) include starter and closing activities as part of lesson plan; (6) support students who miss instruction; (7) engage in positive teacher–teacher and teacher–student interactions; and (8) use screening data to inform instruction. As part of the behavioral component of the primary (Tier 1) plan, teachers are expected to (1) display schoolwide expectations posters, (2) model schoolwide expectations, (3) teach schoolwide expectations, (4) provide praise and reinforcement to students who demonstrate schoolwide expectations, (5) follow the reactive (consequence-based) discipline plan consistently when infractions of expectations occur, and (6) foster a safe environment for all students. As part of the social skills component of the primary (Tier 1) plan, teachers are expected to (1) teach the adopted social skills curriculum (e.g., SSiS SEL Edition Classwide Intervention Program

[CIP]) according to the instructional schedule provided (again, note the level of detail provided in Box 3.2: "Teach social skills curriculum according to school schedule [one new unit weekly, 20–30 minutes, teacher led, counselor supported through rotating schedule or as needed]"; see Lessons Learned 3.5); (2) model skill taught and incorporate these lessons into daily instruction and interactions in noninstructional settings, and (3) provide behavior specific praise and reinforcement to students who demonstrate and use these social skills (e.g., show empathy).

In addition, students, parents, and administrators have responsibilities as part of the primary (Tier 1) prevention efforts to support each of the three components: academic, behavioral, and social. Refer to Boxes 3.2 and 3.3 for sample responsibilities at the elementary and high school levels, respectively.

Thus, all key players—students, faculty and staff, parents, and administrators—have clearly defined roles and responsibilities that support the three components of the primary plan. Once responsibilities are clarified for all parties, the next step is to decide what procedures will be used to teach all components of the plan. In other words, how do we teach everyone about the Ci3T plan?

Procedures for Teaching

When we think about teaching the Ci3T plan, often we only think about teaching the school-wide expectations to the students. However, it is just as important that *all* people involved, including teachers, staff, paraprofessionals, custodians, and parent volunteers, as well as parents and students, be familiar with the full primary (Tier 1) plan—including (but not only!) the schoolwide expectations. So how do you do that? We recommend you not only plan for an initial program kickoff to launch the introduction of the Ci3T model but also establish ongoing procedures and regularly scheduled professional learning opportunities to keep the plan forefront in the minds of everyone.

In terms of kickoff activities, we recommend the Ci3T Leadership Team introduce the plan to the faculty (who will already have provided feedback when constructing the plan) with a presentation that involves modeling the core components. For example, Ci3T Leadership Teams often develop a PowerPoint presentation to introduce the Ci3T model (see Lane, Oakes, Cantwell, & Royer, 2018; see *ci3t.org/building*; Ci3T Trainer Resources). The presentation is designed to offer concrete information about the roles and responsibilities for each of the three domains, plans for providing integrated instruction across these domains, as well as procedures for teaching, reinforcing, and monitoring. The launch focuses on implementing primary (Tier 1) prevention efforts with integrity, with plans to connect students to secondary (Tier 2) and tertiary (Tier 3) supports when needed. When presenting the plan to faculty and staff, the team passed out tickets paired with behavior-specific praise (e.g., "Thank you for asking questions about when to teach the Connect With Kids lessons"). At the end of the presentation, after all questions were addressed, they collected the tickets they had distributed during the presentation and raffled off prizes (reinforcers) that had been displayed in the front of the library. One of our high school partners offered prizes that included an extra 45-minute planning period, a free car wash pass, and a preferred parking space (right next to the principal's spot) for 1 week.

(text resumes on page 80)

LESSONS LEARNED 3.5. Sample Instructional Schedule

Connect With Kids—Ci3T Sequential 2016–2017

Date	Topic	Program Title	Description	Link on Site (customized link redacted)
Lesson 1 August 25, 2016 Thursday, FIRST HOUR	Resilience	Against All Odds—Part 4	Berhane Azage overcomes poverty and hardship by not measuring himself according to what he doesn't have. Instead, he learned from his parents that adversity is not personal and can be overcome.	
Lesson 2 September 7, 2016 Wednesday, SECOND HOUR	Resilience	Against All Odds—Part 5	Kids need to be educated through real-life examples that adversity does not have to be permanent, pervasive, or personal.	
Lesson 3 September 22, 2016 Thursday, THIRD HOUR	Achievement	The Power of Expectations: Motivation—Part 2	Experts discuss the fine line between too much pressure and not enough.	
Lesson 4 October 5, 2016 Wednesday, FOURTH HOUR	Attendance and Achievement	Disconnect: Why Kids Skip School—Part 2	Danielle Anzalone shares her story of not wanting to attend school because of the bullying and harassment that she experienced. Experts say that many students don't want to go to school because they are afraid of what might happen.	
Lesson 5 October 27, 2016 Thursday, FIFTH HOUR	Attendance and Achievement	Disconnect: Why Kids Skip School—Part 5	Explore how keeping kids engaged at school requires the work of not only the entire school administration but also the parents.	
Lesson 6 November 9, 2016 Wednesday, SIXTH HOUR	Life Skills Development	Diligence	Greg Johnson believes that his diligent, disciplined behavior will not only help him with his current academics, leadership roles, and volunteer work but will also prepare him for a future career as a naval officer.	

Lesson	Category	Title	Description
Lesson 7 December 8, 2016 Thursday, SEVENTH HOUR	Life Skills Development	Civility	To Zan Fort, civility means allowing peers to be themselves instead of discriminating against them because of their differences.
Lesson 8 January 12, 2017 Thursday, FIRST HOUR	Bullying Prevention	Sticks and Stones: Cyberbullying—Prevention 4	A female teen shares the rumors and sexual harassment she faced and a subsequent lawsuit against the school system.
Lesson 9 January 25, 2017 Wednesday, SECOND HOUR	Substance Abuse Prevention	Gateway: Drug and Alcohol Prevention—Part 3	Experts explain adolescent brain development and that the earlier kids begin to use drugs, the more detrimental the effects on the individual in the future.
Lesson 10 February 9, 2017 Thursday, THIRD HOUR	Civility	Civil Wars—Part 1	Explore why kids today are deemed less respectful than they were 30 years ago.
Lesson 11 February 22, 2017 Wednesday, FOURTH HOUR	Civility	Civil Wars—Part 2	Experts say feelings of isolation may cause less "civil" or respectful behaviors.
Lesson 12 March 2, 2017 Thursday, FIFTH HOUR	Life Skills Development	Justice/Fairness	Adam Brownfield and Nicole Blakely illustrate two sides of justice. Adam was sentenced to federal prison for taking a teen's life. Nicole was given a second chance at an alternative school for her intent to harm another child.
Lesson 13 March 29, 2017 Wednesday, SIXTH HOUR	Life Skills Development	Kindness	Brian Head's father says his son suffered years of torment from school bullies before he committed suicide at age 15.
Lesson 14 April 6, 2017 Thursday, SEVENTH HOUR	Digital Citizenship	Screen Addicts—Part 4	Daniel Gushue's dream of becoming a surgeon was put on the back burner when he became addicted to online gambling.

Topics: Resilience, Attendance and Achievement, Life Skills Development (Compassion, Citizenship, Civility, Conviction, Cooperation, Courage, Courtesy, Diligence, Freedom, Generosity, Helpfulness, Honesty, Honor, Integrity, Justice/Fairness, Kindness, Loyalty, Patience, Peace, Perseverance, Respect, Responsibility, Self-Control, Togetherness, Tolerance, Trustworthiness), Bullying Prevention, Substance Abuse Prevention, Digital Citizenship, Grief, College and Career Readiness.

Shared by B. DeWitt.

To introduce the program to parents, the team mailed home a letter (see Box 3.7) along with a copy of the primary (Tier 1) plan (including the expectation matrix). Among other things, the letter states that this new plan focuses on acknowledging students for meeting expectations and creating a positive, productive, and safe school environment. And, yes, the primary (Tier 1) plan definitely includes consequences as part of the schools' reactive plan. However, the reactive plan for responding to challenging behaviors subscribes to an instructional approach to behavior that is not punishment based (see Colvin, 2002; Colvin & Scott, 2004). At this point, the school would have a comprehensive plan with proactive strategies for preventing problem behaviors from occurring, as well as reactive strategies for responding to problems that do occur. In the letter, parents can be encouraged to post the expectation matrix in their family communication area (often the refrigerator as the site of most important things in a household, unless, of course, you have a stainless steel refrigerator!) to serve as a reminder for expected behavior and as a communication tool to facilitate the home–school partnership. For example, when a student receives a reinforcement ticket, a parent can say, "Oh, what did you get it for?" If the child does not recall, then the parent can say, "Well, *where* did you get it? . . . Oh, in the hallway for using a quiet voice. Well, that's great!" In this way, a positive parent–child conversation is prompted and the child/adolescent receives additional reinforcement for demonstrating the desired behavior. Similarly, if the student receives an office discipline referral, then the parent can use the information on the expectation matrix to help facilitate a conversation as to how he or she should have behaved and what was expected of him or her. The goal of involving the parent in the primary plan is not to impose values on the family, but to strengthen the home–school partnership by facilitating communication (Lane, Stanton-Chapman, Roorbach, & Phillips, 2007). Parent letters can also be used to clarify the purpose and scope of the Ci3T model—with a focus on the importance of providing equal attention to students' behavioral and social–emotional needs as is currently done for their academic needs (What Works Clearinghouse, 2008; Yudin, 2014; see Box 3.7).

To introduce the program to the students, personnel in one elementary school opened the doors on the first day of school and began passing out tickets paired with verbal praise (e.g., "Thanks for coming to school on time!"; "I appreciate you taking your hat off when coming in the building!"). Students immediately asked questions such as "What is this?"; "What's this for?"; and "What do I do with this?" Students were then ushered into an assembly (one assembly for students in grades 1–3, and another for students in grades 4 and 5) that introduced the Ci3T plan. As students walked into the assembly, they were asked to place their tickets into a large trash can, again prompting lots of questions. The assembly included cheerleaders, skits introducing the expectations for each setting, as well as the schoolwide lessons to be taught as part of the validated social skills lessons (e.g., "During homeroom we'll all be learning about ways to get along even better with our friends and the adults in our life"), and then a drawing. At the end of the assembly, the principal conducted a drawing in which three students received prizes ranging from homework passes, cash, and even a bicycle! Displayed throughout the school were posters illustrating the expectations (see Figures 3.4, 3.5, and 3.6), tickets (see Figure 3.7 and 3.8), and slogans. These visual reminders (prompts, or discriminative stimuli for those of you with formal training in applied behavior analysis!) were present in all key locations: classrooms, hallways, cafeteria, library, and even bathroom stalls. No matter where a student was and whether or not he or she was sitting or standing, the expectations were present.

(text resumes on page 84)

BOX 3.7. Sample Ci3T Family Letter

Dear Families,

As the school year begins, we are excited to introduce new and returning families of Mountain Vista Middle School to our new Comprehensive, Integrated, Three-Tiered (Ci3T) model of prevention! Our faculty and staff are committed to providing an intellectually engaging and safe environment to meet the academic, behavioral, and social skills needs of all students. It is our belief that our commitment to students and our community will show in our Ci3T plan. To maximize the Ci3T plan's effectiveness, we are providing families and our school community with information regarding our Ci3T plan. Thus, a brief description of the Mountain Vista Middle School Ci3T plan and expectations is included in this packet. We hope that you will hear more details about this plan from our students! Please do not hesitate to contact Mountain Vista Middle School faculty and staff if you have any questions and/or comments. And, be sure to check out the information on our school website!

What Is a Ci3T Plan?

A Ci3T model of prevention has at its base a schoolwide primary prevention component. **Every student participates just by virtue of attending our school.** The goal of our Ci3T schoolwide plan is to provide opportunities for all students to be optimally challenged with meaningful academic, behavioral, and social experiences that will support successful school and life outcomes. This plan is also designed to create a positive, productive, and even enjoyable school environment. Students participate in core academic instruction using evidence-based programs. The school community learns the schoolwide expectations, has opportunities to practice these expectations, and is recognized by meeting the expectations by adults. Students may also earn a Bobcat Buck for demonstrating the expected behaviors. Students then trade their Bobcat Bucks in for a variety of activities or prizes. We have also adopted a new social skills program to promote the social interactions we would like to see as a school community.

We will introduce screenings to make sure all students are progressing in their reading, math, and social skills just as we currently screen for hearing, vision, scoliosis, dental health, and overall health (monitoring risk for obesity). We know the primary plan alone may not be enough to meet some students' needs, so we have additional levels of support planned. For example, some students may benefit from small-group instruction on a particular skill (secondary support), whereas others may benefit most from individualized supports (tertiary support). Each of these levels of support, primary (schoolwide), secondary, and tertiary, are part of our Ci3T plan. We aim to foster a positive learning environment for *all* students and support *every* student to the extent necessary for academic, behavioral, and social success in accordance with out purpose.

What Is the Goal of the Ci3T Plan?

The purpose of Mountain Vista Middle School's Ci3T plan is to providing an intellectually engaging and safe environment to meet the academic, behavioral, and social skill needs of all students. To support students' behavior we have identified three Bobcat expectations: (1) Be Respectful, (2) Be Responsible, and (3) Be Your Best. Our Expectation Matrix (see attached) defines what each Bobcat expectation looks like in each school setting. For example, how are we Respectful in the cafeteria, hallways, and classrooms?

The Mountain Vista Middle School community is extremely grateful for the tremendous support of our families. We invite you to be actively involved in your child's middle school experience through volunteering, being present on the school campus, and/or connecting with us on social media and our website. Please see your child's teachers' webpages for detailed information. Thus, your commitment to this Ci3T plan is valuable for your child and our school community! After reading the Ci3T Primary Plan and Bobcat Expectations, we ask that you contact us with any questions, then sign the included Signature of Support form and return to the school office by September 15th.

Thank you for your support and commitment to our school, our students, and our staff. It is with eager anticipation and excitement that we look forward to students' successes of the coming school year.

Sincerely,
Loretta Jackson, Principal and the Mountain Vista Middle School Faculty and Staff

Attachments:
- Ci3T Primary Plan
- Bobcat Expectations

Please detach, complete, and return the "Signature of Support" form to the school office by September 15th.

I, _____, have thoroughly read Mountain Vista Middle School's Ci3T primary plan and Bobcat expectations. I have contacted the school with any questions and agree to support and participate my child and the Mountain Vista Middle School community.

Signature   Date

FIGURE 3.4. Sample PBIS poster—elementary level.

FIGURE 3.5. Sample poster—elementary level. Designed by Kylie Beck, Vanderbilt University Kennedy Center/National Institute of Child Health and Human Development Grant No. P30 HD15052.

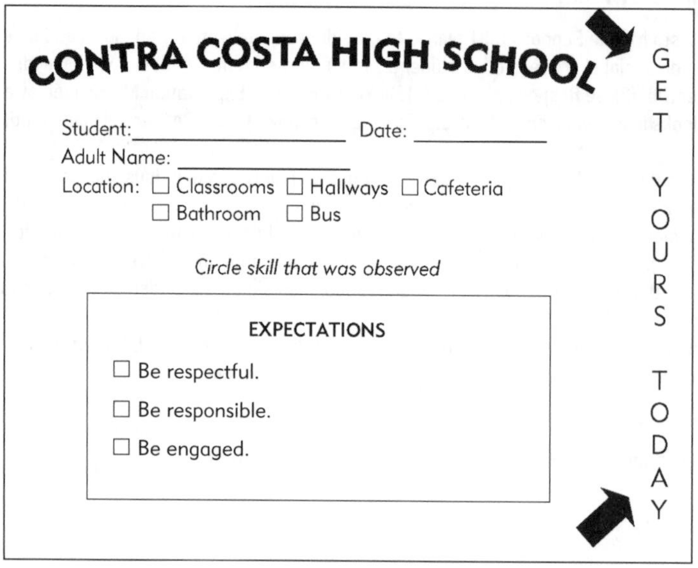

FIGURE 3.6. Sample PBIS poster—high school level.

Orange Elementary School

Student Name: _____ Date: _____

Adult name: _____ Location: ☐ Classroom ☐ Hallway

Grade: _____ ☐ Cafeteria ☐ Playground ☐ Bathroom ☐ Bus

Mark the schoolwide expectation that was shown.

Show respect

Be responsible

Give best effort

FIGURE 3.7. Orange Elementary School ticket.

CONTRA COSTA HIGH SCHOOL

Student: _____ Date: _____

Adult Name: _____

Location: ☐ Classroom ☐ Hallway ☐ Cafeteria ☐ Bathroom ☐ Bus

Circle the skill that was observed

EXPECTATIONS

☐ Be respectful.

☐ Be responsible.

☐ Be engaged.

FIGURE 3.8. Contra Costa High School ticket.

To provide ongoing training for all individuals in the building, various combinations of the following strategies may be used:

- Morning announcements.
- Introduction of new posters and other signage to increase interest.
- Monthly teacher-led lessons to teach behavioral expectations (including all settings; e.g., the cafeteria; see Lessons Learned 3.6).
- Professional learning activities for adults to learn low-intensity supports to increase engagement and minimize disruptions.
- Instructional schedule and regular reminders for teaching the scheduled lessons provided as part of the validated social skills lessons (see Lessons Learned 3.7 and 3.8).
- Daily student-developed videos illustrating expectations (including examples and "non-examples").
- Teacher-led lessons (30 minutes) to reteach expectations for each setting specified in the expectation matrix.
- Bookmarks for substitutes, bus drivers, cafeteria workers, and parent volunteers that contain essential information about Ci3T, including how and when to give out tickets. Bookmarks can be distributed along with a pack of tickets when these adults sign in and enter the building (see Lessons Learned 3.9 and 3.10).
- Emails to teachers to provide reminders about teaching the setting lessons and monthly social skills lessons (see Box 3.8).
- Emails to all adults—employees and volunteers—in the building to provide suggestions about when to give out tickets and the importance of pairing the ticket with behavior-specific praise (see Box 3.8).
- Coaching emails sent out weekly from district Ci3T Coaches to include successes (e.g., shout outs!), tips for success, and action items.

As we mentioned previously, it is important to provide initial and ongoing training for all parties involved: all adults in the building, parents, and teachers. By training broadly and diversely, we promote generalization of the desired skills (Cooper, Heron, & Heward, 2007; Dunlap, 1993; Lane & Beebe-Frankenberger, 2004), which in turn increases the probability of students demonstrating similar behaviors in new environments and in the presence of a variety of people (stimulus generalization).

LESSONS LEARNED 3.6. Implementation Success

To: Bill

Subject: Re: Lesson setting—6th hour today—cafeteria

Thank you to everyone!
It's making a huge difference.
Thanks again.

From: High School Food Service Coordinator

LESSONS LEARNED 3.7. Launching at the High School Level

Below is the letter that is being sent to the teachers at our high school to pump them up for the Connect With Kids rollout. Our first lesson is scheduled to be taught tomorrow, so we will see how it goes. People have been seemingly positive about the experience, so pray for cooperative technology tomorrow morning.

Teachers,

Well, today is the day that we take a step into the *Brave New World* of Connect With Kids. If you have never used a social skills tool to supplement your classroom, then this process will be entirely new. Remember that Connect With Kids is just that—a tool—kind of like a hammer is a tool that can be used to either build things or destroy things, depending on the user. Same with Connect With Kids, it can either be a positive experience or a negative experience, depending on the user. I have complete confidence that you can use this Connect With Kids resource in a way to have deeper conversations with our students and make it extremely positive. Below are the directions to find the video and lesson for the Connect With Kids Session during first hour today, Thursday, August 25.

After logging in to *connectwithkids.com,* click on the button at the bottom of the main page that says "Classroom Resources." Once on the Classroom Resources page, you will find nine options from which to choose, with each option taking you to pages full of different lessons. For the First Lesson of this school year, you will want to click on the "Attendance and Achievement" button (it has a Schoolhouse icon on it) and find the video titled *Against All Odds: Part 4,* which is in the third row of videos. You are now ready to watch the story of Berhane Azage and how not making things personal helped him to succeed in his high school.

If you are ready to roll, then go for it. Nevertheless, here are some notes about the video if you want them:

1. The video series starts at "Part 4" because we lack the time to show all of the lessons in order and sequentially, so we have pulled a sampling of videos and have built a series in that manner. For those of you who are *Star Wars* fans, you know that series started out with Part 4 and it turned out just fine. Also, you could watch *Rocky IV* without having seen the previous three movies and still know exactly what is going on. So I think our students will be OK.

2. In the video, the narrator mentions the third P when he talks about Berhane taking things "Personal." If your students happen to ask what the other two P's are, you can WOW them by answering "Permanence and Pervasive." You can then double-WOW them by giving them an example of what you mean: Pessimistic thinkers tend to think that setbacks are personal ("It's my fault I failed the test"), pervasive ("I am a bad student"), and permanent ("I will never be a good student"). Whereas optimistic thinkers treat setbacks just the opposite: They don't think they are personal ("I bet everyone had a hard time with that test"), pervasive ("I do well normally on tests") or permanent ("It's only the first test; I can make up for it later").

Hope that helps. Thank you for all that you do. Please let me know if you have any questions.

Shared by B. DeWitt.

Also critical to keeping the newly acquired behaviors evident over time (maintenance) and in new situations (stimulus generalization) is reinforcement. It is important that the desired behaviors receive higher rates of reinforcement than the previously undesirable behavior (Umbreit et al., 2007). In the next section we describe a range of procedures for reinforcing behavior.

Procedures for Reinforcing

When we think about reinforcement, it is important to remember that all people with roles and responsibilities need to receive reinforcement as they work toward establishing new practices and habits. You might remember that there are two types of reinforcement: positive reinforcement and negative reinforcement. *Positive reinforcement* occurs when a behavior (e.g., following a teacher's direction) is followed by the contingent introduction of a stimulus (e.g., a ticket paired with verbal praise and a smile) that increases the likelihood that the same behavior (e.g., following a teacher's direction) will occur in the future under similar conditions (Cooper et al., 2007). *Negative reinforcement* also increases the probability of a behavior occurring in the future, but it involves the contingent removal of a stimulus that is aversive.

LESSONS LEARNED 3.8. Supportive Reminders

Subject: Connect With Kids Lesson 3—Thursday THIRD HOUR

Teachers,

   Thursday THIRD HOUR is when the next Connect With Kids Lesson is scheduled. Thank you to everyone for getting this Social Skills initiative started in a positive way for our kids. I know it is homecoming week and it is already haphazard, but the schedule has some extra time built into Thursday anyway, so what an excellent time to engage your students on motivation for coming to school. The first two lessons have focused on resiliency, and now we are moving toward motivators for staying at school.

   Why do kids come to school? Seven thousand students drop out every day, which is 7,000 too many. This video is only 3 minutes, 55 seconds long and focuses on the reasons kids come to school. It ends with one young man saying that he didn't see potential in himself, but others did. That is our challenge with our kids. How do we bring forth the potential that every one of our students has?

   The video link is as follows: Disconnect: Why Kids Skip School—Part 1, *connectwithkids.com/ disconnect-why-kids-skip-school-cv* (this was actually wrong in the guide so I copied it here and have uploaded a corrected guide). This video explores trends in school dropout rates and the reasons that students are disengaged from their education.

   Lesson Plan: *http://content.connectwithkids.com.s3.amazonaws.com/websource/student_ channel/downloads/disconnect/disconnect1.pdf*. This lesson asks teachers to open a group discussion by asking, "Have you ever stopped to think about what keeps you coming back to school? What connects you to this place? Is it the subjects? Is it the chance to see and talk with a particular friend? Is it a teacher? Is it the games in PE? Is it your parents making sure that you show up?"

   You never know, but *you* might be the reason your students show up every day.

   Thank you for all that you do. Any feedback from the conversation with your students is always appreciated.

   Bill

Shared by B. DeWitt.

LESSONS LEARNED 3.9. Ci3T Challenge: Ci3T Leadership Team Member

Attached is a challenge that we are having our staff try out for the month of February. We will see how it goes. Just keeping you in the loop.

Bill
Assistant Principal/Athletic Director

FEBRUARY Ci3T CHALLENGE
WEEK 1 February 1st–7th
Theme: RESPECT

RESPECT	February 1st–7th
OUR BEST EFFORT	February 8th–14th
ACADEMIC ACHIEVEMENT	February 15th–21st
RESPONSIBILITY	February 22nd–29th

Each week of February will have as its theme one of our four schoolwide expectations, and we would like to recognize kids during each week, with each particular theme in mind.

EACH WEEK YOU WILL BE CHALLENGED TO DO THE FOLLOWING:

☐ Give one ROAR ticket each day, preferably with positive praise for an example of **respect,** but any type of ticket will do.

☐ Pick out one student who is quiet or seems unengaged in your class, and make an effort to engage in conversations with that student (get to know him or her).

☐ Write a praise note to at least one staff member and one student in the building who are doing anything **ROAR** related, and put them in their boxes or have an aid deliver them to the student.

☐ Give three specific positive praises each day in and outside of class.

Once you have completed each of these challenges, mark each ☐, and when all of your boxes are marked, turn this sheet in to the Ci3T mailbox in the front office by the end of each week for your chance to win and be recognized. (Yes, there is a Ci3T mailbox—it is on the far right near the bottom.)

Along with this sheet are tickets (can you cut them, please?) and two postcards—one for a staff member and one for a colleague. Each day this week there will be a special announcement specifically related to the theme of the week. We hope that by the end of February, everyone will become more familiar with our expectations of **R**espect, **O**ur Best Effort, **A**cademic Achievement, and **R**esponsibility.

Have fun!

When selecting reinforcers, we recommend incorporating mainly positive reinforcement, although negative reinforcement may also be useful at times. Whereas many people are trying to "get" or "seek" social attention, activities, or tangible items (positive reinforcement; see Table 3.1), others will try to "avoid" or "escape" social attention, activities, or tangible items (Umbreit et al., 2007). So, we encourage you to develop a reinforcement system that appeals to a range of people, such as the attention-seeking elementary student (or, in some instances, graduate students! ☺) and the escape-motivated high school student. And remember that sources of reinforcement change over time. Whereas teacher attention may be highly

(text resumes on page 90)

LESSONS LEARNED 3.10. Feedback on the Ci3T Challenge

To: Bill
Subject: Re: Week 2 Challenge—Ci3T

Bill—

Last week was a failure on my part, but this week is starting out great. The new booklets are great! They are so much easier to carry around and to find on my messy desk! Thanks for fixing the typos on the back and for taking my suggestion and printing directions. The students seem to understand the concept much better.

I gave one to a student today who is at the group home and just started high school on Friday. I said I appreciated her coming to class as a new student with such a positive attitude. She was giddy about being able to shoot photos and have a real camera.

When I gave her the ticket, she said, "No one has ever given me anything like that. Thanks, I am just so excited to be at this school." ☺

BOX 3.8. Sample Ci3T Emails to Faculty and Staff

Reminder to use behavior-specific praise and intermittently use the schoolwide acknowledgment system	Faculty, staff, and volunteers, Thank you for your commitment to our students' academic, behavioral, and social development! We recognize your efforts in teaching student our expectations with behavior-specific praise. When you give a student a ticket, be sure to pair it with behavior-specific praise as well, so that the student knows what you expect and why he or she earned the ticket! For example, last week, I heard Mr. Hightower say, "Gary, I appreciate the way you are showing respect in the hallway by helping a friend with his locker. Way to go!" Keep up the good work, Coach Hughes
Focus on a specific social skill	Greetings! This month we are focusing on self-awareness skills. The lesson this week is learning how to ask for help. After you teach the lesson, please use behavior-specific praise and our STAR tickets to recognize students who are asking for help when needed. Thanks for all you do, Ms. Suzanne
Reminder of the upcoming academic and behavior screening windows	Dear Faculty, Our year has gotten off to a positive start, beginning with our Ci3T kickoff! Please remember to mark your calendars with our assessment windows for this semester. We will conduct academic screenings from August 15th to September 1st, behavior screenings from September 15th to September 25th, and treatment integrity and social validity from October 15th to November 1st. During the last window you may be visited by one of our school Ci3T Data Team members to observe in your classroom. The Ci3T Leadership Team will be available to assist you with any of these assessments—please ask! Thank you for your commitment to our positive school climate and our students' success! Dr. Parker

TABLE 3.1. Reinforcer Menu: Suggested Reinforcers Based on the Function of the Behavior

Function	Students	Faculty and staff	Families
		Persons	

Seeking positive reinforcement

Function	Students	Faculty and staff	Families
Social attention	• Lunch with friend • Lunch with staff member of choice • Preferential seating • Reading time with adult • Meeting with the principal • Tutor/mentor younger class • Award given in front of class/school • Featured in a Ci3T video/skit • Praise postcard sent home	• Preferential parking spot • Award given during faculty meeting • Recognition during assembly • Featured in a Ci3T video/skit	• Student featured on school webpage • Student featured in newsletter or on bulletin board • Phone call home from principal/teacher • Praise postcard sent home • Featured in a Ci3T video/skit
Activity/task	• Lunch with a friend • Lunch with staff member of choice • Movie (on-campus) • Preferential seating • Class helper • Extra reading time • Ci3T assembly • Additional computer time • Additional recess time • Game of choice • Ticket to school event (e.g., sporting, dance, play) • Extra basketball time • Featured spot in Ci3T video	• Draws winning ticket during assemblies • Ticket to school event (e.g., sporting, play, dance) • Feature spot in Ci3T video	• Ticket to school event (e.g., sporting, dance, play) • Feature spot in Ci3T video
Tangible	• School supplies • Fast food gift card coupon • School T-shirt or sweatshirt • Bike, radio, iPad • Candy, soft drinks • Gift cards (e.g., movie, stores, restaurants) • Discounted yearbook, dance ticket, sporting event	• Free yearbook • Gift certificate to local restaurant • Gift cards (e.g., movies, stores, restaurants) • Candy, soft drinks • School T-shirt or sweatshirt • School supplies • Car wash coupon	• Gift certificate (e.g., movies, stores, restaurants) • Postcard sent home regarding student's exemplar behavior • Bumper sticker for car • School T-shirt or sweatshirt
Sensory	• Listen to music • Watch a video • Fidget		

Avoiding negative reinforcement

Function	Students	Faculty and staff	Families
Social attention	• Lunch in private area with peer and staff of choosing • Extra computer time • Quiet time in the library pass • Get out of class participation pass • Get out of PE • Preferential seating during school event	• Supervision at the Ci3T assembly • Before/afterschool supervision • Hallway monitor	• Phone conference instead of on-campus conference • Get out of classroom support duty

(continued)

TABLE 3.1. *(continued)*

Function	Students	Faculty and staff	Families
		Persons	
Activity/task	• Extra computer time (avoid class time) • Homework pass • Front of the lunch line pass • Additional free time • Extra library time • Preferred parking (avoid the long walk to class!)	• Extra planning period • Relief from bus duty • Relief from lunch duty	• Phone conference instead of on-campus conference • Get out of classroom support duty
Tangible	• Certificate to drop lowest grade	• Certificate to avoid walkie-talkie duty in the hallway	• Certificate to avoid supervision duty at extracurricular activities
Sensory	• Noise-canceling headphones • Sunglasses	• Special parking space	

Note. From Umbreit, Ferro, Liaupsin, and Lane (2007, p. 81). Adapted by permission of Pearson Education, Inc., Upper Saddle River, NJ.

reinforcing to early elementary students, peer attention tends to become more meaningful as students transition into middle and high school grades. Adults, too, are motivated in different ways. In Table 3.1, you will see a range of reinforcers that can be used in preschool, elementary, middle, and high schools to reward those students, faculty, staff, and parents who are either trying to "seek" or "avoid" attention, tasks, or tangibles. Some schools have done a great job of combining a range of reinforcers. See Box 3.9 for a description of how one middle school designed a reinforcement system to appeal to its students. See Box 3.10 for some fundraising ideas. See also Lessons Learned 3.11.

As you consider how to develop your reinforcement system, keep in mind that the rate of reinforcement is important. For example, if your initial goal is to teach students the desired behaviors, then it is important to have a rich, thick schedule of reinforcement (for you behaviorists, we're talking about a *variable ratio schedule*) to make sure that students receive reinforcement for demonstrating the desired behaviors. Once the students have learned the desired expectations, we want to make sure these newly acquired behaviors are sustained over time by securing naturally occurring reinforcement (e.g., the absence of the stress that comes with knowing you are going to be late on a project; the extra time you have when your work is completed ahead of schedule; the positive peer interactions that come with being able to choose to work with a partner). At that point, the team will most likely want to introduce a leaner schedule of reinforcement, moving to a more intermitted reinforcement schedule (Cooper et al., 2007).

A few other points to consider are the following. First, not everyone supports the use of tangible reinforcers. If people are opposed to tangible reinforcers, then focus on using social attention and activity reinforcers (see Table 3.1). Social reinforcers such as time with friend, working with a peer, and behavior-specific praise are very convenient, practical, and inexpensive. Second, if you are using primary reinforcers such as edibles (e.g., food or beverages)

BOX 3.9. Description of One Middle School's Reinforcement System

One middle school developed a monthly Ci3T Awards Assembly that was designed to appeal to students with varied interests. The assembly included a variety of components that were attractive to both the seekers and avoiders. In other words, there was something for everyone. See below for how the assembly activities met multiple students' reinforcement preferences.

	Seekers (Positive Reinforcement)	Avoiders (Negative Reinforcement)
Attention	• Opportunities for students to win prizes and have Qheir names called out in front of the entire grade. • Teachers actively engaged in activities with students. • Students could gain attention from peers. • The names of students who earned A's and B's on their report card were posted on the High Flyer Wall.	• Students who wanted to avoid attention from teachers in class could find quiet space to read, listen to music, and hang out with peers.
Activity	• A variety of activities available to engage in (e.g., basketball, ping-pong, dancing, chatting, movie watching, outside sports).	• Avoid class by attending the assembly. • Avoid dressing out for PE.
Tangible/ sensory	• A ticket was drawn from the large bucket of tickets every 10 minutes for a student to win a prize. A variety of prizes were on display. Students could place tickets earned in a box in front of the desired prize to be raffled. • Snacks were on sale for tickets (guaranteed reinforcement!—no "chance" of not getting what you want!).	• Students who did not want to engage in social activity or hear the loud noise of the music and raffles could go to a quiet classroom to watch a movie or play board games.

and sensory stimulation (e.g., music), be careful to remember that many students have food allergies and everyone will eventually satiate on food (yes, even dark chocolate— hard to believe, we know). If you do use edible reinforcers, also make sure to pair food with social reinforcers such as a smile and/or behavior-specific praise (e.g., "Katie Scarlett, you did a great job of _____!"). Third, if you are using secondary reinforcers such as preferred activities and privileges, make sure to vary the choice of reinforcers as the novelty often wears off. Fourth, by using tickets, cards, or tokens that can later be traded for reinforcers, such as time with friends during assemblies, activities, or tangibles, you are also encouraging delayed gratification—another essential skill.

Over the years we have often heard faculty and staff register concerns that giving reinforcement is nothing less that bribery. We respectfully remind people that all behavior is maintained by consequences (Cooper et al., 2007). You do what you do because of what you get or avoid (Umbreit et al., 2007). Whereas bribery is using strategies to increase the likelihood of people doing things that are *not* in their best interest, positive reinforcement is a behavioral principle that involves the contingent introduction of any stimuli that increase the probability of the desired behavior occurring in the future. As adults, it is easy to forget how difficult school can be for some. It is an environment that offers few opportunities for choice and provides real challenges for many students. Helping faculty and staff to remember to pay attention to positive behaviors and recognize students for displaying them helps to fosters an environment in which these behaviors are performed for the intrinsic satisfaction they provide.

BOX 3.10. Fundraising Ideas

Lock-In

Host a "lock-in" in which school personnel supervise students on a weekend evening. School staff members plan various activities (e.g., pizza, basketball, movies, arts and crafts, music) for students in the school gymnasium and cafeteria. The supervised lock-in costs $20 per student, with a discounted rated for families with multiple children.

Silent Auction

A Ci3T Leadership Team member pairs up with the parent organization to organize a silent auction at which various donated items are offered (e.g., dinners, event tickets). Attendees purchase a ticket to attend the auction (and dinner if you can get catering donated too!). The proceeds from the auction are used to acquire reinforcers (e.g., tangibles and events).

Donations

Ci3T Leadership Team members with the parent organization request support from local businesses. Local businesses donate items such as food gift cards, overstocked items at Target or Wal-Mart, or team gear (one school even received NFL tickets!).

Car Wash

High school student groups host a car wash in which all proceeds go to support Ci3T activities.

Holiday-Grams

Student or parent organizations sell small items (e.g., carnations, candy) to students, parents, and school personnel. The items and an accompanying note are delivered to others in the school during the school day (e.g., Valentine's Day, Halloween, finals week, homecoming).

Parking

Schools located near a local university or event center charge a reasonable fee per car to park and walk to the event.

Fall/Spring Festival

A Ci3T Leadership Team subcommittee and parent organization join together to host a festival for students, families, and the local community. The festival may include games, food, rides, or local events (e.g., pony rides, henna tattoos, antique truck show).

LESSONS LEARNED 3.11. Positive Reinforcement in High Schools

Positive reinforcement and positive praise can be difficult items to implement at the high school level, because staff members and students often associate these concepts with elementary school or middle school. However, we found success in getting these concepts implemented once we showed staff members that this is just another way to recognize students for their daily accomplishments. High school personnel all across the country do not think twice about recognizing students for semester-long accomplishments, via the honor roll or season-long accomplishment via a varsity letter. We also found success in getting buy-in from students once we created incentives the students desired. We found two incentives that are particularly popular with the students. Our most popular incentive is the ROAR Zone, special seating behind the end zone at home varsity football games. We select three students to sit in this section, and each of the winners got to bring a friend. We have snacks and beverages for the students; then, during the game, pizza is delivered to them. The second most popular incentive is being able to park in the faculty parking lot. After recognizing our students at home football game for 2 years, we introduced a new concept to recognize community members during Year 3 of our implementation. We created the ROAR fan of the week. We asked community members and staff members to nominate someone in the community who recognized one of our ROAR characteristics (Respect, Our best effort, Academic Achievement, Responsibility). Between the first and second quarter of the game, we asked these patrons to come down to the football field, and we recognize them by reading which of the attributes they exemplify.

Matt Brungardt
High School Principal

Summary

In this chapter, we have provided an overview of a step-by-step, team-based approach for designing and implementing the primary (Tier 1) prevention components of your schools' Ci3T to integrate academic, behavioral, and social components. We described (1) district-level considerations for how to involve district leaders to establish priorities around systems change; (2) how to use a team-based approach with input from faculty, staff, parents, and students to construct a context-sensitive, customized primary (Tier 1) prevention plan that addresses the core values held by the school community; and (3) procedures for implementing the primary (Tier 1) prevention efforts at the school site, namely, procedures for teaching and reinforcing. In Chapter 4, we discuss the final element of primary (Tier 1) prevention efforts: procedures for monitoring. Specifically, we discuss treatment integrity and social validity.

Examining Tier 1 Efforts

MONITORING TREATMENT INTEGRITY
AND SOCIAL VALIDITY

In Chapter 3, we offered an overview of a step-by-step, team-based approach for designing and implementing the primary (Tier 1) prevention components, the base, of your school's Ci3T plan to integrate academic, behavioral, and social learning. Chapter 3 focused primarily on building the base of your Ci3T plan, including drafting of the mission statement, the purpose statement, and expectations for student decorum in key settings throughout the school, as well as establishing roles and responsibilities for all stakeholders (students, faculty and staff, parents, and administrators) in academic, behavioral, and social domains. We also established procedures for teaching and for reinforcing these same stakeholders to support the initial launch, as well as ongoing Ci3T implementation. These components are important, as it is insufficient to build a tiered system without careful consideration of how to support high-fidelity implementation given the model relies on empowering adults who will in turn empower students. In this chapter, we focus on the final section of primary (Tier 1) prevention efforts: procedures for monitoring.

Specifically, we discuss procedures for monitoring Ci3T implementation (treatment integrity) and assessing stakeholder feedback (social validity) to understand how stakeholders view the goals, procedures, and intended outcomes. As part of this process, we explain how Ci3T Leadership Teams build an assessment schedule to serve as an at-a-glance summary of all information collected in a building for both student- and school-level outcomes. This information is important for ensuring students have access to high-quality primary (Tier 1) prevention efforts and establishing entry criteria for secondary (Tier 2) and tertiary (Tier 3) interventions for students who may benefit from more targeted or intensive efforts.

First, we define treatment integrity, explain its importance, introduce a variety of ways to monitor it, and offer logistical considerations for monitoring integrity. Second, we define social validity, explain why it should be considered when designing and implementing your Ci3T model, offer suggestions about whose opinions should be consulted, introduce a few ways of assessing social validity, and offer logistical considerations for monitoring social validity.

Monitoring Ci3T Implementation: Is the Plan Being Put in Place as Designed?

Treatment Integrity: Defined

Once the Ci3T model is designed, the next step is to put the plan in place. Rather than just assuming (remember what your high school teacher said about assuming!) the plan is being used the way you intended, it is necessary to collect information to see whether it is being implemented as originally designed—that is, you ascertain the degree of treatment integrity (Gresham, 1989; Yeaton & Sechrest, 1981). In research terms, *treatment integrity* is a measure of the accuracy with which the independent variable (intervention) is instituted as planned. Without treatment integrity data, it would be difficult (actually, impossible), to draw accurate conclusions regarding intervention outcomes (Peterson, Homer, & Wonderlich, 1982). In other words, you would not be able to tell whether the plan is working.

The Importance of Monitoring Treatment Integrity

Only by measuring treatment integrity can you determine whether the plan is in place and how well it is being used. In the past, interventions were often implemented but not monitored for integrity (Lane, Bocian, MacMillian, & Gresham, 2004). This omission was a critical problem because without treatment integrity data, you cannot draw accurate conclusions about *why* a program did or did not produce the desired outcomes. For example, it could be that ODRs did not decrease because a given intervention did not work (poor program), or it could be that not all intervention components were put in place as originally designed (poor treatment integrity). Similarly, if ODRs decreased but treatment integrity data were not monitored, you could not be sure whether the decrease is attributable to the plan you designed or because the teachers changed the current program, or perhaps even introduced a new program.

Methods of Monitoring Treatment Integrity

Treatment integrity can be measured—and hence monitored—in a variety of ways and from different perspectives. For example, it can be monitored by using behavior checklists that contain key components of the plan. These checklists can be completed by the people at the school site who are responsible for program implementation (e.g., teachers, administrators, office staff). This type of information is referred to as *self-report data*, and it can be less than accurate in some cases, although still useful (some people tend to rate themselves somewhat higher than their actual performance so that they look good to others; Lane, Beebe-Frankenberger, Lambros, & Pierson, 2001). Behavior checklists can also be completed by outside observers to obtain an independent perspective on how the plan is being implemented (Bruhn, 2011).

In our work, we have created the Ci3T Treatment Integrity: Teacher Self-Report (Ci3T TI: TSR). The Ci3T TI: TSR includes 38 items to assess implementation of primary (Tier 1) prevention practices. The measure includes three subscales: Procedures for Teaching (16 items; e.g., "Did I use clear routines for classroom procedures?"), Procedures for Reinforcing (10 items; e.g., "Did I use behavior-specific praise when giving tickets to students?"), and Procedures for Monitoring (12 items; e.g., "Did I use behavior and academic data together [in conjunction with each other] to inform my instruction?"; Lane, 2009a). Educators rate each item in fall and spring using the following Likert-type scale ranging from 0 to 3 (0 = *not at all*, 1 = *some of the time*, 2 = *most of the time*, 3 = *all of the time*). Scores are computed by dividing total score by total possible (adjusted for missing items) and multiplying by 100; school percentages are determined by calculating the mean score for everyone who completed the Ci3T TI: TSR. An initial evaluation of the Ci3T TI: TSR indicated adequate to desirable reliability (see Bruhn, 2011).

In Box 4.1 is an example of a completed Ci3T TI: Direct Observation (Ci3T TI: DO) form. In this case, components 1, 2, 3, 7, 9, 10, 12, and 13 were done *all of the time,* receiving a rating of 3. Yet the teacher received a 0 on component 8, because she did not have a starting activity for the lesson, and a 1 on component 6, because she did not make individual modifications for students' social or behavioral needs. An overall percentage of the score was computed by adding up all the points earned (42) and dividing by the number of points possible (57), to receive an overall score of 73.98%. You can also compute the treatment fidelity for each domain—Procedures for Teaching ($31/39 \times 100 = 79.49\%$; see Box 4.1), and Procedures for Reinforcing ($11/18 \times 100 = 61.11\%$)—if you would like to see where some teachers could benefit from coaching.

In our partnerships with schools, district leaders and Ci3T Leadership Teams at each school examine average component and session scores for educators and for the school as a whole. Component integrity allows you to see how a certain program component (e.g., "Did I use behavior-specific praise when giving tickets to students?") is implemented over the course of a school year. Session integrity allows you to evaluate how a teacher is implementing the program components overall during a certain period of time (e.g., monthly or quarterly). Both pieces of information can be used to determine how the primary (Tier 1) prevention efforts are being implemented. Then this information can be used to shape the Ci3T plan revisions over the summer and professional learning to be offered in next year. For example, you may find that educators are not conducting starting activities (component T.8). The Ci3T Leadership Team can begin the year with a professional learning session on the importance of starting activities, examples of these activities, and even allow time for teachers to plan together to share ideas.

In addition to behavior checklists, standardized measures such as the School-wide Evaluation Tool Version 2.1 (SET; Sugai, Lewis-Palmer, Todd, & Horner, 2005; available from *pbis. org*) and Tiered Fidelity Inventory (TFI; Algozzine et al., 2014; available from *www.pbisassessment.org*) are available to monitor implementation of the primary prevention level of the behavioral (PBIS) component. The SET contains 28 items constituting seven subscales to evaluate the seven key features of PBIS (Horner et al., 2004). The key features evaluated on the subscales include (1) schoolwide behavior expectations are defined, (2) schoolwide expectations are taught to all students in the school, (3) rewards are provided for following schoolwide behavior expectations, (4) a consistently implemented continuum of consequences for problem behavior is in place, (5) problem behavior patterns are monitored and the information is used to inform ongoing decision making, (6) an administrator actively supports and is involved in the PBIS program, and (7) the school district provides support to the school (e.g., functional policies, staff training opportunities, and data collection) (Horner et al., 2004). Each item on the SET is scored on a 3-point Likert-type scale (ranging from 0 (*not implemented*), to 1 (*partially implemented*), to 2 (*fully implemented*). Next, summary scores for each subscale are computed by determining the percentage of possible points for each of the seven key features. Then an overall total summary score is computed by taking the average of the seven subscale scores. The criterion for adequate implementation is 80% on Behavioral Expectations Taught and the overall summary scores. The SET has strong psychometric properties, with an overall alpha coefficient of .96 and test–retest reliability of 97.3% (Horner et al., 2004).

The TFI is a 45-item tool designed to provide information across all three tiers to assess treatment integrity and also support sustainability. The TFI has three sections: Tier I: Universal (15 items); Tier II: Targeted (13 items); and Tier III: Intensive (17 items) SWPBIS features. The sections can be used together or each may be used separately (McIntosh, Massar, et al., 2017). Each section has three subscales: (1) Teams, (2) Implementation, and (3) Evaluation. The Tier III section has an additional subscale to examine support plans. Each item on the TFI is scored on a 3-point Likert-type scale (0 = *not implemented*, 1 = *partially implemented*, 2 = *fully implemented*). The TFI provides a list of possible data sources and scoring criteria for each item. Next, scores for each section are computed by summing the points and dividing by the total points possible. Acceptable implementation is met with 70% earned in each section. The TFI has strong psychometric properties, with an overall internal consistency of .96 (.87, .96, .98 for each section, respectively; McIntosh, Massar, et al., 2017).

We recommend completing the SET or TFI at the beginning (6 weeks into the school year) and end (6 weeks prior to the end of the school year) of the school year. The TFI may also be used more frequently for team planning, if desired. Box 4.2 contains a summary report for hypothetical elementary school SET data. The school had a high level of fidelity during fall 2020, with an overall SET score of 84.11%. The goal for the overall score was 80%, and the SET score for behavioral expectations taught was 70%. As such, the Ci3T Leadership Team would follow up with data sharing, then action planning, which would include addressing elements in need of improvement (e.g., teaching expectations and monitoring and decision making, as well as management; see Box 4.2, Panel A).

In Panel B, you see a school's SET scores over time. The school had a high level of fidelity during fall 2020, with an overall SET score of 84.11%. During the following fall, the level of fidelity as measured by the SET was even higher, with a total SET score of 88.21%. During fall 2020, the school scored 100% on three components: expectations defined, ongoing system for rewarding behavioral expectations, and district-level support. These three components were also fully present during fall 2021. In addition, the school improved in three remaining areas, with only one component—system for responding to behavioral violations (87.5%)—with a score less than 100%.

In our work we rely on a combination of methods to monitor treatment fidelity (see Bruhn, 2011; Lane, Kalberg, Bruhn, et al., 2008; Lane, Oakes, & Magill, 2014). First, in the earlier years of our inquiry, teachers completed monthly component checklists to self-report their implementation of the program. Second, outside observers watched each teacher for a 20- to

(text resumes on page 101)

BOX 4.1. Sample Completed Ci3T Treatment Integrity: Direct Observation Form (Ci3T TI: DO)

Teacher _Sam Smith_   Teacher ID Number _17_   School _Fanning ES_

Subject Taught _Literature Circle_   Grade Level(s) _2nd_   Rater: ☐ School staff member ☒ Ci3T outside observer

Date Completed _10/20/19_   Observation: Start Time _9:15_   End Time _9:45_   Observer: _Jameson Jordan_

Directions: Please evaluate your use of your school's Ci3T plan in the 30-minute observation period that just occurred (when the outside observer was in your classroom). First, please consider if you did (yes) or did not (no) use each element during the 30-minute observation period. If you did not use the element, please circle the 0 for the item. If your response is yes, please circle the frequency that best reflects the extent to which you used that item during today's observation.

| | About how often did you participate? | | | | |
| | No . . . | Yes, I did this . . . | | | |
Procedures for Teaching	Not at All (0)	Some of the Time (1)	Most of the Time (2)	All of the Time (3)	No Opportunity (7)
T.1 Did I have our three to five schoolwide expectations posted and visible in my classroom (e.g., Be Respectful, Be Responsible, Give Best Effort)?	0	1	2	③	7
T.2 Did I have the setting expectations posted in my classroom (expectation matrix with all settings)?	0	1	2	③	7
T.3 Did I model the behaviors (expectations) stated in the schoolwide plan for my students?	0	1	2	③	7
T.4 Was my instruction linked to the district/state standards?	0	1	②	3	7
T.5 Did I differentiate instruction (academic tasks) as needed?	0	1	②	3	7
T.6 Did I make individual modifications to support students' social or behavioral needs?	0	①	2	3	7
T.7 Did I keep students engaged from the beginning to the end of class?	0	1	2	③	7
T.8 Did I conduct a starting activity?	⓪	1	2	3	7
T.9 Did I conduct a closing activity?	0	1	2	③	7

	Not at All (0)	Some of the Time (1)	Most of the Time (2)	All of the Time (3)	No Opportunity (7)
T.10 Did I consistently use a positive tone during student interactions?	0	1	2	③	7
T.11 Did I provide support to students who missed instruction?	0	1	②	3	7
T.12 Did I check for understanding when giving directions to students?	0	1	2	③	7
T.13 Did I use clear routines for classroom procedures?	0	1	2	③	7

Procedures for Teaching Total   31/39 = 79.49%

Procedures for Reinforcing	Not at All (0)	Some of the Time (1)	Most of the Time (2)	All of the Time (3)	No Opportunity (7)
R.1 Did I deliver consequences according to my school's reactive plan (e.g., did I do what I am supposed to do when student behavior is problematic, such as complete an office discipline referral or phone a parent)?	0	1	2	③	7
R.2 Did I give tickets to students demonstrating schoolwide expectations (i.e., in academic, behavioral, and social domains)?	0	①	2	3	7
R.3 Did I use behavior-specific praise during student interactions?	0	1	②	3	7
R.4 Did I use behavior-specific praise when giving tickets to students?	0	1	②	3	7
R.5 Did I allow my students to exchange tickets for rewards (e.g., going to assemblies, going to the store)?	0	1	2	3	⑦
R.6 Did I allow my students to use tickets to participate in ticket classroom or schoolwide drawings?	0	1	2	3	⑦
R.7 Did I refrain from taking away tickets from students who already received them?	0	1	2	③	7
R.8 Did I use tickets to facilitate classroom routines (e.g., select a line leader, messenger)?	⓪	1	2	3	7

Procedures for Reinforcing Total   11/18 = 61.11%

Overall Total   73.68%

Note. From Lane (2009b; see also Lane, Oakes, & Magill, 2014). Available at *www.ci3t.org.*

BOX 4.2. Sample Results from Schoolwide Evaluation Tool Data (SET; Sugai, Lewis-Palmer, Todd, & Horner, 2005)

Panel A. Fall SET Data

Treatment Integrity: SET Results—Orange Elementary

Category	Total Points Earned		Total Points Possible	% Earned	
	Fall 2020	Spring 2021		Fall 2020	Spring 2021
Expectations Defined	4		4	100	
Behavioral Expectations Taught	7		10	70.00	
Ongoing System for Rewarding Behavioral Expectations	6		6	100	
System for Responding to Behavioral Violations	7		8	87.50	
Monitoring and Decision Making	6		8	75.00	
Management	9		16	56.25	
District-Level Support	4		4	100	
TOTAL SCORE	Goal: 80% on Behavioral Expectations Taught and Overall Scores			84.11	

Panel B. Fall and Spring SET Data Over Time

Treatment Integrity: SET Results—Orange Elementary

Category (total points)	Total Points Earned				% Earned			
	Fall 2020	Spring 2021	Fall 2021	Spring 2022	Fall 2020	Spring 2021	Fall 2021	Spring 2022
Expectations Defined (4)	4	4	4		100	100	100	
Behavioral Expectations Taught (10)	7	8	10		70.00	80.00	100	
Ongoing System for Rewarding Behavioral Expectations (6)	6	6	6		100	100	100	
System for Responding to Behavioral Violations (8)	7	7	7		87.50	87.50	87.50	
Monitoring and Decision Making (8)	6	7	8		75.00	75.00	100	
Management (16)	9	12	16		56.25	75.00	100	
District-Level Support (4)	4	4	4		100	100	100	
TOTAL SCORE	Goal: 80% on Behavioral Expectations Taught and Overall Scores				84.11	88.21	98.21	

30-minute period to examine implementation during a randomly selected time period. At the end of this time period, the teacher completed a separate checklist on how he or she viewed his or her implementation during the same observation period. These perspectives are compared to see whether the outside observers' and the teachers' self-ratings are comparable. For example, in Figure 4.1, you can see teachers, on average, rated themselves with higher fidelity as compared to outside observer ratings, with both raters reporting similar levels of fidelity in April and May. This information can be used to provide feedback to teachers and help shape professional learning activities and subsequent revisions for the next academic year (Remember: do not change the plans during a given year, as it is not possible to evaluate a plan that constantly shifts and it creates additional stress for faculty and staff to have shifting targets).

In our current work, most district partners have shifted to collecting treatment integrity data twice a year: once in fall and again in spring. In addition to completing the Ci3T TI: TSR in fall and spring, typically, 25% of educators who instruct students are randomly selected to be observed at the same time points (see Lessons Learned 4.1). Specifically, district leaders use a stratified random selection process to ensure representation from all grade levels at the elementary and department levels at middle and high school levels. Rather than each school having a separate component checklist for direct observations, we have developed the Ci3T TI: DO; Lane, 2009a), which includes a subset of items from the Ci3T TI: TSR (Lane, 2009b; see Figure 4.2). The measure includes 13 items from procedures for teaching and eight from procedures for reinforcing. Trained observers enter a classroom for 30 minutes and score each item using the following Likert-type scale to indicated the level of implementation observed during that session: 0 = *not at all*, 1 = *some of the time*, 2 = *most of the time*, 3 = *all of the time*, to 7 = *no opportunity to observe*. After the observation time and at a natural break in instruction, the teacher completes the same direct observation tool and scores his or her perception of implementation during the same 30-minute time period. Integrity is computed by

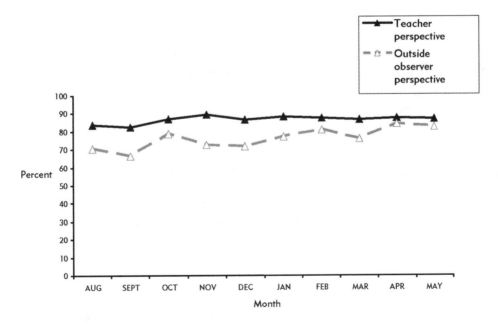

FIGURE 4.1. Treatment integrity data: Teacher and outside observer ratings.

LESSONS LEARNED 4.1. Refining Treatment Integrity Assessment

Time was initially one of our most significant challenges when collecting Treatment Integrity data. The first year, we did not finish in the 1 day we allowed. We needed to use plan time to create opportunities to finish the direct observations and SET data collection. I proposed that we partner with another building's data collection team. With four to six people, instead of two, we were easily able to accomplish what needed to be done. The day we collected data at the second school was much more efficient since all observers had established reliability during our previous set of observations.

We also discovered an added bonus, the opportunity to see how Ci3T implementation looked in another building. While in classrooms, observers discovered new ideas to share with staff members at their own building. The expanded perspective was an invaluable extra.

Ivy Briggs
Student Interventionist

dividing total score by total possible (adjusted for missing items and items rated as no opportunity to observe) and multiplying by 100, with the goal of examining the extent to which observer and teacher converge and diverge in their views of implementing the Ci3T primary plan. Results can be used to celebrate strengths and to inform professional development offerings to support particular components of the plan (Lane, Oakes, & Magill, 2014; see Figure 4.3 and Lessons Learned 4.2).

As you can see, treatment integrity ratings may vary according to who completes the ratings or which rating system is used (Lane, Kalberg, Bruhn, et al., 2008). Educator self-report scores tend to be somewhat higher than outside observer ratings. This is not to suggest faculty and staff should not self-evaluate the degree to which they are implementing the plan as designed. The self-monitoring literature indicates that the simple act of recording and evaluating one's own behavior can actually change and/or improve behavior (DuPaul & Hoff, 1998; Jones, Wickstrom, & Friman, 1997; Peterson, Young, Salzberg, West, & Hill, 2006). From a behavioral perspective, the act of completing these treatment integrity forms monthly, quarterly, or each semester may serve as a prompt (a discriminative stimulus for you BCBA folks!) for program participation (e.g., "Oh yeah, I need to remember to give behavior-specific praise when giving out the ROAR tickets"). However, it is important to consider the potential discrepancy between self-report and outside observer ratings (Lane, Kalberg, Bruhn, et al., 2008).

Logistical Considerations for Monitoring Treatment Integrity

When deciding who will monitor treatment integrity, we recommend that schools measure it from more than one perspective. For example, the district may build a schedule that involves the following:

- Ci3T Treatment Integrity: Teacher Self-Report (Ci3T TI: TSR) completed once in fall and once in spring by faculty and staff.
- Ci3T Treatment Integrity: Direct Observation (Ci3T TI: DO) completed in fall and

(text resumes on page 106)

School _____ Date Completed _____

Name _____ Grade Level or Department _____

The Ci3T Teacher Self-Report is a 38-item component checklist that includes the key features of the Ci3T plan's procedures for teaching, reinforcing, and monitoring. Teachers and staff members rate themselves based on their implementation of the Ci3T plan. The rating is based on a Likert-type scale ranging from *no, not at all* (0); *yes, some of the time* (1); *yes, most of the time* (2); *or yes, all of the time* (3).

Please rate each item to evaluate your use of your school's Ci3T primary plan in two ways. First, please consider if you have (yes) or have not (no) participated in each item from your plan in this school year prior to completing this form. If you have not, please select the 0 for the item. If your response is yes, select the frequency that best reflects the extent to which you have participated in that item during this present academic year (from the onset of this academic year until the date you are completing this form). *If you are not a classroom teacher, please consider your setting (e.g., office, bus, cafeteria) as your "classroom" as you answer each question.*

	About how often did you participate?			
	No ...	Yes, I did this ...		
Procedures for Teaching	**Not at all**	**Some of the time**	**Most of the time**	**All of the time**
T.1 Did I have our three to five schoolwide expectations posted and visible in my classroom (e.g., Be Respectful, Be Responsible, Give Best Effort)?	0	1	2	3
T.2 Did I have the setting expectations posted in my classroom (expectation matrix with all settings)?	0	1	2	3
T.3 Did my students receive instruction (e.g., videos, PowerPoints, formal lessons) about our schoolwide expectations for each setting (e.g., hallway, classroom, and cafeteria)?	0	1	2	3
T.4 Were my students taught (e.g., videos, PowerPoints, formal lessons) the social skills component of our primary plan (e.g., daily, weekly, monthly)?	0	1	2	3
T.5 Did I model the behaviors (expectations) stated in the schoolwide plan for my students?	0	1	2	3
T.6 Was my instruction linked to the district/state standards?	0	1	2	3
T.7 Did I differentiate instruction (academic tasks) as needed?	0	1	2	3
T.8 Did I make individual modifications to support students' social or behavioral needs?	0	1	2	3

(continued)

FIGURE 4.2. Ci3T Treatment Integrity: Teacher Self-Report (Ci3T TI: TSR). Available at *www.ci3t.org.*

From Lane (2009a; see also Lane, Oakes, & Magill, 2014). Reprinted by permission in *Developing a Schoolwide Framework to Prevent and Manage Learning and Behavior Problems, Second Edition* by Kathleen Lynne Lane, Holly Mariah Menzies, Wendy Peia Oakes, and Jemma Robertson Kalberg (The Guilford Press, 2020). Permission to photocopy this material is granted to purchasers of this book for personal use or use with students (see copyright page for details). Purchasers can download additional copies of this material (see the box at the end of the table of contents).

Procedures for Teaching (continued)	Not at all	Some of the time	Most of the time	All of the time
T.9 Did I keep students engaged from the beginning to the end of class?	0	1	2	3
T.10 Did I conduct daily starting activities?	0	1	2	3
T.11 Did I conduct daily closing activities?	0	1	2	3
T.12 Did I consistently use a positive tone during student interactions?	0	1	2	3
T.13 Did my school have procedures in place that foster a safe environment (e.g., emergency or crisis response plan)?	0	1	2	3
T.14 Did I provide support to students who missed instruction?	0	1	2	3
T.15 Did I check for understanding when giving directions to students?	0	1	2	3
T.16 Did I use clear routines for classroom procedures?	0	1	2	3

Procedures for Reinforcing	Not at all	Some of the time	Most of the time	All of the time
R.1 Did I deliver consequences according to my school's reactive plan (e.g., did I do what I am supposed to do when student behavior is problematic, such as complete an office discipline referral or phone a parent)?	0	1	2	3
R.2 Did I give tickets to students demonstrating schoolwide expectations (i.e., in academic, behavioral, and social domains)?	0	1	2	3
R.3 Did I use behavior-specific praise during student interactions?	0	1	2	3
R.4 Did I use behavior-specific praise when giving tickets to students?	0	1	2	3
R.5 Did I allow my students to exchange tickets for rewards (e.g., going to assemblies, going to the store)?	0	1	2	3
R.6 Did I allow my students to use tickets to participate in classroom or schoolwide drawings?	0	1	2	3
R.7 Did I refrain from taking away tickets from students who already received them?	0	1	2	3
R.8 Did I receive positive feedback from my colleagues or administrators about my school's Ci3T plan?	0	1	2	3
R.9 Is the perception of my school's Ci3T plan among my colleagues and administrators favorable or positive?	0	1	2	3
R.10 Did I use tickets to facilitate classroom routines (e.g., select a line leader, messenger)?	0	1	2	3

(continued)

FIGURE 4.2. (continued)

Procedures for Monitoring	Not at all	Some of the time	Most of the time	All of the time
M.1 Have I consistently filled out disciplinary referrals (e.g., office discipline referrals) according to my school's reactive plan?	0	1	2	3
M.2 Did I complete the behavior screeners at each time requested by my principal or Ci3T team?	0	1	2	3
M.3 Did I accurately complete daily attendance as specified by my school's procedures?	0	1	2	3
M.4 Did I accurately administer curriculum-based measures (e.g., AIMSweb, Dynamic Indicators of Basic Early Literacy Skills [DIBELS]) or other assessments to monitor my students' progress in the content I taught?	0	1	2	3
M.5 Did my school (e.g., Ci3T team, an administrator, grade-level team) share schoolwide behavior screening data with the faculty?	0	1	2	3
M.6 Did my school (e.g., Ci3T team, an administrator, grade-level team) share schoolwide academic data with the faculty?	0	1	2	3
M.7 Did I use the behavior data to inform my instruction for at-risk students?	0	1	2	3
M.8 Did I use academic data to inform my instruction?	0	1	2	3
M.9 Did I use behavior and academic data together (in conjunction with each other) to inform my instruction?	0	1	2	3
M.10 Did I make referrals for students who were struggling academically (prereferral intervention teams)?	0	1	2	3
M.11 Did I make referrals for students exhibiting acting-out behaviors?	0	1	2	3
M.12 Did I make referrals for students exhibiting shy or withdrawn behaviors?	0	1	2	3

Please include any other comments you would like to share about how you see your Ci3T plan being put in place at your school in terms of how you teach the skills, reinforce students, and monitor progress:

Comments:

FIGURE 4.2. *(continued)*

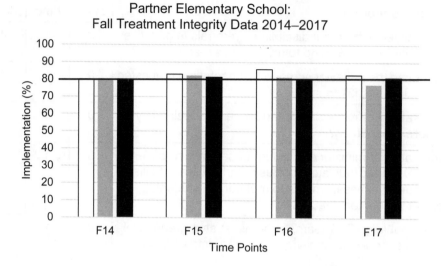

FIGURE 4.3. Treatment integrity data using multiple perspectives.

spring for all or 25% of faculty and staff led by instructional coaches or district leaders trained to criteria.

• School-wide Evaluation Tool (SET; Sugai et al., 2005) or Tiered Fidelity Inventory (TFI; Algozzine et al., 2014) completed in fall and spring by instructional coaches to examine implementation of the behavioral (PBIS) component.

• Treatment integrity checklist accompanying the district-selected reading or mathematics curriculum.

• Treatment integrity checklists accompanying the district-selected social–emotional curriculum.

Self-report checklists of the curricular components completed weekly, monthly, quarterly, or each semester can be used both to monitor implementation and prompt teachers to engage in Tier 1 efforts (Lane, Kalberg, Bruhn, et al., 2008).

LESSONS LEARNED 4.2. Benefit of Treatment Integrity Data

The collection of Treatment Integrity data has become a critical component in moving forward the implementation of Ci3T in our elementary buildings. We quickly realized that in order to systematically sustain this process, it was crucial to build more capacity, and our Instructional Facilitators have taken on the role to assist in collecting Direct Observation data. Our facilitators have gained a better understanding of Ci3T implementation in other buildings and an increased capacity to coach in their respective building around researched-based, successful CI3T strategies that were observed.

Heather Burris
School Improvement Coordinator

For the reasons mentioned earlier, it is essential implementation be measured and not assumed. Once you have decided who will monitor treatment integrity and how often each measure or approach will be assessed, provide the raters (1) training in how to conduct the evaluations and provide formative feedback to the persons rated, (2) time to conduct the evaluations, (3) assistance with the analysis of the information acquired, and (4) time to share feedback with the entire faculty and staff in a manner that informs but does not embarrass anyone. It is very important information be shared back with faculty and staff and is used to inform instruction for students and shape professional learning opportunities for adults. The intent is to build skills and empower educators to implement with fidelity to achieve the intended goals and purposes established.

When doing any type of intervention work, it is important to measure *treatment integrity*—the extent to which the intervention plan was put in place as designed (Gresham, 1989). If treatment integrity is not assessed, then it is not possible to draw accurate conclusions regarding intervention outcomes. Consequently, it is imperative that treatment integrity data be collected using research-based approaches (e.g., the SET or direct observation procedures) and, ideally, from multiple perspectives.

Assessing Stakeholder Feedback: What Do People Think about the Ci3T Model?

Social Validity: Defined

When conducting any type of intervention, it is important to obtain input from the persons involved regarding the intervention goals, procedures, and outcomes to establish social validity. More specifically, *social validity* refers to the social significance of the intervention goals, the social acceptability of intervention procedures, and the social importance of effects produced by the intervention (Kazdin, 1977; Lane & Beebe-Frankenberger, 2004; Wolf, 1978).

Social validity can be measured before an intervention begins, during implementation, and following intervention completion. We recommend assessing social validity of schoolwide models prior to intervention onset, then again in fall and spring of each academic year to give faculty and staff a voice in shaping and refining the plan (Fixsen et al., 2009).

The purpose of assessing social validity before getting started is to make sure that all stakeholders (e.g., faculty, staff, parents, and, in some cases, students) are "on the same page"; that is, do all stakeholders view the goals (e.g., improving attendance, decreasing behaviors that lead to ODRs) as being important? Are the procedures viewed as acceptable? For example, do the required components, such as using tickets paired with behavior-specific praise to acknowledge students who meet expectations, "fit" with teachers' instructional styles? If Tier 1 efforts are implemented as planned, then desired outcomes are likely be achieved; that is, do people think Tier 1 efforts will "work"? If the people involved do not think the intervention is targeting the right goals, if the procedures are viewed as too labor intensive or in conflict with cultural or personal values (e.g., if people do not believe in giving tangible rewards; Lane, Kalberg, Bruhn, et al., 2008), or if people do not think the intervention is likely to work, then it is quite possible the intervention will be implemented with low levels of integrity—which *is* apt to influence programs in a negative way (Gresham & Lopez, 1996; Lane & Beebe-Frankenberger, 2004). In short, if the people do not believe Ci3T holds value, either the school's Ci3T plan needs refinement and/or additional professional learning is needed for faculty and staff to reach consensus on the elements constituting their Ci3T plan. The goal is to ensure persons involved are in agreement that the educational experiences of students and the school climate are apt to improve if the Ci3T plan is implemented as designed, and that Ci3T implementation will provide students with more reliable, efficient strategies for experiencing academic, social, and behavioral success in the school setting (Gresham & Lopez, 1996; Lane, Kalberg, Bruhn, et al., 2009; Vancel, Missall, & Bruhn, 2016).

Furthermore, participants need to view the intervention procedures as being worth the investment (Reimers, Wacker, & Koeppl, 1987). Teachers working in chaotic, violent, or apathetic environments may be more willing to implement the required intervention procedures than teachers working in predictable, safe, productive environments. The most talented teachers may need professional learning around their expanded roles. In years past, the talented teacher was one who could "keep a lid" on student behavior. Often teachers developed unique and idiosyncratic classroom management plans with elaborate and often multifaceted token economies. While these may have "worked" in their individual classrooms, such approaches were not schoolwide efforts. As such, performance feedback was typically only available from the classroom teacher and did not support students in being successful beyond the classroom setting. In other words, these individual classroom management plans did not program for generalization (Cooper et al., 2007). An unintended consequence was that students had to learn multiple systems, which can be challenging for even the most capable students. And it restricted other adults in the building (e.g., custodians, paraprofessionals, office staff) from offering performance feedback because they could not typically participate in the acknowledgment system (e.g., allocating tickets or points); this could only be done by the teacher who created it. The message to all adults working in schools implementing Ci3T: *Our job is now bigger than our own classroom.* Our goals are to create positive, productive, safe, and even joyful environments schoolwide.

In general, the type and severity of a problem; the time, effort, and cost associated with conducting the intervention; the level of training and support provided during implementation; and the extent to which the intervention procedures will influence the environment are all highly predictive of treatment acceptability (Gresham & Kendell, 1987). Finally, to invest the time in implementing the intervention as designed, participants need to view the program as likely to meet the intervention goals, some of which may be immediate (e.g., less disruption and more instructional time) and others that may be more distal (e.g., improved academic outcomes for students) (Fawcett, 1991). By assessing social validity prior to intervention onset (e.g., during the year when the Ci3T model is being designed), it is possible to later determine whether the intervention met, fell short, or even exceeded initial expectations (Lane, Little, Rhodes, Phillips, & Welsch, 2007). It also provides a method to determine whether the intervention was "worth it" in terms of time, money, personnel, and other costs (e.g., Noell & Gresham, 1993). Additionally, social validity measures gathered prior to onset of Ci3T can be used as a baseline and later compared to subsequent time points (e.g., months, years). This information allows comparisons to be drawn regarding the level of social acceptability as the Ci3T plan is modified.

In one study, Lane, Kalberg, Bruhn, and colleagues (2009) found that a school's mean social validity scores on the Primary Intervention Rating Scale (PIRS) during the design year actually predicted teachers' Ci3T TI: TSR during the first year of implementation. Social validity continues to be important as schools implement Ci3T over time. Teachers often rely more on their colleagues' opinion of practices and may be less likely to implement if their colleagues are not in favor. So practices with empirical evidence to support their use may not be implemented with fidelity if the school faculty and staff do not support their use (Burns & Ysseldyke, 2009; Kern & Manz, 2004). This is great news for those responsible for professional learning efforts. Educators' perceptions can be influenced by professional learning and implementation supports that result in positive outcomes with students. The positive student outcomes (socially important effects) serve as reinforcement for teachers to continue to implement the practice with high fidelity (Burns et al., 2013).

We recommend collecting social validity information in fall and spring annually to examine the extent to which these initial expectations were met, and to inform the following year's school plan. The point of the data is to determine whether the intervention targeted worthy goals (social significance of the goals) and if those goals were met (social importance of effects). Were meaningful, lasting changes evident, also referred to as *habilitative validity* (Baer, Wolf, & Risley, 1968, 1987; Hawkins, 1991)? Did the school see improvements in attendance and decreases in ODRs? Over a few years, were there improvements in GPAs? In addition, we again assess social acceptability of intervention (treatment) procedures to determine whether the steps and components were satisfactory to the people involved. For example, it may have been that educators who initially thought it would be burdensome to pass out tickets and pair them with behavior-specific praise to recognize students who met desired behaviors (e.g., using a quiet voice in the hallway) later found that it was quite simple to do so in their classrooms and in noninstructional areas (e.g., cafeteria, hallway). This information can be ascertained from assessing social validity. Once acquired, the information obtained from assessing the social acceptability of the treatment procedures can be used by teams to (1) provide a forum for discussions about primary (Tier 1) prevention efforts; (2) inform professional learning offerings; (3) inform future intervention efforts (e.g., what components to keep or to revise); and (4) predict treatment integrity of similar plans (Lane & Beebe-Frankenberger, 2004; Lane, Kalberg, Bruhn, et al., 2008).

The Importance of Assessing Social Validity

In alignment with current standards for high-quality, treatment–outcome studies to determine which practices are evidence based (i.e., there are sufficient high-quality studies to suggest that a strategy, practice, or program implemented with sufficient integrity will yield the desired changes in students' performance; Cook & Tankersley, 2013), many secondary- (Tier 2) and tertiary-level (Tier 3) intervention studies have begun to assess social validity from various perspectives (Lane, Barton-Arwood, et al., 2007), but relatively few studies of schoolwide intervention efforts include measures of social validity (Farkas et al., 2012; Lane, Kalberg, & Edwards, 2008; Marchant, Heath, & Miramontes, 2013). A review of schoolwide primary prevention efforts at the elementary level (Lane, Kalberg, & Edwards, 2008) revealed that only six of 19 studies mentioned and reported social validity (Ervin et al., 2006; Leff, Costigan, &

Power, 2003; McCurdy et al., 2003; Nelson, 1996; Nelson et al., 2002; Todd et al., 2002). Similarly, a systematic review of primary prevention efforts at the middle and high school levels (Lane, Robertson, & Graham-Bailey, 2006) indicated that eight of 14 studies mentioned social validity from the teacher, student, and/or parent perspective (Cook et al., 1999; Gottfredson et al., 1993; Kartub et al., 2000; Mehas, Boling, Sobieniak, Burke, & Hagan, 1998; Metzler et al., 2001; Skiba & Perterson, 2003; Taylor-Green et al., 1997; Taylor-Greene & Kartub, 2000). Social validity was assessed in a variety of ways (e.g., cost–benefit perceptions, Ervin et al., 2006), but most of the methods were informal, such as ratings scales that were not validated. Though relatively few studies examine social validity, the importance of these data are recognized as an essential source of information for the promotion of high-fidelity implementation and sustainability (Common & Lane, 2017; Marchant et al., 2013; Miramontes, Marchant, Heath, & Fischer, 2011).

We view the absence of social validity information as a possible explanation for why some interventions fail to be implemented as designed. If the intervention agents (e.g., teachers, staff, and parents) do not view the goal as worthy, the procedures as reasonable, and the desired changes as likely to occur, then it should not be surprising that they lack the motivation to implement the plan as designed (Lane & Beebe-Frankenberger, 2004; Miramontes et al., 2011). Therefore, we suggest assessing social validity prior to and after the intervention for a number of reasons (e.g., Ci3T primary [Tier 1] plan in fall and spring each year; for Tier 2 and 3 pre- and postintervention). First, collecting social validity allows people to reach consensus on the target areas for the intervention and to establish a clear picture of the difference between the current and desired level of performance (Bergan & Kratochwill, 1990). Second, social validity data can identify important feasible target areas for primary (Tier 1) prevention efforts. Third, social validity data can be used to inform professional learning offerings (e.g., how to design and deliver integrated lesson plans; the distinctions between consequences and punishment). Fourth, the information can facilitate discussion regarding the procedures and supports necessary to provide natural contingencies and reinforcement for the desired behaviors. Fifth, the information can assist the participants in reaching consensus on goals and procedures to make sure the intended changes in performance (academic, behavior, and social skills) occur. Sixth, social validity data are an important part of program evaluation as it relates to immediate and maintained intervention outcomes (Lane & Beebe-Frankenberger, 2004). When all parties involved participate in choosing intervention goals and procedures, they are more likely to invest effort in paving the path for successful student outcomes that in turn create successful outcomes for faculty, staff, and parents alike. Particularly important to intervention success is attention to the social and cultural values of *all* involved individuals.

Social Validity: Whom to Ask and How

We recommend assessing social validity from multiple perspectives because each participant plays a different role in the intervention (Kern & Mantz, 2004; Lane & Beebe-Frankenberger, 2004). Researchers and practitioners should consider assessing social validity from the following perspectives: Ci3T Leadership Team members, administrators, teachers and support staff, parents, and students. By assessing the extent to which these stakeholders view the goals as significant, procedures as acceptable, and outcomes as important, we can make important predictions about (1) the extent to which their Ci3T plan is apt to be implemented as designed and (2) the likelihood that the new roles, responsibilities, and expectations are likely to generalize and be maintained in other settings (see Lessons Learned 4.3). For example, many teachers and staff have certain academic, behavioral, and social expectations for students in their classroom and in the school setting as a whole (e.g., following directions the first time, asking for help when needed, and controlling oneself in conflict situation with peers; Kerr & Zigmond, 1986; Lane, Givner, & Pierson, 2004; Lane, Wehby, Little, & Cooley, 2005a, 2005b; Walker & Rankin, 1983). Yet teachers also have different teaching styles (Evertson & Weade, 1989) and tolerance levels (Shinn, Tindal, & Spira, 1987). If the schoolwide goals or procedures are in conflict with teachers' instructional styles or tolerance levels, then teachers will be less likely to view the plan as socially valid, which in turn may lead to lower levels of treatment fidelity (Gresham & Kendell, 1987).

Similarly, it is equally important to consider parents' perspectives. (When we say *parent*, we are referring to any significant adult [e.g., guardian, foster parent, grandparent] who assumes primary responsibility for caretaking.) If schoolwide expectations are in conflict with parents' core values for academic and behavioral expectations, it is likely that the student will receive conflicting information as to the importance of meeting the stated schoolwide expectations. It is necessary to enlist parental support in the primary (Tier 1) plan because research evidence indicates that students are apt to be more academically successful when their parents are involved in, and supportive of, their education (Brown, Mounts, Lamborn, & Sternberg, 1993; Dearing, Kreider, Simpkins, & Weiss, 2006). In addition, students are more likely to achieve academic and social success in school if their parents establish boundaries to support these goals (Alexander, Entwisle, & Dauber, 1994; Walker, Zeller, Close, Webber, & Gresham, 1999; Weist et al., 2017). We are not suggesting teachers and parents must have 100% agreement on the specific expectations established in the school setting. However, we want to convey that the best-case scenario is to promote school expectations that are acceptable to both parents and teachers so that students are reinforced for meeting these expectations in the home and school setting. When there are differences in expectations in the home and school settings, these differences should be acknowledged and respectfully approached from a solutions-based perspective (Lane, Stanton-Chapman, et al., 2007; Whitford & Addis, 2017).

We also think it is important to gain student input regarding the plan's social validity. If students view the goals as important and the procedures as reasonable, it is possible that their views or "buy-in" will foster positive intervention outcomes. For example, if students feel that

---

LESSONS LEARNED 4.3. Visible Expectations

Our Ci3T plan has made our expectations visible by increasing our clarity with both students and staff. All stakeholders are clear on the expectations set forth in the plan, as well as the success criteria for meeting those expectations. Ultimately, the plan empowers staff and students to take responsibility for their teaching and learning.

Melissa Blevins
Elementary School Principal

it is essential to communicate their opinions, then a behavioral goal of learning how to begin a conversation respectfully when they disagree with someone is likely to be learned and used. The procedures for teaching the targeted behaviors must also be age appropriate. Middle and high school students who perceive a program as too "babyish" will be unwilling to participate. In addition, student input regarding reinforcement is essential. Social validity information can be used to determine what is (and is not!) reinforcing to students. It is possible that students' motivation for participating in any intervention is enhanced by including reinforcers (e.g., assemblies that afford time with friends) that are "better" than the types of reinforcement they received for *not* meeting the schoolwide expectations (Horner & Billingsley, 1988). Unfortunately, very few studies have investigated the value of assessing social validity from the student perspective (Elliott, Turco, & Gresham, 1987).

Methods of Measuring Social Validity

As we mentioned previously, only a handful of schoolwide intervention studies have assessed social validity (e.g., Cook et al., 1999; Ervin et al., 2006; Fallon, O'Keeffe, Gage, & Sugai, 2015; Farkas et al., 2012; Nelson et al., 2002; Skiba & Peterson, 2003; Taylor-Greene & Kartub, 2000; Todd et al., 2002; Vancel et al., 2016). For example, Cook and colleagues (1999) assessed social validity from three perspectives (teacher, student, and parent). However, many secondary (Tier 2)– and tertiary (Tier 3)–level prevention programs regularly assess social validity. When conducting schoolwide intervention efforts, it is possible to use several techniques also used by targeted (secondary and tertiary)–level supports. These include self-report rating scales and surveys (Finn & Sladeczek, 2001; Kazdin, 1977), interviews (Gresham & Lopez, 1996), and repeated use (i.e., if the intervention is used on an ongoing basis, it is socially valid).

Self-Report Rating Scales and Surveys

In our work, we have collected social validity data from teacher, parent, and student perspectives prior to implementing primary (Tier 1) prevention efforts. To assess different consumer perspectives of social validity, we modified the Intervention Rating Profile–15 (IRP-15; Witt & Elliott, 1985), which is now the PIRS (Lane, Robertson, et al., 2002). The PIRS is used to measure faculty and staff opinion about the social significance of the intervention goals, social acceptability of the intervention procedures, and probability of socially important outcomes (Kazdin, 1997; Wolf, 1978). The IRP-15 is a 15-item, psychometrically sound survey used to measure teachers' perceptions of the intervention. Teachers rate each item on a 6-point Likert-type scale ranging from 1 (*strongly disagree*) to 6 (*strongly agree*). Internal consistency reliabilities range from .88 to .98, suggesting strong psychometric properties. The IRP-15 was adapted for use with primary prevention programs in two ways. First, the wording of some items was changed to reflect a schoolwide, primary (Tier 1) prevention program rather than a targeted intervention for a given student. Second, we added two additional items regarding monitoring procedures (Item 16: "The monitoring procedures are manageable"; Item 17: "The monitoring procedures give the necessary information to evaluate the plan"). With the addition of two new items, total scores of the PIRS ranged from 17 to 102. In addition, the PIRS contains four open-ended questions:

1. "What do you feel is most beneficial about this primary prevention plan's components (Tier 1 efforts)? What is least beneficial part?"
2. "Do you think that your and your students' participation in this Ci3T plan will cause your students' behavior, social, and/or learning problems to improve? Why or why not? Or if so, how?"
3. "What would you change about this plan (components, design, implementation, etc.) to make it more student-friendly and teacher-friendly?"
4. "What other information would you like to contribute about this plan?"

A validation study of the PIRS data completed by elementary, middle, and high school teachers prior to beginning the schoolwide program suggested strong reliability, with internal consistency estimates ranging from .97 to .98 (Lane, Kalberg, Bruhn, et al., 2008). Vancel and colleagues (2016) adapted the PIRS with minor wording changes and by adding a new item to create the Iowa Social Validity Scale (ISVS). Evidence suggested similar reliability of the adapted PIRS with an internal consistency estimate of .97). However, additional studies of the PIRS are warranted before adopting this measure as a reliable, valid tool for monitoring consumers' opinions over the course of program implementation.

Given that few validated social validity forms have been developed for use with school-wide primary prevention programs, another option is to develop and administer social validity surveys to obtain information from administrators, faculty, staff, parents, and students (Farkas et al., 2012; Vancel et al., 2016). For example, the Primary Prevention Plan: Feedback Form (Lane, 2002), was developed to obtain input from faculty and staff (available from *ci3t.org/ measures*). However, it is important to recognize the limitations of using an instrument whose accuracy and consistency of measurement have not been validated. Farkas and colleagues (2012) developed three social validity surveys specific to SWPBIS implementation, one measuring staff and student perceptions of the skills as expectations lessons, another measuring staff and student opinions of positive behavior tickets, and a third measuring staff satisfaction with their schoolwide system.

Interviews

Another option is to conduct interviews with individuals who represent the various parties of interest. Gresham and Lopez (1996) developed a semistructured interview for use with classroom teachers (see Figure 4.4). The three sections included in their interview protocol parallel the three components of social validity: the social significance of the goals, the social acceptability of the treatment procedures, and the social importance of the effects. You might consider making a modified version that can be used to obtain information about your Ci3T model from administrator, faculty and staff, parent, and student perspectives.

Repeated Use

Yet another method of measuring social validity is to examine the degree to which (1) other consumers use the intervention in the future (e.g., when the vice principal is promoted to a principal position at another school and implements a schoolwide plan) or (2) whether the

Name _____ Date _____

Role _____ School _____

A. Social Significance of Goals

1. What school-site concerns led your school to develop a three-tiered model of prevention?
2. Which of these concerns are most problematic?
3. How do these concerns influence student and teacher performance?
4. Describe how these concerns cause classroom problems.
5. What are your goals for this program?
6. If this primary prevention program meets the goals, how will that outcome influence your job or experience at the school?
7. Describe the short-term and long-term benefits of participating in the primary prevention plan.

B. Social Acceptability of Procedures

1. How do you feel about the procedures put in place for the primary plan?
   a. Academic responsibilities: procedures for teaching and reinforcing
   b. Behavioral responsibilities: procedures for teaching and reinforcing
   c. Social responsibilities: procedures for teaching and reinforcing
2. Which components of the primary prevention plan do you like the most? Why?
3. Which components of the primary prevention plan do you like the least? Why?
4. Which components of the primary prevention plan would be the most difficult to implement? Why?
5. Which components of the primary prevention plan would be the least difficult to implement? Why?
6. What, if any, potential negative effects might this primary prevention plan have on students? Teachers? Other persons?
7. How do you feel about the procedures put in place for monitoring:
   a. Student performance: Academically? Behaviorally? Socially?
   b. Treatment integrity?
   c. Social validity?

C. Social Importance of Effects

1. Describe how well you think the primary prevention will work (did work).
2. Are/were the costs (time, personnel, resources) required to implement the plan worth the effort? Explain.
3. How satisfied are you with the outcomes of this primary prevention? Why?
4. What aspects of the primary prevention plan would you change?
5. Would you recommend this type of primary prevention plan to other schools? Why or why not?

FIGURE 4.4. Modified Semistructured Interview for Social Validation.

From Gresham and Lopez (2006). Copyright © 1996 American Psychological Association. Adapted by permission in *Developing a Schoolwide Framework to Prevent and Manage Learning and Behavior Problems, Second Edition* by Kathleen Lynne Lane, Holly Mariah Menzies, Wendy Peia Oakes, and Jemma Robertson Kalberg (The Guilford Press, 2020). Permission to photocopy this material is granted to purchasers of this book for personal use or use with students (see copyright page for details). Purchasers can download additional copies of this material (see the box at the end of the table of contents).

current consumers sustain the schoolwide intervention in the absence of ongoing university or outside support. In brief, if the intervention is used—and used as designed—then it is acceptable. In short, "use" acts a behavioral marker for "acceptability" (Gresham & Lopez, 1996).

Once you have decided how social validity will be assessed, it is necessary to determine who will actually collect the social validity data. For example, some principals have required completion of a social validity survey both at the beginning of the year (before students attend the first day of classes) and again at the end of the year as part of staff check-in/check-out procedures. In other schools, the Ci3T Leadership Team has asked faculty members and randomly selected groups of parents and their students to complete social validity measures.

Social validity is an important, although often overlooked, component of interventions (Gersten, Jordan, & Flojo, 2005; Horner et al., 2005; Lane et al., 2001). We hope you will consider assessing social validity from a range of perspectives to (1) inform intervention construction, (2) predict treatment integrity, (3) assist in interpreting intervention outcomes, and (4) foster a collaborative partnership between all persons involved (Lane, 2017; Lane & Beebe-Frankenberger, 2004). In order to ensure consumers answer surveys accurately and honestly, it is essential to establish both the program's credibility and the credibility of those involved with bringing it to the school site. Creating rapport is also essential in fostering a climate in which everyone feels that his or her suggestions about the design and implementation of the program are valued. Establishing credibility and rapport increases the ability of a school system to accurately measure social validity (Lane & Beebe-Frankenberger, 2004; Whitford & Addis, 2017).

Once decisions are made as to how you will assess treatment integrity and social validity, begin building your at-a-glance assessment schedule to provide a written plan for transparency of all data that will be available for decision making about implementation efforts and student outcomes. The assessment schedule is the one- to two-page table with a section for assessments on the right hand column and the months of the academic year listed across the top row. Ci3T Leadership Teams begin by listing of all schoolwide data sources, such as demographic information; academic, behavioral and social screening; academic, behavioral, and social outcomes measures; and school-level Ci3T implementation measures in the first column. They then indicate the time line for each assessment collection and/or reporting. Some Ci3T Leadership Teams indicate the collection period by adding an "X" in the corresponding month column. Others add dates to the month columns to indicate the open and close of data collection windows. The assessment schedule is part of the Ci3T Implementation Manual and alerts faculty and staff as to when they should expect to participate in assessment procedures and learn about the findings.

Summary

In this chapter, we have provided information for monitoring treatment integrity and assessing social validity. First, we defined treatment integrity, explained its importance, introduced a variety of ways to monitor it, then offered logistical considerations for monitoring integrity. Second, we defined social validity, explained why it should be considered when designing and implementing your Ci3T model, offered suggestions about whose opinions should be consulted, introduced a few ways of assessing social validity, and offered logistical considerations for monitoring social validity. We provided information on how to start your assessment schedule to support transparency and use of data for decision making.

In Chapter 5, we examine procedures for monitoring student progress and systematically screening all students for possible behavior and academic concerns. First, we begin with a practical assessment plan for monitoring how students respond to primary (Tier 1) prevention efforts. Next, we explore the importance of conducting systematic screenings, describe current tools available for use across grades K–12, and offer recommendations for how to put the screenings in place. Then, we discuss the importance of examining schoolwide data, with an emphasis on analyzing multiple sources of data at the same time to inform instruction and professional learning priorities. We feature illustrations across grades PreK–12 to demonstrate how to use schoolwide data to (1) monitor how the school as a whole is responding to the schoolwide plan and (2) determine how different types of students responded to the primary prevention efforts.

PART III

A Focus on Data-Informed Decision Making

As we mentioned at the beginning of Part II, the Ci3T Implementation Manual comprises the following blueprints that are developed over the course of the yearlong professional learning series (see *ci3t.org,* Building your Ci3T Model). Ci3T Blueprint A Primary [Tier 1] Plan):

- Ci3T Blueprint B Reactive Plan
- Ci3T Blueprint C Expectation Matrix
- Ci3T Blueprint D Assessment Schedule
- Ci3T Blueprint E Secondary (Tier 2) Intervention Grid
- Ci3T Blueprint F Tertiary (Tier 3) Intervention Grid

In Part III, we focus on data-informed decision making. In Chapter 5, *Determining How Well Ci3T Is Meeting the Goals: Procedures for Monitoring Overall Student Performance,* we examine procedures for monitoring student progress and systematically screening all students for possible behavior and academic concerns. We start with a practical assessment plan for monitoring how students respond to the primary (Tier 1) prevention efforts. Next we explain the importance of conducting systematic screenings, describe current tools available for use across grades K–12, and offer recommendations for how to put the screenings in place. Then, we discuss the importance of examining schoolwide data, with an emphasis on analyzing multiple sources of data in tandem to inform instruction and professional learning priorities. Then, in Chapter 6, *Empowering Teachers with Low-Intensity, Teacher-Delivered Strategies,* we focus on research-based, low-intensity supports teachers can use to increase engagement and decrease disruption. We begin by discussing practical methods for using data to inform decision making regarding how and when to refine the use of low-intensity, teacher-delivered supports. Then, we introduce seven low-intensity, teacher-delivered strategies that can be used across the tiers. In Chapter 7, *Supporting Students Who Require More Than Primary Prevention Efforts: Tier 2 and Tier 3*, we provide additional information on how to (1) monitor how the school as a whole is responding to the schoolwide plan, (2) determine how different types of students respond, and (3) identify students who require additional supports in the form of secondary and tertiary interventions. In this chapter we feature several illustrations of how to use schoolwide data to identify K–12 students in need of secondary supports. We also discuss a range of supports (academic, social, and behavioral), including options typically available at schools, as well as other research-based programs.

CHAPTER 5

Determining How Well Ci3T Is Meeting the Goals

PROCEDURES FOR MONITORING OVERALL STUDENT PERFORMANCE

We focused in Chapter 4 on primary prevention efforts related to implementation. Specifically, we reviewed procedures for monitoring treatment integrity and social validity. In this chapter, we continue to explore procedures for monitoring as they relate to student performance and achievement. In particular, we examine procedures for monitoring student progress and systematically screening all students for possible behavioral and academic concerns. First, we begin with a practical assessment plan for monitoring how students respond to the primary program. Easy-to-follow guidelines are provided for selecting schoolwide intervention outcomes and monitoring student progress (academic, behavioral, and social). The plan emphasizes the selection of reliable, valid measures to monitor student progress and allows administrators and teachers to determine whether the goals of the primary (Tier 1) prevention efforts are being met. Next, we explain the importance of conducting systematic screenings, describe current tools available for use across grades K–12, and offer recommendations for how to put the screenings in place. Then we discuss the importance of examining schoolwide data, with an emphasis on analyzing multiple sources of data in tandem to inform instruction and professional learning priorities. Several illustrations across grades PreK–12 demonstrate how to use schoolwide data to (1) monitor how the school as a whole is responding to the schoolwide plan and (2) determine how different types of students are responding to the primary prevention efforts.

Monitoring Student Progress: How Are Students Responding to Ci3T?

The next area to monitor is the progress students make in reaching the goals you have set for them. For example, if the goal is to decrease ODRs, improve attendance, and improve academic performance, then it is necessary to collect and monitor data that address these areas. By doing so, you can make judgments about how the plan is influencing student performance and achievement. In essence, the goal is to establish treatment validity (not to be confused with social validity) by linking assessment results to primary (Tier 1) prevention efforts as described in the school's Ci3T Implementation Manual. More specifically, treatment validity refers to the degree to which assessment information contributes to useful treatment outcomes (Gresham, Lane, & Lambros, 2000).

Once you have identified the types of information that will assist you in evaluating the effectiveness of your Ci3T model, the next step is to collect and analyze these data to monitor all aspects of the plan. For example, data sources to examine include: behavior measures (e.g., systematic screenings such as the Systematic Screening for Behavior Disorders [Walker, Severson, & Feil, 2014], ODRs, in-school suspensions, out-of-school suspensions), academic measures (e.g., curriculum-based measures such as the Dynamic Indicators of Basic Early Literacy 8th Edition [DIBELS; Good & Kaminski, 2018] or AIMSweb [Pearson Education, 2015a]), state standardized tests), and referrals for support (e.g., nurse visits, counselor, pre-referral intervention team, and special education), as well as treatment integrity and social validity data, as described earlier. See Figures 5.1, 5.2, and 5.3 for illustrations of sample assessment schedules at the elementary, middle, and high school levels, respectively. You will note assessment schedules for the elementary and high school levels align with the primary (Tier 1) prevention plans introduced in Chapter 3 in Boxes 3.2 and 3.3, respectively. Box 5.1 contains a list of suggestions for how to accurately measure representative variables (outcome measures) presented in these three assessment plans. For example, when monitoring variables such as ODRs and attendance, it is important to compute the rate for each month because not all months have the same number of instructional days.

Central to each assessment schedule is a plan to (1) collect data as part of regular school practices (provided that a reliable system is used to collect the data [e.g., ODRs] to ensure that accurate information is obtained); (2) decide who will monitor each type of data (e.g., the attendance clerk responsible for monitoring attendance data; the assistant principal monitoring ODR data); (3) allot time for the Ci3T Leadership Team, as well as other data teams (e.g., grade-level teams, department teams, professional learning communities) to access, analyze, and interpret data; (4) make sure that data collection procedures are reasonable (if it is too time consuming or difficult, it will not get done); and (5) ensure findings are shared with all parties involved (e.g., teachers, parents, and students) on a regular basis, so they see the value of collecting the information. As these points are deliberated, it is important to consider who has permission to access and view the various data sources. For example, teachers need access to student-level data for students they support (e.g., all students in their sixth-period English course; all students in their advisory period). However, not all adults should have access to all student-level data. It is important to consult your district policies and state and federal laws for guidance on access.

An assessment schedule is essentially an at-a-glance calendar that reminds everyone when the agreed-upon measures are to be collected and by whom. This process provides the district and Ci3T Leadership Teams with timely information to assist them in making objective decisions about how the Ci3T plan is moving toward achieving desired goals and whether any adjustments need to be made during the following academic year. The most effective plan is one that responds quickly to student-specific needs. Establishing an assessment schedule ensures a systematic approach to efficiently evaluating your schoolwide plan.

(text resumes on page 127)

Measure	Aug.	Sept.	Oct.	Nov.	Dec.	Jan.	Feb.	Mar.	Apr.	May
Demographic Information	X	X	X	X	X	X	X	X	X	X
Screening Measures										
Social Skills Improvement System Social–Emotional Learning Edition (SSiS SEL)		9/18 – 10/2			12/2 – 12/16				4/2 – 4/16	
Student Risk Screening Scale—Internalizing and Externalizing (SRSS-IE; Drummond, 1994; Lane & Menzies, 2009)		9/18 – 10/2			12/2 – 12/16				4/2 – 4/16	
Curriculum-based measures (CBMs) (DIBELS® Reading)		9/1 – 9/20			12/2 – 12/20				4/2 – 4/25	
Curriculum-based measures (CBMs) (easyCBM Math®)		9/1 – 9/20			12/2 – 12/20				4/2 – 4/25	
Academic Measures										
Report cards and progress reports	X	X	X	X	X	X	X	X	X	X
Writing assessment		9/21 – 10/8				1/15 – 1/31		3/5 – 3/19		
Statewide assessment								X	X	
Social Skills and Behavioral Measures										
Attendance	X	X	X	X	X	X	X	X	X	X
Office discipline referrals (ODRs)	X	X	X	X	X	X	X	X	X	X
Counseling referrals	X	X	X	X	X	X	X	X	X	X
Bullying referrals	X	X	X	X	X	X	X	X	X	X
Mental health referrals	X	X	X	X	X	X	X	X	X	X
Nurse visits	X	X	X	X	X	X	X	X	X	X
Program Measures (School Level)										
Social Validity Survey: Primary Intervention Rating Scale (PIRS; Lane, Robertson, & Wehby, 2002)			10/15 – 10/30				2/15 – 3/2	2/15 – 3/2		
Parent survey of Social Skills Improvement System (SSiS) Social–Emotional Learning (SEL) Edition Classwide Intervention Program (CIP; Gresham & Elliott, 2017)	X	X	X	X	X	X	X	X	X	X
Tiered Fidelity Inventory (TFI; Algozzine et al., 2014)			10/15 – 10/30				2/15 – 3/2	2/15 – 3/2		

(continued)

FIGURE 5.1. Orange Elementary School assessment schedule.

Measure	Aug.	Sept.	Oct.	Nov.	Dec.	Jan.	Feb.	Mar.	Apr.	May
Ci3T Treatment Integrity Teacher Self-Report (Ci3T TI: TSR) and Ci3T Treatment Integrity Direct Observations (Ci3T TI: DO)			10/15 – 10/30				2/15 – 3/2	2/15 – 3/2		
Curricula fidelity—walk-throughs by instructional coach	X	X	X	X	X	X	X	X	X	X
Curricula fidelity—self-report checklists	X	X	X	X	X	X	X	X	X	X
Curricula fidelity—log of social skills lessons taught	X	X	X	X	X	X	X	X	X	X

FIGURE 5.1. *(continued)*

Measure	Aug.	Sept.	Oct.	Nov.	Dec.	Jan.	Feb.	Mar.	Apr.	May
Demographic Information	X	X	X	X	X	X	X	X	X	X
Screening Measures										
Student Risk Screening Scale—Internalizing and Externalizing (SRSS-IE; Drummond, 1994; Lane & Menzies, 2009)		9/18 – 10/2			12/2 – 12/16				4/2 – 4/16	
Curriculum-based measures (CBMs) (DIBELS® Reading)		9/1 – 9/20			12/2 – 12/20				4/2 – 4/25	
Curriculum-based measures (CBMs) (easyCBM Math®–CCSS)		9/1 – 9/20			12/2 – 12/20				4/2 – 4/25	
Academic Measures										
Report cards and progress reports	X	X	X	X	X	X	X	X	X	X
Writing assessment		9/21 – 10/8				1/15 – 1/31		3/5 – 3/19		
Statewide assessment								X	X	
Pre-ACT (8th grade)			X		X				X	
Social Skills and Behavioral Measures										
Attendance	X	X	X	X	X	X	X	X	X	X
Tardies to class	X	X	X	X	X	X	X	X	X	X
Office discipline referrals (ODRs)	X	X	X	X	X	X	X	X	X	X
ODR outcomes: In- and out-of-school suspensions	X	X	X	X	X	X	X	X	X	X
Counseling referrals	X	X	X	X	X	X	X	X	X	X

(continued)

FIGURE 5.2. Sample Middle School assessment schedule. CCSS, Common Core State Standards.

Measure	Aug.	Sept.	Oct.	Nov.	Dec.	Jan.	Feb.	Mar.	Apr.	May
Bullying referrals	X	X	X	X	X	X	X	X	X	X
Mental health referrals	X	X	X	X	X	X	X	X	X	X
Nurse visits	X	X	X	X	X	X	X	X	X	X
Program Measures (school-level)										
Social Validity Survey: Primary Intervention Rating Scale (PIRS; Lane, Robertson, & Wehby, 2002)			10/15 – 10/30				2/15 – 3/2	2/15 – 3/2		
Tiered Fidelity Inventory (TFI; Algozzine et al., 2014)			10/15 – 10/30				2/15 – 3/2	2/15 – 3/2		
Ci3T Treatment Integrity: Teacher Self-Report (Ci3T TI: TSR) and Ci3T Treatment Integrity: Direct Observations (Ci3T TI: DO)			10/15 – 10/30				2/15 – 3/2	2/15 – 3/2		
Curricula fidelity—walk-throughs by instructional coach	X	X	X	X	X	X	X	X	X	X
Curricula fidelity—log of social skills lessons taught	X	X	X	X	X	X	X	X	X	X

FIGURE 5.2. *(continued)*

Measure	Aug.	Sept.	Oct.	Nov.	Dec.	Jan.	Feb.	Mar.	Apr.	May
Demographic Information	X	X	X	X	X	X	X	X	X	X
Screening Measures										
Student Risk Screening Scale—Internalizing and Externalizing (SRSS-IE; Drummond, 1994; Lane & Menzies, 2009)		9/18 – 10/2			12/2 – 12/16				4/2 – 4/16	
Credit accrual	X				X					X
Academic Measures										
Grade point average (GPA)		X			X			X		X
Quarterly grades		X			X			X		X
Writing assessment	X	X	X	X	X	X	X	X	X	X
Advance placement enrollment	X	X	X	X	X	X	X	X	X	X
Statewide assessment								X	X	
ACT/SAT • 9th grade: Pre-ACT • 10th grade: PSAT • 11th and 12th grades: ACT/SAT			X		X				X	
Graduation (completion with diploma)										X

(continued)

FIGURE 5.3. Contra Costa High School's assessment schedule.

Measure	Aug.	Sept.	Oct.	Nov.	Dec.	Jan.	Feb.	Mar.	Apr.	May
Social Skills and Behavioral Measures										
Attendance	X	X	X	X	X	X	X	X	X	X
Tardies (to class)	X	X	X	X	X	X	X	X	X	X
Office discipline referrals (ODRs)	X	X	X	X	X	X	X	X	X	X
ODR outcomes: In- and out-of-school suspensions	X	X	X	X	X	X	X	X	X	X
Counseling referrals	X	X	X	X	X	X	X	X	X	X
Bullying referrals	X	X	X	X	X	X	X	X	X	X
Mental health referrals	X	X	X	X	X	X	X	X	X	X
Program Measures (School-Level)										
Social Validity Survey: Primary Intervention Rating Scale (PIRS; Lane, Robertson, & Wehby, 2002)			10/15 – 10/30				2/15 – 3/2	2/15 – 3/2		
Student surveys of Lions Quest lessons (weekly)	X	X	X	X	X	X	X	X	X	X
Schoolwide Evaluation Tool Version 2.1 (SET; Sugai, Lewis-Palmer, Todd, & Horner, 2005)			10/15 – 10/30				2/15 – 3/2	2/15 – 3/2		
Ci3T Treatment Integrity: Teacher Self-Report (Ci3T TI: TSR) and Ci3T Treatment Integrity: Direct Observations (Ci3T TI: DO)			10/15 – 10/30				2/15 – 3/2	2/15 – 3/2		
Monthly student survey (e.g., expectations, access to Contra Costa Cash, feedback from adults, interest in current reinforcers, additional ideas for reinforcement)	X	X	X	X	X	X	X	X	X	X

FIGURE 5.3. *(continued)*

BOX 5.1. Assessment Schedule Information: Logistical Considerations

Measure	Frequency of Data Collection	Suggestions on How to Analyze Data
Report cards and progress reports	Each grading period	• Determine which content or behavior areas of the report card to monitor (e.g., language arts, math, listening skills). • Decide which grades or proficiency levels signal at risk status on the report and progress reports. • Aggregate number of at-risk level grades each grading period. Track and compare aggregated numbers over time.
Grade point average (GPA)	Each grading period	• Identify when GPA signals unacceptably low level of academic achievement (e.g., below 2.0). • Compute schoolwide average GPA. Track and compare over time (e.g., compare annual GPAs, see Figure 7.4 in Chapter 7).
Course failures	Each grading period	• Grade of D or F in one or more course indicates at risk status and warrants further investigation. • Aggregate number failed courses each grading period. Track and compare aggregated course failures over time.
Writing assessment	3 times per year	• Establish proficiency levels. Those below acceptable performance signal at-risk status. • Aggregate number of scores below proficient. Track and compare aggregated scores over time.
Curriculum-based measures (CBMs)	Monthly	• Establish proficiency levels. Those below acceptable performance signal at risk status. • Aggregate number of scores below proficient. Track and compare aggregated scores over time.
ACT scores	Annually	• Identify the minimum acceptable score. • Aggregate number of scores in the unacceptable range. Track and compare aggregated scores over time.
Statewide assessment	Annually	• Scores in the bottom quartile indicate at-risk performance. • Aggregate number of scores in the bottom quartile. Track and compare aggregated scores over time.
Office discipline referrals (ODRs)	Monthly	• When collecting ODR data, use a reliable system such as the Schoolwide Information System (SWIS © 6.7.0 b42; May et al., 2003) for monitoring major and minor infractions. When analyzing data, be sure to do a variety of comparison with minor and major offenses (e.g., Quarter 1, Fall 2020 to Quarter 1, Fall 2021; see Figure 7.1 in Chapter 7). This provides for a more sensitive analysis and allows you to observe differences in the number of minor referrals versus major referrals (e.g., the number of major referrals may have decreased as minor referrals increase). Also look at context (e.g., settings, time of day). • Compute rate across months, quarters, semesters, and/or years.
Student Risk Screening Scale— Internalizing and Externalizing (SRSS-IE; Drummond, 1994; Lane & Menzies, 2009)	3 times per year	• Compute total scores for each subscale and then compare percentages across risk categories (low, moderate, and high). • Examine comparisons (e.g., Fall scores over time, see Figure 7.2 in Chapter 7) or compare Fall to Winter data to identify students for additional supports.

(continued)

BOX 5.1. *(continued)*

Measure	Frequency of Data Collection	Suggestions on How to Analyze Data
Systematic Screening for Behavior Disorders (SSBD; Walker & Severson, 1992)	3 times per year	• Compute percentage of students in the school that exceed normative criteria on the internalizing and externalizing dimensions according to the rating scales completed in Stage 2. • Compare percentages across time (e.g., Fall 2010 to Fall 2011; see Figure 7.7 in Chapter 7).
Strengths and Difficulties Questionnaire (SDQ; Goodman, 1997)	3 times per year	• Compute total score and subscale scores for each student. Aggregate data and compute percentage of students in each level of risk category. • Compare percentage of students by category over time (see Figures 7.8, 7.9, and 7.10 in Chapter 7).
Social Skills Improvement System Social–Emotional Learning Edition (SSiS SEL; Elliott & Gresham, 2017b)	3 times per year	• Compute scale and composite (Social–Emotional, Academic Functioning) scores. • Compare the percentage of students by category over time.
Attendance	Monthly	• Compute rate across months and/or years to examine tardiness and absenteeism (see Figure 7.3 in Chapter 7).
Referrals for support (e.g., mental health, bullying, intervention team, special education)	Monthly	• Compute rate across months and/or years by type of referral.
Social Validity Survey (e.g., Primary Intervention Rating Scale; Lane, Robertson, & Wehby, 2002)	2 times per year (start and near end of year)	• Compute averages both at the item level and the total scores for each time point. • Compare averages across time (e.g., preimplementation Fall 2010 to postimplementation Spring 2011).
Treatment Integrity: Tiered Fidelity Inventory (TFI; Algozzine et al., 2014)	Onset and end of the academic year	• Compute subscale scores (percentage of the possible points for each feature) as well as the overall total summary score (average of the seven subscale scores). • Compare subscale and total summary scores over time.
Ci3T Treatment Integrity: Teacher Self Report (Ci3T TI: TSR)	Fall and Spring semester	• Use behavioral checklists completed by all faculty and staff and compute percentages across semesters and/or years.
Ci3T Treatment Integrity: Direct Observation (Ci3T TI: DO)	Fall and Spring semester	• Use behavioral checklists completed for a 30-minute observation by an independent observer and the educator, and compute percentages across semesters and/or years. • Compute percentages by observers across semesters and/or years.

Note. Frequency of data collection may vary among schools. Rate is computed by taking the total number of occurrences (e.g., ODRs, referrals, absences) and dividing it by the number of instructional days (per month or year). Average is computed by summing all components and dividing that number by the total number of components (e.g., sum all individual students' GPA scores and divide by total number of students). Percentage is computed by taking the number earned/present and dividing it by the total possible and multiplying by 100 (e.g., the number of students who fall into the high-risk category and dividing by the total number of students and multiplying by 100).

In the next section, we introduce a variety of assessment measures that can be used for systematic screening of students for behavioral and academic concerns. These assessments help the team identify students who would benefit from more intensive intervention than the primary plan provides. The chapter concludes with guidelines for putting a screening system into place.

Screening for Early Detection: Who Needs More Support?

The Importance of Systematic Screening

In addition to collecting extant schoolwide data to monitor student performance, schools should incorporate systematic screening tools and procedures to detect students for whom primary prevention efforts are insufficient to meet their needs. By using validated screening tools and procedures, students can more quickly be directed toward participation in focused interventions efforts such as secondary (Tier 2) and tertiary (Tier 3) prevention efforts (the focus of Chapter 7; see Lessons Learned 5.1).

Ideally, effective screening tools and procedures should possess certain core features (Gresham et al., 2000; NCII, 2017). First, to reduce the potential for false positives and false negatives, systematic screeners need to be psychometrically sound (Kauffman, 1999). This means that the measures should have reliable and valid *cut scores* (i.e., the score that identifies a student to be in a particular category). A measure's *validity* refers to the extent to which theory and evidence support the interpretations of the test scores for the test's intended use (American Educational Research Association, 1999; NCII, 2017). For a measure to be valid, it must also be reliable. *Reliability* refers to the extent to which a particular test, when administered repeatedly over time, produces the same (or similar) results.

Ideally, systematic screeners should have evidence of the following characteristics (Lane, Kalberg, Parks, & Carter, 2008; Lane, Parks, Kalberg, & Carter, 2007). First, they should have high internal consistency (a Cronbach's alpha of .80 or higher; or see more current recommendations using Omega; McNeish, 2018) to make sure that the measure is actually assessing the defined construct of interest (e.g., behavior disorders). Second, a screener should evidence convergent validity with other established instruments that measure the same construct of interest (when both measures are completed at the same time). Third, a systematic screening tool should have both *positive predictive value* (the probability that a student above a selected

---

LESSONS LEARNED 5.1. Hooked by Screening

I was initially very skeptical of the Ci3T concept. The hook that initially got me to the table was the idea of having screening data for both internalizing behavior and externalizing behavior. I was hoping that is could somehow help us identify students who were slipping between the cracks. We administer the screener three times a year . . . teams meet weekly to review student attendance, behavioral data, and academic data.

Matt Brungardt
High School Principal

cut score is actually a member of the target group) and *negative predictive value* (the probability that a student below a selected cutoff score is a member of the control or nonclinical group) (Lanyon, 2006). Fourth, a systematic screener should have specificity (proportion of the comparison or typical group that is not identified, given the same cut score) and sensitivity (proportion of the target population correctly identified) (Lane, Parks, et al., 2007; Lanyon, 2006). Recently, the NCII (2017) established specific guidelines for examining behavior screening and academic screening tools (e.g., classification accuracy as well as technical standards for reliability, validity, sample representativeness, and bias analysis).

In addition to having strong psychometric properties, systematic screeners also need to be reasonable for teachers and administrators to administer and process with respect to available resources (e.g., personnel, time, and money; Oakes, Lane, Cantwell, & Royer, 2017). Ideally, a feasible screener is a reliable screening tool that also (1) costs little to no money and (2) takes limited time to administer, score, and analyze (Oakes et al., 2017; Walker et al., 2004). No matter how wonderful the instrument, if it is too cumbersome to administer, score, and analyze, then school sites are less likely to put such a screener in place.

We review in the next section the existing tools and procedures for monitoring students' behavioral and academic performance. The examples offered are all psychometrically sound but have a range in terms of feasibility.

Existing Tools and Procedures for Monitoring Students' Behavior and Social Performance

Researchers have developed several user-friendly, empirically validated instruments to detect students at risk for emotional and behavioral disorders, with screeners available for use from preschool through high school (Oakes et al., 2017). Since the first edition of this book was published, there have been several new tools developed, and systematic screening for behavior and social–emotional concerns has become a priority (Yudin, 2014). Examples of currently available tools include the Behavior Assessment System for Children, Third Edition: Behavioral and Emotional Screening System (BASC-3: BESS; Kamphaus & Reynolds, 2015); the Social, Academic, and Emotional Behavior Risk Screener (SAEBRS; Kilgus, Chafouleas, Riley-Tillman, & von der Embse, 2013); the Social Skills Improvement System—Social–Emotional Learning Edition (SSiS-SEL; Elliott & Gresham, 2017b); the Strengths and Difficulties Questionnaire (SDQ; Goodman, 2001); the Student Risk Screening Scale (SRSS; Drummond, 1994); the Student Risk Screening Scale—Internalizing and Externalizing (SRSS-IE; Drummond, 1994; Lane & Menzies, 2009); and the Systematic Screening for Behavior Disorders, Second Edition (SSBD; Walker et al., 2014). See Box 5.2 for summary information.

Behavior Assessment System for Children, Third Edition: Behavioral and Emotional Screening System

The BASC-3: BESS, a commercially available screening tool, is designed to assess behavioral and emotional functioning for PreK–12 students. Teachers can complete the BASC-3: BESS on Scantron forms and score the results manually, with software (scanned or hand-entered).

(text resumes on page 133)

BOX 5.2. Systematic Screening Tools for Behavior and Academic Performance

Behavior Screening Tools

For additional information, see

- Comprehensive, Integrated Three-Tiered Model of Prevention (Ci3T) *www.ci3t.org/screening*
- National Center for Intensive Interventions at the American Institutes for Research *https://intensiveintervention.org*
- Schoolwide Integrated Framework for Transformation (SWIFT Center) *http://guide.swiftschools.org/resource/examples-behavior-screeners*

Reference	Description	Contact Information and Technical Adequacy
Behavior Assessment System For Children, Third Edition: Behavioral and Emotional Screening System (BASC-3: BESS; Kamphaus & Reynolds, 2015)	• Purpose: Measures behavioral and emotional functioning with potential to negatively impact academics/social relationships • Scores: Total scale • Grades: Preschool–12 • Time: 30–45 minutes per class • Rater: teacher, parent, student • Format: Forms or online • Additional tools: • BASC-3 Rating Scales • Intervention Guide and Materials (Vannest, Reynolds, & Kamphaus, 2015)	• *www.pearsonclinical.com/education* • Split-half reliability estimates range from .94 (preschool) to .97 (child/adolescent) teacher-rated, combined scores • Sensitivity range preschool .44–.82, child/adolescent .53–.80; specificity > .90 across all scales • Predictive validity longitudinal zero-order correlations, teacher report: .27 reading, .31 math, .11 GPA, $p > .05$ (Kamphaus & Reynolds, 2007)
Social, Academic, and Emotional Behavior Risk Screener (SAEBRS; Kilgus, Chafouleas, Riley-Tillman, & von der Embse, 2013)	• Purpose: Differentiate between students with few behavioral concerns and those with moderate/high rates • Scores: Social Behavior (SB), Academic Behavior (AB), Emotional Behavior (EB), Total Behavior (TB) • Grades: K–12 • Time: 1–3 minutes per student; up to five times per year • Rater: Teacher, student • Format: online	• *www.fastbridge.org/assessments/behavior/behavior* • Internal consistency reliability estimates for ES: Cronbach's alpha .92 (SB), .93 (AB), .84 (EB), .94 (TB; Kilgus, von der Embse, Allen, Taylor, & Eklund, 2018) • Content validity with BESS statistically significant correlation coefficients with highest TB and lowest EB all above .69 threshold • Diagnostic accuracy: ES AUC range = .89 (EB) to .98 (TB); MS AUC range = .88 (EB) to .98 (TB; Kilgus et al., 2016)
Social Skills Improvement System—Social–Emotional Learning Edition (SSiS-SEL; Elliott & Gresham, 2017b)	• Purpose: Screening and progress monitoring of Social–Emotional (SE): Self-Awareness, Self-Management, Social Awareness, Relationship Skills, Responsible Decision Making; and Academic Functioning (AF): Motivation to Learn, Reading Skills, and Math Skills • Scores: Each items and composite score for the two domains (SE and AF) • Grades: PreK–12 • •Time: 30–40 minutes per class • •Rater: Teacher • Format: Booklets with hand scoring and/or online scoring • Additional tools: • SSiS SEL Rating Forms (Gresham & Elliott, 2017) • Classwide Intervention Program (ages 4–14; Elliott & Gresham, 2017b)	• *www.pearsonclinical.com/education* • Internal consistency .93 full scale; .91 SE, .90 AF; test–retest correlations .89 SE, .91 AF • Positive predictive power: socially at risk 60.47%; academically at risk 86.67% reading, 84.44% math. Negative predictive power: socially at risk 92.44%; academically at risk 91.03% reading, 83.86% math (Elliott, Davies, Frey, Gresham, & Cooper, 2018) • ROC AUC range: socially at risk 0.90 SE; 0.92 AF. Academically at risk 0.78 SE; 0.90 AF–reading; 0.76 SE; 0.90 AF–math • Feasible and easy to use in school settings (elementary sample; Elliott et al., 2018)

(continued)

BOX 5.2. *(continued)*		
Reference	**Description**	**Contact Information and Technical Adequacy**
Strengths and Difficulties Questionnaire (SDQ; Goodman, 2001)	• Purpose: Screening for five domains: Emotional Symptoms, Conduct Problems, Hyperactivity/Inattention (H/I), Peer Problems (PP), Prosocial Behavior • Scores: Total Difficulties and subscale scores • Ages: 2–17 • Time: estimate 3–5 minutes per student • Raters: Teacher, parent, student • Format: printable from online, online entry	• *www.sdqinfo.com* • Internal consistency estimates: alpha range = .70 (PP)–.88 (H/I; Goodman, 2001) • Specificity 94.6%, Sensitivity 63.3% (Goodman, 1997)
Student Risk Screening Scale (SRSS; Drummond, 1994)	• Purpose: Screen for students' antisocial behavior risk • Score: Total scale score • Grades: K–12 • Time: 10–15 minutes per class • Format: One sheet per class (can be built in an online worksheet or other school management system)	• *https://miblsi.org* • Internal consistency estimates: alpha > 80 (Lane, Bruhn, Eisner, & Robertson Kalberg, 2010) • Content validity with Child Behavior Checklist: $r = .79$ (Drummond, Eddy, Reid, & Bank, 1994) • Convergent validity with SSBD AUC .95–.96 externalizing, .76–.82 internalizing (Lane, Kalberg, et al., 2010)
Student Risk Screening Scale—Internalizing and Externalizing (SRSS-IE; Drummond, 1994; Lane & Menzies, 2009)	• Purpose: Screen students for internalizing and externalizing risk • Scores: Subscale scores Externalizing (SRSS-E7) and Internalizing (SRSS-I5 ES and SRSS-I6 MS/HS) • Grades: K–12 • Time: 15–20 minutes per class • Format: One sheet per class (can be built in an online worksheet or other school management system)	• *www.ci3t.org* • Internal consistency established at MS and HS levels: .84 SRSS-E7; .84 SRSS-I6 (Lane, Oakes, Cantwell, et al., 2017) • Convergent validity with SDQ and SSBD scores: ES (correlation coefficients; AUC range .82–.95; Lane, Oakes, et al., 2012) • Predictive Validity: MS and HS, GPA, course failures, nurse visits, in school suspensions (Lane, Oakes, Cantwell, Royer, et al., 2019); ES, ORF, formative academic assessments, nurse visits, in-school suspension (Lane, Oakes, Cantwell, Common, et al., 2018)
Systematic Screening for Behavior Disorders, Second Edition (SSBD; Walker, Severson, & Feil, 2014)	• Purpose: Screen students for risk in externalizing and internalizing behavior patterns: three scales: Critical Events Index, Adaptive Behavior Rating Scale, Maladaptive Behavior Rating Scales • Scores: subscale scores of internalizing and externalizing risk • Grades: PreK–9 • Time: 40 minutes per class, plus optional observation time • Rater: teacher • Format: online and paper format	• *www.ancorapublishing.com/product/ssbd-classroom-screen-packet-grades-1-9* • Cross-validation of SSBD screening stages (e.g., School Archival Records Search, SARS; Walker et al., 2014) • Convergent validity with SRSS and SRSS-IE scores (e.g., Lane, Oakes, et al., 2014) • Updated norms available in the technical manual—Stages 1 and 2, 6,743 cases (Walker et al., 2014)

Academic Screening Tools

For additional information, see

• Response to Intervention at American Institute for Research (AIR) *www.rti4success.org/resou rces/tools-charts/screening-tools-chart*
• National Center for Intensive Interventions (NCII) at the AIR *https://charts.intensiveintervention.org/chart/academic-screening*

(continued)

BOX 5.2. *(continued)*

Reference	Description	Contact Information and Technical Adequacy
i-Ready Diagnostics–Math (Curriculum Associates)	• Purpose: An adaptive diagnostic assessment to monitor student growth by math domain • Scores: National percentiles. Scaled scores. Developmental benchmarks (on level, level below, 2 or 3+ levels below) and grade-level scores. Individual, class and school reports. • Grades: 3–8 • Time: 30–60 minutes, group administration • Administrator: trained tester–paraprofessional or teacher • Format: Online • Additional tools: • A full package of tools available for assessment and online instruction (whole-class, small-group, and personalized instruction). Teacher and student materials. • iReady has reading assessments with comparable psychometric evidence.	• *www.curriculumassociates.com* • Classification accuracy met full evidence across studies and time points by NCII review panel. • Classification accuracy, reliability, and validity met full evidence by the AIR review panel. • Sample representativeness was not met (AIR). • Classification accuracy: False-positive rates across studies ≥ .20. False negative rate across studies ≥ .30; AUC ≤ .89 (NCII). • Reliability internal consistency estimates .95 (AIR)
Measures of Academic Progress® (MAP) Growth Math Assessment (Northwest Evaluation Association [NWEA])	• Purpose: An adaptive measure of mathematics growth between testing administrations • Scores: Scaled scores based on difficulty of item. Percentile, benchmark scores, RIT scale scores, composite scored, subscale scores. • Grades: K–12 • Children's Progress Academic Assessment (CPAA) PreK early numeracy • Time: 45 minutes per student (untimed) • Administrator: trained tester–paraprofessional or teacher • Format: online (computer or tablet) accessible • Additional tools: • MAP Skills assessments • MAP has reading assessments with similar psychometric evidence.	• *www.nwea.org* • Classification accuracy for grades K–2, and 3–7, reliability and validity met full evidence for grades K–8 (by NCII review panel) • Sample representativeness met partial evidence (NCII) • Classification accuracy met full evidence; reliability and validity met partial evidence by the AIR review panel. • Classification accuracy: False-positive rates across studies and grade levels ≥ .14, higher for black students ≥ .30 and Hispanic students ≥ .26. False-negative rate across studies and grade levels ≥ .34; higher for Asian Pacific Islander ≥ .36 students.
Standardized Testing and Reporting® (STAR) Math® (Renaissance)	• Purpose: Adaptive assessment of math domains and subskills. • Scores: Percentile, benchmark scores (at or above benchmark, on watch, intervention, urgent intervention), composite scales scores, subscale scores. • Grades: K–12 • Time: <20 minutes • Administrator: trained tester–paraprofessional or teacher • Format: online • Additional tools: • STAR Reading, Spanish • Programs for personalized practice • STAR reading assessments have comparable psychometric evidence.	• *www.renaissance.com* • Classification accuracy met full evidence across studies and time points for grades 2, 3, 5–8 and partial evidence for remaining grades; Reliability and validity met full evidence for all grade levels by NCII review panel. • Classification accuracy, reliability, and validity met full evidence by the AIR review panel. • Sample representativeness was met for the majority of grade levels (NCII). • Classification accuracy: False-positive rates across studies 0.26 ($n = 29,594$ in seven states). False-negative rate 0.25; AUC ≤ .80 across grade levels (AIR) • Reliability coefficient .947 (AIR)

(continued)

BOX 5.2. (continued)

Reference	Description	Contact Information and Technical Adequacy
Formative Assessment System for Teachers® (FAST) Adaptive Reading	• Purpose: Adaptive assessment of reading skills (e.g., print, phonemic awareness, phonics, vocabulary, comprehension); 30 items presented in audio and visual format • Scores: Benchmark criterion scores by grade level. Predictive scores of risk in meeting end-of-year state assessment expectations • Grades: K–12 • Time: 15–30 minutes per student; individual or group-administered • Administrator: trained tester • Format: online • Additional tools: • A full range of assessment tools for reading, math, and social–emotional behavioral skills • CBM Reading for Progress Monitoring • CBM for Reading Comprehension (CBMcomp) • earlyReading (grades PreK–1) • aMath	• www.fastbridge.org • Classification accuracy data available for grades 1–3 (Spring) met full evidence. Reliability met full evidence, as did validity for grades 2–4 by the NCII review panel. • Sample representativeness was not met (NCII). • Classification accuracy, reliability, and validity met full evidence by the AIR review panel. • Classification accuracy: False-positive rates grades 1–5 $\geq$ .20. False-negative rate $\geq$ .26 using the Gates–MacGinitie Reading Test; AUC $\leq$ .87 across grade levels (AIR). • Reliability: internal consistency alpha coefficient .95 (grades K–5; AIR) • Construct validity demonstrated using Gates–MacGinitie, CBM-ORF, and MAP (AIR)
easyCBM Reading (University of Oregon Center on Teaching and Learning)	• Purpose: A comprehensive benchmark and progress monitoring system of early literacy skills • Scores: Raw scores for each measure, Need for Support (intensive, strategic, core) by grade level and time of year, cutoff points based on percentile scores • Grades: K–6 • Time: varies by measure (25–40 minutes for group or individual reading comprehension test; 3- to 4-minute individual passage reading fluency) • Administrator: trained educator, including paraprofessionals • Format: online and paper-and-pencil versions available; app available for data collection and management • Additional tools: • A full range of assessment tools for reading, math, and Spanish • Lite version available for free to individual teachers	• www.easycbm.com • https://dibels.uoregon.edu/assessment • Classification accuracy met evidence for the three measures reviewed reading comprehension, vocabulary and passage reading fluency by the AIR review panel • Classification accuracy: False-positive rates $\geq$ 0.49. False-negative rate $\geq$ .30 using two state assessments; AUC .66–.91 (AIR) • Validity: concurrent .65–.69 with state test across grades 3–7 • Technical reports available on the website (information disaggregated by ethnicity, race, and English status)

Additional Resources for Systematic Screening

• AIR www.air.org/resource/essa-multi-tiered-systems-support-mtss-response-intervention-rti
• Iowa Resource for International Service (IRIS) Center (screening in mathematics) http://irisdashboarddemo.org/module/rti-math/#content
• IRIS Center (An Introduction to Monitoring Academic Achievement in the Classroom) https://iris.peabody.vanderbilt.edu/module/gpm/#content

Note. AUC, area under the curve; ES, elementary school; GPA, grade point average; HS, high school; K, kindergarten; MS, middle school; PreK, prekindergarten; ORF, oral reading fluency; CBM, curriculum-based measure; ROC, receiver operating characteristic; RIT, Rasch unIT. Representative psychometric evidence included. We do not endorse any specific tools; we encourage decision makers to review available evidence to explore more fully the screening tools to ensure they are appropriate for use within the given school context.

Another option is for teachers to complete the screener through an online administration, scoring, and reporting system (Q-Global; Pearson Education, 2015b). Teachers rate each item (25–30 depending on the form) using a 4-point Likert-type scale of *never, sometimes, often,* and *almost always* (some items are reverse-scored). Using the scoring process, each student receives one score to reflect six indices or patterns: behavioral and emotional risk, externalizing risk, internalizing risk, adaptive skills risk, self-regulation risk (student), and personal adjustment risk (student). Scores include raw scores, percentiles, and risk classifications according to *T*-scores ($M = 50$, $SD = 10$): normal (0–60), elevated (61–70), or extremely elevated (71 or higher). The BASC-3: BESS is one component of a family of tools that also include rating scales for in-depth student assessment (BASC-3; Reynolds & Kamphaus, 2015), as well as intervention materials for use classwide and in small groups (BASC-3 Behavioral and Emotional Skill Building Guide; Vannest, Reynolds, & Kamphaus, 2015).

Social, Academic, and Emotional Behavior Risk Screener

The SAEBRS, another commercially available tool (Kilgus, Chafouleas, Riley-Tillman, et al., 2013), assesses K–12 students' performance in three domains: Social Behavior (SB), Academic Behavior (AB), and Emotional Behavior (EB). Teachers rated each of 19 items using a 4-point Likert-type scale of *never, sometimes, often,* or *almost always,* with some items reverse-scored (see FastBridge Learning [*www.fastbridge.org*]). Ratings indicate the frequency with which each student exhibited specific behaviors during the prior month. The SAEBRS yields three subscale scores and a Total Behavior score, with scores used to indicate risk or no risk. Evidence suggests the SAEBRS is reliable and valid for use in determining risk (Kilgus, Chafouleas, & Riley-Tillman, 2013; Kilgus, Eklund, von der Embse, Taylor, & Sims, 2016).

Social Skills Improvement System— Social–Emotional Learning Edition

The SSiS-SEL is a commercially available tool, for students in preschool (age 3 and older), elementary, and middle school (through eighth grade). The teacher-completed screening tool focuses on student performance in two domains: Social–Emotional and Academic Functioning. Composite scores for the domains comprise subscales: Social–Emotional—self-awareness, self-management, social awareness, relationship skills, and responsible decision making; and Academic Functioning—motivation to learn, reading skills, and math skills. The social–emotional domain is based on the CASEL framework (Elliott, Davies, Frey, Gresham, & Cooper, 2018). Teachers use the criterion-reference performance levels to guide to scoring as follows: 1 (red band; *significant difficulty*), 2–3 (yellow band; *moderate difficulty*), and 4–5 (green band; *adequate performance*). Subscale scores are summed and interpreted using the following cut scores: Social–Emotional composite ≤ 10 indicates at risk and Academic Functioning composite scores ≤ 6 indicates at risk. This tool is available in two forms (online or in paper booklet form), with each booklet used to screen a class including up to 25 students. The booklet includes an interpretation and action sheet in which teachers write each student's name, skills area rated with a 1 or 2/3, and make notes regarding an action plan.

Like the BASC-3: BESS, the SSiS SEL is one component of a family of tools. Other materials include rating scales for in-depth student assessment (SSiS Rating Scales; Gresham & Elliott, 2008), as well as schoolwide instruction (SSiS–SEL Edition Classwide Intervention Program; Elliott & Gresham, 2017a).

Strengths and Difficulties Questionnaire

The SDQ (Goodman, 1997) is a systematic screener designed to examine students' (ages 2–17) strengths and deficits in sociobehavioral domains (Goodman, 2001; Goodman, Meltzer, & Bailey, 1998). The SDQ includes a number of forms available at no cost online. Specifically, there are teacher-completed (ages 2–4; 4–10; 11–17), parent-completed (ages 2–4; 4–10; 11–17), and self-report forms (ages 11–17). The teacher version requires teachers to fill out one page for *each* student in his or her class. The 25 items on the SDQ are equally distributed across five factors: emotional symptoms, conduct problems, hyperactivity, peer problems, and prosocial behavior. Teachers evaluate each item, some of which are positively phrased and others that are negatively phrased, on the following 3-point, Likert-type scale: *not true* = 0, *somewhat true* = 1, *certainly true* = 2. The authors estimate that it takes a teacher approximately 60 minutes to rate an entire class.

Subscale scores range from 0 to 10, with high scores indicating higher degrees of risk for emotional symptoms, conduct problems, hyperactivity, and peer problems, as well as higher degrees of prosocial behavior. The total score ranges from 0 to 40 and reflects the scores of the first four subscales. Each student is placed into one of three categories, which were recently updated from normal, borderline, or abnormal (three-band categories) to *close to average, slightly raised, high,* and *very high* (four-band risk categories) as established for each domain in the Total Difficulties score (Youth in Mind, 2012). Updates also include more general categories of externalizing (conduct problems and hyperactivity) and internalizing (emotional symptoms and peer problems) behavior patterns, placing students in the same risk categories (A. Goodman & Goodman, 2009).

Student Risk Screening Scale

The SRSS (Drummond, 1994) is a free-access, brief, mass screening tool originally designed to identify K–6 students at risk for antisocial behavior. This one-page instrument includes a list of all students in the first column, with seven items listed across the top row. Homeroom teachers rate each student in their class on the following items: steal; lie, cheat, sneak; behavior problem; peer rejection; low academic achievement; negative attitude; and aggressive behavior. Teachers rate each item on a 4-point Likert-type scale as follows: *never* = 0, *occasionally* = 1, *sometimes* = 2, or *frequently* = 3. Total scores are used to classify students into three levels of risk: low (0–3), moderate (4–8), and high (9–21). Administration time is 10–15 minutes for an entire class. The SRSS is a practical, psychometrically sound tool for distinguishing between students who do and do not exhibit behaviors indicative of antisocial behavior (Drummond, Eddy, & Reid, 1998a, 1998b). In our work, we have placed this information into an Excel file and included formulas to compute total scores for each students (see *www.ci3t.org* for additional details related to screening and the SRSS).

Student Risk Screening Scale—Internalizing and Externalizing

The SRSS was adapted to expand the SRSS to better detect students with internalizing behaviors. The SRSS-IE includes five additional items rated by teachers using the same 4-point Likert-type scale developed for the SRSS (Drummond, 1994; Lane & Menzies, 2009; Lane, Oakes, Swogger, et al., 2015). At the elementary level (grades K–5) the 12 total items are scored to offer two subscale scores: the SRSS original items (Externalizing, SRSS-E7) and five additional items (Internalizing, SRSS-I5). Each total score is used to place students in one of three risk categories. SRSS-E7 Externalizing are as follows: low (0–3), moderate (4–8), and high (9–21), and SRSS-I5 Internalizing categories are as follows: low (0–1), moderate (2–3), or high (4–15). When screening in middle and high schools, teachers complete the same 12 items that also offer two subscale scores. However, the scoring is different (SRSS-E7 and SRSS-I6; Lane, Oakes, Cantwell, Schatschneider, et al., 2016). For middle and high school students, the original SRSS item Peer Rejection is also added into the Internalizing scale (resulting in the SRSS-I6). SRSS-I6 categories are as follows: low (0–3), moderate (4–5), or high (6–18). SRSS-IE scores predict important outcomes in elementary (e.g., suspensions and oral reading fluency scores) and secondary students (e.g., GPA, course failure, and in school suspensions (Lane, Oakes, Cantwell, Menzies, et al., 2017; Lane, Oakes, Cantwell, Royer, Leko, et al., 2018). This tool is still being studied, so we encourage Ci3T Leadership Teams and district leaders who have selected the SRSS-IE to stay apprised regarding ongoing research related to the Internalizing subscale (Oakes, Lane, Cantwell, & Royer, 2017).

Systematic Screening for Behavior Disorders, Second Edition

The second edition of the SSBD (Walker et al., 2014) was recently released. We continue to view the SSBD to be the "gold standard" of systematic screening. This multigated screening tool is for use in grades PreK–9 to detect students showing soft signs of internalizing or externalizing behaviors. In Stage 1, teachers compare their students' externalizing and internalizing behaviors to provided definitions. Teachers nominate (list) five students whose behavior patterns are most similar to the definitions and examples for each domain. Next, teachers rank-order the five students listed under the externalizing category and the five students listed under the internalizing category from most like to least like. The top three students (ranks 1, 2, and 3) on each list pass through Gate 1 to Stage 2. As part of Stage 2, two nationally normed rating scales, the Critical Events Index (CEI) and the Combined Frequency Index (CFI) for the six students, the goal is to gain more specific information regarding the students' behavior patterns. The CEI is a 33-item checklist of high-intensity, low-frequency behaviors (e.g., sets fires, steals, vomits after eating). Teachers record the presence or absence of each behavior, with total scores ranging from 0 to 33. The CFI assesses low-intensity, high-frequency behaviors on adaptive (e.g., does seatwork as directed) and maladaptive (e.g., pouts or sulks) domains. CEI and CFI scores are interpreted according to established guidelines, with students exceeding normative criteria passing through Gate 2 to Stage 3. In Stage 3, a professional observes students' behaviors in classroom and playground settings and reviews students' educational records using the School Archival Records Search (SARS). Walker and colleagues indicate Stage 3 is optional for systematic screening purposes, yet information from this stage can be useful.

These validated screeners can be used to detect students who are at risk for various behavior concerns. In Chapters 6 and 7 we explore the possibility of using these systematic screening tools as part of K–12 primary (Tier 1) prevention programs to (1) assess the overall index of risk; (2) inform the use of teacher-delivered, low-intensity supports; and (3) identify how different types of students respond to the primary plan over time (Lane, Kalberg, Bruhn, et al., 2008). In the section that follows, we illustrate how to monitor students' academic progress.

Existing Tools and Procedures for Monitoring Students' Academic Performance

Just like behavioral measures, academic screeners need be technically sound and easy to administer, score, and interpret. It is also essential they be a valid measure of the curriculum your school site implements. Both norm-referenced assessments and curriculum-based assessments (CBAs) may be used as screeners, but curriculum-based measurements (CBMs) provides the most accurate information about educational growth because they deliver specific information that is sensitive to what students learn in their classes. CBMs also offer a more sensitive measure of growth than norm-referenced tests, which means that they detect smaller increases in student progress. However, group norm-referenced tests, such as those used to assess a school's yearly academic progress, also can be used initially to identify students who need further monitoring. We discuss in this next section the use of norm-referenced tests, CBAs, and CBMs as systematic screeners to identify students who are not making adequate academic progress.

Norm-Referenced Assessments

Wide-scale norm-referenced assessments are intended to compare an individual student's performance to a statistically constructed "average" student. These measures provide a benchmark for a parent, teacher, or other school personnel to use when evaluating student achievement. However, norm-referenced tests do not necessarily measure what a student learns at his or her school (Popham, 1999). Because the assessments are constructed to create a distribution of scores, they are not intended to monitor individual student progress but rather to furnish an approximate estimate of how, overall, an entire school is doing. Yet when used carefully, it is possible to employ these assessments as a very rough guide in identifying students who may be at risk for school failure. For example, if a student scores in the bottom quartile on a state-administered reading achievement test, this performance may be a cause for concern. Relying on norm-referenced assessments or CBAs might be most beneficial at the high school level, where academic screening tools are less available at this time.

The Ci3T Leadership Team (as well as other school-site teams that engage in data-informed decision-making activities) will want to use norm-referenced tests in conjunction with CBM for a measure of performance more sensitive to student growth. For example, the team may decide to establish an at-risk category of all students who score below the 25th percentile on the districtwide norm-referenced assessment and look for students who have scored below benchmark on a reading or math CBM. Once these students have been identified, the team can examine additional measures such as GPA or grades in language arts or mathematics for a fuller picture of academic progress. If students are doing poorly on all the measures thought to be important indicators of student progress, then this group is established as being at risk and will require additional monitoring and/or intervention.

CBA and CBM

CBAs directly measure a student's progress in the school's formal curriculum. They include a variety of measures, such as chapter tests from textbooks, teacher-made quizzes, portfolios, and anecdotal notes. They may also include capstone projects or final exams. An advantage of using CBAs as part of your systematic screening plan is that they are often already in place, are feasible, and provide a relatively easy-to-interpret measure of a student's academic skills. When choosing which assessments to use as screeners, several issues need to be considered. The Ci3T Leadership Team will have to make decisions about reliability and validity, as well as ease of administration, scoring, and aggregation of data.

For example, the team must identify assessments that are common across grade levels, so all students in a grade are measured using the same criterion. This uniformity makes it possible to establish "local norms"—that is, what a school's typical student performance looks like at a particular grade level at a particular point in the academic year. If each teacher uses a different CBA, a school is likely to either over- or underidentify students. Teacher A may use an advanced reading passage, whereas Teacher B uses a connect-the-dots worksheet. In this case, Teacher A will probably have more students who appear to be at risk than does Teacher B. This issue is also related to concerns about validity. Teachers must agree the measure accurately represents the key academic demands in a particular grade level. The assessment should be appropriately difficult and in the appropriate domain (e.g., reading and not physical education). The assessment must also be administered frequently enough, so it is possible to monitor student progress throughout and across the years.

Many school districts now employ CBM of academic progress or interim assessments that are administered at all their school sites to track progress across the district (January & Ardoin, 2015; Klingbeil, Nelson, Van Norman, & Birr, 2017). These measures are most often given in reading and mathematics, are leveled by grade, and provide cut scores that establish above-average, average, and below-average performance. In addition, they are typically administered several (e.g., three) times a year. These are a good choice as academic screeners because they establish local norms and address many of the issues related to reliability and validity. Teachers are already familiar with administering them and collecting and analyzing the data that they produce. Parents, too, are often familiar with these assessments, and because they are curriculum based, it is easy to discuss what performance means in terms of student achievement.

CBMs were originally designed as a formative evaluation tool to assist teachers in adjusting instruction to better meet students' needs. Increasingly, they are used to screen students who may be at risk academically (Deno, 2003). While CBM does reflect a school's general curriculum, it differs from CBA in that it is a standardized set of procedures that has established technical adequacy, uses stimulus materials that are representative and equivalent, is efficient in terms of time, and consists of short probes that are easy to administer. Because of their design, CBMs are ideal for use as academic screeners. School sites can create their own CBMs, but some are commercially available and others are accessible at no cost on websites. For example, the DIBELS 8th Edition (Good & Kaminski, 2018), developed by the University of Oregon's Center on Teaching and Learning, is a series of CBMs for reading that include fluency probes for initial sounds, letter naming, phoneme segmentation, nonsense words, oral reading, retelling, and word use. DIBELS measures are considered to have good reliability and validity, and are predictive of later reading success. Extensive information about the measure is available at *https://dibels.uoregon.edu/research*.

Similarly, AIMSweb, a commercially available assessment system for grades K–8, provides CBM in numeracy and literacy, spelling, written expression, mathematics, and reading. It is organized for use with multi-tiered intervention models and generates progress monitoring data that can be used to identify at-risk students. More information about these measures can be accessed at *www.aimsweb.com*.

When using CBM, be sure to note the cut scores that indicate risk. Cut[au scores are different for each of the subtests *within* a program as well as *between* them (e.g., DIBELS 8th Edition and AIMSweb). For example, at the beginning of first grade, a score of ≤ 37 on the DIBELS Phonemic Segmentation Fluency probe indicates at-risk performance; however, for the Nonsense Word Fluency: Words Read Correctly, a probe score of ≤ 7 is at-risk performance.

A variety of assessments can be used as academic screeners. District leaders and Ci3T Leadership Teams must choose those that are a good fit with the school's curriculum, and consider their validity and reliability. Equally important is that teachers, parents, and students find the assessments a meaningful and significant indicator of academic progress.

Recommendations for Conducting Screenings

When conducting systematic screenings in behavioral and academic domains, consider logistical issues such as (1) when to do them, (2) who should prepare them, (3) who should administer them, (4) who completes them, (5) who should score them, and (6) when and how to share results with educators. We have put together some suggestions based on our work in K–12 schools (see Boxes 5.3 and 5.4; however, these are just suggestions, and there are many "right ways" to conduct screenings; Ci3T Leadership Teams may create a similar table with their specific answers as an informational tool for educators and parents).

Examining the Schoolwide Data: Analyzing Multiple Sources of Data in Tandem

As demonstrated in this chapter, there are multiple sources of student-level data to inform decision making. It is important to consider multiple sources of data at the same time when analyzing student performance to make decisions based on the most complete picture of a student's performance in academic, behavioral, and social domains (see Lessons Learned 5.2). For example, only attending to behavioral risk and *not* considering academic risk, attendance, and fidelity of primary (Tier 1) prevention efforts could result in flawed decisions. Consider the student who is in the high-risk category for externalizing and internalizing behaviors, with reading fluency below benchmark, missing more than 10 days of instruction during the first quarter of the school year, and who is in a class with adequate levels of integrity of primary (Tier 1) prevention efforts. These multiple sources of data suggest the importance of an intervention to improve attendance and address both academic and behavioral needs. To have a complete picture or all the puzzle pieces, we need to access and interpret multiple sources of data. Fortunately, many districts now use dashboards that allow easy access to multiple sources of data. We return to data-informed decision making and corresponding professional learning needs in Chapters 6, 7, and 8.

BOX 5.3. Suggestions for Conducting Systematic Behavior Screeners	
Questions	**Suggestions**
When to do them?	• Conduct screenings three times each year (Fall, Winter, and Spring), following guidelines for administrations (e.g., 4–6 weeks after the school begins, prior to winter break, and 4–6 weeks before year end). • Once you have chosen dates to complete the screeners, include these on your assessment schedule. This may avoid scheduling several assessments during the same time period. • It is important to give teachers time to complete the screeners and sufficient professional learning to understand the rationale for screening. Consider allocating time during regularly scheduled faculty meetings or during department/grade-level meetings.
Who should prepare them?	• The Ci3T Leadership Team should determine a representative to coordinate the behavior screeners (i.e., administrative assistant responsible for attendance, counselor, administrator, district technology and evaluation team). This person should have access to school attendance and teacher rosters, as they will need to prepare forms that include all student names.
Who should administer them?	• The behavior screeners should be administered by the Ci3T Leadership Team after they have received training in administration, scoring, and interpretation.
Who completes them?	• All classroom teachers. • In an elementary school, teachers rate all students in their class. Support teachers (i.e., art, music, physical education) do not complete the screeners, as their students are rated by their homeroom teachers. • In a middle school, consider having the homeroom teachers complete the screeners on their group of students (see Lane, Parks, Kalberg, & Carter, 2007). • In a high school, consider choosing a teacher in a content area that students are required to take for 4 years (e.g., English teacher). Or perhaps choose a period (e.g., second period, fifth period; see Lane, Kalberg, Parks, et al., 2008) in which everyone teaching during that time will administer the screening to all students on their roster. • Note that whatever method you choose, it is necessary that every student be rated at least once. Some schools have chosen to have two different teachers complete screeners on students to offer multiple perspectives (Lane, Kalberg, Parks, et al., 2008).
Who should score them?	• Behavioral screeners should be scored by the Ci3T Leadership Team after they have received training in administration, scoring, and interpretation. • We also encourage the Ci3T Leadership Team to do reliability checks on the scoring to make sure that systematic screeners were scored accurately (e.g., all scores within range, all items completed).
When and how should results be shared?	• Once the data team member has aggregated the information, it should first be shared with an administrator and/or the Ci3T Leadership Team to determine how to share the results with the full faculty. • Consider spending some time during a regularly scheduled faculty meeting to share this information.

BOX 5.4. Suggestions for Conducting Systematic Academic Screeners

Questions	Suggestions
When to do them?	• Identify districtwide assessments that can be used as screeners. As these are administered at predetermined times, they should be listed in your assessment schedule. • Designate curriculum-based measures (CBMs) to administer three times per year with a plan or progress monitoring more frequently. • Be sure to consider your assessment schedule for behavior screeners to avoid too many items being collected at the same time.
Who should prepare them?	• Academic screening tools are prepared in accordance with state and/or district guidelines. • CBMs that are an integral part of teachers' instruction may be prepared by each teacher or by the assessment team. • If CBMs have been purchased, they may be Web based and can be downloaded by teachers or a designated Ci3T Leadership Team member.
Who should administer them?	• Teachers or the school data team. • Make certain that teachers and Ci3T Leadership Team members receive necessary training in administration, scoring, and interpretation.
Who completes them?	• Students
Who should score them?	• Screeners are scored in accordance with publisher guidelines. Teachers typically score district assessments (e.g., writing assessments) and report the results to administrators or test coordinators. • Make certain that teachers and Ci3T Leadership Team members receive necessary training in scoring.
When and how should results be shared?	• Administrators should develop systems for aggregating and sharing schoolwide academic screening data. Graphs or charts can be developed to clearly display how the school is performing. • The administrator may want to report results to the Ci3T Leadership Team and then with the full faculty. • Consider dedicating time during a regularly scheduled faculty meeting to share this information.

LESSONS LEARNED 5.2. Data-Informed Decision Making

For years, our staff has spent time looking at academic data to make instructional decisions. When we implemented the social–emotional and behavioral aspects of our Ci3T plan, we now have data points in these areas that provide more comprehensive data about our students. Our staff has yearly assessment reviews and student support meetings multiple times a year. Each year, we have students who need social–emotional or behavioral support before we can fully focus on their academic success.

Tammy Becker
Elementary School Principal

Summary

In this chapter, we have explored procedures for monitoring related to student performance—specifically, screening all students for possible behavior and academic concerns. First, we presented a practical assessment plan for monitoring how students respond to primary (Tier 1) prevention. We emphasized the importance of selecting valid, reliable tools to monitor student progress and allowing administrators and teachers to determine whether the goals of the primary (Tier 1) prevention efforts are being met. Next, we described a few of the current tools available in grades PreK–12 to benchmark student performance, and provided recommendations for installing screenings. Then, we discussed the importance of examining schoolwide data, with an emphasis on analyzing multiple sources of data in tandem to inform instruction and professional learning priorities. In Chapter 6, we examine how to use data to inform teacher-delivered supports and in Chapter 7, we discuss how to detect students who require additional supports in the form of secondary (Tier 2) and tertiary (Tier 3) interventions.

Empowering Teachers with Low-Intensity, Teacher-Delivered Strategies

As we have discussed in earlier chapters, the goal of Tier 1 is to prevent challenges from occurring in the first place. The roles and responsibilities established for each stakeholder—students, faculty and staff, parents and other family members, as well as administrators—are intended to create transparency, so each stakeholder is aware of the multiple contributions made by others. Ideally, Tier 1 efforts comprise evidence-based strategies, practices, and programs (Cook, Smith, et al., 2012). Yet, even when Tier 1 efforts are implemented as planned, there will still be students who require more than primary prevention efforts have to offer. Screening data help to determine which students may benefit from Tier 2 and Tier 3 supports, which should also feature strategies, practices, and programs with sufficient evidence to suggest that if implemented as planned, they are likely to achieve the desired outcome (a topic we discuss in more detail in Chapter 8).

Yet before using data to connect students to appropriate Tier 2 and Tier 3 supports, educators should consider proactive changes that set the stage for desired student performance and create positive, productive learning environments. In their work, Geoff Colvin and Terry Scott (2004) have taught the field that a teacher's first reaction to challenging behavior is highly predictive of how the student will respond. Using the right strategies at the right time can prevent students' behavior from escalating, and increase the likelihood of smooth instructional experiences for all.

Building on these lessons learned, we recommend educators use screening data to (1) examine overall level of risk in their building and (2) consider low-intensity, teacher-delivered supports before moving to more student-directed Tier 2 and Tier 3 supports. Although there will be instances when students should be supported immediately and directly with Tier 2 and Tier 3 supports, too often insufficient attention is devoted to empowering teachers to acquire tools for their toolkit that require far less effort and appropriately address students' needs.

As such, we encourage teachers to carefully consider their classroom management and instructional techniques in relation to student performance. The good news is that teachers' behaviors or actions influence student performance, and simple shifts in management practices that require relatively little time and effort can lead to improvements in student behavior and academic outcomes (Colvin & Scott, 2004; Lane, Menzies, et al., 2015). For example, when teachers increase their use of behavior-specific praise (Ennis, Royer, et al., 2018), incorporate instructional choice (e.g., Royer, Lane, Cantwell, & Messenger, 2017), engage in active supervision (e.g., Allen et al., in press), and increase students' opportunities to respond (e.g., Common, Lane, Cantwell, Brunsting, & Oakes, 2019), student outcomes often improve. These improvements are seen from preschool to high school, influencing a range of outcomes: engagement, disruption, work completion, and work accuracy, to name a few. Wonderful resources are now available such as the classroom management briefs on *pbis.org*, the guide on classroom strategies from the Office of Education Programs (OSEP) Ideas That Work (Simonsen et al., 2015), and practice guides from the IES (What Works Clearinghouse, 2008). These resources feature several strategies and practices with illustrations on how to use them in elementary, middle, and high school settings (Simonsen et al., 2015). In addition, there are well-produced, free-access videos developed with funding from the IES by Terrance (Terry) Scott at the Center for Instructional and Behavioral Research in Schools (CIBRS; *www.cibrs.com*).

We focus in this chapter on research-based, low-intensity supports that teachers can use to increase engagement and decrease disruption. First, we discuss practical methods for using data to inform decision making about how and when to refine the use of low-intensity, teacher-delivered supports. Second, we introduce seven low-intensity, teacher-delivered strategies that can be used across the tiers.

Data-Informed Decision Making: Using Teacher-Delivered Strategies

As we discussed in Chapter 3, Ci3T Implementation Manuals would feature research-based, low-intensity strategies to facilitate engagement during instruction and decrease disruption. For example, in Boxes 3.2 and 3.3 in Chapter 3, you see such strategies listed as Tier 1 components of the academic domain. These supports are intended for use as part of primary prevention efforts. For example, from preschool through high school, as part of integrated lesson plans, teachers could use precorrection to remind students of the expectations listed in the expectation matrix (see Boxes 3.5 and 3.6 in Chapter 3) or relevant skills taught during schoolwide instruction of SEL (e.g., how to show empathy or resolve conflict with others) *before* engaging in cooperative learning activities. With multiple tools such as precorrection, behavior-specific praise, instructional choice, and so on, teachers are well equipped to construct positive, productive learning environments that meet students' multiple needs.

Yet even with well-designed lessons with clearly defined academic and social skills objectives, as well as defined behavioral expectations, there will certainly be some students who engage in behaviors such as noncompliance, off-task behavior, or disruptive behavior that impedes instruction and disrupt the classroom (Menzies et al., 2018). Fortunately, we know that teachers' first responses to challenging behavior are highly predictive of how students respond (Colvin & Scott, 2004). This is good news for teachers; that is, if teachers have a well-defined, well-practiced set of skills they can implement early on in the acting-out cycle, before students' negative behavior accelerates, it is possible to interrupt the cycle and prevent students from engaging in serious peak behaviors that lead to unsafe behaviors—for themselves and others (Colvin & Scott, 2004).

Before using screening data to connect students to supports, we encourage you to examine systematic academic and behavior screening data in conjunction with treatment integrity and social validity data for the school. Specifically, we suggest district leaders work closely with Ci3T Leadership Teams to explore the relations among implementation (integrity); stakeholders views about goals, procedures, and intended outcomes (social validity); and student performance on screening data, as well as other data collected as part of regular school practices (e.g., ODRs, attendance, course completion), as discussed in Chapter 5. Then, Ci3T Leadership Teams can work with faculty members to unpackage these same data for the individual teacher's classes.

For example, with the use of data management systems, teachers would ideally access data to answer the following questions:

- "To what extent am I implementing Tier 1 efforts as planned [source: treatment integrity data]? How does my level of implementation compare to other teachers in my school or district?"
- "How do I feel about the goals, procedures, and intended outcomes of Tier 1 efforts [source: social validity data]? How does my level of social validity compare to other teachers in my school or district?"
- "How are students performing in my class(es) [sources: academic and behavior screening scores, office discipline referrals, tardies, attendance]?

In reviewing these data, teachers would consider multiple sources of information to determine the percentage of students responding to primary prevention efforts. When more than 20% of students in a given class appear to be struggling, teachers may visit their treatment integrity and social validity data to identify a target area for refinement in their own practice. For example, if treatment integrity data suggest expectations are not reinforced with the delivery of a PBIS ticket and specific information as to why the student received it or if social skill lessons are being taught but not revisited during instruction, teachers may identify one or more low-intensity supports to refine. In this illustration, teachers may decide to refocus their instruction by designing integrated lesson plans that involve (1) precorrection, (2) behavior-specific praise, and (3) instructional feedback (described in detail below). At the elementary level, a teacher might review the social skills and behavioral expectations that students will need for success in the particular lesson activity in addition to the academic objectives for the lesson. For example, the teacher may plan to have students engage in a collaborative activity where they work together to identify and create a map that details the journeys of the characters in their novel. To support students in successfully engaging in this activity the teacher uses precorrection. She reminds students of the social skills of how to be respectful of others' ideas, and how to come to agreement when ideas differ. She also reminds students of the behavioral expectations, such as using a conversational voice, and having one person talk at a time. Then as she circulates while they work, she can be specific in her praise statements: "Jameson, thank you for talking through your disagreement with Carlos. It sounds like you came to good solution together." She might give both students a PBIS ticket. Behavior-specific praise is one type of instructional feedback, in addition to offering guidance on academic work: "How might you label the route so we know which character made that journey?" or "I see you used different colors for each route, good idea. Remember the part of the map that lets us know what character each of those colors refers to? . . . Yes! It is called the key. Please remember to add that important detail to your map." At high school, it will look very similar. The teacher plans for the social skills and behavioral objectives, along with the academic objectives appropriate for a lesson (see Figure 2.1 in Chapter 2 and Lessons Learned 6.1). For example, the journalism teacher may use precorrection to remind students that when story assignments are made, they may not get their first choice but should show respect for others by accepting their assignment. Then, when students are in the process of selecting and being assigned assignments, and they graciously take their second or third choice, the teacher uses behavior-specific praise to recognize the expectation was met: "Savannah, thank you for accepting your third choice so graciously. I appreciate you showing such professionalism and respect." Along with this feedback, the teacher would make sure to circulate and provide additional feedback to students as they are developing the plan for their stories: "I see you are considering your time as well as your interviewee"; "That sounds like an interesting idea to take a surprising new angle on the story." Collectively, these low-intensity strategies prompt teachers to look for and promote expected social and academic behaviors, creating an engaging and positive learning environment.

In other instances, a review of these multiple sources of data might indicate the vast majority of students are responding to Tier 1 efforts. It may be just a few students are screening into the moderate risk category on the behavior screening. In this instance, the teacher may decide to provide Tier 2 support that involves more intentional delivery of these same low-intensity supports. For example, if schoolwide data indicate three students are scoring at moderate risk on the SRSS-IE for externalizing behaviors and have earned more than six ODRs in the hallways during transitions in the past month, the teacher might employ precorrection. To do this, the teacher stands near the door as students are getting ready to enter the hallway. She will have the full expectation matrix posted near the door. Then she simply says, "Before you enter the hallway, let's review the expectations, so you can all have a successful transition to your next class." Then she states the expectations and calls on the three students to restate them. Ideally, the teacher is available in the hallway or preplans with another

---

LESSONS LEARNED 6.1. Behavior-Specific Praise in Secondary Schools

The Ci3T Leadership Team grew exponentially in its capacity to facilitate school improvement through the process of writing the Ci3T plan. Seasoned educators learned the power of big ideas, such as using feedback loops and making data-driven decisions across academic, behavioral, and social–emotional domains. Even the most skeptical of secondary teachers learned that an intervention as simple as behavior-specific praise could shift our school culture from one that focused on punitive systems to one that focused on relationships among students and adults in the building.

Laura Lyons, PhD
High School Assistant Principal

teacher to provide behavior-specific praise when the students meet expectations. If this easy-to-implement strategy was effective in decreasing ODRs for two of the students, but not quite robust enough for the third student, then an functional assessment-based intervention (FABI) might be developed to learn more about the function of the student's behavior (e.g., the student is trying to access adult attention) and provide more intensive intervention efforts (an intervention we discuss in Chapter 7). As one element of FABIs, the intervention might include precorrection as one of the antecedent adjustments (adjustments made to prevent challenges from happening in the first place; Cooper et al., 2007). For example, the student is given a copy of the hallway expectations to keep on his or her desk. Before students line up or prepare to transition, the teacher stops at the student's desk to review the hallway expectations one-on-one (providing some adult attention prior to entering the hallway). These examples illustrate how to use your data to determine which students may need you to use the low-intensity strategies more intentionally and intensively.

Low-Intensity, Teacher-Delivered Strategies

Next, we review seven teacher-led strategies that can be used as either a Tier 1 support for all students or a more intensive support for an individual student. Each support is theoretically grounded in applied behavior analysis (ABA) principles (Baer et al., 1968; Cooper et al., 2007), with evidence to suggest that if implemented as designed, the desired change in student performance is likely to be achieved. Each strategy is defined and explained in enough detail to use it in the classroom the next day. Illustrations from research studies are also included to show how the strategies have been used in different settings. In the illustration noted earlier and in those that follow, we focus on the principle of reinforcement—a central technique for shaping desired behaviors that facilitate instruction and learning. However, for those interested in more information on the topic, a chapter-length discussion of each strategy is available in *Behavior for School Success: A Step-by-Step Guide to Key Strategies* (Lane, Menzies, et al., 2015). A special issue of *Beyond Behavior* provides extensive information on the topic, and the website *ci3t.org* provides resources for putting these practices into place. When using these strategies, we recommend allowing students to offer feedback on them. Students are our best source of information on how to adjust instruction to better meet their needs. The additional resources listed earlier include comprehensive information on how to elicit structured feedback from students on each of the strategies.

Behavior-Specific Praise

Acknowledging appropriate behavior is one of the most powerful strategies a teacher can use. We all appreciate hearing when we have done something well (which is why I so appreciated my dentist, who said I had a "nice bite"! Thank you, Dr. Averbush! [K. L. L.]), and students are no exception. Teachers tend to be more familiar with general praise statements such as "Good job" or "Nice work," but behavior-specific praise or explicit feedback for performance on a particular task or act is even more potent. Behavior-specific praise improves behavioral and academic performance, and enhances effective classroom management (Brophy & Good, 1986; Floress, Jenkins, Reinke, & McKnown, 2018; Sutherland, Wehby, & Copeland, 2000).

Using Behavior-Specific Praise

Initially, it is helpful to know how often you may already be using behavior-specific praise. Teachers are sometimes surprised at the relatively low rates of verbal praise they use when not being intentional about it. Noticing patterns of usage is informative because you may be overlooking the opportunity to praise students who would benefit greatly from the strategy. A colleague or instructional coach could observe during an instructional period and provide input on the rate or specificity of praise used, or you could self-monitor by keeping an informal tally. After determining whether you need to increase or enhance the use of behavior-specific praise, it is productive to think in advance about the behaviors you want to reinforce (Fullerton, Conroy, & Correa, 2009). This may be specific to a particular lesson format as in the earlier examples or more generally applied to expected classroom behaviors. For example, if your priority is on-task behavior, then that is a great starting point. Practicing behavior-specific praise praise statements is also a good idea as it makes it easier to deliver the behavior-specific praise phrase in the moment. Practicing the statements and identifying the behaviors in advance will make you more accurate in delivering behavior-specific praise rather than general praise, which although beneficial, is not as effective. After determining the target behavior, the teacher simply watches for the opportunity to deliver behavior-specific praise making sure to connect explicitly the feedback to the behavior the student has performed, and to do so as quickly after the behavior occurs as possible (Sutherland et al., 2000). For example, if a student who has had difficulty with task completion finishes an assignment, a teacher would say, "Thank you, Steven, for completing your work. I appreciate you finishing it before recess." This makes it clear to the student that the teacher wanted him to finish his work, and that she noticed, and appreciated, when he did so. This is more effective than saying, "Good work, Steven," because Steven may not realize exactly what it is he did to receive the teacher's praise. If he was being quieter than usual, he might think his teacher was commenting on that behavior instead of task completion. By noting the specific action important to her, the teacher increases the likelihood of Steven completing his work in the future if he is motivated by teacher praise.

An understanding of a student's skills level is necessary because it is appropriate to use behavior-specific praise when a student has partial mastery of the desired behavior (Haydon & Musti-Rao, 2011; Marchant & Anderson, 2012). For example, if Steven did not finish all his work, but he completed more than he usually does, the teacher could write, "Steven, I see you finished more than half of the assignment before recess. Thank you for concentrating on it. I think tomorrow you may be able to finish even more during math class. ☺" Behavior-specific praise can shape a student's behavior by communicating the expectation and reinforcing him for successive approximations of it until he performs the task as desired. Similarly, once a student has mastered a target skill, he or she should be acknowledged periodically to ensure fluency of the behavior is maintained. The final step of using behavior-specific praise is to self-monitor one's own use of it to see whether it is being used frequently enough to shape students' behavior.

Behavior-Specific Praise in Practice

Behavior-specific praise is impactful from preschool to high school. Next, we illustrate two applications: the first in preschool, and the second is an elementary school setting.

Preschool

Our first example of using behavior-specific praise is from a Head Start preschool setting with students between 3 and 5 years old (Stormont, Smith, & Lewis, 2007). Preschool may seem very early to be concerned about misbehavior, but there has been an increase in behavior problems such as aggression, and there is evidence that approximately 50% of students who exhibit behavioral challenges in preschool will also manifest them once they reach kindergarten and beyond (Campbell, 2002). In this study, three teachers who were identified as using more reprimands than praise in their preschool classrooms took part in a 4-hour training about using behavior-specific praise as a Tier 1 practice. Researchers observed before the intervention started (baseline), then again after the training to see whether teachers were able to increase their use of behavior-specific praise and whether behavior-specific praise reduced behavior problems. They found that while two of three teachers did not reduce the number of reprimands they used, all three teachers did increase their use of behavior-specific praise, and overall student behavior issues were reduced in all three classes. So even brief teacher trainings on behavior-specific praise were effective in helping teachers improve their use of behavior-specific praise and were an effective classroom strategy for reducing behavior problems.

Elementary School

In another illustration of behavior-specific praise, four elementary teachers (kindergarten, and first, second, and sixth grades) worked with university researchers to use behavior-specific praise with their students (Allday et al., 2012). The goals of the study were threefold. The first was to see whether it was possible to increase each teacher's use of behavior-specific praise with a brief training and minimal feedback. The second was to determine whether a general increase of behavior-specific praise in the classroom resulted in an improvement of on-task behavior for at-risk students, even if those students were not always the recipient of the behavior-specific praise. The third goal was to see whether teachers decreased their use of corrective statements when they was focused on using behavior-specific praise.

The 40-minute training had five elements. The first was to provide the teachers with a definition of behavior-specific praise. Then the researchers gave examples and nonexamples of behavior-specific praise to differentiate between behavior-specific praise and general praise. They also provided specific examples of behavior-specific praise from observations in each of the classrooms. Next, researchers showed teachers a graph of their baseline use of behavior-specific praise during the observations. Finally, teachers identified instances in which they could use more behavior-specific praise.

Once the intervention began, each class was observed 18 times during a designated activity period. During the observations, on-task and off-task behaviors were recorded for seven students who had been identified as having high rates of off-task behavior. Teacher use of behavior-specific praise was coded from audio recordings made during the same activity period. After every third day of data collection, researchers provided teachers with feedback that included their rate of behavior-specific praise compared to their goal, as well as students' task engagement rates.

The results showed that a single training and minimal feedback did increase the use of behavior-specific praise, although there were high rates of variability from session to session for three of the four teachers. One of the most interesting findings was that on-task behavior of all the at-risk students improved even though they were not targeted for behavior-specific praise. In fact, some of the at-risk students received less direct praise posttraining compared to baseline, but their on-task behavior still increased. This strongly suggests that a general increase in the use of behavior-specific praise positively impacted their engagement. Finally, teachers were able to reduce their use of corrective statements, partly because they delivered behavior-specific praise to one student to signal to other students what they should be doing. This eliminated the need to give a corrective statement to noncompliant students. Although teachers gave behavior-specific praise a high favorable rating, said they would recommend it to a colleague, and were likely to use the technique again, they also said they found it difficult to increase their use of behavior-specific praise.

Summary

Behavior-specific praise is a strategy easily used by teachers to provide students with sincere and accurate feedback about their work and behavior. Because it is a powerful reinforcer, it can increase students' engagement and participation in the classroom, including those at risk for behavior problems. One of the best aspects of behavior-specific praise is the minimal amount of time and energy it takes to learn how to use it. Behavior-specific praise can be paired with several other low-intensity supports, including precorrection.

Precorrection

In its simplest form, *precorrection* is a brief reminder of how to behave, but surprisingly, it is an underused strategy despite its effectiveness. Using antecedent strategies (Crosby, Jolivette, & Patterson, 2006) such as precorrection is a shift away from controlling behavior with consequences and punishment. Rather than trying to handle a behavior problem after it has occurred, precorrection anticipates and prevents it from happening in the first place. This is part of a proactive and instructive approach to behavior. More time, reflection, and planning is done to adjust the environment, so it promotes positive behavior, in order to reduce the number of behavior issues that occur.

Using Precorrection

Precorrection can be used without any planning at all, but the most effective use comes from reflecting on the activities or times when problem behavior is likely to occur. Thinking in advance about precorrection allows the teacher to clearly define the behavioral expectations and determine whether the environment requires adjustment. For example, if the teacher has determined that lining up to go to lunch is a good target for precorrection, she might decide where students will line up, then examine the area carefully to be sure there are no environmental barriers. If she notices there is not enough space for students to line up without jostling one another, she should adjust the procedure or rearrange the space. After any needed adjustments have been made, the teacher reviews the procedure and the expected behavior with her students. Modeling and practice are essential to ensure students understand the procedure. Once the teacher is confident students understand the routine, she can use precorrection when students line up. This could be one of many types of prompts, including verbal (e.g., restating schoolwide expectations, counting down from 10), gestural (e.g., pointing, holding up the quiet sign), environmental (e.g., posting signs, sectioning off areas of the room with tape or dividers), and manual (e.g., facing students, using proximity control) prompts (Haydon & Scott, 2008). When students perform the routine correctly, lining up behind one another without pushing, they should be praised. Praise can be used strategically with individual students or it can be addressed to the entire class. Acknowledging students' appropriate behavior not only reinforces its future use, but the praise itself serves as a prompt. When students see others around them being praised, they are likely to engage in the expected behavior as well. In schools implementing Ci3T, precorrection can be used to prompt the use of behavioral expectations (Ci3T Blueprint C Expectation Matrix) or skills acquired from the social–emotional skills curriculum (e.g., Connect with Kids Network, 2016) to facilitate a harmonious environment.

Precorrection in Practice

Precorrection is another easy-to-use, effective strategy from preschool to high school. Next, we illustrate two applications: the first in preschool, and the second is an elementary school setting.

Preschool

The intervention by Stormont and colleagues (2007) that we featured earlier for behavior-specific praise also included the use of precorrection. Teachers in a Head Start center, who were observed to have high levels of reprimands, were invited by the researchers to participate in a study to reduce problem behaviors in their classes. After the researchers took baseline data on the number of behavioral incidents and the teachers' and assistant's rate of praise and reprimands, each was provided with a 30-minute individual session on how to (1) use precorrective statements during a review of expectations of students prior to the small-group lesson, and (2) increase use of behavior-specific praise with students meeting behavioral expectations. The training included examples of precorrection and behavior-specific praise statements, and teachers were given the opportunity to practice using these statements. Researchers also provided teachers with feedback during class on whether they had used the precorrection strategy and their frequency of praise statements.

The intervention took place during daily teacher-directed, small-group activities (79 students in a group) in which children ranged in age from 3 to 5 years. Data collected showed that before the intervention, the participants seldom used precorrection, and instead relied on a high level of reprimands. After the intervention, the assistant and both teachers decreased their use of reprimands and increased their use of both precorrection and behavior-specific praise statements. As a result, student problem behavior decreased in all three small groups. In addition, the teachers and assistant indicated that they believed the intervention to be both effective and worthwhile.

Upper Elementary School

At an elementary school in the Midwest, school personnel were concerned about the commotion occurring each morning when students lined up in the gymnasium after finishing breakfast in the cafeteria or arriving to school. More than 400 students in grades 3–5 congregated in this area before going to class at the start of the school day. In the year before the intervention took place, over 77 ODRs were generated because of yelling, hitting, and being out of line. To address the problem, the staff adopted a seven-step precorrection strategy developed by Colvin, Kameenui, and Sugai (1993) to decrease problems behaviors during noninstructional settings. After establishing and modeling the expected behaviors for students, supervisors used the following precorrections: (1) At the top of the stairs, students were reminded to be quiet; (2) walkers and bus riders were greeted, then reminded to walk in the gym; (3) a supervisor who walked around with a sign printed on one side with the phrase "use an inside voice" and on the other side with "use self control" asked students if they knew what was on the side of the sign they could not see. If students answered correctly, they received immediate positive feedback; incorrect responses received a correction. On Thursdays, supervisors told students they tended to be louder on Fridays and reminded them to keep the noise level low. Supervisors also did this the day before a special event was held.

During the first year of implementation, only 12 ODRs were written. This was a huge improvement over the 77 referrals given the year before. In addition, the calmer morning routine was appreciated by staff supervisors, who had previously dreaded this portion of the day. Precorrection was effective in helping students maintain prosocial behavior in this noninstructional setting.

Summary

Precorrection is another simple but effective strategy that takes little time to implement. In addition to being easy to use, it improves the classroom climate when teachers cue students in advance about good behavior rather than reprimanding for misbehavior afterward. Most teachers use this strategy instinctively, but being intentional with precorrection is even more productive. Strategic use includes establishing your objectives, modifying the environment if needed, and rehearsing the behavior. Once these elements are in place, gentle cues and prompts will keep most students on track. Precorrection is a foundational component of another low-intensity support: active supervision.

Active Supervision

Active supervision is the intentional and planned use of supervisory activities to diminish behavior problems and promote prosocial behavior. Schools are dynamic places, teeming with energy, and require the careful attention of adult personnel to maintain the safety of its students. When teachers and other school personnel actively scan classrooms and public spaces in schools, and interact with students proactively, they are nurturing an environment of care and concern. Sites that have deliberate, and respectful, procedures in place for supervising students promote a positive school climate. Interacting positively with students is an essential element in active supervision. It provides the opportunity to remind students of school/classroom expectations and how to avoid misbehavior.

Using Active Supervision

Active supervision has several distinct steps. The first is to identify the activity or transition period that would benefit most from active supervision. Sometimes this is already in place, such as during lunch or recess. However, teachers can review their classroom transitions to see whether there are some that would benefit from active supervision. This is also a good time to determine whether the routine for the target activity is familiar and understood by students. For example, if students are not allowed to run in the hallways, then specific instructions should be given about that policy (precorrections or reminders about expectations). Even if expectations appear to be common sense and should already be known, they must be explained to students. Once students have been given the cue to begin an activity, such as leaving for the lunchroom or transitioning to another activity, then the teacher or school personnel circulate so they are a noticeable presence as they scan the area. Moving about is important because it signals to students that adults are attentive. It also allows for better visibility in large spaces such as the schoolyard or recess area. The next step is to interact strategically with students while circulating and scanning. This is the opportunity to remind students of expected behavior (precorrection) and offer prompts to stay on task or to avoid problem behavior. Prompts can be nonverbal, a shake of the head, or verbal: "Remember to pick up your lunch tray." If needed, teachers and other adults provide corrections or apply consequences for problem behaviors that arise. Equally important is communicating what students are doing well. These, too, can be either verbal or nonverbal, and a smile, thumbs-up, or thank you quickly lets students know their prosocial behavior is recognized and appreciated. It is an easy way to reinforce students for their positive actions. Active supervision is also a great time for spontaneous interactions. Students value attention from their teacher and other adults, and these brief interactions are important opportunities to make connections that build positive school relationships.

Active Supervision in Practice

Active supervision is a strategy for use in a range of settings within and beyond the classroom (e.g., cafeterias, hallways, arrival and dismissal, as well as assemblies and sporting events).

Next, we illustrate two applications: the first in an elementary school and the second in a high school setting.

Elementary School

One of the earliest research studies on active supervision was conducted by Colvin and colleagues in 1997. The school staff were concerned with the high number of behavioral problems during three transition periods, as they averaged about 40 incidents a transition. The first transition of concern was when students arrived in the morning and crossed through a courtyard into their classrooms. The next difficult transitions were when students left their classrooms to go to the cafeteria at lunchtime and when they left the school building at the end of the day. The main problems during each of these transitions were running, pushing, hitting, yelling, screaming, and crossing prohibited areas. The intervention included staff members reminding students of the expectations before and during the transition (walk, keep hands and feet to self, and use a quiet voice), then moving around the transition areas, scanning the area, and interacting with students. Once active supervision was used regularly, problem incidents during transitions were dramatically reduced to an average of only eight per session when arriving to and leaving school, and 15 incidents during lunch. The intervention dramatically increased staff members' effectiveness when supervising students, and as a result, greatly decreased student misbehavior.

High School

In an urban high school in the Midwest, ninth grade teachers were concerned with the transition from lunch back to classrooms (Haydon & Kroeger, 2016). Two educators who cotaught an interdisciplinary language arts and history course to a group of 60 students wanted to reduce the number of problem behaviors, such as pushing, shouting, whistling, and throwing things, and decrease the amount of time it took students to begin their classwork. Researchers helped the teachers design an intervention based on precorrection and active supervision. Students were expected to enter the classroom and begin a silent warm-up activity. They were to remain seated and take out a pen and binder. One of the teachers and a student–teacher reminded students of the expected behavior as they entered the classroom. As the teacher and student–teacher offered the precorrection, the other teacher circulated through the classroom and reinforced the expectations by giving verbal praise to those who were on task. In addition, a prompt was projected onto a screen at the front of the room for the first 15 minutes of class. It included the following reminder: Enter and Focus, Remain Seated, Must Have Pen and Binder, and Silent Warm Up. The teachers also reminded students how many minutes were left in the transition time. These simple procedures made a significant change in students' behavior when transitioning from lunch to the classroom. Transition time was reduced from an average of nearly 9 minutes to an average of 3 minutes and 24 seconds. Before the intervention, problem behavior was quite high, with an average of 18 occurrences during the transition. After the intervention, problem behavior was reduced to an average of less than two occurrences and remained low. Both teachers and the student teacher reported that using active supervision was not only easy but also very successful.

Summary

Active supervision is an easy-to-use tool for reducing problem behaviors in classrooms and other school areas, such as the playground, cafeteria, and hallways. Not only is it important in ensuring overall school-site safety, but active supervision can also be used to address specific problems such as bullying and tardiness (e.g., Johnson-Gros, Lyons, & Griffin, 2008; Ttofi & Farrington, 2011). Another strategy that can be used in both recreational activities (e.g., playground and sporting events) and the classroom is to increase students' opportunities to respond.

Increasing Opportunities to Respond

Increasing students' opportunities to respond is a powerful tool for promoting engagement. It is typically used with material requiring practice or review. The teacher initiates a high number of questions or prompts about the material within a predetermined amount of time, and all students answer, either individually or in unison, depending on how the lesson has been structured. A variety of response formats can be used such as thumbs-up or -down, an electronic response system, or small whiteboards (Sutherland & Wright, 2013). The teacher gives immediate corrective feedback on the students' responses. For example, after learning new vocabulary, a review could be done using opportunity to respond. The teacher would provide students in the class with a set of the vocabulary terms they had studied printed on cards. She would project a definition on a screen, and students would choose from their selection of terms and hold it up for her to see. After giving enough time for everyone to hold up the chosen vocabulary card, she would scan the responses and say, "I see many of you know the definition of *immediately* is right away." This review of material is superior to calling on students individually because with opportunity to respond, all students have the chance both to demonstrate their understanding and be actively involved in the lesson. The teacher can also use this activity to assess quickly which students may need additional instruction or practice.

Using Opportunities to Respond

An important first step when using opportunity to respond is deciding on the lesson's content and instructional objective. Opportunity to respond is best used for practicing skills and reviewing facts, but it can be used with new material if students have the prerequisite skills. An example is when students read a new story but are asked to perform a familiar task such as identifying characters, setting, and plot. In this instance, opportunity to respond could be used for new information. Once the material is identified, the teacher develops a list of questions, prompts, or cues related to the content. The ideal rate is three opportunities to respond per minute (Sutherland & Wehby, 2001), so multiplying the number of minutes in the instructional period by three will give you an idea of how many prompts or questions to prepare. After choosing the content, the next step is to determine how to present it. Although verbal presentation may be the easiest, a visual presentation using a projector or document camera may be better, as it avoids issues with noise and the projection makes it is easier for students to see the prompts. However, if using opportunity to respond with a small group, then a verbal presentation may work fine. The response mode must also be decided in advance, whether it is text written on mini-whiteboards, preprinted cards, or a simple thumbs-up or -down. Before using opportunity to respond with students, a brief explanation of the procedures will avoid confusion and disruption. Students should be clear about the content to be covered, as well as both the presentation and response formats. They should also know that the pace will be rapid and their participation is required, but that incorrect responses are fine, as the point of the lesson it to learn the material, and the teacher will review the correct answers. One of the benefits of opportunity to respond is that is can reduce student anxiety about having to produce the right answer. Since everyone responds at the same time, individuals are not "put on the spot" if their answers are wrong. The lesson should move along quickly, as the goal is to offer three opportunities per minute to respond. Once the activity starts, the item is presented and students respond, the teacher provides corrective feedback before moving to the next item. Once a sufficient review has been conducted, the lesson ends.

Opportunities to Respond in Practice

Increasing students' opportunities to respond is another effective strategy for use from preschool to high school. Next, we illustrate two applications: the first in an early elementary school and the second is an upper elementary school setting.

Early Elementary School

There have been several studies examining the relation between student engagement and the use of opportunity to respond. One recent study (MacSuga-Gage, & Gage, 2015) took place in an elementary school where five teachers, in first through third grades, took part in a professional development opportunity to respond, then used the strategy during reading instruction. The training session was designed to be as efficient as possible. The researchers provided a 1-hour presentation that reviewed how to increase opportunities to respond, self-monitor use of opportunities to respond with a golf counter, and how to enter that data into a spreadsheet set up to automatically graph the information. This gave teachers a visual of their performance. During the training, teachers learned the definition of opportunity to respond, were given examples of it, and were told the optimal number of opportunities to respond was three per minute. Researchers then had teachers practice opportunities to respond while they observed.

After the training, teachers began using and monitoring their use of opportunity to respond during phonics or spelling instruction. As they collected data on their use, they entered and reviewed their progress. The researchers assessed each teacher's per-minute rate by reviewing video recordings of each session. Twenty-one days of video were recorded, and after the first 5 days of intervention, each teacher's opportunity to respond rate was assessed. One teacher who was below the target rate of three opportunities to respond per minute received additional professional development until she raised her rate to the criterion.

To determine the effectiveness of opportunities to respond, researchers tracked the level of disruptive behavior, engagement, and improvement in oral reading fluency (ORF) for six target students in each class, as well as each teacher's rate of opportunity to respond. Using the Student Risk Screening Scale (SRSS; Drummond, 1994), teachers identified three students who were considered to be at low risk and three students at either moderate or high risk for problem behavior.

By the end of the intervention, there was a clear relation between teachers' use of opportunity to respond and the outcome measures of disruption and engagement. As the rate of opportunities to respond increased, so did engagement, while the rate of disruptive behavior decreased. This effect occurred regardless of risk status, indicating that opportunity to respond worked for all students, a very positive finding. There was, however, no increase in students' ORF. The researchers hypothesized that, on its own, opportunity to respond may not be powerful enough to affect ORF, but it is clearly an effective tool as part of a repertoire of strategies for promoting high levels of student engagement.

Upper Elementary School

This example of opportunity to respond, which took place in a fifth-grade science class, was designed to see whether it would improve the behavior of a girl, Bree, who had chronic and very disruptive behavior, including fighting (Haydon, Mancil, & Van Loan, 2009). She scored at risk on the SSBD (Walker & Severson, 1992), although academically she was at grade level. The researchers met with Bree's teacher, Mr. Smith, a first-year teacher, and provided a 30-minute training for him that included understanding the definition and purpose of opportunity to respond, and practice with delivering opportunities to respond at a rate of three questions per minute.

Prior to the start of the intervention (baseline condition), the researchers observed Mr. Smith and measured Bree's disruptive and on-task behavior, the number of times she offered a correct response, and Mr. Smith's rate of opportunities to respond, which was approximately one per minute.

Mr. Smith began using choral responding for reviewing science definitions instead of the traditional question-and-answer format he had been using (i.e., posing a question, then calling on one student at a time). He increased his rate of opportunities to respond to three per minute. As a result, Bree's performance during the class period improved significantly. The median percentage for on-task behavior increased from 34 to 67% (almost double from the baseline condition); the median rate of disruptive behavior decreased to 0.25 per minute from 1.9, and correct responses increased to 0.90 per minute compared to 0.025 at baseline. Changing the questioning technique to opportunities to respond had a strongly positive impact on Bree's behavior and engagement, as well as her ability to review the science terms accurately.

Summary

As both of the examples illustrate, opportunity to respond can greatly increase active participation and students' engagement in a lesson, with very little advanced training. Compared to typical instruction, students have several chances to offer an answer and receive immediate feedback, which automatically promotes their engagement. Answering a teacher's questions during a lesson can feel like high stakes for students, but opportunity to respond reduces that pressure, as the entire class is replying at the same time. However, the teacher can still see how individual students are performing and provide the whole class with corrective feedback. It does take time to prepare content for an opportunity to respond presentation, but increasing all students' participation in a lesson is a great return on that investment. Similarly, offering instructional choices can also provide a feasible approach for increasing engagement.

Instructional Choice

Being able to make choices is an important contributor to a student's sense of autonomy and freedom. Schools are typically environments that offer little in the way of independence, sometimes with good reason, for students' safety, or because of other aspects of schooling such as the pressures of covering a designated curriculum. However, teachers can easily incorporate more choice into the school day, and it turns out offering even minimal choices positively impacts students' behavior. Jolivette, Stichter, and McCormick (2002) define instructional choice as follows: "Opportunities to make choices means that the student is provided with two or more options, is allowed to independently select an option, and is provided with the selected option" (p. 28). Choice may include (1) which assignment to tackle first; (2) the presentation mode (book report or PowerPoint presentation); (3) materials used to complete an assignment, crayons or markers; or (4) working independently or alone.

Using Instructional Choice

Teachers begin by deciding which types of choice they will feel most comfortable offering. Classroom management is affected by how and when choice is offered, so teachers must feel confident about managing choice options in the classroom. For example, some teachers let students choose where they do their independent reading: at their desk, in the book corner, or at an activity table. Others may want students to remain at their desk while they read but give students the choice of how they summarize what they have read: an illustration, a paragraph, or a graphic organizer. Once the teacher decides when and where to offer choice, he or she can develop a menu of choices such as those mentioned earlier: different materials, order of completion, and so forth. The next step is to incorporate the options into the lesson and offer the available choices to students. Classroom management issues can be addressed by planning in advance the materials or arrangements that will be needed. After students have been offered a choice, teachers must provide wait time because students need sufficient time to make their selection. Some choices can be made quickly, such as choice of materials, whereas others require more time for thought, such as how to present material about a topic. Plan how to deal with situations such as students changing their mind about their choice and how to document choices. Depending on the activity, the teacher may need to approve the choice and do some record keeping to track the chosen option. Last, communicating clearly to students that they can proceed with their choice will reduce misunderstandings.

Instructional Choice in Practice

Instructional choice is an efficient strategy, easily incorporated to daily routines from pre-school through high school. Next, we illustrate applications in two middle school settings.

Middle School Special Day Class

One fascinating study looked at whether choice would improve the ORF of two seventh graders with behavioral disorders, Tina and Jacob, who attended a special day class in a public school (Daly, Garbacz, Olson, Persampieri, & Ni, 2006). The choice students could make was whether to receive 10 minutes of reading instruction before reading a text passage aloud for 30 seconds. Students could earn points if they read the passage with two or fewer errors. Points could be turned in for items such as chocolates and mints, pens, and barrettes. In addition to instruction, students could choose the type of instruction they preferred from the following options: modeling, practice, error correction, or performance feedback. Perhaps surprisingly, both students mostly opted for instruction each time they were offered the opportunity. Tina chose not to be instructed the first time, but then chose practice (71%) and error correction (29%) the other 11 times. Jacob chose instruction all 12 times and selected practice (77%), error correction (12%), and modeling (11%). As a result, both students increased their ORF rate. It might be argued earning points was so motivating it influenced students to choose instruction, but it also indicates students believed the feedback was valuable and would enhance their performance. What is more unusual is the study focused on two students whose disability (behavioral disorders) made it less likely they would cooperate or be able to sustain attention. While the sample was small, with only two students, it is rewarding to see students themselves believe teacher feedback is valuable.

Inclusive Middle School Setting

Another study on the use of choice looked at whether choice could improve both engagement and academic performance for students with emotional and behavioral disorders who were included in general education classes. The intervention took place during language arts instruction, in which the teacher provided lessons on vocabulary development. Each day, Monday through Thursday, students took out their vocabulary workbook at their teacher's direction. They followed along with a taped song created for that day's vocabulary assignment. Then the teacher passed out the daily assignment to all students, who were given 7 minutes to complete the assignment. After 7 minutes, the teacher collected all assignments. In the no-choice condition, students were given one of four assignments each day: (1) cloze sentences and multiple-choice items, (2) sentence writing, (3) fill in the blanks and yes–no items, and (4) word maps. By the end of the week, they had completed all four assignments.

In the choice condition, students were given all four assignments as a stapled packet on Monday. Each day, they could choose which of the four they wanted to work on, but all assignments had to be completed by the end of the week. While all 25 students in the class participated in both the no-choice and choice conditions, five students were observed for academic engagement, academic scores, and time to complete the assignment. Of the five, four showed improvement on all measures. Simply allowing students to decide the order in which they completed required assignments improved their engagement and increased their scores, while reducing the time to complete the task. On a measure of social validity, both students and teacher were positive about the intervention.

Summary

Instructional choice is an antecedent-based strategy that improves engagement and reduces disruptive behavior (Ramsey, Jolivette, Patterson, & Kennedy, 2010). Choice increases students' sense of autonomy by giving them some control over their educational experiences (Jolivette, Wehby, Canale, & Massey, 2001). Although it requires reflection and advance planning, once choice is integrated into lesson planning, it is relatively easy to use. One of the many benefits of using instructional choice is that it can be used as an extra support for some students while enhancing the experience of all students in the class. Another strategy easily woven into daily practice is instructional feedback.

Instructional Feedback

A critical part of instruction is having students practice newly learned material so they develop fluency with the skills and/or concepts and can use them independently. After initial lessons on new material, instructional feedback is used to inform students about their performance by confirming understandings, clearing up confusion, and restructuring schemas (Butler & Winne, 1995). When used consistently, instructional feedback is a proactive, dynamic mode of instruction because the teacher's feedback is immediate, specific, and focused on the lesson's objectives.

Using Instructional Feedback

The first steps for using instructional feedback include regular lesson planning and instructional delivery. The teacher must have a clear understanding of the lesson objective and how he or she expects students to demonstrate their understanding of it. Then the lesson is developed and taught. Teachers may choose from a variety of instructional designs, including direct instruction, problem-based learning, or cooperative learning, but regardless of the lesson design, it should be structured so the teacher is confident students can acquire the concepts. Checking for understanding at the end of the lesson (or series of lessons) is necessary to be sure students have mastered the basic skills and/or concepts. It is at this point students begin practice. Practice opportunities are essential for becoming proficient in the knowledge, skills, or behaviors that are the lesson's objective. In fact, multiple opportunities for practice are needed for almost all types of learning, whether it is academic or behavioral. The type of practice a teacher plans for is crucial in determining whether students actually learn the new content, and the instructional feedback provided during practice refines and enhances that learning.

As the teacher observes a student practicing content or skills, he or she offers information on performance by either confirming its accuracy or offering error correction. Whereas some activities make it easy to provide feedback, others are more nuanced. For example, if a student is practicing multiplication facts, the teacher can scan a worksheet or listen to a verbal recitation and indicate whether the answers are correct or incorrect. A task such as solving a word problem accurately may take more time. The teacher needs to listen to the student's thinking to understand where an error occurred, and feedback will probably be more extensive. Two characteristics of instructional feedback are important to keep in mind. One is that feedback is offered during practice. This means practice sessions have to be scheduled when the teacher can work with students in the classroom. The second is that feedback is individualized. A general comment to the whole class is always helpful, but the most effective feedback is personalized, based on the teacher's observation of an individual's specific performance.

Observations made during practice allow a teacher to gather valuable information about how well students have mastered the content and whether additional instruction, reteaching, or practice is needed. Although teachers often feel pressure to move through the curriculum, it is essential students have time to respond to the instructional feedback that has been provided. The best teaching offers students a feedback loop in which they can apply the feedback and the teacher checks to see whether their understanding has increased (Hattie & Timperley, 2007; Sadler, 1989).

Instructional Feedback in Practice

Instructional feedback is an effective, feasible strategy. This strategy can be used in inclusive and restrictive settings, with a range of content areas. Next, we illustrate two applications: the first in an elementary school in the primary grades and the second in a residential school.

Primary Grades

Researchers looked at the use of two types of instructional feedback when solving math equivalence problems. They examined how outcome feedback, focused on the accuracy of the learner's *response,* and strategy feedback, focused on the *process* the learner uses when tackling a math problem, impacted students' problem-solving ability. A group of 87 second and third graders used *exploratory problem solving,* a form of discovery learning in which students have the opportunity to solve problems before receiving instruction on the topic. The idea is that the exploration will result in a deeper understanding of the concepts. In this study, there were three conditions: (1) exploratory problem solving with outcome feedback, (2) exploratory problem solving with strategy feedback, and (3) exploratory problem solving with no feedback.

Each child attended a one-to-one, 45-minute tutoring session in one of the three conditions. All worked on 12 mathematical equivalence problems using exploratory problem solving. An example of outcome feedback: "Good job! You got the right answer—X is the correct answer"; "Good try, but you did not get the right answer—X is the correct answer." An example of strategy feedback: "Good job! That is one correct way to solve that problem"; "Good try, but that is not a correct way to solve the problem" (Fyfe, Rittle-Johnson, & DeCaro, 2012, p. 1097). The students were presented with the feedback both verbally and projected on a screen (the problems to be solved were also presented on a screen). Students in the no-feedback condition were not given any feedback and were asked to move to the next problem. All students were assessed using a pre- and posttest measure to determine which condition had an effect on performance.

Results indicated it did not matter which type of instructional feedback was used, and either type of feedback had a positive impact on students with low prior knowledge, but not for those who already had moderate knowledge of the topic. This indicates the need to think about how feedback accompanies different types of instruction, and for whom. In a discovery model of learning, in which students explore concepts before formal instruction, those who lack prior knowledge benefit from the feedback, but other students may not. The next study shows how instructional feedback had a significant positive impact when the authors used direct instruction to improve students' writing.

Residential School

A study conducted in a residential school for students with emotional and behavioral disorders illustrates how instructional feedback improved the writing performance of students with behavioral issues and mood disorders (McKeown, Kimball, & Ledford, 2015). The goal of the intervention was to provide students with individualized audio feedback that would improve their ability to write and revise independently, as well as produce higher quality written products. Using an audio recording meant students could listen to and access the feedback as many times as needed.

One teacher administered the intervention in her classroom with six students. The teacher attended 10 hours of one-on-one professional development to learn how to use self-regulated strategy development (SRSD; developed by Karen Harris) model of writing instruction and the audio technology, teach revision using SRSD, and provide genre-based feedback. She also learned how to assess student writing, so that her results would be consistent and focus on the targeted elements.

The intervention involved teaching students how to use SRSD to produce a written text; then, after producing the text, teaching students how to use the personalized audio feedback to revise it. The teacher read through each student's essay, guided by a revising checklist. She first took notes, then produced an audio recording based on the notes. The recording included suggestions students could make for each element listed on the checklist. Students were taught to use the pause button to stop the audio recording while they made changes to their draft and consulted the checklist. They could listen to the recording as many times as they wanted. The teacher modeled how to revise using the checklist and audio feedback before students tried it independently.

Not only did the intervention result in essays that were longer and of better quality, but students learned revising skills that would help them with future assignments. One of the best outcomes was that students reported enjoying writing, whereas before they had felt they were not good at it and disliked having to write.

Summary

Without feedback, it is hard to improve one's performance or skills level in any endeavor—from the classroom to the CrossFit Box. After students have been introduced to new material, it is essential they have adequate opportunities for practice and receive feedback on how well they have mastered the skill or topic. Instructional feedback routinely built into practice sessions provides a structure students can anticipate and rely on for receiving information to help them correctly execute newly learned skills and content. In addition, monitoring student performance through direct observation allows the teacher to collect formative assessment data that enhances planning for future instruction. Providing prompt feedback during the practice time increases the likelihood that students will not adopt misconceptions and will learn new material more quickly. Another strategy that can support a positive trajectory for student behavior is the use of high probability requests.

High-Probability Requests

High-probability (high-p) requests are a form of behavioral momentum (Nevin, Mandell, & Atak, 1983). The idea is that by starting with tasks or activities a student finds easy to comply with, paired with reinforcement, it is more likely the student will complete harder or less desirable tasks. The teacher begins by requesting behaviors with which a student will comply, providing reinforcement for appropriate responding, then making a low-probability (low-p) request close to the previous reinforcement. A student's compliance with the high-p requests increases compliance with the low-p request (Mace et al., 1988). Initially, this strategy was used with young children (Davis, Brady, Williams, & Hamilton, 1992) in clinics or special education settings but more recently, it has been used in general education settings to improve task completion, increase the use of social skills, and decrease the amount of time needed for transition between activities (Banda & Kubina, 2006; Lee, Belfiore, Scheeler, Hua, & Smith, 2004; Lee & Laspe, 2003; Wehby & Hollahan, 2000).

Using High-Probability Requests

First, a teacher must determine the target behavior he or she wants to improve. For example, a common issue with children who are noncompliant is starting an assignment. Once the target behavior has been identified (e.g., beginning a math worksheet), a list of high-p behaviors that are topographically similar is created. In a math example, the low-p behavior might be subtraction problems with regrouping, while a topographically high-p behavior might be subtraction *without* regrouping. To be sure the high-p behavior is identified accurately, it should be tested by seeing whether the student complies with the high-p request more than 80% of the time. If this is not the case, it is a low-p request and will not provide the behavioral momentum necessary. After a high-p request is identified, three to five high-p requests should be delivered followed by one low-p request. If possible, behavior-specific praise should be offered right after the high-p requests have been completed. In the case of the math worksheet, the teacher would create a series of problems using the pattern of three to five subtraction without regrouping problems followed by one subtraction with regrouping problem and work with the student while he or she finished the first three, then offer behavior-specific praise. When the entire worksheet is completed, the teacher should offer behavior-specific praise for completion, such as "I noticed you finished all the problems on your math worksheet today. That was good work." Even if the student did not finish all problems but tackled them diligently, behavior-specific praise can be offered for compliance: "You attempted to solve all the problems on your math worksheet. Thank you for working so hard."

High-Probability Requests in Practice

In these final two illustrations, we highlight the feasibility and effectiveness of this easy-to-use strategy. We offer two illustrations: one in an upper elementary setting, and the other in an alternative education setting.

Upper Elementary School

Wehby and Hollahan (2000) described how the high-*p* strategy helped a student begin and complete math assignments. Meg, a 13-year-old with learning disabilities in general education, had difficulty with starting and finishing assignments. The teacher and researchers identified high-*p* requests for Meg that included "Take out a paper," "Put your name on the paper," and "Take out a pencil," among others. In the intervention, the teacher gave directions to the entire class about starting the assignment, then walked to Meg's desk to deliver a high-*p* request and praise her if she completed it within 10 seconds. If Meg did not complete the high-*p* request, the teacher would offer another one until she complied. Once she complied with three consecutive requests, the teacher would deliver the low-*p* request, which was "Begin independent seatwork." Before the intervention, it took Meg an average of 11 minutes to begin an assignment. This was reduced to less than 1 minute with use of the high-*p* strategy. It also increased the amount of time Meg spent working on the assignment, although there was more variability in this outcome.

Alternative School Setting

One of the first studies to examine the use of the high-*p* strategy also addressed engagement with a math assignment, but it took place at an alternative school (Belfiore, Lee, Vargas, & Skinner, 1997). The intervention was conducted with two students, Allison (age 14) and Robert (age 15), who had been expelled from school for noncompliant behavior (e.g., failure to complete schoolwork and follow rules). The goal of the intervention was to decrease the amount of time it took students to begin their math assignments. In this case, the high-*p* requests were math problems, not a verbal directive. Packets that were created contained three high-*p* cards, each with a single-digit multiplication problem, followed by five low-*p* cards, which had multiple-digit multiplication problems. This simple switch to mixed difficulty problems rather than an assignment of only multiple-digit multiplication resulted in better performance for Allison and Robert. They both decreased the amount of time it took to begin their math assignments and reduced their noncompliant behavior.

Summary

The high-p request is a useful tool for working with students who are noncompliant. It reduces confrontation and helps students perceive a task or direction to be less onerous than they may have thought. High-p requests are another relatively simple technique that improves performance on both behavioral and academic tasks. Having a variety of strategies readily available that focus on the positive is an important step in establishing a classroom praxis that honors a proactive approach to classroom management and dealing with behavioral issues. The most successful teacher is the one who can adjust the environment to minimize or ameliorate behavioral challenges, so students spend the majority of their time actively engaged in productive work.

Summary

We have worked with several talented district and school-site leaders who have done a stellar job of developing primary (Tier 1) prevention plans that feature several—if not all—of these strategies (see Lessons Learned 6.2). Many have shared their successes with empowering general and special education teachers to use these strategies at Tier 1 (e.g., Lessons Learned 6.3), as well as featuring these strategies as a dedicated Tier 2 support in which the strategy is applied with greater intensity for students needing additional assistance.

In this chapter, we have featured research-based, low-intensity supports to increase engagement and decrease disruption. First, we discussed practical methods for using data to inform decision making about how and when to refine the use of low-intensity, teacher-delivered supports. Second, we introduced six low-intensity, teacher-delivered strategies for

---

LESSONS LEARNED 6.2. Success of Low-Intensity Supports

I wholeheartedly believe in our school's Ci3T plan. As a building, we have been able to implement the low-intensity strategies, and the behavior of our students has greatly improved. By using the three components of Ci3T (behavioral, academic, and social), we are able to teach and meet the needs of each student individually.

LeAnn Deters
Elementary Interventionist/Ci3T District Trainer

LESSONS LEARNED 6.3. Low-Intensity Supports—Day to Day

Utilizing Ci3T and low-intensity strategies is a way of life in my classroom. Finding small ways to offer my most challenging students' choice and safe ways to respond has decreased disruptive behaviors in my classroom and increased positive relationships and student accountability by creating small, positive choices to celebrate, and celebrating feels great.

Laura Leonard
Middle School Secondary Language Arts Teacher

use with Tiers 1, 2, and 3. In Chapter 7, we build on the content in Chapters 5 and 6 to provide additional information on how to (1) monitor how the school as a whole is responding to the schoolwide plan, (2) determine how different types of students responded, and (3) identify students who require additional supports in the form of secondary (Tier 2) and tertiary (Tier 3) intervention efforts. In Chapter 7, we provide several illustrations of how to use schoolwide data to determine which students may benefit from secondary supports. We also discuss a range of supports (academic, social, and behavioral) that include options typically available at schools, as well as other research-based programs.

Supporting Students Who Require More Than Primary Prevention Efforts

TIER 2 AND TIER 3

In Chapter 5, we reviewed the importance of collecting and analyzing schoolwide data as a means of (1) monitoring how the school as a whole is responding to the schoolwide plan, (2) determining how different types of students respond, and (3) identifying students who require additional supports in the form of secondary and tertiary interventions. In Chapter 6, we discussed practical methods for using data to inform decision making. We introduced several research-based, low-intensity supports teachers can use to increase engagement and decrease disruption as they weave these strategies into the fabric of daily instruction. These strategies can be used at Tier 1 as well as with greater intensity at Tier 2. They can also be used as components of rigorous Tier 3 supports (e.g., functional assessment-based interventions [FABIs]).

In this chapter, we continue the conversation by providing additional information on how to move forward with data-informed decision-making efforts across the tiers, offering several detailed illustrations of how to use schoolwide data to identify preschool, elementary, middle, and high school students in need of secondary supports. We also discuss a range of supports (academic, social, and behavioral) that includes options typically available at schools, as well as other research-based programs.

Examining the Schoolwide Data

As we discussed in Chapter 5, collecting data that address the purpose statement or main goals of the primary (Tier 1) prevention plan is essential if you want to know whether your schoolwide Ci3T plan is working. If the goals are to improve students' grades or reading skills, decrease office discipline referrals (ODRs) and instances of bullying, or improve attendance, then the team must monitor student progress on each of these variables (See Lessons Learned 7.1). For example, Contra Costa High School's assessment schedule (see Figure 5.3 in Chapter 5) shows us the types of information the team is monitoring. During the planning process (see Chapter 3), the Ci3T Leadership Team identified three main objectives to operationalize the school's purpose statement:

1. Decreased problem behaviors as measured by ODRs and SRSS-IE risk scores (a goal 80% of students with low risk; a reduction in ODRs by 20%) (Drummond, 1994; Lane & Menzies, 2009).
2. Improved attendance, as measured by unexcused tardies and absences (a goal of 95% of students with fewer than seven absences).
3. Improved academic outcomes as measured by GPA (goal increase students with 2.5 or higher by 10%).

Collecting and monitoring this information for each student in the school offers the team a clear picture of how the school as a whole is responding. Many schools already collect large amounts of information, such as daily attendance, ODRs, curriculum-based measures (CBM) of academic performance (e.g., reading, writing, and math skills), standardized state and district assessments, and, in some cases, behavioral screeners. Yet questions arise as to how well (or whether) these data are used to inform instructional decision making and subsequently support students who need assistance. In our work, teachers have expressed concern that they are asked to conduct a plethora of assessments, but the information is rarely used and the results are not shared. When information is collected but not analyzed and used, it can be a source of frustration both to teachers and to those who are asked to complete the assessments. Therefore, practitioners and researchers alike must *use* the information they collect and *share it* in a timely and meaningful way with the parties involved. This can be done with brief reports that include clear graphics displaying trends in the collected data.

Consider Contra Costa High School's first goal to decrease problem behaviors as measured by ODRs and the SRSS-IE. Figure 7.1 presents one method of sharing data with faculty, which shows the estimated rate of ODRs per instructional day during the beginning of the

---

LESSONS LEARNED 7.1. Improved Student Performance

Our high school implemented the Ci3T framework and immediately saw positive change. The opportunity and structure to purposefully plan supports and interventions around academic, behavioral, and social–emotional needs are powerful in improving outcomes for students. Teachers found success in being more purposeful in action and content; students' behavior referrals declined while their passing grades improved. The work in creating and implementing the plan creates more and more positive outcomes. As students are more successful and teachers, counselors, and administrators move from being reactive to proactive, there is more time to build positive interventions and improve practice, leading to even more successful outcomes.

Alan Penrose
High School Principal

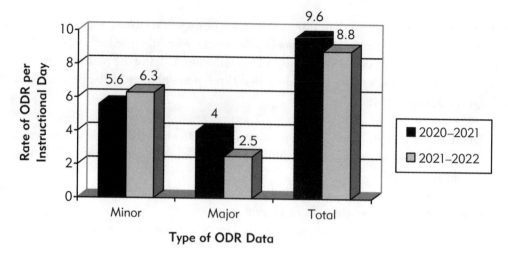

FIGURE 7.1. ODR data across school years for Contra Costa High School: Quarter 1 of 2020 to Quarter 1 of 2021.

first year of implementation (Quarter 1 of 2020) compared to the beginning of the second year of implementation (Quarter 1 of 2021). In this graph, you can see that when looking at combined ODRs (for both minor and major infractions; the two bars on the right-hand side of the graph), the rate of ODRs during Quarter 1 has declined over this time frame. However, closer inspection of the data shows that although the rate of major offenses has decreased, the rate of minor offenses has increased. This information could be shared to help inform practices. For example, the Ci3T Leadership Team might recommend that teachers adjust the rate of reinforcement (in terms of PBIS tickets paired with behavior-specific praise) by acknowledging students who are meeting the schoolwide expectations more frequently. Had the Ci3T Leadership Team not looked at both major and minor infractions, they would not have become aware of this increasing trend in minor infractions.

Figure 7.2 presents a graphic of SRSS-IE estimated Fall results over the first 4 years of implementation. Panel A illustrates SRSS-E (seven externalizing items) data, and Panel B illustrates SRSS-I (six internalizing items) data. In Panel A, the lower portion of each bar contains the percentage of students scoring in the low-risk category (0–3) for externalizing behaviors, the middle portion of each bar contains the percentage of students scoring in the moderate-risk category (4–8), and the upper portion of each bar contains the percentage of students scoring in the high-risk category (9–21). In looking at the low-risk category over time, the percentage of students in the low-risk category has increased steadily over the past 4 years. For example, in the Fall of 2020, 72% of students placed in the low-risk category, 77% in the Fall of 2021, 84% in the Fall of 2022, and 86% in the Fall of 2023. The percentage of students in the moderate-risk category has declined from 21% in the Fall of 2020 to 11% in the Fall of 2023. Furthermore, the percentage of students in the high-risk category has also declined, from 7% in the Fall of 2020 to 3% in the Fall of 2023. In Panel B, a similar pattern is seen for internalizing behaviors. The lower portion of each bar contains the percentage of students scoring in the low-risk category (0–3) for internalizing behaviors, the middle portion of each bar contains the

Panel A. SRSS-E7

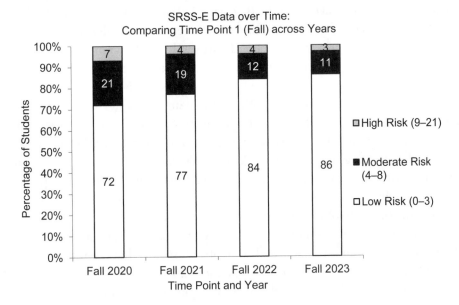

Panel B. SRSS-I6

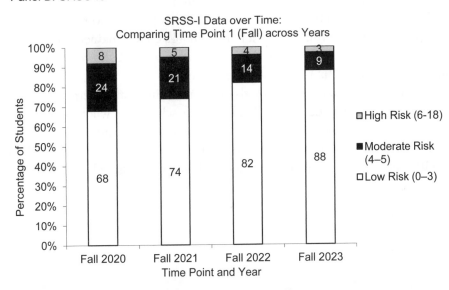

FIGURE 7.2. Contra Costa High School Graph—SRSS-IE Data. Panel A: SRSS-E7; Panel B: SRSS-I6.

percentage of students scoring in the moderate-risk category (4–5), and the upper portion of each bar contains the percentage of students scoring in the high-risk category (6–18). Overall, SRSS-IE data suggest that risk for externalizing and internalizing behaviors has declined over the past 4 years at Contra Costa High School. However, be certain *not* to draw causal conclusions that the primary (Tier 1) prevention plan caused these changes because an experimental design was not used. But you *can* say that results of the descriptive analyses suggest a decline in the percentage of students at risk for both externalizing and internalizing behaviors since introducing Ci3T. It is also important to note the scores used to form categories of risk status differ between externalizing and internalizing scores, and there are different cut scores and procedures for determining internalizing risk at the elementary level as well. For any screening tool, it is important to provide professional learning to ensure teachers compute and interpret scores accurately.

Contra Costa High School's second goal was to improve attendance, as measured by unexcused tardies and unexcused absences. Figure 7.3, which presents one method of sharing this information with faculty, staff, parents, and students, illustrates that the rate of unexcused tardies decreased, from a rate of 67 per day in November 2020 to a rate of 43 per day in November 2021. Also, unexcused absences declined, from a rate of 40 per day to a rate of 30 per day during this same period of time.

Contra Costa High School's third goal was to improve academic performance, as measured by GPA. Figure 7.4 is a bar graph of the student body's GPA over the course of the first 3 years of implementation. In this illustration, the school's GPA remained relatively stable during the first 2 academic years. However, the school's average GPA showed an increasing trend during the 2022–2023 and 2023–2024 academic years.

These illustrations are but a few methods of summarizing data. There are numerous other comparisons that could be made to examine how your school as a whole is responding to the plan (e.g., see Lessons Learned 7.2). For example, you could examine ODR data in different settings, compare SRSS-IE data from Fall and Winter time points, and compare Quarter 1 and Quarter 2 GPA data. Just remember to stay focused on your goals, collect the necessary data,

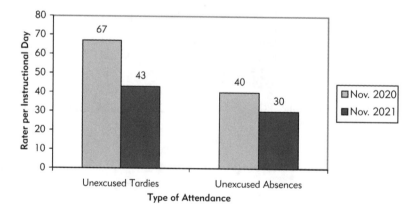

FIGURE 7.3. Unexcused tardies and absences data across school years for Contra Costa High School Graph: November 2020 to November 2021.

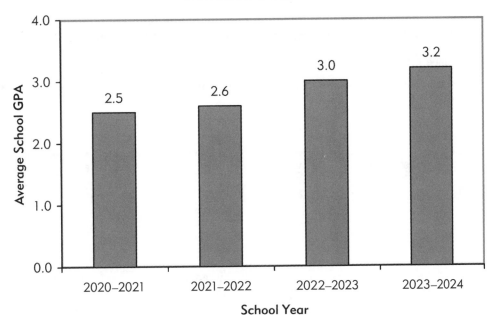

FIGURE 7.4. GPA data for Contra Costa High School.

then share findings with all consumers in a meaningful, easy-to-understand way that does not overstate or understate the case.

Interpreting your data so that you know how well your schoolwide Ci3T plan is working provides very useful information, but another important objective is to understand how different types of students are responding to your Ci3T primary (Tier 1) prevention program (e.g., Lane & Menzies, 2005; Lane, Wehby, et al., 2007). For example, it is highly likely that not all students will respond the same way to Tier 1 efforts; it may be that students with externalizing (e.g., aggression, noncompliance), internalizing (e.g., anxiety, depression), or comorbid behavior patterns respond differently to primary prevention efforts (Lane, Kalberg, Bruhn, et al., 2008; Lane, Wehby, Robertson, & Rogers, 2007). Therefore, looking closely at how different groups of students respond offers information about how to work more effectively with them.

Determining How Different Students Respond

Only a handful of studies has examined how different types of students, such as those at risk for behavioral difficulties, those with typical behavior patterns, and those with high-incidence disabilities, have responded to schoolwide Ci3T primary (Tier 1) prevention plan. Furthermore, most of these investigations have been conducted at the elementary level (e.g., Cheney, Blum, & Walker, 2004; Lane, Kalberg, et al., 2011; Lane & Menzies, 2005; Walker, Cheney, Stage, Blum, & Horner, 2005), leaving us with limited information about middle and high school settings. In this section, we briefly review a few of our studies to illustrate how different types of students in elementary and high school settings respond to primary prevention efforts.

LESSONS LEARNED 7.2. Success in Summarizing Screening Data

Bill and Kathleen,

Here are our 3-year trend dates. I pulled this document together today. Looks like we are making some gains.

Matt

Fall- SRSSIE-I	Low	Moderate	High		Fall- SRSSIE-E	Low	Moderate	High
2016	80.28%	10.36%	9.36%		2016	89.56%	8.02%	2.42%
2017	90.18%	4.16%	5.66%		2017	91.29%	6.18%	2.54%
2018	90.91%	3.86%	5.23%		2018	92.22%	6.20%	1.58%

WTR-SRSSIE-I	Low	Moderate	High		WTR-SRSSIE-E	Low	Moderate	High
2016	87.25%	9.49%	3.26%		2016	87.25%	9.49%	3.26%
2017	86.14%	9.02%	4.85%		2017	86.14%	9.02%	4.85%
2018	88.79%	8.52%	2.69%		2018	88.79%	8.52%	2.69%

Couldn't resist looking at this one more time . . . REALLY great to see!
Rest easy, gentlemen!

Take care,
Kathleen

Thank you for the kind words. A math teacher on our team pointed out that we had enough years to establish trend data. Bill and I pulled it together and we were a little surprised at the story the data told. We hope that the data can be used to convince other high schools to participate in Ci3T.

Matt

How Students Respond at the Elementary School Level

Lane and Menzies (2005) examined the degree to which elementary-age students with and without academic and behavioral problems ($n = 86$) responded to a multi-tiered intervention program. Teachers nominated up to three students from their classrooms in each of four categories: academic concerns only, behavioral concerns only, academic and behavioral concerns, and typical performance. Nomination procedures followed a modified version of Walker and Severson's (1992) Systematic Screening for Behavior Disorders (SSBD), with a goal of identifying students with early literacy and/or behavioral concerns.

Analysis of student outcome data suggested that the program was not equally effective for all types of students; there were differences in how students responded. For example, in terms of reading, students in the academic and behavioral concerns group made significantly more progress on the reading measures than did students in the typical performance group. So students who were at risk benefited more from the academic reading intervention than did those who were not at risk. In terms of behavioral performance, student risk scores (as measured by the SRSS) in the combined concerns group showed improvement. The combined group showed significant decreases in risk and improvement in written expression, despite the lack of a significant improvement in reading skills. In addition, students in the combined concerns group and those in the academic concerns group showed significant improvement in attendance as compared to students in the typical performance and behavioral concerns groups. Perhaps the combination of the literacy and behavioral components provided enough reinforcement and individualized focus to make school a less aversive place for students with academic concerns, with and without behavioral concerns, thereby promoting attendance (Lane & Menzies, 2005).

How Students Respond at the High School Level

Lane, Wehby, and colleagues (2007) conducted a similar study at the high school level to determine how high school students (*n* = 178) with externalizing, internalizing, comorbid, and typical behavior patterns, as well as students receiving special education services for high-incidence disabilities, responded to a Ci3T model that included academic, behavioral (PBIS), and social skills (Character Under Construction for one school) plan. In this study, English teachers from two high schools with SWPBS programs nominated one student from each class period for each of the following categories: externalizing, internalizing, comorbid (externalizing and internalizing), and typical, using a modified version of the SSBD (Walker & Severson, 1992).

Results suggested that while students in the externalizing, internalizing, and typical groups all showed improved GPA, decreased unexcused tardies, and decreased suspension, students with internalizing behaviors appeared to be the most responsive group. Findings also suggested that students in the comorbid group (with both externalizing and internalizing behaviors) were perhaps the least responsive. This is not surprising given that students with comorbid concerns are often highly resistant to intervention efforts (Gresham et al., 2000).

How Students Respond across K–12 Settings

Lane, Kalberg, and colleagues (2011) offered three illustrations across K–12 to explore how students with varying behavioral risk responded to their school's Ci3T model that included academic, behavioral (PBIS), and social skills components (Character Under Construction at the middle and high schools). Screening data were monitored over time to examine shifts in student risk.

At the elementary level, teachers monitored screening data for students (*n* = 482) in grades K–4 using the SSBD (Walker & Severson, 1992) and the SRSS (Drummond, 1994). Results suggested that risk decreased during the first semester of implementation, with fewer students identified as having increased risk for either externalizing or internalizing behaviors from Fall to Winter screening time points. This illustration shows how data were used to select students in need of more intensive supports. Specifically, in this study, two students who were rated in high-risk categories on both measures were supported with a Tier 3 FABI (Umbreit et al., 2007).

At the middle school level, teachers screened students ($n = 500$) in grades 6–8 using the Strengths and Difficulties Questionnaire (SDQ; Goodman, 1997). Results suggested improvements, as measured by two subscales of the SDQ; students' prosocial behavior improved from Fall of their first year of implementation to Fall 1 year later. They also observed fewer students identified as having increased risk for peer problems, although the decreases were not as dramatic. This illustration shows how data were used to select students in need of more intensive supports. Specifically, in this study, determination of secondary interventions was based on the specific subscale scores; for example, students identified with peer problems could participate in small-group social skills instruction targeting these skills.

At the high school level, teacher screened students ($n = 674$) in grades 9–12 using the SRSS (Drummond, 1997). Two teachers rated each student, one a teacher of a content-area class, who provided students with grades, and another who led a noninstructional course (e.g., study hall). Results suggested increases in the percentage of students in the low-risk category from Fall of Year 1 implementation to Fall of the next year. Improvements were observed for both teacher groups; however, teachers saw greater improvements during noninstructional periods even though their scores indicated that risk remained higher. Over the course of 1 year, about 81% of students demonstrated a stable risk status, 15% of students showed behavioral improvements, and about 4% showed worsening behavioral patterns according to the instructional raters. Similar patterns were observed for noninstructional raters; about 74% of students were stable, about 18% improved, and about 9% worsened.

Summary

These are just a few of the studies that examined how different types of students respond to Ci3T primary (Tier 1) prevention efforts. While replication is needed to see whether the differences noted earlier are consistent in other geographic areas and in programs implemented without university support, these initial findings suggest that not all students respond in the same way. Therefore, be sure to collect and analyze data to determine whether particular groups of students are responding differently to Ci3T primary (Tier 1) prevention efforts (e.g., Lane, Kalberg, Bruhn, et al., 2008). These same types of data can also be used to determine which students will require additional support in the form of targeted prevention efforts.

Identifying Students Who Need Targeted Supports

As discussed throughout this book, three-tiered models include secondary (Tier 2)- and tertiary (Tier 3)-level prevention efforts for students for whom primary prevention efforts alone are insufficient. Due to its intensive nature, tertiary (Tier 3) prevention efforts are reserved for students with multiple risk factors as well as those for whom secondary (Tier 2) prevention efforts are deemed to be insufficient (Horner & Sugai, 2015; Lane & Walker, 2015), for example, a middle or high school student reading well below grade level. Central to this model is data-informed decision making (Sugai & Horner, 2015). Rather than relying solely on teacher

LESSONS LEARNED 7.3. Stronger Intervention Groups

The Ci3T model has transformed the way we do business for kids at SWMS. One of the biggest benefits going through the implementation process was bringing everyone together to talk the same language for kids in the areas of academics, behavior, and social skills. The Ci3T process has created stronger intervention groups and has allowed us to analyze data in many different ways. One of my personal celebrations is that our staff members have stepped into many different leadership opportunities to improve our school.

Kristen Ryan
Middle School Principal

judgment, data collected to monitor Tier 1 implementation are also used to determine which students require secondary (Tier 2) and tertiary (Tier 3) intervention efforts (Lane, Oakes, Ennis, et al., 2014).

For Ci3T Leadership Teams to maximize the use of data to place students in appropriate interventions, they should develop two intervention grids (see Lessons Learned 7.3). One would contain all of the secondary (Tier 2) prevention efforts currently available at the school or in the community (for examples at the elementary and the middle and high school levels, see Boxes 7.1 and 7.2, respectively), and the other containing all of the tertiary (Tier 3) prevention interventions currently available at the school or in partnership with the community (see Boxes 7.3 and 7.4 for examples at the elementary, middle, and high school levels). As you will see in Boxes 7.1–7.4, each intervention grid contains five pieces of information. The first column identifies the type and name of the support (e.g., the Direct Behavior Rating [DBR; Chafouleas, 2013; Chafouleas, Riley-Tillman, & Christ, 2009]; see Box 7.1). This column does not include the name of a person (e.g., school social worker or school psychologist); rather it includes what the person does—the support he or she can offer. The second column contains a brief description of each intervention. The description includes information such as (1) the content of the intervention; (2) the treatment dosage (e.g., the number of days per week, the length of each intervention session) and context (e.g., in the classroom, in the cafeteria after school, in the conference room during Friday preferred activity time); and (3) the person responsible for conducting the intervention (e.g., guidance counselors, paraprofessionals, teachers). For example, in Box 7.1 the DBR is a secondary intervention that includes both teacher and parent support. Each day a student's teacher completes a DBR to provide immediate feedback about the student's academic engagement, respect, and disruption that day. The student takes the report home or the teacher emails it home for parents' review and signature.

The third column contains the entry criteria: the specific cutoff scores on schoolwide data used to place students in the targeted support groups. These data specify data profiles for students for whom the intervention may be appropriate. For example, elementary school students participate in the DBR intervention when they demonstrate either academic problems (e.g., a failing or near failing [C–] grade due to low work completion) and behavior problems (e.g., moderate-risk score on the SRSS-I7 and/or SRSS-I5).

(text resumes on page 179)

BOX 7.1. Secondary Intervention Grid: Elementary Level

Support	Description	Schoolwide Data: Entry Criteria	Data to Monitor Progress	Exit Criteria
Direct Behavior Rating (DBR; Chafouleas, Riley-Tillman, & Christ, 2009)	DBR implemented daily by teacher or other school staff (e.g., reading specialist, social worker) during daily observation periods (e.g., during English language arts). The completed DBR is shared with parents, who are asked to sign the form each day. DBR is used to monitor academic engagement, respect, and disruption. At the conclusion of each observation period, the teacher uses the provided scale to indicate the degree to which the student displayed each behavior. The teacher meets briefly with the student to share the teacher's DBR rating. Home–school communication procedures are established (e.g., student takes a paper copy or it is emailed to parent or caregiver each day). The DBR is then signed and returned to the teacher. If emailed, the parent/caregiver replies to the email.	**Academic** ☐ Failing or near failing (C–) grade due to low work completion **AND** **Behavior** ☐ SRSS-E7 score: Moderate (4–8) and/or ☐ SRSS-I5 score: Moderate (2–3) **AND** ☐ Evidence of teacher implementation of Ci3T primary (Tier 1) plan [treatment integrity: direct observation] **AND** ☐ Parent permission	**Student Measures** • DBR (daily) • Attendance and tardies • Weekly grades • Monitored by the teacher **Social Validity** • Teacher: IRP-15 • Student: CIRP • Completed pre–post • Collected by the school DBR intervention lead **Treatment Integrity** • DBR treatment integrity measure • Collected daily by the teacher and reviewed in collaboration with the school DBR intervention lead	☐ Student goals met for 10–12 weeks (team review of progress to determine) ☐ SRSS-E7 and I5 scores are in the low-risk category ☐ Passing grades
Behavior Education Program (BEP; Crone, Hawken, & Horner, 2010)	The student is assigned to a mentor for daily contact. The student meets with the mentor upon arrival to check in and pick up the Daily Progress Report (DPR). Then the teacher(s) complete the BEP for each class period. The teacher provides immediate feedback on the student's behavior by completing a DPR and is intentional about having additional positive interactions with the student. The student meets with the mentor at the end of the day to check out by reviewing the day's progress. Parents participate by signing off on daily sheets.	**Academic** ☐ Report cards: earned a "needs improvement" score on study skills or a C– or lower in any academic content area, or ☐ Below proficient on curriculum-based measures (CBMs) **OR** **Behavior** ☐ Systematic Screening for Behavior Disorders (SSBD) score exceeding normative criteria on externalizing, or internalizing behavior on Stage 2 rating scales **AND** ☐ Parent permission	**Student Measures** • Daily progress monitoring forms collected by teacher and viewed by parent • Progress in academic content area grades used as entry criteria • Three or more CBM progress monitoring data points at or above the trend line for meeting end of year expectations **Social Validity** • Mentor and Teacher(s): IRP-15 • Student: CIRP • Completed pre–post • Collected by the school BEP intervention lead **Treatment Integrity** • Completed BEP • Collected daily by the mentor and reviewed with teacher(s) and the weekly school BEP intervention	☐ Maintenance self-monitoring phase after the student meets their goals for 3 consecutive weeks ☐ Self-monitoring phase ends when the next screening benchmark results indicate the absence of risk following the same criteria stated in the inclusion criteria

176

Program	Description	Entry Criteria	Progress Monitoring / Social Validity / Treatment Integrity	Exit Criteria
Incredible Years (IY) Small Group Dinosaur Program	Small group instruction with the classroom teacher or other trained educator. This curriculum builds skills in anger management, school success, and interpersonal problem solving. Two hours of weekly small-group instruction for 18–22 weeks. Two-hour parenting group session. See Blueprints for Violence Prevention (*www.colorado.edu/cspv/index.html*) of What Works Clearinghouse (*https://ies.ed.gov/ncee/wwc/evidencesnapshot/590*) for further details.	☐ Students ages 4–8 **Behavior/Social Skills** ☐ Scored in the slightly raised risk range on the Social Skills Improvement System—Social–Emotional Learning Progress Monitoring Scales (Elliott & Gresham, 2017b) **OR** ☐ Two or more bullying referrals **OR** ☐ Three or more major ODRs **AND** ☐ Parent permission and participation	• Monthly progress monitoring using the SSiS-SEL **Social Validity** • Parent and Teacher(s): IRP-15 • Student: CIRP • Completed pre–post • Collected by the school IY intervention lead **Treatment Integrity** • Program-specific fidelity scale/checklist • Collected daily by the teacher and reviewed with the IY weekly intervention	☐ Completion of the program ☐ Monitor entry criteria after completion to ensure that desired shifts in performance are achieved and maintained
Self-Regulated Strategy Development (SRSD) for Writing (Harris, Graham, Mason, & Friedlander, 2008)	Explicit strategy instruction to improve writing. Students work one-on-one with a trained interventionist three times per week or 30 minutes (20–60 recommended). SRSD includes: develop background knowledge; discuss, model, and memorize the strategy; support the student in applying the strategy; and then students apply and adapt the strategy independently.	☐ Students in grades 2–5 **Academic** ☐ Below grade level on writing assessments; **OR** ☐ Earning a failing grade in writing or another content area due to difficulty with writing assignments ☐ Progress on early learning standards: Insufficient with Tier 1 and Tier 2 efforts **Behavior** ☐ Strengths and Difficulties Questionnaire scores of *high* or *very high* for Hyperactivity or Conduct Problems, or Total Difficulties	• Student measures • Progress monitoring with weekly writing probes scored for number of writing elements and a quality rubric • Attendance and tardies **Social Validity** • IRP-15 (pre–post; teacher and parent) • Student-completed survey (pre–post) **Treatment Integrity** • SRSD completion log • SRSD component checklist completed daily by interventionist • Second rater for 33% of probe scoring (interrater agreement 90% or higher)	☐ Meeting writing benchmark scores for 3 consecutive weeks ☐ Completion of lessons

Note. From *www.ci3t.org/fabi*. The examples are not intended to represent one school's completed intervention grid. To provide a variety of examples with different assessment tools, each row could be part of a different school's grid; that is, we are not recommending that schools use multiple screeners for entry criteria. We recommend that schools use the schoolwide measures they have adopted. See Blueprints for Violence Prevention (*www.colorado.edu/cspv/index.html*) and What Works Clearinghouse (*http://ies.ed.gov/ncee/wwc*) for overviews of additional model and promising programs. IRP-15, Intervention Rating Profile; CIRP, Child Intervention Rating Profile. We include an illustration for preschool (Incredible Years® Small Group Dinosaur Program) for elementary schools that also include preschool-age students and for preschool centers).

BOX 7.2. Secondary Intervention Grid: Middle and High School Level

Support	Description	Schoolwide Data: Entry Criteria	Data to Monitor Progress	Exit Criteria
Targeted Algebra II Study Hall	Direct, targeted instruction of Algebra II learning targets by math teachers. Time will be used to reteach concepts, provide one-on-one or small-group instruction and offer greater supports for students struggling to pass the graduation requirement course; 50 minutes per day until exit criteria are met.	☐ 11th or 12th graders ☐ Algebra II grade below a 75 at any point in the semester (checked weekly) ☐ Permission of fifth period teacher	• Algebra II classroom grades • Daily class average if grade is ≤ 75 **Treatment Integrity** • Daily checklist of the lessons covered • Student attendance **Social Validity** • Survey: Student (survey) • Algebra II pass rate	☐ Algebra II grade increases to above 75% for 2 consistent weeks.
Social Skills Group	Focuses on improving students' social skills. Connect With Kids lessons used as a starting point for consistent language across Tier 1 and 2. Two days a week, 45 minutes to address students' specific acquisition deficits; sessions conducted by school psychologist, counselor, or social worker, or as part of an elective course taught by the teacher	**Behavior** ☐ Three or more ODRs that reflect social problems, **OR** ☐ SRSS-E7 score: Moderate (4–8) ☐ SRSS-I6 score: Moderate (4–5) **AND/OR** ☐ Two or more tardies or absences per quarter	• Weekly number of ODRs • Weekly teacher completed social skills checklist • Daily class participation collected by the social skills teacher **Treatment Integrity** • Sessions offered, duration, and attendance at sessions (dosage) **Social Validity** • Teacher: IRP-15 (pre- and postintervention) • Student: CIRP (pre- and postintervention)	☐ SRSS-E7 score: Low (0–3) ☐ SRSS-I6 score: Low (0–3) ☐ No ODRs ☐ Fewer than two tardies or absences in a quarter
Behavior Education Program (BEP; Crone, Hawken, & Horner, 2010)	Students check in and out with a mentor each day to establish and review progress toward targeted goals. During check-in, students receive a daily progress report form that they take to each class for teacher feedback on their progress meeting the targeted schoolwide Ci3T model expectations.	**Behavior** ☐ SRSS-E7 score: Moderate (4–8) ☐ SRSS-I6 score: Moderate (4–5) **OR** ☐ SRSS-E7 score: High (9–21) ☐ SRSS-I6 score: High (6–18) **OR** ☐ Two or more ODRs in a 5-week period **OR** ☐ Two or more tardies or absences per quarter **AND/OR** **Academic** ☐ Progress report: one or more course failures	**Student Measures** • Daily progress reports • Weekly grades • Weekly ODRs **Treatment Integrity** • Coach or mentor completes a component checklist of all BEP steps and whether they were completed each day (percentage of completion computed) • Daily completion of the Daily Progress Report form **Social Validity** • Teacher: IRP-15 (pre- and postintervention) • Student: CIRP (pre- and postintervention)	☐ SRSS-E7 score: Low (0–3) ☐ SRSS-I6 score: Low (0–3) ☐ Passing grades in all classes (C or better) ☐ With a minimum of 8 weeks of data, if a student has made his or her BEP goal 90% of the time and there have not been any ODRs, consideration of ending the daily check-in/check-out is made with teachers, parents, and student.

Note. From *www.ci3t.org.* The examples are not intended to represent one school's completed intervention grid. In order to provide a variety of examples with different assessment tools, each row could be part of a different school's grid; that is, we are not recommending that schools use multiple screeners for entry criteria. We recommend that schools use the schoolwide measures they have adopted. See Blueprints for Violence Prevention (*www.colorado.edu/cspv/index.html*) and What Works Clearinghouse (*http://ies.ed.gov/ncee/wwc*) for overviews of additional model and promising programs. SRSS, Student Risk Screening Scale (Drummond, 1994); SRSS-IE, Student Risk Screening Scale for Internalizing and Externalizing (SRSS-IE; Drummond, 1994; Lane & Menzies, 2009); E7, Externalizing 7 items; I6, Internalizing 6 items (for middle and high school use); SSiS-SEL, Social Skills Improvement System—Social–Emotional Learning Progress Monitoring Scales (Elliott & Gresham, 2017b); IRP-15, Intervention Rating Profile; CIRP, Child Intervention Rating Profile.

The fourth column contains data monitoring procedures, such as the information that will be collected, by whom, and how often to determine whether the intervention is appropriate to make desired shifts in student performance. For example, the teacher examines the student's DBR, attendance/tardies, and weekly grades to monitor the degree to which the student's performance is improving. This column also includes information on how treatment integrity and social validity will be assessed, when, and by whom. As recommended previously, ideally, each tiered intervention has at least two faculty or staff leaders who maintain the most current training on an intervention. These leaders could then provide feedback to the teacher on the use of the intervention (e.g., reviewing treatment integrity data together) and coaching, if needed (e.g., role playing, providing clarifications, modeling).

The fifth column contains information regarding exit criteria—that is, the criteria and performance levels that must be met before the intervention is concluded. In other words, how will you determine when a student no longer needs the intervention? Once students participating in the DBR have met their designated goals for 10–12 consecutive weeks, have passing grades, and the next behavior screening period indicates the absence of risk following the same criteria stated in the inclusion criteria, they are exited from the program.

When you are ready to design these secondary (Tier 2) and tertiary (Tier 3) intervention support grids, begin by making a master list of all the supports (strategies, practices, and programs) you already have available at your school (again, see Boxes 7.1–7.4), as well as those you would like to employ. Select interventions that are evidence-based practices, or at least those that are promising practices (e.g., function-based interventions for students with EBD; Common, Lane, Oakes, et al., 2019; What Works Clearinghouse, 2008), which means that scientifically rigorous evaluations support the use of such practices (CEC, 2014; Gersten, Fuchs, et al., 2005; Horner et al., 2005). We also suggest you see the What Works Clearinghouse (*https:// ies.ed.gov/ncee/wwc/fww*), the NCII (*https://intensiveintervention.org*), Blueprints for Healthy Youth Development at the University of Colorado Boulder, Center for the Study and Prevention of Violence at (*www.blueprintsprograms.org/search*), and CASEL (*https://casel.org*) for overviews of additional models and promising programs.

If the practices in which you are interested have not been validated yet, then consider testing these practices using either single-case or group-design methodologies; you also might partner with your local university researchers or your regional technical assistance providers. In short, incorporate practices that are supported by scientific testing and are feasible in relation to the multiple demands placed on teachers (Lane, 2007).

In the sections that follow are illustrations of how to identify and support students across the PreK–12 continuum who require secondary and tertiary levels of prevention. We describe different approaches to analyzing (1) academic data in isolation, (2) behavioral data in isolation, and (3) academic and behavioral data together. The goal in each of these approaches is to identify students who require additional support by using data-based decision making. In addition, we recommend that you rely on scientifically rigorous, defensible designs to determine the extent to which these extra supports meet the intended goals.

(text resumes on page 184)

BOX 7.3. Tertiary Intervention Grid: Elementary Level

Support	Description	Schoolwide Data: Entry Criteria	Data to Monitor Progress	Exit Criteria
Wilson Reading System® (Comprehensive program)	Intensive reading intervention delivered by a certified Wilson therapist or practitioner (e.g., trained reading specialist or intervention coach). Six 20- to 30-minute sessions weekly (to complete two lessons per week). • Word structure • Word recognition • Vocabulary • Sentence level text reading • Listening comprehension • Reading comprehension • Narrative and informational text structure • Oral and written expression • Proofreading skills • Self-monitoring	Elementary grades 2–5 **Academic** ☐ AIMSweb reading: intensive ☐ Writing assessment: below 25th percentile ☐ Tier 2 intervention in place but AIMSweb progress monitoring aim line inconsistent with growth pattern toward grade-level benchmark	Program End-of-Step Assessments* with progress monitored using the Student Progression Recording Form* and My Step Progress Booklet* (*part of program materials from Wilson Language Training)	Completion of the curriculum. AIMSweb reading progress monitoring at or above the aim line to meet grade level benchmark, for at least three consecutive data points. Continued growth maintained after reducing intensity of support—progress monitoring weekly through the end of the academic year.
Functional Assessment-Based Intervention (FABI)	Individualized interventions based on the function of the students' problematic behavior as determined by the functional behavioral assessment (FBA) and summarized in the *Function Matrix*. A prosocial replacement behavior is selected. *The Function-Based Intervention Decision Model* is used to determine the intervention focus as one of the following: Method 1: Teach the replacement behavior; Method 2: Improve the environment; Method 3: Adjust the contingencies;	One or more of the following: **Behavior** ☐ SRSS-E7: High (9–21) ☐ SRSS-I5: High (4–15) ☐ SSiS-SEL Ranking of 1, 2, or 3 on the Motivation to Learn ☐ Six or more ODRs within a grading period	Improvement of behavior targeted for improvement (e.g., target or replacement behavior) using direct observation **Treatment Integrity** • FABI Step checklists for procedural fidelity (completed by the intervention team) • Treatment integrity checklist of intervention tactics (teacher completed daily)	The FABI will be faded once a functional relation is demonstrated using a validated single-case research design (e.g., withdrawal) and: • Student meets the behavior objective (see BIP)

	AND/OR		
and a combination of Method 1 and Method 2. Each Behavior Intervention Plan (BIP) includes antecedent adjustments, reinforcement adjustments, and extinction procedures directly linked to the function of the target (problem) behavior. The intervention team and teacher design, implement, and monitor implementation and student outcomes.	**Academic** □ Progress report: one or more course failures □ Missing assignments: five or more within a grading period □ AIMSweb: intensive level (math or reading)	**Social Validity** • Checklist: IRP-15 (teacher, parent) • Checklist: CIRP (student) • Collected by the intervention team leader	Services are maintained until parents, school personnel, and mental health providers agree on appropriate course of action.
Mental Health Support—Counseling	School psychologist facilitates services with local mental health services representative and parents/guardians. Mental health provider provides individual and small-group counseling services at the school site within the school day.	□ Counseling referral for serious mental health or behavior issues made by parent or teacher □ Exceed internalizing or externalizing normative criteria on the Systematic Screening for Behavior Disorders (SSBD)	• Checklist of critical indicators (as identified by team) completed by teacher and parent, collected daily • School psychologist- and mental health provider-identified measures • Weekly teacher report on academic status **Treatment Integrity** • Sessions offered, duration, and attendance at sessions (dosage) **Social Validity** • Education team interview (teacher, parent) • Family interview (student) • Conducted by the mental health provider

Note. From *www.ci3t.org/fabi.* The examples are not intended to represent one school's completed intervention grid. To provide a variety of examples with different assessment tools, each row could be part of a different school's grid; that is, we are not recommending that schools use multiple screeners for entry criteria. We recommend that schools use the schoolwide measures they have adopted. See Blueprints for Violence Prevention (*www.colorado.edu/cspv/index.html*) and What Works Clearinghouse (*http://ies.ed.gov/ncee/wwc/*) for overviews of additional model and promising programs. SRSS, Student Risk Screening Scale (Drummond, 1994); SRSS-IE, Student Risk Screening Scale for Internalizing and Externalizing (SRSS-IE; Drummond, 1994; Lane & Menzies, 2009); E7, Externalizing 7 items; I5, Internalizing 5 items; SSiS-SEL, Social Skills Improvement System—Social–Emotional Learning Progress Monitoring Scales (Elliott & Gresham, 2017b); IRP-15, Intervention Rating Profile; CIRP, Child Intervention Rating Profile.

BOX 7.4. Tertiary Intervention Grid: Middle and High School Level

Support	Description	Schoolwide Data: Entry Criteria	Data to Monitor Progress	Exit Criteria
Functional Assessment-Based Intervention (FABI)	Individualized interventions based on the function of the target (problem) behavior as determined by the functional behavioral assessment (FBA) summarized using the *Function Matrix. The Function-Based Intervention Decision Model* is used to determine the intervention focus: Method 1: Teach the replacement behavior; Method 2: Improve the environment; Method 3: Adjust the contingencies; and a combination of Method 1 and Method 2. The behavioral intervention plan, including antecedent adjustments, reinforcement adjustments, and extinction procedures, is designed and implemented, and student progress is monitored.	**Behavior** One or more of the following: ☐ SRSS-E7: High (9–21) ☐ SRSS-I6: High (6–18) ☐ Six or more ODRs within a grading period **AND/OR** **Academic** ☐ Progress report: one or more course failures ☐ Missing assignments: five or more within a grading period ☐ AIMSweb: intensive level (math or reading) ☐ Below 2.5 GPA	Student behavior targeted for improvement (e.g., target or replacement behavior) using direct observation **Treatment Integrity** • Procedural fidelity using the FABI Step Checklists (completed by the intervention team after each step) • Treatment Integrity Checklist (completed daily by the teacher) **Social Validity** • IRP-15 (teacher; pre- and postintervention) • CIRP (student; pre- and postintervention)	The FABI will be faded once a functional relation is demonstrated using a validated single-case research design (e.g., withdrawal) • Behavioral objective for the student is met.
Individualized Deescalation Plan	Individualized strategy that involves identifying specific student characteristics for each phase of the deescalation cycles and implementing appropriate and evidence-based adult responses to managing student acting-out behavior. Identify a target behavior for the individual student. Include (1) label for the behavior, (2) definition, (3) examples, and (4)	**Behavior** One or more of the following: ☐ SRSS-E7: High (9–21) ☐ Six or more ODRs within a grading period	• Direct observation of the target behavior with data points graphed for decision making **Treatment Integrity** • Treatment integrity intervention component checklist (completed by all teachers)	• SRSS-E7 score: Low (0–3) • No ODRs earned in the quarter • Observation data demonstrate that behavior is consistently within the expected level (per goal; three consecutive data

points), then transition to maintenance plan and monitor behavior during transition.

Social Validity
- Teachers: IRP-15 (pre- and postintervention)
- Student: CIRP (pre- and postintervention)

- Meets individual READ 180 reading goals.
- Reading scores on benchmark assessments demonstrate proficiency.
- Meets expectations for reading performance on state assessment.

non-examples. Set behavioral goal based on baseline performance of the behavior.

Developed with the intervention team and implemented by all of the students' teachers.

READ 180 (Stage C) Reading Intervention (Houghton Mifflin Harcourt)

Individualized intensive reading instruction. Students participate in a 50-minute reading instructional block during their intervention period. Students meet in the computer lab for participation in the online portion for 20 minutes daily. Students use a progress management system to monitor and track their own progress. Special education teachers or general education teachers facilitate instruction with training in the READ 180 curriculum.

Academic
☐ Reading performance basic or below basic on state assessment (but above fourth-grade reading level).

- Progress Monitoring with Scholastic Reading Inventory of individual goals
- Writing Assessments
- Progress Monitoring AIMSweb (vocabulary, comprehension, and spelling)
- Attendance in class

Treatment Integrity
- Teachers monitor performance and attendance in class.
- Completion of weekly checklists for activities completed.

Social Validity
- Students and teachers complete surveys pre- and postintervention

Note. From *www.ci3t.org/fabi.* The examples are not intended to represent one school's completed intervention grid. In order to provide a variety of examples with different assessment tools, each row could be part of a different school's grid; that is, we are not recommending that schools use multiple screeners for entry criteria. We recommend that schools use the schoolwide measures they have adopted. See Blueprints for Violence Prevention (*www.colorado.edu/cspv/index.html*) and What Works Clearinghouse (*http://ies.ed.gov/ncee/wwc*) for overviews of additional model and promising programs. SRSS-IE, Student Risk Screening Scale for Internalizing and Externalizing (SRSS-IE; Drummond, 1994; Lane & Menzies, 2009); E7, Externalizing 7 items; I6, Internalizing 6 items (for middle and high school use); IRP-15, Intervention Rating Profile; CIRP, Child Intervention Rating Profile.

Analyzing Academic Data

A vast amount of academic data is collected on a regular basis: CBM, work samples, standardized assessments, and grades. In this section we provide two illustrations, one traditional and the other nontraditional, for using existing schoolwide data to identify and support elementary and high school students who require additional academic supports.

Identifying and Supporting Elementary School Students with Varying Reading Skills

Curriculum-based assessment data can be used across the PreK–12 continuum as a practical, cost-effective, accurate method of identifying students who require additional supports. In this section, we illustrate practices from an elementary school that used curriculum-based reading data as part of their Ci3T primary (Tier 1) prevention program to monitor student progress, then identify students who required either remediation or enrichment (Lane, Robertson, et al., 2006).

At this particular school, three CBM probes were administered to each student at three time points: at the onset of the school year (Time 1), prior to Winter break (Time 2), and at year end (Time 3). The median probe was the score to be compared. In addition, teachers administered one probe per student each week (progress monitoring) to use when making instructional decisions in the classroom (Lane, Robertson, et al., 2006).

Figures 7.5 and 7.6 present graphs with four quadrants showing results of Time 1 and Time 2 administrations (Lane, Robertson, et al., 2006). Specifically, data were analyzed to determine how students responded to instruction between Time 1 and Time 2 CBM administrations to help determine how to shape instruction. The vertical and horizontal lines that divide the graph into four quadrants represent the benchmarks for performance. Students whose benchmark scores placed them in Quadrant I were identified as needing enrichment activities beyond the scope of the current reading program, as evidenced by above benchmark scores at Time 1 and Time 2 (Responders: High—Grow). Students placing in Quadrant II showed improvement by moving from below benchmark at Time 1 to at or above benchmark at Time 2 (Responders: Low—Grow), indicating that the present curriculum and instruction were sufficient. Students placing in Quadrant III were identified as needing remediation in the form of either secondary or tertiary intervention efforts, as evidenced by below benchmark scores at Time 1 and Time 2 (Nonresponders: Low—No Grow). Finally, students placing in Quadrant IV were also identified as needing remediation in the form of either secondary or tertiary intervention efforts, given that although they initially scored above benchmark at Time 1, they now scored below benchmark at Time 2, indicating that they were not making the necessary gains in reading fluency (Nonresponders: High—No Grow).

In the kindergarten illustration (Figure 7.5), you'll see that although some students responded to the program (Quadrant II Responders: Low—Grow), the majority of the class was still below benchmark at Time 2 (Quadrant III Nonresponders: Low—No Grow). Given this profile, one suggestion is to supplement the kindergarten reading curriculum with a program aimed at improving early literacy skills, such as Phonological Awareness Training for Reading (PATR; Torgesen & Bryant, 1994) or Ladders to Literacy: A Kindergarten Activity

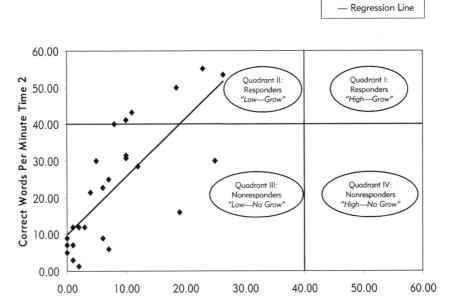

FIGURE 7.5. Analyzing CBM data for kindergarten.

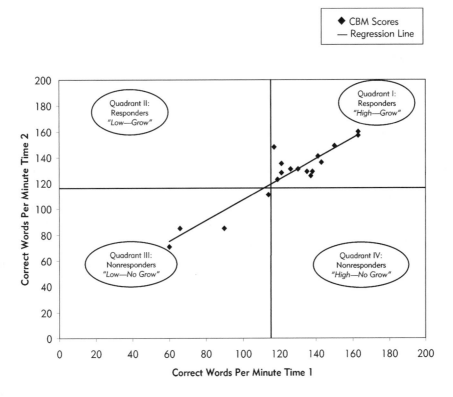

FIGURE 7.6. Analyzing CBM data for fourth grade.

Book (O'Connor, Notari-Syverson, & Vadasy, 2005). Either intervention could be implemented immediately following Winter break.

In the fourth-grade illustration (Figure 7.6), all but a few students met or exceeded the benchmark requirements (Quadrant I Responders: High—Grow; Lane, Robertson, Parks, et al., 2006). Only four students required additional supports (Quadrant III Nonresponders: Low—No Grow). In this case, you might consider a one-to-one reading intervention to provide intensive support for students in Quadrant III. A multiple baseline across-participants design could be used to evaluate how these students respond to the tertiary level support (a great thesis option!).

Supporting High School Students as They Prepare for the ACT Test

Several of us (Lane, Robertson, Mofield, Wehby, & Parks, 2009) took a less traditional approach to secondary interventions by supporting an entire subgroup of students—11th-grade students taking the ACT Test—who historically had been less than successful on college entrance exams. In this study, we conducted a targeted, secondary intervention implemented within the context of a three-tiered model to prepare 11th-grade students for the ACT college entrance exam. Rather than waiting for some students to perform poorly on the ACT, then providing support, this intervention was conducted with the entire 11th-grade class. Although it is not typical to offer a secondary intervention to a group that includes students for whom the primary plan is working, this was a proactive measure based on data that indicated the previous years' 11th-grade students had not performed as desired on the ACT and that participation would likely benefit *all* students as they prepared for the test.

The principal and leadership team at a rural high school elected to implement an ACT preparation program, Preparing for the ACT (see Lane, Robertson, Mofield, et al., 2009, for a detailed description of the curriculum). Homeroom teachers taught an ACT preparation program to all 11th-grade students 1 day per week. As part of this program, students ($N = 126$) completed practice probes with sample ACT items and took a practice test before and after completing the curriculum. One aspect of this intervention was a quasi-experimental study that compared actual ACT performance of students who did and did not participate in the intervention (current academic year vs. previous academic year). Results suggested improved performance on the ACT for students who did participate in the program. Also, there was an increase in the percentage of students who met or exceeded the district target scores, and school mean ACT scores exceeded state mean scores following intervention participation.

Summary

These are just two illustrations of how to use schoolwide academic data to determine which groups of students are in need of additional supports, building on some of the evidence of tiered systems we presented in Chapter 2. There are a multitude of options for how to develop more focused intervention efforts to support students who need more than what is offered in the primary prevention program. The same is true when analyzing behavioral data, which we consider next.

Analyzing Behavioral Data

As we mentioned in Chapter 4, empirically validated screening tools are available for use across the K–12 continuum. In this section, we provide three illustrations of how to analyze screening data at the elementary, middle, and high school levels to identify students who require more targeted or intensive supports. Then we review a secondary intervention conducted as part of a three-tiered model of prevention at the elementary level.

Identifying Elementary School Students Using the SSBD

Figure 7.7 illustrates how to analyze data from the SSBD to determine which students require additional supports (Lane, Kalberg, Menzies, et al., 2011). One school reported in this study implemented the SSBD at three times as part of regular school practices: 6 weeks after school started (Fall), prior to winter break (Winter), and again at year end (Spring). Figure 7.7 contains the data for the first two time points: Fall 2007 and Winter 2007.

The first two bars contain information about students who were nominated in the externalizing category. During the fall of 2007, 69 students received a ranking of 1, 2, or 3 for externalizing behaviors on the SSBD. Of these 69 students, 29 students (6.23% of the school) exceeded normative criteria for externalizing behavior during Stage 2, as determined by scores on the Critical Events Index and Combined Frequency Index rating scales (see Chapter 5 for

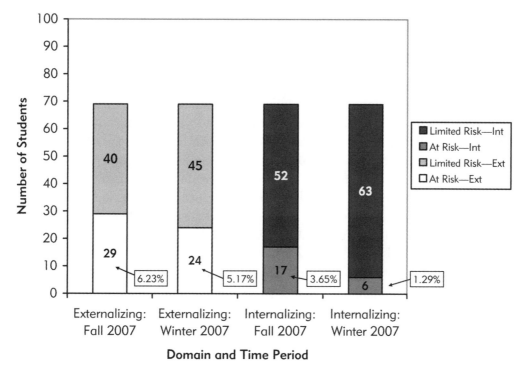

FIGURE 7.7. SSBD data Fall 2007 to Winter 2007 for Payton Povey Elementary School: Comparing limited-risk to at-risk students for both externalizing and internalizing domains.

a detailed description of the SSBD screening tool). A few months later, another 69 students were ranked 1, 2, or 3 on the externalizing dimension of the SSBD. Of these 69 students, 24 (5.17% of the school) exceeded normative criteria for externalizing behavior during Stage 2. Thus, there was a small reduction in the percentage of students exceeding normative criteria with regard to externalizing behaviors.

The next two bars contain information about students nominated in the internalizing category. During the Fall of 2007, a total of 69 students received a ranking of 1, 2, or 3 for internalizing behaviors on the SSBD. Of these 69 students, 17 students (3.65% of the school) exceeded normative criteria for internalizing behavior during Stage 2, as measured by scores on the Critical Events Index and Combined Frequency Index rating scales. A few months later, another 69 students were ranked 1, 2, or 3 on the internalizing dimension of the SSBD. Of these 69 students, only 6 (1.29% of the school) exceeded normative criteria for internalizing behavior during Stage 2. This suggests that the primary prevention program was particularly effective for students with internalizing behavior patterns.

In terms of secondary prevention efforts, the 24 students exceeding normative criteria for externalizing behavior and the six students exceeding normative criteria for internalizing behavior at the Winter 2007 time point could be supported by either secondary or tertiary levels of prevention. The information examined by grade level indicated that the majority of students with externalizing concerns are in first grade, and the majority of students with internalizing concerns are in third grade. In looking at the secondary intervention grid (see Box 7.1), these students may be eligible for participation in Behavior Education Program (BEP; Crone, Hawken, & Horner, 2010), depending on the extent to which the other inclusionary criteria are met for the secondary prevention efforts.

Identifying Middle School Students Using the SDQ

Figures 7.8 (Total Difficulties scores), 7.9 (Peer Problems subscale scores) and 7.10 (Prosocial Behavior subscale scores) are examples of how to analyze data from the SDQ to see how the middle school as a whole is responding and to determine which students require additional supports (Lane, Kalberg, Menzies, et al., 2011). At this particular school, the SDQ and the SRSS were implemented at three time points as part of regular school practices: 6 weeks after school started (Fall), prior to winter break (Winter), and again at year end (Spring).

Figure 7.8 reflects the Total Difficulties score (a composite score reflecting the first four subscales), with normal, borderline, and abnormal ranges for Fall 2005 and Fall 2006 (Lane, Kalberg, Menzies, et al., 2011). Figures 7.9 and 7.10 present the same results for Peer Problems (Figure 7.9) and Prosocial Behavior subscales (Figure 7.10). You can complete similar figures for all five subscales: Emotional Symptoms, Conduct Problems, Hyperactivity, Peer Problems, and Prosocial Behavior. One of the outcomes you will notice is that the percentage of students in the school in the normal category for Prosocial Behavior scores increased from 73% in the Fall of 2005 to 82% in the Fall of 2006, with the percentage of students in the borderline category decreasing from 14 to 6%. Furthermore, the percentage of students in the abnormal category decreased from 13 to 12%. Thus, prosocial behavior is increasing for the school as a whole.

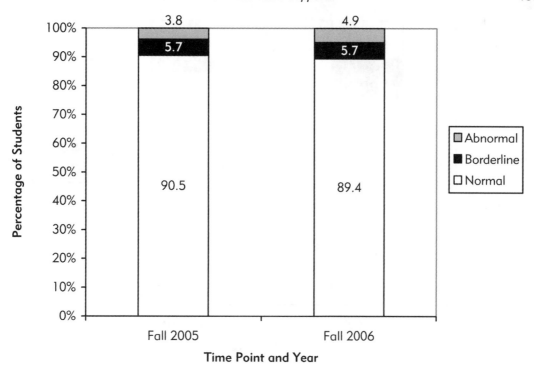

FIGURE 7.8. SDQ Total Difficulties data over time for Foster Middle School: Fall 2005 to Fall 2006.

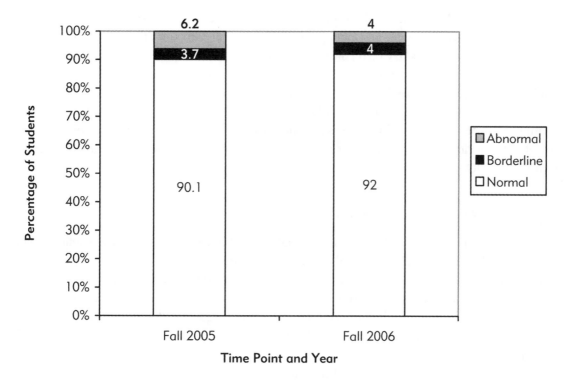

FIGURE 7.9. SDQ Peer Problems data over time for Foster Middle School: Fall 2005 to Fall 2006.

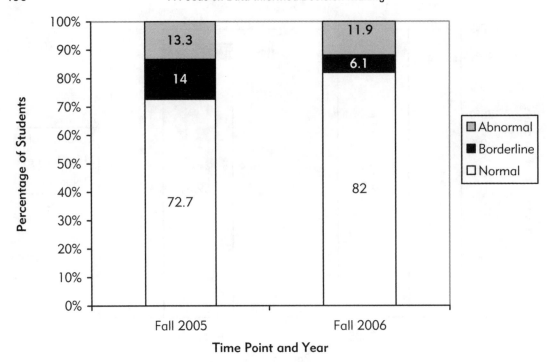

FIGURE 7.10. SDQ Prosocial Behavior data over time for Foster Middle School: Fall 2005 to Fall 2006.

Additionally, these data can be used to identify students with emotional symptoms, conduct problems, hyperactivity, and peer problems, who fall into the abnormal category and could benefit from secondary or tertiary interventions. For example, students scoring in the abnormal range for conduct problems, hyperactivity, or total difficulties, who also are experiencing academic difficulties in writing, may be eligible for an academic intervention to teach self-regulated strategy development (SRSD; Harris, Graham, Mason, & Friedlander; 2008) for writing. We note that since this particular school used the SDQ to screen, the tool has been updated to include four risk categories with new names (see Chapter 5 for a detailed description of the SDQ).

Identifying High School Students Using the SRSS-IE

Figure 7.11 is an example of how to analyze data from the SRSS-IE at the high school level to see how the school as a whole is responding and determine which students require additional supports (see Lane, Oakes, Cantwell, Royer, et al., 2018). At this particular school, the SRSS-IE was implemented three times as part of regular school practices: 6 weeks after school started (Fall), prior to winter break (Winter), and again at year end (Spring). Figure 7.11 contains the data for two time points: Fall of 2015 (first year of implementation and Fall of 2016 (second year of implementation).

As you may recall from earlier in this chapter, the lower portion of each bar contains the percentage of students scoring in the low-risk category (E7 and I6 0–3), the middle portion of

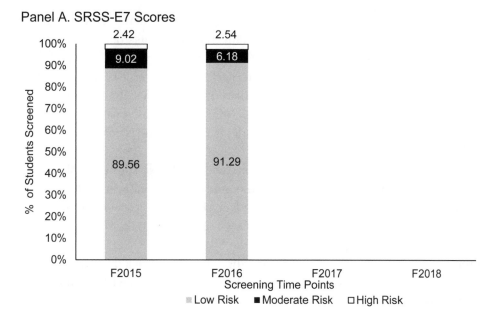

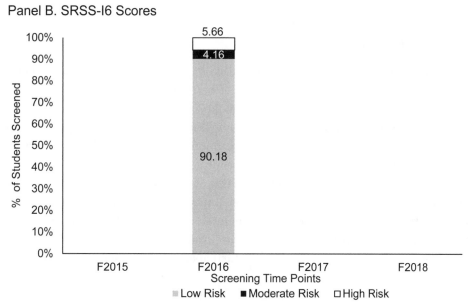

FIGURE 7.11. Finlay High School Graph—Student Risk Screening Scale (SRSS-IE) data: Fall 2015 to Fall 2016. Panel A: SRSS-E7 Scores; Panel B: SRSS-I6 Scores. The scores for the SRSS-I6 were available beginning Fall 2016 for middle and high school use.

each bar contains the percentage of students scoring in the moderate-risk category (E7 4–8; I6 4–5), and the upper portion of each bar contains the percentage of students scoring in the high-risk category (E7 9–21; I6 6–18). One of the outcomes you will notice is that the percentage of students in the low-risk category for externalizing behavior (SRSS-E7) increased from 89.56% in the Fall of 2015 to 91.29% in the Fall of 2016, after just 1 year of implementation. The percentage of students in the moderate-risk category decreased (suggesting a lowering of risk) from 9.02 to 6.18%. The percentage of students in the high-risk category remained relatively stable.

These data can be used to identify students with high-risk status for placement in tertiary (Tier 3) prevention efforts and those in the moderate-risk category into secondary-level prevention programs. For example, you might place students in a secondary-level prevention program such as the BEP, as discussed earlier. Or you might place them in a social skills group if they (1) score in the moderate-risk range on the SRSS-IE, (2) earn three or more ODRs for social problems, and/or (3) have two or more tardies or absences in a quarter (see Box 7.2). You might also consider more intensive supports such as tertiary-level FABI (Umbreit et al., 2007) if the student meets those inclusion criteria.

Identifying and Supporting Elementary School Students with Behavioral Concerns

A more formal study developed a targeted social skills training program to support elementary school-age students identified by their teachers as being at risk for challenging behavior (Lane et al., 2003). Specifically, they designed a secondary-level social skills program to determine the degree to which participation in the program (1) improved behavior in the classroom and playground setting and (2) the degree to which improved social competence influenced the amount of time students were engaged academically.

Students in grades 2–4 were selected for this study based on how they responded to a schoolwide primary prevention program that contained literacy and behavioral components as determined by the SRSS data. Students who maintained or moved into high-risk status (scores of 9–21) after the first 4 months of the school year, in addition to a problem behavior rating of 2 (*sometimes*) or 3 (*frequently*), were invited to participate in this social skills prevention effort. Eight students met these criteria; however, one was expelled, so seven at-risk students, along with seven peers who were not at risk, were placed in one of three social skills groups. These groups were conducted 2 days per week (for 30 minutes) for a total of 10 weeks (10 hours) by doctoral students in a school psychology program. Non-at-risk peers served as models for their at-risk peers during the intervention sessions to help students at risk learn the new skills and to provide prompts for them in other settings (e.g., playground) to encourage generalization of the skills learned in the intervention sessions. Each intervention group focused on students' specific social skills deficits, as determined by the Social Skills Rating Scale (SSRS; Gresham & Elliott, 1990; see Lane et al., 2003, for a detailed discussion of the curriculum). The lessons to address the specific acquisition deficits, which came from Elliott and Gresham's (1991) *Social Skills Intervention Guide: Practical Strategies for Social Skills Training*, were taught during 17 of the 20 sessions, with the additional three sessions used for review and to plan for generalization.

Results of this multiple-baseline across-intervention group design study indicated that students in the three groups experienced lasting decreases in disruptive classroom behavior and negative social interactions on the playground. In addition, there were increases in academic engaged time in the classroom. Social validity results revealed that students rated the intervention procedures favorably and used their new skills in several settings.

Summary

The previous illustrations are practical examples of how to analyze behavioral data to identify students who require additional behavioral supports. These examples range from more global (e.g., social skills) to more specific (e.g., emotional problems) supports. It is also possible to analyze academic and behavioral data to identify and support students with multiple needs.

Analyzing Academic and Behavioral Data Together

In the material that follows, we provide examples from our work of how to analyze academic and behavioral data together to identify and assist students in elementary and secondary schools who have deficits in both areas. However, there are also a number of studies by other researchers offering illustrations of how to examine academic and behavioral data together (e.g., Cheney et al., 2004; Frick et al., 1991; Lane, Barton-Arwood, et al., 2007; Lane & Menzies, 2005; Walker et al., 2005).

Identifying and Supporting First-Grade Students with Literacy and Behavioral Concerns

Several of us (Lane et al., 2003) conducted a supplemental early literacy program for first-grade students identified by their teachers as being at risk for antisocial behavior and not responding to a schoolwide program that contained both behavioral and academic components. Students were invited to receive this extra literacy instruction if they met two criteria. First, students had to be rated by their teachers as at high risk (scores 9–21) on the SRSS (which was completed by all teachers as part of the schoolwide assessment plan) at the midpoint assessment. Second, students had to be identified by their teachers as being in the bottom third of their class in terms of early literacy skills.

In this study, the intervention was conducted in a general education classroom during the course of the regular school day. The seven participants were assigned randomly to one of two intervention groups (Group 1: $n = 4$; Group 2: $n = 3$) and evaluated using a multiple-baseline design. The school literacy leader, a doctoral candidate, conducted both intervention groups in a general education classroom. Thirty lessons, 30 minutes in length, were held 3–4 days per week over a 9-week period. Although students showed initial variability in their decoding skills and behavior in the classroom, all students showed improved word attack skills and decreased levels of disruptive behavior in the classroom following the completion of the intervention. Improved early literacy skills were associated with lasting decreases in disruptive classroom behavior, which has also been observed in other academic interventions in relation to students with EBD (Falk & Wehby, 2001; Wehby et al., 2003).

Identifying and Supporting Elementary School Students with Reading and Behavioral Concerns

We also investigated the effects of a schoolwide program on the academic and behavioral skills of all students in an urban elementary school (Lane & Menzies, 2002). The primary-level behavior intervention included the teaching and reinforcement of 10 social skills the teachers identified as necessary for school success. In addition, a common discipline plan was used by all teachers. The plan was created by the teaching staff and used elements from both the Lee Canter (1990) and Harry Wong (Wong & Wong, 1998) approaches to student discipline. The schoolwide academic plan relied on the use of small-group instruction in language arts to target the particular needs and strengths of students (see Menzies, Mahdavi, & Lewis, 2008, for a complete description of the small-group program used in first grade). Small-group instruction supplemented and supported the school's regular whole-group language arts instruction.

Students were administered the SRSS at three time points to examine changes in risk status. Academic risk status was assessed using district multiple measures, as well as standardized CBM. These were administered at the same time as the behavioral measures. Results indicated that the program may have positively influenced students' behavior and academic growth by promoting academic gains and maintaining stability in prosocial behaviors.

Students who were nonresponsive to the primary intervention efforts and who were still identified as being at high risk for antisocial behavior at the midpoint were invited to participate in secondary interventions. Paraprofessionals were trained to use a social skills curriculum (Elliott & Gresham, 1991) to provide 20 lessons that were focused on students' areas of deficit as identified by their teachers. Students attended the lessons two times a week for 30 minutes each session. These were conducted in small groups that included two to three target children, as well as two model students. The results indicated that students were responsive to the secondary intervention. At the study's end, they displayed higher rates of academic engaged time, lower rates of disruptive behavior during instructional times, and lower rates of negative social interactions on the playground.

Identifying and Supporting First-Grade Students with Writing and Behavioral Concerns

We examined the effects of an academic intervention focused on improving the writing skills of second-grade students with poor writing skills, who were also at risk for EBD (Lane, Harris, et al., 2008). This study was conducted in a large rural elementary school that had a three-tiered model of positive behavior interventions and supports.

Lane, Harris, and colleagues (2008) selected second-grade students for possible participation in the secondary intervention by analyzing both the behavior screening data and the standardized writing measures, each of which was collected as part of regular school practices. Specifically, students who (1) scored at high or moderate risk on the SRSS or who exceeded normative criteria on Stage 2 of the SSBD and (2) scored at or below the 25th percentile on a standardized measures of writing (the Test of Written Language–3; Hammil & Larsen, 1996) were invited to receive this extra support. Of the 11 second-grade students who had both writing and behavior concerns, parental consent and student assent were received for eight students. Six students completed the program (one student moved and one did not finish before year end).

Once students were identified and the necessary permissions were obtained, research assistants worked individually with students to teach them how to plan and write a story using the SRSD model. The research assistants worked with the students three to four times per week for 30 minutes each session. Students needed between 13 and 15 lessons to learn the strategies, knowledge, and skills necessary to write stories.

Results of this multiple-probe design suggested that the six students improved in story completeness, length, and quality. Moreover, the improvements were sustained into the main-tenance phase. Social validity data indicated that the students and teachers found the inter-vention acceptable, with some raters indicating that the intervention actually exceeded their expectations.

Identifying and Supporting Middle School Students with Academic and Behavioral Concerns

In another study students nonresponsive to Tier 1 efforts were identified using existing schoolwide data (Robertson & Lane, 2007). Sixty-five students were selected as having both academic and behavioral concerns. A *behavioral concern* was operationally defined as scor-ing moderate or high on the midpoint administration of the SRSS or obtaining one or more ODRs within the first 4 months of school. Furthermore, an *academic concern* was defined as obtaining one or more failing grades or a low GPA (< 2.7) during the second quarter. Upon selection, any student with poor reading skills (defined by enrollment in a remedial reading program) was excluded because the curriculum required independent reading skills. Selected students were assigned randomly to one of two intervention groups: (1) a study skills program or a (2) study skills plus conflict resolution skills program. Students remained in the intervention group led by teachers with the support of counselors for 21 weeks, or 56 lessons. Results suggested that students in both intervention groups showed similar patterns of responding in terms of their knowledge of study skills, but they did not display significant gains in study habits. According to behavioral outcome measures, students who received the conflict resolution skills curriculum demonstrated improvements in their knowledge of these skills. However, changes in their *knowledge* of skills did not generalize to changes in conflict resolution *styles*. This study illustrates one way to identify nonresponsive students using exist-ing schoolwide data.

Identifying and Supporting Elementary and Middle School Students with Tier 3 Needs

In another study, we used schoolwide data to identify students who were nonresponsive to both primary and secondary prevention efforts (Lane, Rogers, et al., 2007). Two students, one at the elementary level and the other at the middle school level, received FABIs using a systematic approach to (1) identify the function of the target behavior, (2) select an appropriate intervention focus, and (3) design an intervention with the components necessary to accurately interpret intervention outcomes (e.g., treatment integrity, social validity, and generalization and maintenance; Umbreit et al., 2007).

The elementary student, Claire, was identified for a secondary intervention due to high levels of internalizing behaviors, as measured by the SSBD. She went on to receive a behavior intervention that did produce some decreases in internalizing behavior (e.g., isolating herself from others), but she still showed very high levels of internalizing behaviors, as measured by the Internalizing subscale of the SSRS (Gresham & Elliott, 1990). In addition, Claire continued to perform below average in reading skills, as evidenced by earning a broad reading score below the 25th percentile (Woodcock–Johnson III Tests of Achievement; Woodcock, McGrew, & Mather, 2001).

To increase her participation in class, Claire next received a function-based intervention that was measured using event recording. Functional assessment data were analyzed by placing the data into a *function matrix* (see Umbreit et al., 2007) to determine whether the target behavior occurred to either seek (positive reinforcement) or avoid (negative reinforcement) attention from others, activities or tasks, or tangibles. Based on results of the function matrix, Claire's nonparticipation served to help her avoid attention from her teacher and peers. Her intervention was designed using the *function-based intervention decision model* (Umbreit et al., 2007). This model guides the intervention design process using two key questions: (1) Is the student able to perform the replacement behavior? and (2) Does the classroom environment represent effective practices? It was determined that Claire was able to participate in class (the replacement behavior) and that the classroom environment did represent effective practices. Claire's intervention focused on *adjusting the contingencies*. In accordance with this intervention method, Adjust the Contingencies, as defined within the intervention decision model, conditions within the environment were structured to increase the likelihood that Claire would participate in class. Furthermore, when she did participate, the consequences that previously reinforced the target behavior (nonparticipation) were provided. Finally, the same consequences were withheld when Claire did not participate.

Results of a changing criterion design demonstrated a functional relation between the introduction of the intervention and increases in Claire's participation. In short—it worked! Furthermore, both Claire and her teacher rated the intervention procedures favorably.

Aaron, a middle school student receiving special education services, was identified for a secondary intervention because he was initially nonresponsive to the primary prevention program. Nonresponsiveness to the primary plan was defined as having concerns in both academic (low GPA [$\leq$ 2.7] or one or more failing grades, according to the second quarter) and behavioral (one or more ODRs within the first 4 months of the school year or scoring in the moderate- or high-risk status on the SRSS) domains. As a result, Aaron was placed in a secondary intervention, as described earlier (see "Identifying and Supporting Middle School Students with Academic and Behavioral Concerns"). Aaron met the academic inclusion criteria by earning one failing grade, and he met the behavioral inclusion criteria by earning a score of 9 (high risk) on the SRSS, as well as four ODRs. Aaron's secondary intervention consisted of 21 weeks of instruction (28 hours) in study skills and conflict resolution skills, which were conducted by credentialed teachers as part of an elective class during the second semester (see Robertson & Lane, 2007). However, although Aaron showed changes in his knowledge of study skills, he was considered nonresponsive to the secondary plan because he continued to demonstrate concerns in academic (a GPA of 2.17 and one failing grade) and behavioral (year-end SRSS score of 14 and nine ODRs) domains. According to schoolwide data, Aaron was *the* least responsive of all students in the secondary prevention plan, which is why he was selected to receive a function-based intervention.

To increase his compliance during his science class, Aaron received a function-based intervention that was measured using whole-interval recording. Based on the results of the functional assessment data, which were analyzed using the function matrix, noncompliance was maintained by teacher attention. When applying the function-based intervention decision model (Umbreit et al., 2007) to Aaron's case, the team decided that he was capable of performing the replacement behavior, but that the classroom environment and methods could be improved to support Aaron better. Therefore, the intervention focused on *improving the environment.* In accordance with the Improve the Environment method of the intervention decision model, antecedents were adjusted to increase the likelihood that Aaron would comply during class, while decreasing the likelihood of his noncompliant behavior. Additionally, positive reinforcement was given when Aaron complied, whereas noncompliance was placed on extinction (no reinforcement).

Results of a withdrawal design also revealed a functional relation between the introduction of the intervention and increases in compliance, with dramatic increases in compliance during the intervention phases as compared to baseline. Furthermore, Aaron's teachers reported that Aaron's overall science grade increased from a 55% during the first 9-week session to an 82% during the third 9-week session. His cumulative GPA also increased.

Low-Intensity, Teacher-Delivered Supports

It is also possible to empower teachers with low-intensity strategies to support academic engagement as Tier 2 supports. For example, Lane, Royer, Messenger, and colleagues (2015) used instructional choices during writing time to assist students in an inclusive elementary setting. As part of this study, they examined the effectiveness of two types of instructional choice—across-task and within-task choices—implemented during writing instruction by the classroom teacher.

While the choices were offered to the entire class, the focus was on seeing how choices impacted academic engagement of two students—Neal and Tina. Both students were identified as having academic and behavioral concerns according to academic (report card grades) and Student Risk Screening Scale (Drummond, 1994) screening procedures. After securing teacher and parent consent, as well as student assent, the teachers introduced two types of choices: (1) across-task choices (e.g., choosing the order in which various tasks were completed) and (2) within-task choices (e.g., choosing your writing tool—pencil or pen?), collecting treatment integrity data to make certain the procedures were taking place as planned. The teachers (general and special education teachers) collected academic engaged time and disruption data using momentary time sampling procedures (which is feasible for a teacher to do while teaching). This information was collected on only these two students, although the entire class received choices. For Tina, a functional relation was established between the introduction of the choices and increases in engagement and decreases in disruption. For Neal, the intervention was less successful, suggesting a more intensive intervention was needed.

Summary

As you can see from these illustrations, there are a number of methods for using academic and behavioral data to identify and support students with secondary and tertiary interventions (see Boxes 7.1–7.4 for additional suggestions). When getting started with the identification process, we encourage you to consider the suggestions that follow for managing data.

Guidelines for Establishing Secondary (Tier 2) and Tertiary (Tier 3) Supports

The first step for intervention team members is to identify the secondary (Tier 2) and tertiary (Tier 3) levels of prevention already in place at the school site. Also, they need to decide the criteria for determining which students are placed in the more intensive programs. Criteria for entry and exit need to be established, as well as procedures for monitoring student progress. In addition, the team members decide who should be assigned to teach the interventions. Another consideration is when and where the intervention will be offered. As team members begin this process, they should create secondary (Tier 2) and tertiary (Tier 3) intervention grids to serve as a graphic reminder of the resources available and the specific criteria for providing them to students. This structure facilitates transparent communication between school leaders, parents and families, and students themselves. Essentially, these grids help to demystify options for remediation *and* enrichment beyond Tier 1 efforts.

The second step for the school-site team is to decide on additional secondary (Tier 2) and tertiary (Tier 3) levels of prevention they might like to consider. There may be resources available in the community, in addition to published programs or research-based recommendations, ideally those that are established as an evidenced-based practice (Cook et al., 2013; Gersten, Fuchs, et al., 2005; Horner et al., 2005). A team member might take on the task of vetting programs to determine which are validated, feasible, and fit well with school goals and philosophies. These can then be brought to the team for further discussion and a final decision. Finally, it is critical to make sure procedures are manageable—do not attempt to start all secondary and tertiary interventions at the same time. Begin by putting in one or two secondary (Tier 2) supports. Ci3T Leadership Teams are often tempted to put all elements in place rapidly. However, if primary and secondary prevention efforts are not firmly established, then the percentage of students requiring tertiary prevention will be larger. In the end, this preemptive approach makes it more difficult to provide the most at-risk students the supports they need to be successful. The review of Ci3T Treatment Integrity data will help the team members decide whether they need to primarily focus efforts on (1) increasing Ci3T Primary (Tier 1) Prevention implementation or (2) supporting faculty and staff members in making data-informed decisions for identifying students with tiered intervention needs, implementing the interventions with high treatment integrity, and monitoring the social validity of the interventions in the school's Ci3T plan.

Guidelines for Managing Data

We offer the following guidelines for managing data within the school day, based on recommendations from Sugai and Horner (2002, 2006), as well as our own work. First, schools have access to a plethora of data; use the data collected as part of regular school practice (taking steps to ensure that the data are collected in a reliable and efficient manner) and focus on adopting validated behavioral and academic screening tools (see Assessment Schedules in Figures 5.1–5.3).

Second, as a general rule of thumb, handle the data as few times as possible. In other words, instead of "pushing papers," refine your system so that data are entered immediately, when data entry is needed. For example, many schools have systems in which teachers enter ODRs or attendance records online (e.g., School Wide Information Systems [SWIS]; May et al., 2003). This is an efficient and effective way of entering data. Instead of the teacher filling out a piece of paper, sending a copy to the office and a copy into a filing system later, do it all just one time (whenever possible).

Third, devote no more than 1% of the school day to collecting and analyzing data (Sugai & Horner, 2002). Similar to handing data as few times as possible, be efficient with time and personnel resources when collecting data. Feasible, effective data collection systems are much more likely to be adopted and maintained over time. If you find yourself devoting a significant amount of the school day to data management, consider ways to monitor student outcomes more efficiently or consider developing the expertise of faculty and staff for more efficient use of the systems in place.

Fourth, build data collection into daily routines. In other words, make it a part of the job or the school day for certain personnel (e.g., attendance clerk and assistant principals), so that it is not considered one more *extra* thing. So, if a teacher assesses his or her students on reading probes, allow him or her to build the assessment and data entry into his or her routine if not using applications that allow for recording of scores in the management system at the time of screening.

Fifth, establish data collection procedures. When designing your Ci3T Primary (Tier 1) Prevention Plan (which is a working document, remember), include data collection procedures so that if the person in charge of entering the data is absent, another person can still carry on the job. This will also give others a chance to read over procedures and perhaps develop more efficient methods.

Finally, regularly share findings with faculty. Updates on schoolwide data should be reviewed at each faculty meeting (or at a minimum, distributed via email, being careful not to include individual students' names to maintain confidentiality). This sharing of data does not need to take up a lot of time, but presenting the information often will make faculty and staff alike aware of the changes that are occurring. Box 7.5 provides some other ways in which the Ci3T team may want to disseminate findings, either through email or PowerPoint presentations. We have also included images of reports summarizing Fall and Spring treatment integrity and social validity data, as well as student-level data. Consider these guidelines when creating and refining procedures in which your school collects, analyzes, and shares schoolwide data.

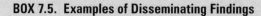

	BOX 7.5. **Examples of Disseminating Findings**
Handout in Faculty Meeting	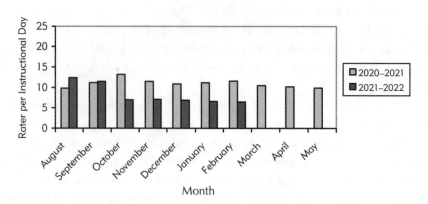 Check out our current schoolwide unexcused tardy data as compared to last year. Note that the first bars represent the rate of tardies per instructional day each month during last school year, and the second bars represent this year! We've heard many students say that they love the new morning announcement drawings! Keep up the good work! Mr. Nathan Principal, Finlay High School
Email to faculty and staff	Dear Staff, • Thought I'd send this along before we go home until 2021! • Through 11/30, 877 students (94%) have NO OFFICE REFERRALS! • Behavior Screeners: Student Risk Screening Scale—Remember our goal of 80% + scoring in the low-risk category? Well, we exceeded that goal! 92% of our students scored in the low-risk category this December! • Thank you for all of your efforts this fall. Have a wonderful and relaxing break. See you in 2021! Katie Scarlett, Principal, Fanning Elementary School

(continued)

BOX 7.5. *(continued)*

PowerPoint presentation	Here is a slide from one of our faculty PowerPoint presentations in which the results of the behavior screeners for the most recent time point (December 2020) are compared to last year's data from December! Nice job, Jaguars! Keep up the good work and behavior-specific praise and enjoy your holiday break. Lulu Lemon Principal, Payton Povey Elementary

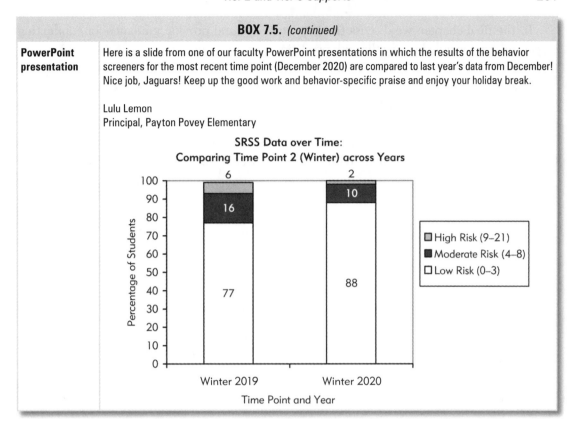

Summary

In this chapter, we have discussed the importance of collecting and analyzing schoolwide data to (1) monitor how the school as a whole is responding to your Ci3T Primary (Tier 1) Prevention Plan, (2) determine how different types of students responded, and (3) identify students who require additional supports in the form of secondary and tertiary interventions. To accomplish these objectives, we provided several illustrations on how to use schoolwide data to identify elementary, middle, and high school students in need of secondary supports, inclusive of academic, behavioral, and social domains. We do not presume to think that these comprise a comprehensive list of illustrations; rather this is a starting point to shape your thinking as you continue to focus on meeting students' academic, behavioral, and social needs in an integrated fashion across the tiers (see Lessons Learned 7.4).

LESSONS LEARNED 7.4. Data-Based Decision Making

Ci3T's emphasis on targeted strategies and supports for academics, behavior, and social skills has been powerful in widening our lens to teach the whole child.

I have seen strength in implementing the Ci3T plan in our school, as we now have a clear system for making data-based decisions for student learning supports.

Rebecca Hummer
Elementary School Principal

In the final chapter, we discuss the importance of and provide guidance for conducting respectful, responsible inquiry through practitioner–researcher partnerships. Next, we situate the important work of designing, installing, and evaluating tiered prevention models within an implementation science framework (Fixsen, Naoom, Blase, Friedman, & Wallace, 2005). We close the final chapter with recommendations for each stage of implementation. These will assist schools as they engage in designing, implementing, and evaluating Ci3T models of prevention by providing practical information that addresses logistical issues. Please read on! Consider this final chapter a ROM WOD . . . time to relax and consider next steps!

PART IV

Moving Forward

CONSIDERATIONS FOR SUCCESSFUL IMPLEMENTATION

In Part IV, we provide considerations for implementation. Although we have completed the important task of designing a Ci3T model, implementing it with fidelity required clear strategic priorities and a commitment of resources (e.g., personnel time, professional learning, and materials) to initial and sustained implementation.

In Chapter 8, *Understanding Implementation Science: Responsible Implementation of System Change Efforts,* we discuss how to conduct respectful, responsible inquiry through practitioner–researcher partnerships. Specifically, we situate the important work of designing, installing, and evaluating tiered prevention models within an implementation science framework (Fixsen et al., 2005). Then we discuss the importance of professional learning to support not only the design of Ci3T models of prevention but also its implementation and sustainability. Here we highlight the importance of empowering all educators with the tools necessary to weave low-intensity, teacher-delivered strategies into the fabric of instruction as part of integrated lesson plans to meet students' academic, behavioral, and social needs (Lane, Oakes, Buckman, & Lane, 2018). We close this chapter with practical information about addressing logistical issues at each stage of implementation when designing, implementing, and evaluating Ci3T models of prevention.

CHAPTER 8

Understanding Implementation Science

RESPONSIBLE IMPLEMENTATION
OF SYSTEM CHANGE EFFORTS

In this second edition of *Developing a Schoolwide Framework to Prevent and Manage Learning and Behavior Problems*, we explain how to design, implement, and assess the Ci3T model of prevention—a tiered model addressing academic, behavioral, and social–emotional domains for a comprehensive approach to student support and school improvement (Lane, Oakes, & Menzies,2014). Across the United States, federal, state, and local education agency leaders have moved toward the design, implementation, and evaluation of integrated systems to address all students' multiple needs proactively (Lane, Oakes, & Menzies, 2014; McIntosh & Goodman, 2016; Yudin, 2014). This is a wonderful shift in focus given the magnitude of the number of students with academic, behavioral, and social–emotional challenges. It is imperative educators build effective, efficient systems to facilitate collaborative practice among general and special educators to prevent and respond to learning and behavioral challenges (Ervin et al., 2006; Gage et al., 2015).

To empower educators in effectively and efficiently serving an increasingly diverse group of students, coupled with the increased demand for academic accountability while maintaining positive, productive learning environments, we wrote this second edition. In Chapter 1, we provided an overview of Ci3T, explaining the benefits of using one unified model for meeting students' academic, behavioral, and social–emotional needs. In Chapter 2, we detailed the evidence regarding tiered systems. We shared lessons learned about Tier 1 practices, low-intensity supports delivered by teachers to facilitate engagement and minimize disruption, and representative studies from Tier 2 and Tier 3 interventions designed to improve student performance. In addition, we shared lessons learned from studies providing insight on data-informed professional learning and teachers' sense of efficacy when working in Ci3T models. In Chapter 3, we provided an updated, step-by-step approach for designing and implementing a comprehensive primary prevention model containing academic, behavioral, and social–emotional components. We described a team-based process for designing Tier 1 elements of the Ci3T model. First, we explained how to define the mission, purpose, roles, and responsibilities of students, faculty and staff, parents, and administrators in academic, behavioral, and social domains. As part of Tier 1 efforts, Ci3T Leadership Teams develop a reactive plan to provide explicit guidance on how to respond when challenging behavior occurs, as well as expectations for specific settings to facilitate school success. After establishing these roles and responsibilities, we focused on procedures for teaching and reinforcing all stakeholders. Chapter 4 offered guidance for determining whether the plan has been put in place as designed (treatment integrity), as well as how to solicit stakeholders' views of the goals, procedures, and intended outcomes (social validity). We discussed procedures for monitoring implementation. This includes assessing the degree to which Tier 1 plans are put in place as designed (treatment integrity) and stakeholders' views about the goals, procedures, and outcomes (social validity). We also discussed the rationale for building an assessment schedule to ensure that all stakeholders know when programmatic and student-level information will be collected each year. Chapter 5, focused on student performance in tiered systems. We reviewed the use of academic and behavioral screening tools to determine how students are responding to Tier 1 efforts. We introduced existing tools and procedures, recommendations for conducting screenings, and examples of how to analyze multiple sources of data in tandem to examine student performance. In Chapter 6, we introduced research-based, low-intensity supports teacher can use to increase engagement and decrease disruption, with a rich discussion of practical methods for using data to inform decision making and empower faculty and staff with the knowledge and confidence to implement these easy-to-use strategies with integrity. In Chapter 7, we provided guidance for establishing transparency of secondary and tertiary supports, offering a range of illustrations of how to design, implement, and evaluate these supplemental supports. We included illustrations from academic, behavioral, and social domains, with an emphasis on integrating them.

In this final chapter, we discuss how to conduct respectful, responsible inquiry through practitioner–researcher partnerships. Next, we situate the important work of designing, installing, and evaluating tiered prevention models within an implementation science framework (Fixsen et al., 2005). Then we discuss the importance of professional learning to support not only the design of Ci3T models of prevention but also its implementation and sustainability. Here we highlight the importance of empowering all educators with the tools necessary to weave low-intensity, teacher-delivered strategies into the fabric of instruction as part of integrated lesson plans to meet students' academic, behavioral, and social needs (Lane, Oakes, Buckman, et al., 2018). We close this chapter with practical information about addressing logistical issues at each stage of implementation when designing, implementing, and evaluating Ci3T models of prevention.

Respectful, Responsible Inquiry through Practitioner–Researcher Partnerships

As discussed throughout this book, Ci3T models of prevention offer promising benefits for administrators, teachers, students, and families. These models build clarity and efficiencies for preventing the development of learning and behavioral challenges and responding swiftly when challenges arise. Ci3T enables each stakeholder to meet students' academic, behavioral, and social needs in an integrated fashion using evidence-based strategies at each level of prevention (Tiers 1, 2, and 3). As is evident in this book, designing, implementing, and evaluating any tiered system is indeed a formidable task. Fortunately, practitioner–researcher partnerships harness a range of talented individuals to meet this charge. Partnerships can be helpful—especially in times of political and economic uncertainty as educational priorities wax and wane (Lane, 2017).

With shared goals of meeting students' multiple needs, practitioners and researcher have an opportunity to learn and grow together (Lane, 2017). The Institute for Education Sciences (IES) has prioritized building strong partnerships by creating opportunities for practitioners and researchers to collaborate from design to implementation to dissemination (e.g., What Works Clearinghouse, 2008). Specifically, the IES established a request for applications (RFA) titled *Partnerships and Collaborations Focus on Problems of Practice or Policy* (Research Collaborations Program, CFDA 84.305H). This topic was designed to facilitate collaborative inquiry by "research institutions and U.S. state and local education agencies working collaboratively on problems or issues that are a high priority for education agencies" (IES RFA FY 2017, 2016). The overarching goal is to improve educational outcomes—academic, behavioral, and social–emotional—for all learners, including students at risk and students receiving special education serveries. As part of the Research Collaborations Program, the intent is to increase the relevance of education inquiry, as well as the accessibility and usability of research outcomes for the day-to-day practices and decision making conducted by educators and policymakers. As part of this process, educational leaders working in schools (and other educational settings) partner with researchers to generate shared questions of interest, design feasible and methodologically sound studies, conduct inquiry with integrity in authentic educational settings, share findings with a range of audiences, and weave lessons learned into the fabric of daily instruction (IES RFA FY 2017, 2016; Lane, 2017).

In this chapter, we highlight a few suggestions to facilitate respectful, responsible inquiry committed to meeting students' multiple needs in tiered systems of support. While there are many points to be made, we offer three considerations for working in a partnership.

Assemble a Team of Honorable Individuals with Shared Goals

When engaging in inquiry related to Ci3T, we encourage everyone to recognize this is a complex system that, when done well, can be beneficial for students and teachers alike. However, implementation takes time—a point to which we return later in this chapter. Establish partnerships with individuals you respect and enjoy; understanding this is a long-term commitment that will involve several years (see Lessons Learned 8.1). As teams are developed, it is important to create clearly articulated, reasonable management plans and enlist sufficient resources (e.g., time, money, professional learning) to ensure on-time completion of project objectives. Similar to how expectations are established in schools (Horner & Sugai, 2015), it is important to develop expectations for collaboration (e.g., clearly defined goals and objectives, norms for contributions). At times some teams lose focus on their "why?" and become focused

> **LESSONS LEARNED 8.1.** Moving Away from Punishment
>
> As we have implemented the Ci3T process over the last 6 years, I have seen our staff members change their focus from punishing student misbehavior to changing our classroom and school culture to change student behavior.
>
>   Ci3T has given us a consistent way to measure our success in meeting academic, social, and behavior goals.
>
> Howard Diacon
> *Principal, Sunflower Elementary School*

on "getting the next grant" rather than on the important questions and priorities driving the inquiry (e.g., Ci3T: collaborative inquiry focused on meeting students' multiple needs). Losing focus is dangerous—life is precious and simply too short not to live with purpose (Lane, 2017). Develop a team of focused, ethical, respectful, and committed partners with the collective set of skills needed to pose and answer questions of shared interest. Then, take steps to ensure the "why" stays at the forefront of the work and team members are acknowledged regularly and feel valued for their contributions.

Secure Necessary Permission and Supports

When establishing the partnership and assembling teams, remember to secure necessary permissions and supports from each partner (e.g., university, district, state). Respectful, responsible inquiry necessarily involves a commitment to the highest level of ethical behavior (Lane, 2017). If you are unfamiliar with research integrity issues, you can learn more about Institutional Review Board (IRB) procedures through the Office for Human Research Protections (OHRP; *www.hhs.gov/ohrp*). As new regulations go into effect, it is important to participate in ongoing education and create opportunities for your team members to conduct day-to-day activities in accordance with the federal, state, and local laws. In short, engage in honorable inquiry.

Remember that despite the best of intentions, people are human, and errors occur and need to be addressed (e.g., reporting new information [RNI] to the IRB). We encourage you to choose team members who are ready to create an environment in which people feel comfortable being transparent when challenges arise (e.g., protocol deviations). Ideally, you will establish group norms that encourage others to be respectful to those not present and assume the best of intentions (e.g., Center for Research on Learning, University of Kansas, as directed by Don Deshler). In addition, you will establish a team committed to keeping current on regulations (e.g., common rule; *www.hhs.gov/ohrp/regulations-and-policy/regulations/finalized-revisions-common-rule/index.html*) to facilitate honorable inquiry. Mistakes happen. We need to create positive, productive environments in which mistakes (e.g., incorrect scoring of a measure, data entry errors, or incorrect set up of screening time point) are brought to the forefront—corrected when possible and a plan established to reduce the future probability of a similar error occurring (e.g., conducting trainings in data with checks for understanding; performance-based assessments).

Disseminate Lessons Learned with Integrity

Teams should disseminate widely, and with integrity, lessons learned from the inquiry conducted (Lane, 2017). By *widely*, we mean it is important to consider the various audiences that could benefit from what you are learning: researchers, practitioners, parents, community members, students, and policymakers. Then, consider how these stakeholders access information. This will require dissemination in not only peer-reviewed journal outlets but also other venues: conference presentations, workshops, technical guides, practice guides, social media (Facebook, Twitter), and posting on the project website. We advise thinking about dissemination when project ideas are being developed, so dissemination plans can be included in the initial approval process.

The timing of dissemination activities is also important. In our Ci3T Partnerships we provide summative information in the form of research- and practitioner-oriented articles (see special issues of *Beyond Behavior*, 2014, 2018), as well as formative feedback. For example, during the Ci3T design process, Ci3T Leadership Teams use information from faculty and staff to shape the Ci3T blueprint. Data from the Schoolwide Expectations Survey for Specific Settings (SESSS) are used to learn about faculty and staff expectations for student behavior. The Primary Intervention Rating Scale (PIRS; Lane, Kalberg, Bruhn, et al., 2009; Lane, Robertson, et al., 2002) and Ci3T Feedback Form offer information about faculty and staff views of the goals, procedures, and intended outcomes. Data from each source inform the building, revising, and finalizing of the Ci3T blueprints.

During implementation, similar data-informed professional learning activities take place. For example, under the direction of district leaders, Ci3T Leadership Teams receive Fall and Spring Ci3T implementation reports that provide the treatment integrity and social validity data that are used to shape professional learning efforts. Ci3T Leadership Teams also review screening data (aggregated and student-level) in Fall, Winter, and Spring to monitor student performance over time to inform instruction. Furthermore, each Spring, the district leadership team reviews collective data to inform professional learning and implementation goals for the following year. This iterative process requires dedicated time to analyze data, shape instruction and professional learning efforts, and seek funding (as appropriate) to continue collaborative inquiry (Walker, Forness, et al., 2014).

Summary

These are just some features of respectful, responsible inquiry. We view this to be the antithesis of "hit-and-run" research, in which researchers approach district and/or school-site leaders with plans to answer a set of questions without taking into account district and school goals, needs, and questions. As we said at the outset of the book, teaching is both an art and a science. We remain committed to positive, productive partnerships dedicated to building local capacity to sustain meaningful, lasting change to improve students' academic, behavioral, and social performance (Baer et al., 1968; Fixsen et al., 2013; Lane, 2017). As such, the work of Ci3T is situated within the context of an implementation science framework, and theoretically grounded in applied behavior analysis (Cooper et al., 2007).

Professional Learning to Support Installation and Sustainability: A Focus on Low-Intensity Supports

In our collaborations with professionals over the last 30 years, we have been nothing but impressed by district and school leaders' commitment to ensuring faculty and staff have a range of opportunities to acquire and refine the skills and confidence needed to implement these strategies in a range of contexts across the PreK–12 continuum. In this section, we discuss a variety of professional learning opportunities to empower faculty and staff in mastering these low-intensity, teacher-delivered supports (Lane, Menzies, et al., 2015). We focus on these strategies as an illustration; however, these same professional learning approaches can—and should—be applied to other facets of the Ci3T model (e.g., literacy and math instruction, social–emotional learning lessons, procedures for teaching, and procedures for reinforcing). In this section, we discuss the following approaches to professional learning: in-person trainings, book studies, on-demand resources, practice-based professional learning opportunities, as well as on-site coaching and performance feedback.

In-Person Trainings

First, consider developing a range of in-person professional learning presentations for a range of stakeholders. In our work with Ci3T, we have traditionally introduced low-intensity supports when Ci3T Leadership Teams are initially designing their Ci3T blueprints, as described in Chapters 1 and 3 (see Figure 3.1). Typically, Ci3T Leadership Teams include most—if not all—low-intensity, teacher-delivered supports described in the chapter as strategies to be implemented by faculty and staff as part of their roles and responsibilities for increasing engagement and decreasing the likelihood of undesirable behaviors (e.g., off-task, disruption, noncompliance). When Ci3T Leadership Team lead their schools into implementation the following year, they discuss these strategies in greater detail during dedicated professional learning sessions designed for the teams (see the colorful implementation graphic on Implementing Ci3T page at *ci3t.org*).

In addition to these dedicated offerings to Ci3T Leadership Teams, additional professional learning opportunities are provided for all faculty and staff as part of districtwide professional learning days and during evening Project EMPOWER sessions, the latter of which are designed to reach families, as well as educators. Typically, Project EMPOWER sessions are offered from 5:00 to 7:00 P.M., allowing attendees time to take care of family commitments (e.g., picking up their own children after school or day care, running errands), then arrive at the training location. Sessions should be held at an easy-to-access location such as a community center or even a country club. The goal is to make sure parking is simple and the location is not filled with distractions or reminders of other commitments (which is why we encourage that these sessions not be held at a school building or university setting). Under ideal circumstances, we recommend that food be provided to create a welcoming and relaxing environment, and to allow people to enjoy others' company and fully engage during the sessions.

During districtwide professional learning days, we have seen creative offerings, such as (1) traditional 1-hour in-depth sessions on one strategy, (2) ignite sessions offering brief, 10- to 15-minute introductions to a series of strategies in a single session, (3) 10-minute minisessions offered during passing periods, in which faculty and staff literally sit down in arranged chairs in a hallway to secure a brief introduction to a single strategy, and (4) poster sessions describing one strategy. Some district leaders also offer what they refer to as "genius bars"—similar to technology bars—where people can stop by for a brief consultation on strategy (e.g., "What is behavior-specific praise? How is it different from general praise? Can you give me a few quick examples?"; Lane, Edgecomb, & Burris, 2018). We encourage you to read Lessons Learned 6.2 and 6.3 in Chapter 6 to hear from our district partners how they have supported the installation of these strategies as part of districtwide professional development days.

Book Studies

Another popular professional learning option has been the use of book studies to teach these strategies, with some organized at the school level and others offered at the district level. For example, one forward-thinking principal created an opportunity for her faculty to learn these strategies while the Ci3T Leadership Team was designing their Ci3T blueprint. She provided the book *Supporting Behavior for School Success: A Step-by-Step Guide to Key Strategies* (Lane, Menzies, et al., 2015) to each faculty member and developed an instructional schedule for moving through the book. They focused on one strategy a month and dedicated time during their monthly faculty meetings to introduce and discuss the featured strategy. Each month, two different faculty members introduced each strategy and often used prepared professional learning materials (e.g., PowerPoint and resources guides) available at *ci3t.org*. The principal chose this particular emphasis on low-intensity strategies, as they were core components of the Ci3T Tier 1 plan being developed and were well-researched elements of Tier 2 and 3 supports as well. She felt that these learning opportunities would provide faculty (and staff) with research-based strategies that were feasible and effective for supporting engagement and minimizing disruption.

In terms of district-level efforts, it is also possible to conduct similar offerings—but districtwide. By conducting book studies featuring these same strategies districtwide, all faculty and staff can be empowered with the same strategies on the same schedule. Then, principals can support the installation of these strategies as part of their regularly scheduled walk-throughs. We have learned from forward-thinking district leaders that some prefer to focus on fewer strategies (e.g., one strategy per semester), with priority placed on supporting implementation, as well as knowledge acquisition.

On-Demand Resources

Another popular option for professional learning is connecting professionals and students' caregivers and parents to on-demand resources. Examples of on-demand resources include presentation materials, instructional videos, technical and practitioner guides, research briefs, and policy guides (see Lessons Learned 8.2). These materials can be accessed at convenient times (e.g., when our own children are taking a nap or out on a date, while watching our spouses play on a softball league, or relaxing after dinner before heading to sleep).

On *ci3t.org*, you will find a professional learning tab, with a series of folders featuring several of the low-intensity, teacher-delivered strategies described earlier. These materials

> **LESSONS LEARNED 8.2.** Online Resources
>
> We were able to support our local high school in the beginning phases of developing a Ci3T model of prevention using the professional learning resources of Kathleen Lane's professional learning series provided to our elementary and middle school. The online coaching resources found at *Ci3T. org* were used to systematically move through the process.
>
> Laura Boudreau
> *Assistant Superintendent*

include a video explaining the strategy, a description, an introductory brief, a PowerPoint presentation, an intervention grid (see Chapter 7 for details), an implementation checklist, a treatment integrity checklist, social validity surveys, and a resource guide. On this page you will also notice other items to add to your tiered intervention library: (1) a behavior education program (BEP)/check-in/check-out (CICO), (2) a direct behavior rating (DBR), (3) repeated readings (to support reading fluency), (4) self-regulated strategy development (SRSD) for writing, and (5) Tier 3: Individual deescalation support plan for managing the acting-out cycle. There is also a separate page (functional assessment-based interventions (FABI; *www.ci3t.org/fabi*) with the full scope of tools needed to design, implement, and evaluate FABIs for students with the most intensive intervention needs. In addition to the benefit of having on-demand professional learning materials that can be accessed at one's convenience, they also support procedural integrity of the professional learning content. In addition to these materials, our Ci3T Strategic Leadership Team (Ci3T: SLT) is currently developing checks-for-understanding that people can complete to make certain the necessary knowledge is acquired.

Similarly, there are the previously mentioned videos developed by Terry Scott with funding from IES, explaining and illustrating these low-intensity, teacher-delivered supports. For example, the high-quality videos feature content knowledge as well as excellent footage of teachers implementing these strategies in authentic educational settings. These videos also are linked, in addition to other resources, in the OSEP IDEAs That Work publication, *Supporting and Responding to Behavior: Evidence-Based Classroom Strategies for Teachers* (Simonsen et al., 2015). The guide offers an interactive map of core features for classroom interventions and supports in three areas: (1) foundational systems addressing the physical layout, routines, and expectations; (2) practices, including strategies listed in this chapter; and (3) data systems with procedures for collecting student data. When you click on the interactive map practice link, you will see critical features of the practice or strategy, elementary and secondary examples, non-examples, and links to additional resources. Additional tips and scenarios for practice are also included in the guide.

The official website for the Positive Behavior Interventions and Supports OSEP Technical Assistance Center (*pbis.org*) has multiple resources to support implementation of these and other strategies and practices. For example, on this website, you will find several technical guides to support classroom management. Brandi Simonsen, Jennifer Freeman, and colleagues developed a technology guide for classroom management practices (Simonsen et al., 2015). Jessica Swain-Bradway and colleagues (2017) developed a companion guide on collecting and interpreting classroom data. Similarly, they offer briefs such as *Getting Back to School after Disruptions: Resources for Making Your School Year Safer, More Predictable, and More Positive* (McIntosh, Simonsen, et al., 2017). Such briefs are highly useful for communicating with educators, family members, and policymakers.

Practice-Based Professional Learning

Another well-researched approach to supporting teachers in mastering these and other skills necessary for successful implementation (e.g., data-informed decision making) is practice-based professional learning (Ball & Cohen, 1999; Grossman & McDonald, 2008). Practice-based professional development provides opportunities for teachers to practice the skills needed to implement an effective educational strategy, as well as receive coaching. This type of professional learning is more than building knowledge: It prepares and supports those working with students to implement the strategy or practice with integrity.

Under optimal conditions, teachers in the same school (or district) identify strategies they would like to learn. For example, teachers may be interested in learning how to incorporate instructional choice to increase engagement of students with externalizing issues during writing instruction or increase opportunities to respond for students with externalizing issues who struggle to stay engaged during math instruction (Messenger et al., 2017). Professional learning sessions include an analysis of the characteristics, strengths, and areas of concerns of students in the teachers' classrooms. In addition, time is spent focusing on content knowledge needs, including pedagogical content knowledge. Teachers participate in activities designed to practice the new methods being learned, which involves accessing examples of successful implementation (e.g., modeling or videos of stellar exemplars). The materials used in professional development are the same as those used in the classroom (e.g., intervention materials, treatment integrity forms) to support positive practice. Then, teachers receive feedback during their practice opportunities to develop their knowledge, confidence, and skills sets before implementing in their classrooms. This rich, comprehensive approach to professional learning is highly effective and has been used to support the installation of several other strategies, practices, and programs (e.g., SRSD for writing; Harris et al., 2012; Lane, Harris, et al., 2011, 2008).

On-Site Coaching and Performance Feedback

As a final illustration, on-site coaching and performance feedback during implementation in the classroom are valuable approaches to professional learning as well. Fallon, Collier-Meek, Maggin, Sanetti, and Johnson (2015) conducted a systematic review of the performance feedback literature and determined performance feedback is an evidence-based practice applying What Works Clearinghouse standards (Kratochwill et al., 2010). In a review specifically examining social behavior interventions, Stormont, Reinke, Newcomer, Marchese, and Lewis (2015) found that teachers rated coaching as socially valid and improved their use of effective practices.

For example, Duchaine, Jolivette, and Fredrick (2011) used coaching and performance feedback to help three high school math inclusion teachers increase their use of behavior-specific praise. Authors used a multistep process in which teachers and coaches identified the skill; teachers learned about the skill, discussed it, practiced it; coaches collected observational data in the authentic context; and teachers received written performance feedback from the coaches. Teachers reported a positive view of the coaching intervention. Teachers received performance feedback every three sessions (about one time per week with block scheduling). Improvements in the use of behavior-specific praise were observed for all three teachers. When planning for coaching and performance feedback to support teachers in new or refined practices, it is important to consider "fit" (Barton, Kinder, Casey, & Artman, 2011). There are also multiple issues to be considered before implementing performance feedback, such as the climate for giving and receiving feedback, time available for observations and collaboration, established relationships, current level of teacher performance, and purpose of the feedback, to name just a few (Barton et al., 2011). So while coaching and performance feedback is an evidence-based practice to improve teacher performance, contextual issues must be considered.

In our partnership with district and school leaders, many talented individuals have developed comprehensive professional learning plans that include the installation of these research-based, low-intensity, teacher-delivered supports. Often, they will invite two faculty or staff members from each school to take on the role of "on-site coach" for a single strategy. For example, Holly and David may be the on-site coaches for instructional choice; whereas, Mark and Kathleen may be the on-site coaches for behavior-specific praise. This does not mean that Mark and Kathleen are the only ones giving behavior-specific praise, but it does mean they are the go-to people if other faculty and staff members want to learn more about behavior-specific praise. In addition to taking on the role of being a strategy coach, each person agrees to take on the role of a learner for a different strategy. For example, Mark may focus on learning high-p requests, and Kathleen may focus on increasing students' opportunities to respond. By having faculty and staff serve as a coach for one strategy and a learner on another, this professional learning approach supports knowledge and skills acquisition among adults. Participants often report feeling valued for their skills sets and supported to learn new skills. Historically, some teachers we have supported in the past felt coaching opportunities were reserved for a selected few. Furthermore, some indicated they were concerned about not being expert in the strategies and skills not yet fully acquired for fear it would lead to negative evaluations. Lane, Menzies, Bruhn, and Crnobori's (2012) text, *Managing Challenging Behaviors in Schools,* includes a scale to determine faculty and staff knowledge, confidence, and use of these and other strategies. When faculty and staff complete this measure, the content can be used to inform decision making when determining coaches and learning targets.

Summary

It has been a gift to work with talented leaders from coast to coast to create and offer professional learning opportunities for faculty and staff committed to learning these and other low-intensity supports. We have been impressed by the range of professional learning opportunities to assist faculty and staff in mastering these low-intensity, teacher-delivered supports (Lane, Menzies, et al., 2018). Approaches featured here included in-person trainings, book studies, on-demand resources, and practice-based professional learning opportunities, as well as on-site coaching and performance feedback. We recognize that these efforts take time to design, install, and refine. Fortunately, there have been wonderful lessons learned from the implementation sciences community.

Systems Change within an Implementation Science Framework

The intent of the Ci3T model is to improve the educational experiences and outcomes for all students, including those with exceptionalities, and to create positive, productive, collaborative experiences for practitioners to achieve this goal. To achieve the remarkable goal of improving long-term outcomes for all students, schools must work toward implementing evidence-based practices with fidelity as regular practice. As schools undertake the work of adopting, designing, implementing, and evaluating Ci3T models of prevention, they move through several phases of systems change. Implementation science offers guidance to understand and support this change process. Given the importance of the intended goal and the investment of district and school resources, it is essential these practices be conducted with a high level of fidelity and a commitment to achieve sustainability (Fixsen et al., 2005). For investments to achieve the desired outcomes, Ci3T Leadership Teams, district leaders, and Ci3T trainers and coaches must focus on both the selection of EBPs and the systems and structures for implementation (Fixsen et al., 2013). Attention must also be given to increasing the capacity of school personnel to address complex student needs. It is simply not enough to design a prevention framework such as Ci3T with evidence-based practices (e.g., practices, strategies, and programs) in place and assume the desired changes will occur. Purposeful planning for increasing capacity and working toward sustainability are important tasks.

In the sections to follow, we situate Chapters 1–7 within an implementation science framework. To begin, implementation science defines the phases organizations work through as they implement evidence-based practices and bring them to scale to produce meaningful outcomes for individuals and systems (e.g., at the school level, districtwide, or state level; Fixsen et al., 2013). Meaningful systems change requires that changes occur from macro (state or district) to micro (practices within classrooms) levels. District leaders provide the systems, structures, policies, resources, professional learning, and leadership. School personnel enact these with fidelity through ongoing professional learning and coaching support at the site level. This process is defined by six implementation stages: (1) exploration and adoption, (2) installation, (3) initial implementation, (4) full operation, (5) innovation, and (6) sustainability (Fixsen et al., 2005).

Exploration

Self-identified need most often drives the decision to seek changes in the systems and adopt a Ci3T model of prevention. For example, a school site may identify concerns related to the percentage of students graduating from high school; reading at grade level; requiring mental health services; being excluded from school through disciplinary actions; or excelling in the areas of science, technology, math, and engineering. School personnel begin to seek information related to changes that may improve the desired outcomes. To assist with this, Ci3T Trainers provide open access to professional learning. The monthly professional learning sessions (we call them Project EMPOWER sessions) allow school personnel, community members, families, or any interested person to attend and learn about the Ci3T model of prevention and proactive practices adopted for use within the framework. We use what Fixsen and colleagues (2009) call an "active process" for moving evidence-based practices to scale in schools. This means we advocate for professional, respectful partnerships between university research teams and school-based professionals, in which university partners take an active role in creating systems change through the implementation of Ci3T models of prevention (Fixsen et al., 2009; Lane, 2017).

Exploration is prompted by readiness for change, with attention to resources, leadership, efficacy and feasibility. District or school leaders consider the resources required in a systems change effort. For Ci3T models of prevention, resources are needed for school Ci3T Leadership Teams to attend a professional learning series to design their Ci3T plan and continued professional learning for all faculty and staff throughout implementation. School leaders must allocate for any needed evidence-based curricula for reading, mathematics, other academic areas, and social–emotional learning. Current assessments are reviewed to ensure data are available to monitor improvement goals and student progress and outcomes. New data systems to collect and manage data may also require resources.

Strong leadership is required for successful implementation (McIntosh et al., 2014, 2016; Menzies et al., 2019). Leaders must be ready to commit time to engage fully in the Ci3T design, implementation, and evaluation efforts, as they are the decision makers for their districts and schools. Districts will identify Ci3T Coaches to support each school's Ci3T Leadership Team, so current duties of current coaches may need to be redefined to allow time for Ci3T activities (e.g., attending Ci3T Leadership Team meetings, gathering evidence and data to support team decisions, examining data, continuing to develop their own knowledge and skills). District and schools leaders must consider not only the resources required for investments of money and time but also the efficacy and feasibility of the practices, strategies, and curricula they will include as part of their Ci3T plan. As discussed in Chapter 3, each Ci3T Leadership Team designs its Ci3T plan to be respectful and responsive to the priorities of the school community (e.g., equitable access to tiered interventions; bullying prevention program) and the district's requirements (e.g., all schools include systematic screening practices for academics and behavior).

For primary (Tier 1) prevention, schools have flexibility with the selection of practices and curricula, so they will want to examine the efficacy and feasibility of those selected in meeting the desired goals. Many districts have standing policies and procedures for adopting new curricula. Otherwise, district and school leaders will want to establish a plan to ensure input from multiple stakeholders (e.g., investigating options, collecting and reviewing evidence for the intended purpose, narrowing the selection, providing time for review by school personnel and public comment, making a final decision and adoption of the plan). Similar procedures could be applied when choosing new assessment and data collection systems, according to district policies.

For Tier 2 and Tier 3 interventions, the exploration phase involves Ci3T Leadership Team members working with existing data and their faculty and staff on the specific types of strategies, practices, programs, and interventions to address student needs, and specific resources necessary to support high-fidelity implementation (Odom, Cox, Brock, & National Professional

Development Center on Autism Spectrum Disorder, 2013). In the Ci3T model, tiered intervention grids are designed to make transparent all supports offered, and data are used to identify others that may be needed. The process for adopting curricula and structures at Tiers 2 and 3 is similar to that at Tier 1. As supports are considered, the Ci3T Leadership Team gathers information to ensure there is evidence the Tier 2 and Tier 3 strategies, practices, programs, and interventions are likely to achieve the desired outcomes if implemented with integrity. The team must also determine whether the interventions are feasible (or socially valid) within the school's particular context (Oakes, Lane, & Germer, 2014). Implementation science phases are revisited as needed. For example, when the Ci3T model is in place in a school, the Ci3T Leadership Team may identify the need to update curricula, add additional or new assessment tools, or add tiered interventions available to meet data-identified student needs (Fixsen et al., 2015). Again, newly identified needs would prompt Ci3T Leadership Team members and district leaders to consider resources, leadership, efficacy, and feasibility.

Installation

When the decision has been made to move forward with adopting a Ci3T model of prevention at the district or school level, preparation for installation begins. Districts and schools plan for and engage in a yearlong professional learning series (described in detail in Chapters 3 and 4). The yearlong process allows time to convene a Ci3T Leadership Team; identify a Ci3T Coach for each school-site team; design the Ci3T plan; and acquire needed curriculum, assessment tools, and data management systems. The design process also allows time for the entire school faculty and staff to contribute to the schoolwide Ci3T plan (Ci3T Blueprints A–D) and Tier 2 and Tier 3 supports (Ci3T Blueprints E–F; Lane, Oakes, Ennis, et al., 2014). As part of readiness activities, leaders provide opportunities for faculty and staff to participate in "readiness" activities—professional learning for high-fidelity practices (e.g., low-intensity strategies, curricula use, screening purposes and procedures).

Resources planned for during the exploration and adoption phase are committed (e.g., substituting funds for Ci3T Team members to attend the professional learning series, supporting team meetings between sessions, purchasing curricula and data management systems). Initially, selected resources may need to be revisited for adequacy and availability. Of primary concern is that school and district leaders support Ci3T Leadership Team members so they feel efficacious in their role as active members of the team (Fixsen et al., 2015). Part of this support is that district-level decisions affecting the school sites are made in advance and communicated clearly. The selected curricula, screening tools, and tiered intervention materials should be purchased and on hand. Decisions about expectations for the instructional schedule need to be made. For example, Ci3T Leadership Teams must know the expected number of minutes for academic and social–emotional curriculum instruction (e.g., 90 minutes of uninterrupted reading instruction, two 30-minute lessons weekly for social–emotional learning). A district assessment schedule (Ci3T Blueprint D) will have to be established, so that school personnel are conducting assessments within expected time frames and according to recommendations (e.g., Fall, Winter, and Spring screening for academic progress and behavioral performance). Having these decisions ready will facilitate the Ci3T Leadership Team in ensuring that the school's Ci3T plan is consistent with district expectations.

Initial Implementation

Following the yearlong design process, schools are ready for rollout efforts for their first year of implementation, enacting their Ci3T plan. Putting the entire model in place takes time before full operation occurs. Substantial effort to communicate with all stakeholders is required. We recommend that Ci3T Leadership Teams make the full plan and all tiered intervention supports easily available, so all school personnel, families, and students, as appropriate, know about the Ci3T plan, their roles and responsibilities, and how students with identified needs will be served through Tiers 2 and 3 (Lane, Oakes, Ennis, et al., 2014). For example, many schools hang a large poster of the full Ci3T plan (Ci3T Blueprints A–F) in a main hallway or front office, send a copy of the plan or a brochure and the Expectation Matrix home to families at the beginning of the year, and regularly share updates at faculty and staff meetings and family functions.

We focus on a 2-year initial implementation phase as the Ci3T Leadership Teams, faculty, and staff use the new procedures of their Ci3T prevention plan. During this phase, Ci3T Leadership Teams collect and examine school-level (e.g., Ci3T Treatment Integrity and social validity data, graduation rates, number of students taking ACT or SAT exams); teacher-level (e.g., fidelity, overall levels of academic and behavioral risk evident in a given classroom); and student-level (e.g., screening data, grades, attendance) data to determine progress toward goals.

Staff buy-in continues to be developed during initial implementation. Faculty, staff, students, and parents "buy in" at different times. Early adopters, about one-third of people, will eagerly support and implement new practices during initial implementation, while late adopters will want evidence that this change will produce desired effects (Rogers, 1995, 2002). Ci3T Leadership Teams should understand this phenomenon so as not be discouraged when 100% of their school community is not onboard initially. Likewise, it takes 3–5 years to implement tiered models in schools that sustain (Horner et al., 2017). However, schools with onongoing professional learning reached optimal levels of PBIS fidelity in just 2 years (Bradshaw, Reinke, et al., 2008). As such, assessing social validity of the Ci3T plan during this stage (ideally, twice a year) is essential to obtain stakeholder input, plan for professional learning, determine the adequacy of data-sharing efforts, and inform plan revisions that occur at the end of each academic year. As a reminder, it is not wise to modify Ci3T plans midyear, as doing so impedes your ability to know "what works."

Initial installation is marked by competing priorities between the identified need for change and the hesitancy by some to engage in new and unfamiliar practices (Fixsen et al., 2005). Ongoing professional learning opportunities support faculty and staff as they adopt and implement the new practices. For example, teachers are asked to remove behavior management systems that are inconsistent with PBIS (e.g., clipping down, card flipping). For a teacher who may have used these systems successfully for many years, it is hard to let go of such practices (Menzies et al., 2019). Teachers must be supported in implementing the schoolwide reinforcement system and reactive plan in place of the previous systems.

To build capacity, we recommend school teams and leaders access the expertise in their own building. Ci3T Leadership Teams can identify two faculty or staff members to serve as the lead for specific low-intensity strategies (see Chapter 6), screening or assessment practices, and Tier 2 and Tier 3 supports. For example, an instructional coach and a data literacy teacher may take the lead in becoming screening experts and supporting faculty with behavior screeners. Or a sixth-grade teacher and a reading specialist may take the lead on a Tier 2 reading fluency intervention (e.g., repeated readings; see *ci3t.org/pl* for free access to materials). They do not become the school's reading fluency interventionists, however. Instead, they serve as on-site consultants or experts. They also acquire additional expertise in this practice by participating in high-quality professional learning activities, develop or acquire materials, and offer assistance such as modeling and coaching as they implement the reading fluency interventions for students in their own class who may benefit from this support (Lane, Carter, et al., 2015; Odom et al., 2013). We recommend that at least two people serve as experts for each strategy, practice, or intervention to ensure sustained assistance over time, even as some people transition beyond their current position (e.g., move into other positions, retire, take leave from work after having a child; Oakes, Lane, & Germer, 2014). Developing on-site experts has the added benefit of supporting late adopters. Peers and social networks, rather than published evidence, often influence this group more (Rogers, 2002).

Full Operation

Full operation occurs when the Ci3T plan becomes regular school practice used with fidelity (Sugai & Horner, 2009). All new initiatives are consistent with the school's mission and purpose statements, and are placed within the Ci3T framework. During this time, professional learning is in alignment with the Ci3T plan (resources are not spent on shiny new things without supporting evidence! [Lane, Menzies, Oakes, et al., 2014]). As the Ci3T Leadership Team identifies new needs, the team, school, or district returns to the exploration and adoption stage for selecting interventions (e.g., an intervention to support students with anxiety). The Ci3T Leadership Team, Ci3T Coaches, and District Leaders keep apprised of new evidence-based practices consistent with the proactive, prevention-minded philosophy of their Ci3T plan. They revise the school's Ci3T plan at the end of each year with data-informed decisions regarding professional learning needs, new or additional Tier 2 and 3 interventions, needs of individuals or small groups of students, and new priorities of the school community (Lane, Oakes, Cantwell, & Royer, 2018). During the full operation phase, fidelity measures and social validity data are regularly above the expected criterion. With high-fidelity implementation, the school should see progress or achievement of initial goals, and new goals are set.

Innovation

Once the Ci3T plan is regular school practice with sustained high levels of fidelity, innovations may occur (Fixsen et al., 2005). Faculty and staff ebring in new evidence-based practices, shifting practices to meet local needs and testing new strategies, assessments, or practices. However, Ci3T Leadership Teams will want to be vigilant, as not all innovation is productive and consistent with a school's mission and purpose, or fits within the Ci3T framework (Fixsen et al., 2005; Horner et al., 2017). Some represent drift; as new faculty and staff come on board, the purposes and science behind Ci3T practices may be lost. For example, new teachers should understand the importance and purpose behind a unified schoolwide reinforcement system; otherwise, they may bring practices learned in teacher preparation or at their previous school (e.g., marble jars!) that are not a good fit with the local model. Sustained, focused professional learning opportunities and intentional onboarding of new faculty, staff, and administrators will support positive innovation efforts (Lane, 2017). Ci3T Leadership Teams monitor data to ensure the efforts result in the intended positive outcomes.

Sustainability

Over time, schools move into the sustainability phase by maintaining established practices with fidelity. Research on multi-tiered models indicates school personnel consider administrator support and effective teaming, as well as high fidelity of implementation, critical for sustainability (see Lessons Learned 8.3). Barriers include staff buy-in, particularly for low-implementing schools, and neglecting to use data (Kincaid, Childs, Blase, & Wallace, 2007; McIntosh et al., 2014; Sugai & Horner, 2006). Issues related to sustainability of Ci3T practices are planned for during the installation (designing the plan) and initial implementation phases.

First, Ci3T district and school leaders must be engaged in the design and implementation of the school's Ci3T plan. Both district and school-site leaders provide the leadership, resources, and sustained commitment for high-fidelity implementation of the Ci3T plan and evidence-based practices within the plan (Sugai & Horner, 2006). The school-site administrator is part of the Ci3T Leadership Team from the start; he or she fully participates in the design process and all professional learning sessions. Often, district leaders also attend the professional learning sessions during the design year. This shows commitment, keeps all leaders current with the school-site team's decisions and resource needs, and allows a Ci3T Leadership Team's questions to be answered quickly (e.g., "What is the district expectation for . . . ?"). Strong, committed leaders are essential for successful initial implementation and sustainability (Coffey & Horner, 2012; see Lessons Learned 8.4). Successful leaders often collaborate with outside experts who can offer technical assistance and support with professional learning (Kincaid et al., 2007; Lane, 2017). For these reasons, we believe it is important to have careful plans for hiring new leaders at the district and school levels. Some of our district partners share Ci3T Implementation Manuals and District Ci3T masters (blueprints from the district with "certainties" or non-negotiables as to strategies, practices, and programs that need to be including in each school's Ci3T model) during the hiring process to make sure new leaders are well prepared (and philosophically aligned) to lead these comprehensive, integrated systems. The onboarding process of new leaders needs to involve continued learning and mentorship to ensure a smooth transition in leadership.

LESSONS LEARNED 8.3. Change and Sustainability

The level of Ci3T success depends on the level of teacher, building, and on the district buy-in, implementation, and reinforcement. Opportunities for continuous professional development and conversations surrounding daily implementation are essential for the culture shifts needed for effective change and sustainability.

Mena Hill
Instructional Learning Coach

LESSONS LEARNED 8.4. Leadership

There are multiple ingredients that comprise a Ci3T plan that is efficacious and manageable. Initially, it is easy to become overwhelmed by the resources/supports available; it is therefore imperative that teams distill the process down and anchor their efforts by honestly and authentically looking at areas of deficit that are impeding the progress of students. This is where leadership comes into play—harnessing the enthusiasm, utilizing the data, and designing a plan that is sustainable. The plan will become an integral part of the school culture, and stakeholders will see their efforts come to fruition and deem the process to be a value-added result of their efforts.

Darcy Kraus
Director of Elementary Schools

Second, the Ci3T Leadership Team is representative of the school faculty and staff. The team is established during installation (the design year) and continues to serve through initial implementation. New members join, and some members need to move on to other activities. However, most often, the majority of team members persist into full operation. Ci3T implementation professional learning sessions focus on productive Ci3T Leadership Team functioning (e.g., meetings on a predictable schedule; us of a standard agenda with prompts for all model components; recording of tasks to be completed, by whom, and with a due date; established roles). As part of ongoing implementation, Ci3T Leadership Teams need both regularly scheduled monthly meetings as well as regularly scheduled team-based professional learning sessions to hone their leadership skills (e.g., data-informed decision making, connecting their faculty and staff to ongoing professional learning efforts).

Third, fidelity of implementation can be a facilitator to sustainability when it is high and a barrier if it is low. The Ci3T primary (Tier 1) plan articulates Procedures for Monitoring (see Chapters 3 and 4). The procedures are planned for during the design year, then revisited at the end of each school year to ensure collected data support school goals, student outcomes, and sustainability of the model. Procedures for Monitoring specifies the tools used to assess fidelity. The Assessment Schedule details when those measures are conducted, ideally, twice each academic year. Two tools are available to examine Ci3T models at the teacher level, the Ci3T Treatment Integrity: Teacher Self-Report (Ci3T TI: TSR) and Ci3T Treatment Integrity: Direct Observation (Ci3T TI: DO) (tools are available free at *ci3t.org*). Schools may also select schoolwide measures for treatment integrity of tiered prevention models such as the Tiered Fidelity Inventory (TFI; Algozzine et al., 2014; available from *www.pbisapps.org*) or the Schoolwide Evaluation Tool (SET; Sugai et al., 2005; available from *pbis.org*). Collecting and using treatment integrity data are not just district compliance or research practices; they are an "active influencer of effective implementation" (Horner et al., 2017, p. 217; see Lessons Learned 8.5).

Fourth, Ci3T Leadership Teams consider and work toward full faculty and staff acceptance and participation (McIntosh et al., 2014). Keep in mind, as previously discussed, this takes time and communication. One communication tool is the twice-yearly faculty and staff social validity assessment, also part of Ci3T Procedures for Monitoring. Careful attention must be paid to ensuring the procedures are socially valid initially and over time (Burns et al., 2013).

LESSONS LEARNED 8.5. Annual Revisions

Our district administers the Ci3T treatment integrity/social validity survey to school-based staff twice a year. The data are easily organized with the tools supplied by *Ci3T.org.* School leadership teams share the collected data with faculty and staff members, and update implementation manuals annually.

Laura Boudreau
Assistant Superintendent

Ci3T Leadership Teams schedule time to share the treatment integrity and social validity results with faculty and staff . Sharing data in a timely way shows those who completed the surveys that their time investment is valued and provides evidence of successes and needed adjustments.

Fifth, data sources available for decision making are made transparent and accessible, as appropriate for student data, and are reported in the Assessment Schedule (Lane, Kalberg, & Menzies, 2009). Team members review data at the identified intervals to determine program implementation, students' responses to the primary prevention plan, the need for additional professional development or coaching for individual teachers, and the need for Tier 2 or Tier 3 supports for individual students. The Ci3T Leadership Team shares data updates at least quarterly or more often as appropriate (Sugai et al., 2005). Ci3T Coaches can also support teachers and departments or grade-level teams in using data to make decisions about which students require tiered supports. The Ci3T Tier 2 and 3 Intervention Grids specify the data source and criteria for decision making. Ease of access to data is imperative for efficient decision making and use of data. Districts and schools will see their initial investments in data management systems, planned for during exploration, continue to pay off (see Lessons Learned 8.6)!

We believe families play an important role in any system change effort, so a parent serves as a member of the Ci3T Leadership Team. Larger schools may want to include two parents on the team. The parent(s) attend the professional learning series during installation as part of the team and offer families' perspectives as the Ci3T plan is developing. They continue to serve on the team, ideally, until their children have matriculated out of the school building and onto the next school level or graduation. The role of families in the Ci3T process becomes even more important as the school moves into full operation (McIntosh et al., 2014). The parent member may serve as a liaison between school-based members of the Ci3T Leadership Team

LESSONS LEARNED 8.6. Structure

Our school district has benefited from the structured guidance to develop implementation manuals based on the Ci3T model of prevention to house and monitor our multi-tiered systems of support. We require the implementation manuals at leadership team meetings as a reference when discussions are focused on academics, behavior, and social–emotional data and learning.

Laura Boudreau
Assistant Superintendent

and the family–school organization. A partnership with the family–school organization allows for maximized resources and the missions of the two groups to be complementary. The parent Ci3T Leadership Team member(s) provides a valuable perspective on the cultural appropriateness of practices, and offers guidance on and facilitates communication with the school community families. A system change effort must embrace the perspectives and concerns of the entire school community and plan for consistent two-way communication for a truly inclusive schoolwide approach.

Considerations for Design, Implementation, and Evaluation of the Ci3T Model of Prevention: Closing Thoughts

In this final chapter, we have discussed the importance of respectful and responsible inquiry and have situated design, implementation, and evaluation of Ci3T within an implementation sciences framework. We have made several suggestions to facilitate productive and effective implementation and have connected you with several lessons learned by our talented and forward-thinking partners (see Lessons Learned 8.7 and 8.8). We would also like to offer some final considerations.

First, we applaud you for your decision to meet students' academic, behavioral, and social–emotional needs. We firmly believe high-fidelity implementation of a well-constructed Ci3T plan results in improved student outcomes. However, we also know that creating and implementing a Ci3T plan for your school site requires hard work and commitment. Our experience with schools has provided us with insight into some of the obstacles and challenges you may encounter as you put your plan into place. We offer the following final suggestions:

- Reach consensus in terms of goals and procedures.
- Establish an active Ci3T Leadership team to promote long-term continuity.
- Make decisions based on data.
- Share ongoing findings with the entire school community.
- Stay the course: Commit to a full year of implementation before revising the plan.
- Implement the entire Ci3T plan (proactive and reactive components) with fidelity.
- Acknowledge adults as they move through the design, install, and disseminate stages (see Lessons Learned 8.9).
- Make sure every adult in the building regularly accesses the Ci3T Implementation Manual and receives ongoing, high-quality professional learning to support implementation (see Lessons Learned 8.10).
- Consider available resources to make the best use of existing programs.

When you design your Ci3T model based on the values held by faculty, staff, parents, students, and administrators, you have the potential to effect powerful change at your school academically, behaviorally, and socially, provided the plan is implemented with fidelity. We hope this book will be a useful tool as you move through the process. Although it may seem overwhelming at points, we encourage you to focus your resources and energy on this proactive approach (see Lessons Learned 8.11). Rather than losing valuable instructional time by

LESSONS LEARNED 8.7. Supporting Successful Instruction

Subject: CWK—Wednesday SECOND HOUR

Teachers,

Today, Wednesday, SECOND HOUR is when the next Connect With Kids Lesson (9) is scheduled. We will send out a survey at the end of second hour to follow up on the lesson.

This video and subsequent lessons are kind of a "scared straight" attempt addressing the dangers of driving while intoxicated. An additional theme that accompanies the obvious and disastrous consequences of driving drunk is the "invincibility" mentality that teenagers often have about "things not happening to them."

The video link is as follows: Shattered—Part 1

Video: *https://lps.connectwithkids.com/shattered-cv*

Lesson Plan: *http://content.connectwithkids.com.s3.amazonaws.com/websource/student_channel/downloads/shattered/shattered_segment1.pdf*

This resource guide has a tremendous amount of information about the topic, plus the worksheets that help you complete the lesson, if you choose: *http://content.connectwithkids.com.s3.amazonaws.com/websource/student_channel/downloads/shattered/shattered1up.pdf*

A few facts about alcohol and automobiles . . .

- There is approximately one fatal alcohol-related motor vehicle crash every 30 minutes.
- Although 16- to 24-year-olds comprise only 15% of licensed drivers, they are involved in more than 25% of all fatal alcohol-related crashes.
- Nearly one-fourth of fatally injured teenage drivers were drinking prior to their crashes, with nearly two-thirds of these at legally intoxicated levels.

Just remember . . . *you* might be the reason why your students show up every day.

Thank you for all that you do. Any feedback from the conversations with your students is always appreciated.

Bill

LESSONS LEARNED 8.8. Supporting Sustainability

Great and timely lesson today. Lots of discussion about the recent accidents in the Dominican Republic. These videos are so well done that we never want to stop at the first one.

High School Teacher

LESSONS LEARNED 8.9. Sharing Successes

Matt and Bill—You both rocked it today presenting at the PBIS leadership forum! I was so impressed by your ability to share candidly and effectively articulate the successes and challenges at your high school with implementation! You are doing great things, and it was wonderful for others to hear and learn from your experience! Well done!

Leah
Sent from my iPhone

LESSONS LEARNED 8.10. Remembering the "Why"

While I'm here in Chicago, I reminded my teachers about the CWK lesson that was supposed to be taught today, see below . . .

> Bill
> Sent from my iPhone

Begin forwarded message:

Subject: today

So we had a gut-wrenching talk in class today. Some of these students have to overcome a lot. Thanks for giving us the avenue to talk about some of these things.

> From: a high school teacher

LESSONS LEARNED 8.11. Managing Bumps

During the planning phase of our Ci3T implementation, we selected Connect With Kids as our Social Skills curriculum. We determined that we would teach seven lessons each semester during first period. We selected first period, because we did our Ci3T screening during this period. We spent our summer working with the team to identify which topics and lessons we would teach all students in the Fall. We returned to school in the Fall, ready to implement our social skills curriculum, and found out the union had filed a grievance and we could not begin our implementation. The grievance centered around lost planning time with the way we were planning to implement our social skills curriculum. We then spent the Fall semester working through the issue with our teachers' association. We decided we would teach seven lesson each semester, and each lesson would be taught during a different period. For example, Connect With Kids, Lesson 1 during first period and Connect With Kids, Lesson 2 during second period, and so on. We are now in our third year of successfully implementing our Connect With Kids curriculum. It is important that you do not let a little bump in the road derail the entire process.

> Matt Brungardt
> *High School Principal*

LESSONS LEARNED 8.12. Substitutes

During the last 2 years, I have had substitute teachers comment about how well our students follow our established school expectations. They share how easy it is to come work at Hillcrest due to the consistency and everyone knowing what is expected. All substitutes receive our buildingwide expectations as part of their daily plans. This has happened due to our comprehensive Ci3T implementation.

> Tammy Becker
> *Elementary School Principal*

having to respond to behavior problems, use of primary prevention refocuses your efforts, so you spend more time noticing and reinforcing students who adhere to the academic, behavioral, and social expectations established in your plan. A primary (Tier 1) intervention plan helps to level the playing field because it explicitly teaches all students the schoolwide expectations. In this way, it motivates many students who, in the past, may not have had the ability or opportunity to earn positive recognition. We have had numerous teachers tell us they feel less frustrated, more productive, and pleased with the changes at their school sites (Menzies et al., 2019). In short, instead of trying to survive the school day, design, implement, and evaluate a plan that makes it possible for all parties involved to thrive (see Lessons Learned 8.12). We wish you the best as you move forward with Ci3T and thank you for taking such good care of your students! We admire and appreciate your commitment to meeting students' academic, behavioral, and social–emotional needs in positive, productive systems.

References

Achenbach, T. M. (1991). *Integrative guide for the 1991 CBCL/4–18, YRS, and TRF profiles*. Burlington: University of Vermont Department of Psychiatry.

Aitken, A., Harlan, A., Hankins, K., Michels, J., Moore, T. C., Oakes, W. P., & Lane, K. L. (2011). Increasing academic engagement during writing activities in an urban elementary classroom. *Beyond Behavior, 20*, 31–43.

Alexander, K., Entwisle, D., & Dauber, S. (1994). *On the success of failure: A measurement of the effects of primary grade retention*. New York: Cambridge University Press.

Algozzine, R. F., Barrett, S., Eber, L., George, H., Horner, R. H., Lewis, T. J., & Sugai, G. (2014). *SWPBIS Tiered Fidelity Inventory*. Eugene, OR: OSEP Technical Assistance Center on Positive Behavioral Interventions and Supports. Retrieved from *www.pbis.org*.

Allday, A. R., Hinkson-Lee, K., Hudson, T., Neilsen-Gatti, S., Kleinke, A., & Russel, C. S. (2012). Training general educators to increase behavior-specific praise: Effects on students with EBD. *Behavioral Disorders, 37*, 87–98.

Allen, G. E., Common, E. A., Germer, K. A., Lane, K. L., Buckman, M. M., Oakes, W. P., & Menzies, H. M. (in press). A systematic review of the evidence base for active supervision in PK–12 settings. *Behavioral Disorders*.

American Educational Research Association. (1999). *Standards for educational and psychological testing*. Washington, DC: Author.

American Psychiatric Association. (2000). *Diagnostic and statistical manual of mental disorders* (4th ed., text rev.). Washington, DC: Author.

Andreou, T. E., McIntosh, K., Ross, S. W., & Kahn, J. D. (2015). Critical incidents in sustaining schoolwide positive behavioral interventions and supports. *Journal of Special Education, 49*, 157–167.

Baer, D. M., Wolf, M. M., & Risley, T. R. (1968). Some current dimensions of applied behavior analysis. *Journal of Applied Behavior Analysis, 1*, 91–97.

Baer, D. M., Wolf, M. M., & Risley, T. R. (1987). Some still-current dimensions of applied behavior analysis. *Journal of Applied Behavior Analysis, 20*, 313–327.

Bal, A., Thorius, K. K., & Kozleski, E. (2012). *Culturally responsive positive behavioral support matters*. Tempe: Equity Alliance at Arizona State University.

Ball, D. L., & Cohen, D. K. (1999). Developing practice, developing practitioners: Toward a practice-based theory of professional education. In G. Sykes & L. Darling-Hammond (Eds.), *Teaching as the learning profession: Handbook of policy and practice* (pp. 3–22). San Francisco: Jossey-Bass.

Banda, D. R., & Kubina, R. M. (2006). The effects of a high-probability request sequencing technique in enhancing transition behaviors. *Education and Treatment of Children, 29,* 507–516.

Bandura, A. (1993). Perceived self-efficacy in cognitive development and functioning. *Educational Psychologist, 28,* 117–148.

Barrett, S., Eber, L., & Weist, M. (Eds.). (2013). *Advancing education effectiveness: Interconnecting school mental health and school-wide positive behavior support.* Baltimore: Center for School Mental Health.

Barton, E. E., Kinder, K., Casey, A. M., & Artman, K. M. (2011). Finding your feedback fit: Strategies for designing and delivering performance feedback systems. *Young Exceptional Children, 14,* 29–46.

Batsche, G., Elliott, J., Graden, J. L., Grimes, J., Kovaleski, J. F., Prasse, D., . . . Tilly, W. D. (2006). *Response to intervention policy considerations and implementation.* Alexandria, VA: National Association of State Directors of Special Education.

Bavarian, N., Lewis, K. M., Acock, A., DuBois, D. L., Yan, Z., Vuchinich, S., . . . Flay, B. R. (2016). Effects of a school-based social–emotional and character development program on health behaviors: A matched-pair, cluster-randomized controlled trial. *Journal of Primary Prevention, 37,* 87–105.

Belfirore, P. J., Lee, D. L., Vargas, A. U., & Skinner, C. H. (1997). Effects of high-preference single-digit mathematics problem completion on multiple-digit mathematics problem performance. *Journal of Applied Behavior Analysis, 30,* 327–330.

Bell, S. K., Coleman, J. K., Anderson, A., Whelan, J. P., & Wilder, C. (2000). The effectiveness of peer mediation in a low-SES rural elementary school. *Psychology in the Schools, 37,* 505–516.

Bergan, J., & Kratochwill, T. (1990). *Behavioral consultation and therapy.* New York: Plenum Press.

Bernstein-Yamashiro, B., & Noam, G. G. (2013). Teacher–student relationships: A growing field of study. *New Directions for Youth Development, 2013*(137), 15–26.

Board of Education v. Rowley, 458 U.S. 176 (1982). Retrieved from *https://supreme.justia.com/cases/federal/us/458/176.*

Bradshaw, C. P., Koth, C. W., Bevans, K. B., Ialongo, N., & Leaf, P. J. (2008). The impact of school-wide positive behavioral interventions and supports (PBIS) on the organizational health of elementary schools. *School Psychology Quarterly, 23,* 462–473.

Bradshaw, C. P., Mitchell, M. M., & Leaf, P. J. (2010). Examining the effects of schoolwide positive behavioral interventions and supports on student outcomes. *Journal of Positive Behavior Interventions, 12,* 133–148.

Bradshaw, C. P., & Pas, E. T. (2011). A statewide scale up of positive behavioral interventions and supports: A description of the development of systems of support and analysis of adoption and implementation. *School Psychology Review, 40,* 530–548.

Bradshaw, C. P., Reinke, W. M., Brown, L. D., Bevans, K. B., & Leaf, P. J. (2008). Implementation of school-wide positive behavioral interventions and supports (PBIS) in elementary schools: Observations from a randomized trial. *Education and Treatment of Children, 31,* 1–26.

Briesch, A., Chafouleas, S., & Chaffee, R. (2018). Analysis of state-level guidance regarding school-based, universal screening for social, emotional, and behavioral risk. *School Mental Health, 10,* 147–162.

Brophy, J., & Good, T. L. (1986). Teacher behavior and student achievement. In M. C. Wittrock (Ed.), *Handbook of research on teaching* (3rd ed., pp. 933–958). New York: Macmillan.

Brouwers, A., & Tomic, W. (2000). A longitudinal study of teacher burnout and perceived self-efficacy in classroom management. *Teaching and Teacher Education, 16,* 239–253.

Brown, B. B., Mounts, N., Lamborn, S. D., & Steinberg, L. (1993). Parenting practices and peer group affiliation in adolescence. *Child Development, 64,* 467–482.

Bruhn, A. L. (2011). *Measuring primary plan treatment integrity of comprehensive, integrated three-tiered prevention models.* Unpublished doctoral dissertation, Vanderbilt University, Nashville, TN.

Brunsting, N. C., Sreckovic, M. A., & Lane, K. L. (2014). Special education teacher burnout: A synthesis of research from 1979 to 2013. *Education and Treatment of Children, 37,* 681–712.

Burns, M. K., Egan, A. M., Kunkel, A. K., McComas, J., Peterson, M. M., Rahn, N. L., & Wilson, J. (2013). Training for generalization and maintenance in RtI implementation: Front-loading for sustainability. *Learning Disabilities Research and Practice, 28,* 81–88.

Burns, M. K., & Ysseldyke, J. E. (2009). Reported prevalence of evidence-based instructional practices in special education. *Journal of Special Education, 43*(1), 3–11.

Butler, D. L., & Winne, P. H. (1995). Feedback and self-regulated learning: A theoretical synthesis. *Review of Educational Research, 65,* 245–281.

Campbell, S. B. (2002). *Behavior problems in preschool children: Clinical and developmental issues* (2nd ed.). New York: Guilford Press.

Canter, L. (1990). *Lee Canter's back to school with assertive discipline.* Santa Monica, CA: Canter & Associates.

Chafouleas, S. M. (2013, November). *Direct behavior rating: Overview of use in assessing student behavior within multi-tiered models of service delivery.* Paper presented at the annual meeting of the Rhode Island School Psychologists Association, Providence, RI.

Chafouleas, S. M., Riley-Tillman, T. C., & Christ, T. J. (2009). Direct Behavior Rating (DBR): An emerging method for assessing social behavior within a tiered intervention system. *Assessment for Effective Intervention, 34,* 195–200.

Chang, M. (2009). An appraisal perspective of teacher burnout: Examining the emotional work of teachers. *Educational Psychology Review, 21,* 193–218.

Cheney, D., Blum, C., & Walker, B. (2004). An analysis of leadership teams' perceptions of positive behavior support and the outcomes of typically developing and at-risk in their schools. *Assessment for Effective Intervention, 30,* 7–24.

Coffey, J. H., & Horner, R. (2012). The sustainability of schoolwide positive behavior interventions and supports. *Exceptional Children, 79,* 407–422.

Collaborative for Academic, Social, and Emotional Learning [CASEL]. (2019). What is SEL? Retrieved from *https://casel.org.*

Colvin, G. (2002). Designing classroom organization and structure. In K. L. Lane, F. M. Gresham, & T. E. O'Shaughnessy (Eds.), *Interventions for children with or at risk for emotional and behavioral disorders* (pp. 159–174). Boston: Allyn & Bacon.

Colvin, G., Kameenui, E. J., & Sugai, G. (1993). Reconceptualizing behavior management and school-wide discipline in general education. *Education and Treatment of Children, 16,* 361–381.

Colvin, G., & Scott, T. M. (2004). *Managing the cycle of acting out behavior in the classroom.* Eugene, OR: Behavior Associates.

Colvin, G., Sugai, G., Good, R. H., & Lee, Y. (1997). Using active supervision and precorrection to improve transition behaviors in an elementary school. *School Psychology Quarterly, 12,* 344–363.

Committee for Children. (2013). *Second steps violence prevention.* Seattle, WA: Author.

Common, E. A., Buckman, M. M., Lane, K. L., Leko, M., Royer, D. J., Oakes, W. P., & Allen, G. E. (2019). *Exploring solutions to address students' social competencies to facilitate school success: A usability and feasibility study.* Manuscript in review.

Common, E. A., & Lane, K. L. (2017). Social validity assessment. In J. K. Luiselli (Ed.), *Applied behavior analysis advanced guidebook* (pp. 73–92). San Diego, CA: Academic Press.

Common, E. A., Lane, K. L., Cantwell, E. D., Brunsting, N., & Oakes, W. P. (2019). Teacher-delivered strategies to increase students' opportunities to respond: A systematic methodological review. *Behavioral Disorders.* [Epub ahead of print]

Common, E. A., Lane, K. L., Oakes, W. P., Schellman, L. E., Shogren, K., Germer, K. A., & Quell, A. E. (2019). *Building site-level capacity for functional assessment-based interventions: Outcomes of a professional learning series.* Manuscript under review.

Conduct Problems Prevention Research Group. (2010). The effects of a multi-year randomized clinical trial of a universal social-emotional learning program: The role of student and school characteristics. *Journal of Consulting and Clinical Psychology, 78,* 156–168.

Connect with Kids Network. (2017). *Connect with Kids.* New York: Author.

Cook, B. G., & Cook, S. C. (2013). Unraveling evidence-based practices in special education. *Journal of Special Education, 47,* 71–82.

Cook, B. G., Smith, G. J., & Tankersley, M. (2012). Evidence-based practices in education. In K. R. Harris, S. Graham, T. Urdan, C. B. McCormick, G. M. Sinatra, & J. Sweller (Eds.), *APA educational psychology handbook: Vol 1. Theories, constructs, and critical issues* (pp. 495–527). Washington, DC: American Psychological Association.

Cook, B. G., & Tankersley, M. (2013). *Effective practices in special education.* Boston: Pearson.

Cook, B. G., Tankersley, M., & Landrum, T. J. (2013). *Advances in learning and behavioral disabilities.* Bingley, UK: Emerald Group.

Cook, T. D., Habib, F. N., Phillips, M., Settersten, R. A., Shagle, S. C., & Degimencioglu, S. M. (1999). Comer's school development program in Prince George's County, Maryland: A theory-based evaluation. *American Educational Research Journal, 36,* 543–597.

Cooper, J. O., Heron, T. E., & Heward, W. L. (2007). *Applied behavior analysis.* Upper Saddle River, NJ: Pearson Education.

Cooper, J. T., Gage, N. A., Alter, P. J., LaPolla, S., MacSuga-Gage, A. S., & Scott, T. M. (2018). Educators' self-reported training, use, and perceived effectiveness of evidence-based classroom management practices. *Preventing School Failure, 62,* 13–24.

Corcoran, R. P., Cheung, A. C. K., Kim, E., & Xie, C. (2018). Effective universal school-based social and emotional learning programs for improving academic achievement: A systematic review and meta-analysis of 50-years of research. *Educational Research Review, 25,* 56–72.

Council for Exceptional Children. (2014). *CEC standards for evidence-based practices in special education.* Arlington, VA: Author.

Cox, M., Griffin, M. M., Hall, R., Oakes, W. P., & Lane, K. L. (2011). Using a functional assessment-based intervention to increase academic engaged time in an inclusive middle school setting. *Beyond Behavior, 20,* 44–54.

Crick, N. R., Grotpeter, J. K., & Bigbee, M. A. (2002). Relationally and physically aggressive children's intent attributions and feelings of distress for relational and instrumental peer provocations. *Child Development, 73,* 1134–1142.

Crone, D. A., Hawken, L. S., & Horner, R. H. (2010). *Responding to problem behavior in schools: The Behavior Education Program* (2nd ed.). New York: Guilford Press.

Crosby, S., Jolivette, K., & Patterson, D. (2006). Using precorrection to manage inappropriate academic and social behaviors. *Beyond Behavior, 16,* 14–17.

Daly, E. J., Garbacz, S. A., Olson, S. C., Persampieri, M., & Ni, H. (2006). Improving oral reading fluency by influencing students' choice of instructional procedures: An experimental analysis with two students with behavioral disorders. *Behavioral Interventions, 21,* 13–30.

Davis, C. A., Brady, M. P., Williams, R. E., & Hamilton, R. (1992). Effects of high-probability requests on the acquisition and generalization of responses to requests in young children with behavior disorders. *Journal of Applied Behavior Analysis, 25,* 905–916.

Dearing, E., Kreider, H., Simpkins, S., & Weiss, H. B. (2006). Family involvement in school and low-income children's literacy: Longitudinal associations between and within families. *Journal of Educational Psychology, 98,* 653–664.

Deno, S. L. (2003). Developments in curriculum-based measurement. *Journal of Special Education, 37,* 184–192.

Denton, C. A. (2012). Response to intervention for reading difficulties in the primary grades: Some answers and lingering questions. *Journal of Learning Disabilities, 45,* 232–243.

DiGangi, S., Maag, J., & Rutherford, R. (1991). Self-graphing of on-task behavior: Enhancing the reactive effects of self-monitoring on on-task behavior and academic performance. *Learning Disability Quarterly, 14,* 221–230.

Dolph, D. (2017). Challenges and opportunities for school improvement: Recommendations for urban school principals. *Education and Urban Society, 49,* 363–387.

Drevon, D. D., Hixson, M. D., Wyse, R. D., & Rigney, A. M. (2019). A meta-analytic review of the evidence for check-in check-out. *Psychology in the Schools, 56*(3), 393–412.

Drugli, M. B., Larsson, B., Fossum, S., & Morch, W. T. (2010). Five- to six-year outcome and its prediction for children with ODD/CD treated with parent training. *Journal of Child Psychology and Psychiatry, 51,* 559–566.

Drummond, T. (1994). *The Student Risk Screening Scale (SRSS).* Grants Pass, OR: Josephine County Mental Health Program.

Drummond, T., Eddy, J. M., & Reid, J. B. (1998a). *Follow-up study #3: Risk screening scale: Prediction of negative outcomes by 10th grade from 2nd grade screening.* Unpublished technical report, Oregon Social Learning Center, Eugene, OR.

Drummond, T., Eddy, J. M., & Reid, J. B. (1998b). *Follow-up study #4: Risk screening scale: Prediction of negative outcomes in two longitudinal samples.* Unpublished technical report, Oregon Social Learning Center, Eugene, OR.

Drummond, T., Eddy, J. M., Reid, J. B., & Bank, L. (1994, November). *The Student Risk Screening Scale: A brief teacher screening instrument for conduct disorder.* Paper presented at the fourth annual Prevention Conference, Washington, DC.

Duchaine, E. L., Jolivette, K., & Fredrick, L. D. (2011). The effect of teacher coaching with performance feedback on behavior-specific praise in inclusion classrooms. *Education and Treatment of Children, 34,* 209–227.

Dunlap, G. (1993). Promoting generalization: Current status and functional considerations. In R. V. Houten & S. Axelrod (Eds.), *Behavior analysis and treatment* (pp. 269–296). New York: Plenum Press.

DuPaul, G. J., & Hoff, K. E. (1998). Reducing disruptive behavior in general education classrooms: The use of self-management strategies. *School Psychology Review, 27,* 290–303.

Durlak, J. A., Weissberg, R. P., Dymnicki, A. B., Taylor, R. D., & Schellinger, K. B. (2011). The impact of enhancing students' social and emotional learning: A meta-analysis of school-based universal interventions. *Child Development, 82,* 405–432.

Eagle, J. W., Dowd-Eagle, S. E., Snyder, A., & Holtzman, E. G. (2015). Implementing a multi-tiered system of support (MTSS): Collaboration between school psychologists and administrators to promote systems-level change. *Journal of Educational and Psychological Consultation, 25,* 160–177.

Eisen, M., Zellman, G. L., & Murray, D. M. (2003). Evaluating the Lions-Quest Skills for Adolescence drug education program: Second-year behavior outcomes. *Addictive Behaviors, 28,* 883–897.

Elliott, S. N., Davies, M. D., Frey, J. R., Gresham, F., & Cooper, G. (2018). Development and initial validation of a social emotional learning assessment for universal screening. *Journal of Applied Developmental Psychology, 55,* 39–51.

Elliott, S. N., & Gresham, F. M. (1991). *Social skills intervention guide: Practical strategies for social skills training.* Circle Pines, MN: American Guidance Services.

Elliott, S. N., & Gresham, F. (2008a). *Social Skills Improvement System (SSiS)—Intervention Guide.* San Antonio, TX: PsychCorp Pearson Education.

Elliott, S. N., & Gresham, F. (2008b). *Social Skills Improvement System (SSiS)—Performance Screening Guide.* San Antonio, TX: PsychCorp Pearson Education.

Elliott, S. N., & Gresham, F. M. (2017a). *Social Skills Improvement System (SSiS)—SEL Edition Classwide Intervention Program.* San Antonio, TX: PsychCorp Pearson Education.

Elliott, S. N., & Gresham, F. M. (2017b). *Social Skills Improvement System—Social–Emotional Learning Edition.* San Antonio, TX: PsychCorp Pearson Education.

Elliott, S. N., Turco, T. L., & Gresham, F. M. (1987). Consumers' and clients' pretreatment acceptability ratings of classroom-based group contingencies. *Journal of School Psychology, 25,* 145–154.

Endrew F. v. Douglas County School District, 798 F. 3d 1329 § 10th Cir. 2015.

Ennis, R. P., Lane, K. L., & Oakes, W. P. (2012). Score reliability and validity of the Student Risk Screening Scale: A psychometrically sound, feasible tool for use in urban elementary school. *Journal of Emotional and Behavioral Disorders, 20,* 241–259.

Ennis, R. P., Lane, K. L., & Oakes, W. P. (2018). Empowering teachers with low-intensity strategies to support instruction: Self-monitoring in an elementary resource classroom. *Preventing School Failure, 62,* 176–189.

Ennis, R. P., Royer, D. J., Lane, K. L., Menzies, H. M., Oakes, W. P., & Schellman, L. E. (2018). Behavior-specific praise: An effective, efficient, low-intensity strategy to support student success. *Beyond Behavior, 27,* 134–139.

Ervin, R. A., Schaughency, E., Goodman, S. D., McGlinchey, M. T., & Matthews, A. (2006). Merging research and practice agendas to address reading and behavior school-wide. *School Psychology Review, 35,* 198–223.

Espelage, D. L., Polanin, J. R., & Rose, C. A. (2015). Social–emotional learning program to reduce bullying, fighting, and victimization among middle school students with disabilities. *Remedial and Special Education, 36,* 299–311.

Evertson, C. M., & Weade, R. (1989). Classroom management and teaching style: Instructional stability vvand variability in two junior high English classrooms. *Elementary School Journal, 89,* 379–393.

Every Student Succeeds Act of 2015, Public Law No. 114-95 § 114, 1177 (2015).

Falk, K. B., & Wehby, J. (2001). The effects of peer-assisted learning strategies on the beginning reading skills of young children with emotional or behavioral disorders. *Behavioral Disorders, 26,* 344–359.

Fallon, L. M., Collier-Meek, M. A., Maggin, D. M., Sanetti, L. M. H., & Johnson, A. H. (2015). Is performance feedback for educators an evidence-based practice?: A systematic review and evaluation based on single-case research. *Exceptional Children, 81,* 227–246.

Fallon, L. M., O'Keeffe, B. V., Gage, N. A., & Sugai, G. (2015). Brief report: Assessing attitudes toward culturally and contextually relevant schoolwide positive behavior support strategies. *Behavioral Disorders, 40,* 251–260.

Farkas, M. S., Simonsen, B., Migdole, S., Donovan, M. E., Clemens, K., & Cicchese, V. (2012). School-wide positive behavior support in an alternative school setting: An evaluation of fidelity, outcomes, and social validity of Tier 1 implementation. *Journal of Emotional and Behavioral Disorders, 20,* 275–288.

Farrell, A. D., Meyer, A. L., Sullivan, T. N., & Kung, E. M. (2003). Evaluation of the Responding in Peaceful and Positive Ways (RIPP) seventh grade violence prevention curriculum. *Journal of Child and Family Studies, 12,* 101–120.

Farrell, A. D., Valois, R. F., Meyer, A. L., & Tidwell, R. P. (2003). Impact of the RIPP Violence Prevention Program on rural middle school students. *Journal of Primary Prevention, 24,* 143–167.

Fawcett, S. (1991). Social validity: A note on methodology. *Journal of Applied Behavior Analysis, 24,* 235–239.

Finn, C. A., & Sladeczek, I. E. (2001). Assessing the social validity of behavior interventions: A review of treatment acceptability measures. *School Psychology Quarterly, 16,* 176–206.

Fixsen, D., Blasé, K., Metz, A., & Van Dyke, M. (2013). Statewide implementation of evidence-based programs. *Exceptional Children, 79,* 213–230.

Fixsen, D. L., Blasé, K. A., Naoom, S. F., & Wallace, F. (2009). Core implementation components. *Research on Social Work Practice, 19,* 531–540.

Fixsen, D. L., Naoom, S. F., Blasé, K. A., Friedman, R. M., & Wallace, F. (2005). *Implementation research: A synthesis of the literature.* Tampa: University of South Florida, Louis de la Parte Florida Mental Health Institute, the National Implementation Research Network.

Flay, B. R., Allred, C. G., & Ordway, N. (2001). Effects of the positive action program on achievement and discipline: Two matched-control comparisons. *Prevention Science, 2,* 71–89.

Fletcher, J. M., & Vaughn, S. (2009). Response to intervention: Preventing and remediating academic difficulties. *Child Development Perspectives, 3,* 30–37.

Floress, M. T., Jenkins, L. N., Reinke, W. M., & McKown, L. (2018). General education teachers' natural rates of praise: A preliminary investigation. *Behavioral Disorders, 43,* 411–422.

Foorman, B. R., Francis, D. J., Shaywitz, S. E., Shaywitz, B. A., & Fletcher, J. M. (1997). The case for early reading intervention. In B. A. Blachman (Ed.), *Foundations of reading acquisition and dyslexia: Implications for early intervention* (pp. 243–264). Mahwah, NJ: Erlbaum.

Forness, S. R., Freeman, S. F. N., Paparella, T., Kauffman, J. M., & Walker, H. M. (2012). Special education implications of point and cumulative prevalence for children with emotional or behavioral disorders. *Journal of Emotional and Behavioral Disorders, 20,* 4–18.

Freeman, J. (2018). Effective low-intensity strategies to enhance school success: What every educator needs to know—a closing commentary. *Beyond Behavior, 27,* 175–176.

Frick, P., Kamphaus, R., Lahey, B., Loebert, R., Christ, M., Hart, E., & Tannenbaum, L. E. (1991). Academic underachievement and the disruptive behavior disorders. *Journal of Consulting and Clinical Psychology, 59,* 289–294.

Fuchs, D., & Fuchs, L. S. (2017). Critique of the national evaluation of response to intervention: A case for simpler frameworks. *Exceptional Children, 83,* 255–268.

Fuchs, D., Fuchs, L. S., & Compton, D. L. (2012). Smart RTI: A next-generation approach to multilevel prevention. *Exceptional Children, 78,* 263–279.

Fuchs, D., Fuchs, L. S., & Vaughn, S. (2014). What is intensive instruction and why is it important? *Teaching Exceptional Children, 46,* 13–18.

Fuchs, L. S. (2003). Assessing intervention responsiveness: Conceptual and technical issues. *Learning Disabilities Research and Practice, 18,* 172–186.

Fuchs, L. S., & Fuchs, D. (2007). A model for implementing response to intervention. *Teaching Exceptional Children, 39,* 14–20.

Fullerton, E. K., Conroy, M. A., & Correa, V. I. (2009). Early childhood teachers' use of specific praise statements with young children at risk for behavioral disorders. *Behavioral Disorders, 34,* 118–135.

Fyfe, E. R., Rittle-Johnson, B., & DeCaro, M. S. (2012). The effects of feedback during exploratory mathematics problem solving: Prior knowledge matters. *Journal of Educational Psychology, 104,* 1094–1108.

Gage, N. A., Sugai, G., Lewis, T. J., & Brzozowy, S. (2015). Academic achievement and school-wide positive behavior supports. *Journal of Disability Policy Studies, 25,* 199–209.

George, H. P., Cox, K. E., Minch, D., & Sandomierski, T. (2018). District practices associated with successful SWPBIS implementation. *Behavioral Disorders, 43,* 393–406.

George, M. P., White, G. P., & Schlaffer, J. J. (2007). Implementing school-wide behavior change: Lessons from the field. *Psychology in the Schools, 44,* 41–51.

Germer, K. A., Kaplan, L. M., Giroux, L. N., Markham, E. H., Ferris, G., Oakes, W., & Lane, K. L. (2011). A function-based intervention to increase a second-grade student's on-task behavior in a general education classroom. *Beyond Behavior, 20,* 19–30.

Gersten, R. (2016). What we are learning about mathematics interventions and conducting research on mathematics interventions. *Journal of Research on Educational Effectiveness, 9,* 684–688.

Gersten, R., Fuchs, L. S., Compton, D., Coyne, M., Greenwood, C., & Innocenti, M. S. (2005). Quality indicators for group experimental and quasi-experimental research in special education. *Exceptional Children, 71,* 149–164.

Gersten, R., Jordan, N. C., & Flojo, J. R. (2005). Early identification and interventions for students with mathematics difficulties. *Journal of Learning Disabilities, 38,* 293–304.

Gersten, R., & Newman-Gonchar, R. (2011). *Understanding RTI in mathematics: Proven methods and applications.* Baltimore: Brookes.

Good, R. H., & Kaminski, R. A. (2018). *Dynamic Indicators of Basic Early Literacy Skills* (8th ed.). Eugene: University of Oregon.

Goodman, A., & Goodman, R. (2009). Strengths and Difficulties Questionnaire as a dimensional measure of child mental health. *Journal of the American Academy of Child and Adolescent Psychiatry, 48,* 400–403.

Goodman, R. (1997). The Strengths and Difficulties Questionnaire: A research note. *Journal of Child Psychology and Psychiatry, 38,* 581–586.

Goodman, R. (2001). Psychometric properties of the Strengths and Difficulties Questionnaire (SDQ). *Journal of the American Academy of Child and Adolescent Psychiatry, 40,* 1337–1345.

Goodman, R., Meltzer, H., & Bailey, V. (1998). The Strengths and Difficulties Questionnaire: A pilot study on the validity of the self-report version. *European Child and Adolescent Psychiatry, 7,* 125–130.

Gottfredson, D. C., Gottfredson, G. D., & Hybl, L. G. (1993). Managing adolescent behavior: A multiyear, multischool study. *American Educational Research Journal, 30,* 179–215.

Greenbaum, P. E., Dedrick, R. R., Friedman, R. M., Kutash, K., Brown, E. C., Lardieri, S. R., . . . Pugh, M. (1996). National Adolescent and Child Treatment Study (NCATS): Outcomes for children with serious emotional and behavioral disturbance. *Journal of Emotional and Behavioral Disorders, 4,* 130–146.

Gresham, F. M. (1989). Assessment of treatment integrity in school consultation and prereferral intervention. *School Psychology Review, 18,* 37–50.

Gresham, F. M., & Elliott, S. N. (1990). *Social Skills Rating System.* Circle Pines, MN: American Guidance Service.

Gresham, F. M., & Elliott, S. N. (2008). *Social Skills Improvement System (SSiS) Rating Scales.* San Antonio, TX: PsychCorp Pearson Education.

Gresham, F. M., & Elliott, S. N. (2017). *SSIS Social Emotional Learning Edition Classwide Intervention Program.* New York: Pearson Education.

Gresham, F. M., Elliott, S. N., & Kettler, R. J. (2010). Base rates of social skills acquisition/performance deficits, strengths, and problem behaviors: An analysis of the Social Skills Improvement System—Rating Scales. *Psychological Assessment, 22,* 809–815.

Gresham, F. M., & Kendell, G. K. (1987). School consultation research: Methodological critique and future directions. *School Psychology Review, 16,* 306–316.

Gresham, F. M., Lane, K. L., & Lambros, K. M. (2000). Comorbidity of conduct problems and ADHD: Identification of "fledgling psychopaths." *Journal of Emotional and Behavioral Disorders, 8,* 83–93.

Gresham, F. M., & Lopez, M. F. (1996). Social validation: A unifying construct for school-based consultation research and practice. *School Psychology Quarterly, 11,* 204–227.

Gresham, F. M., Sugai, G., Horner, R. H., McInerney, M., & Quinn, M. (1998). *Classroom and schoolwide practices that support students' social competence: A synthesis of research.* Washington, DC: Office of Special Education Programs.

Grossman, P., & McDonald, M. (2008). Back to the future: Directions for research in teaching and teacher education. *American Educational Research Journal, 45,* 184–205.

Hammill, D., & Larsen, S. (1996). *Test of Written Language–3.* Austin, TX: PRO-ED.

Harris, K. R., Graham, S., Mason, L., & Friedlander, B. (2008). *Powerful writing strategies for all students.* Baltimore: Brookes.

Harris, K. R., Lane, K. L., Graham, S., Driscoll, S., Wilson, K., Sandmel, K., . . . Schatschneider, C. (2012). Practice-based professional development for self-regulated strategies instruction in writing: A randomized controlled study. *Journal of Teacher Education, 63,* 103–119.

Hattie, J., & Timperley, H. (2007). The power of feedback. *Review of Educational Research, 77*(1), 81–112.

Hawken, L. S., MacLeod, K. S., & Rawlings, L. (2007). Effects of the Behavior Education Program (BEP) on office discipline referrals of elementary school students. *Journal of Positive Behavior Interventions, 9,* 94–101.

Hawken, L. S., O'Neill, R. E., & MacLeod, K. S. (2011). An investigation of the impact of function of problem behavior on effectiveness of the Behavior Education Program (BEP). *Education and Treatment of Children, 34,* 551–574.

Hawkins, R. (1991). Is social validity what we are interested in?: Argument for a functional approach. *Journal of Applied Behavior Analysis, 24,* 205–213.

Haydon, T., & Kroeger, S. D. (2016). Active supervision, precorrection, and explicit timing: A high school case study on classroom behavior. *Preventing School Failure, 60,* 70–78.

Haydon, T., Mancil, G. R., & Van Loan, C. (2009). Using opportunities to respond in a general education classroom: A case study. *Education and Treatment of Children, 32,* 267–278.

Haydon, T., & Musti-Rao, S. (2011). Effective use of behavior-specific praise: A middle school case study. *Beyond Behavior, 20,* 31–39.

Haydon, T., & Scott, T. M. (2008). Using common sense in common settings: Active supervision and precorrection in the morning gym. *Intervention in School and Clinic, 43,* 283–290.

Henggeler, S. (1998). Multisystemic therapy. In D. S. Elliott (Ed.), *Blueprints for violence prevention.* Boulder: Center for the Study and Prevention of Violence, Institute of Behavioral Science, University of Colorado.

Hinshaw, S. P. (1982). Academic underachievement, attention deficits, and aggression: Comorbidity and implications for intervention. *Journal of Consulting and Clinical Psychology, 60,* 893–903.

Horner, R. H., & Billingsley, F. F. (1988). The effect of competing behavior on the generalization and maintenance of adaptive behavior in applied settings. In R. H. Horner, G. Dunlap, & R. L. Koegel (Eds.), *Generalization and maintenance: Lifestyle changes in applied settings* (pp. 197–220). Baltimore: Brookes.

Horner, R. H., Carr, E. C., Halle, J., McGee, G., Odom, S., & Wolery, M. (2005). The use of single-subject research to identify evidence-based practice in special education. *Exceptional Children, 71,* 165–179.

Horner, R. H., & Sugai, G. (2015). School-wide PBIS: An example of applied behavior analysis implemented at a scale of social importance. *Behavior Analysis in Practice, 8,* 80–85.

Horner, R. H., Sugai, G., & Fixsen, D. L. (2017). Implementing effective educational practices at scales of social importance. *Clinical Child and Family Psychology Review, 20,* 25–35.

Horner, R. H., Todd, A. W., Lewis-Palmer, T., Irvin, L. K., Sugai, G., & Boland, J. B. (2004). The School-wide Evaluation Tool (SET): A research instrument for assessing school-wide positive behavior support. *Journal of Positive Behavior Intervention, 6,* 3–12.

Horner, R. H., Ward, C. S., Fixsen, D. L., Sugai, G., McIntosh, K., Putnam, R., & Little, H. D. (2019). Resource leveraging to achieve large-scale implementation of effective educational practices. *Journal of Positive Behavior Interventions, 21*(2), 67–76.

Hoy, W. K. (2003). The Organizational Health Inventory for Elementary Schools (OHI-E). Retrieved from *http://waynekhoy.com/pdfs/ohi-e.pdf.*

Hughes, K., Bellis, M. A., Hardcastle, K. A., Sethi, D., Butchart, A., Mikton, C., . . . Dunne, M. P. (2017). The effect of multiple adverse childhood experiences on health: A systematic review and meta-analysis. *Lancet Public Health, 2,* 356–366.

Individuals with Disabilities Education Improvement Act of 2004, Public Law No. 20 U.S.C. 1400 et esq. (2004).

January, A. M., Casey, R. J., & Paulson, D. (2011). A meta-analysis of classroom-wide interventions to build social skills: Do they work? *School Psychology Review, 40,* 242–256.

January, S. A., & Ardoin, S. P. (2015). Technical adequacy and acceptability of curriculum-based measurement and the measures of academic progress. *Assessment for Effective Intervention, 41,* 3–15.

Johnson, E., Mellard, D. F., Fuchs, D., & McKnight, M. A. (2006). *Responsiveness to Intervention (RTI): How to do it.* Lawrence, KS: National Research Center on Learning Disabilities. Retrieved from *https://files.eric.ed.gov/fulltext/ED496979.pdf.*

Johnson-Gros, K. N., Lyons, E. A., & Griffin, J. R. (2008). Active supervision: An intervention to reduce high school tardiness. *Education and Treatment of Children, 31,* 39–53.

Jolivette, K., Strichter, J. P., & McCormick, K. M. (2002). Making choices–improving behavior– engaging in learning. *Teaching Exceptional Children, 34,* 24–30.

Jolivette, K., Wehby, J. H., Canale, J., & Massey, N. G. (2001). Effects of choice-making opportunities on the behavior of students with emotional and behavioral disorders. *Behavioral Disorders, 26,* 131–145.

Jones, K. M., Wickstrom, K. F., & Friman, P. C. (1997). The effects of observational feedback on treatment integrity in school-based behavioral consultation. *School Psychology Quarterly, 12,* 316–326.

Joyce-Beaulieu, D., & Sulkowski, M. L. (2015). *Cognitive behavioral therapy in K–12 school settings: A practitioner's toolkit.* New York: Springer.

Kamphaus, R. W., & Reynolds, C. R. (2007). *Behavior Assessment System for Children (BASC-2) Behavioral and Emotional Screening System (BESS).* San Antonio, TX: Pearson.

Kamphaus, R. W., & Reynolds, C. R. (2015). *Behavior Assessment System for Children (BASC-3): Behavioral and Emotional Screening System (BESS)* (3rd ed.). Bloomington, MN: Pearson.

Kartub, D. T., Taylor-Greene, S., March, R. E., & Horner, R. H. (2000). Reducing hallway noise: A systems approach. *Journal of Positive Behavior Interventions, 2,* 179–182.

Kauffman, J. M. (1999). How we prevent the prevention of emotional and behavioral disorders. *Exceptional Children, 65,* 448–468.

Kauffman, J. M. (2004). The president's commission and the devaluation of special education. *Education and Treatment of Children, 27,* 307–324.

Kauffman, J. M. (2005). *Characteristics of emotional and behavioral disorders of children and youth* (Vol. 8). Upper Saddle River, NJ: Pearson.

Kazdin, A. E. (1977). Assessing the clinical or applied importance of behavior change through social validation. *Behavior Modification, 1,* 427–452.

Kern, L., & Manz, P. (2004). A look at current validity issues of school-wide behavior support. *Behavioral Disorders, 30,* 47–59.

Kerr, M. M., & Zigmond, N. (1986). Assessment for instructional planning. *Exceptional Children, 52,* 501–509.

Kilgus, S. P., Chafouleas, S. M., & Riley-Tillman, T. C. (2013). Development and initial validation of the social and academic behavior risk screener for elementary grades. *School Psychology Quarterly, 28,* 210–226.

Kilgus, S. P., Chafouleas, S. M., Riley-Tillman, T. C., & von der Embse, N. P. (2013). *Social, Academic, and Emotional Behavior Risk Screener©: Teacher Rating Form.* Columbia: University of Missouri.

Kilgus, S. P., Eklund, K., von der Embse, N. P., Taylor, C. N., & Sims, W. A. (2016). Psychometric defensibility of the Social, Academic, and Emotional Behavior Risk Screener (SAEBRS) Teacher Rating Scale and multiple gating procedure within elementary and middle school samples. *Journal of School Psychology, 58,* 21–39.

Kilgus, S. P., von der Embse, N. P., Allen, A. N., Taylor, C. N., & Eklund, K. (2018). Examining SAEBRS Technical Adequacy and the moderating influence of criterion type on cut score performance. *Remedial and Special Education, 39,* 377–388.

Kincaid, D., Childs, K., Blasé, K. A., & Wallace, F. (2007). Identifying barriers and facilitators in implementing schoolwide positive behavior support. *Journal of Positive Behavior Interventions, 9,* 174–184.

Klingbeil, D. L., Nelson, P. M., Van Norman, E. R., & Birr, C. (2017). Diagnostic accuracy of multivariate universal screening procedures for reading in upper elementary grades. *Remedial and Special Education, 38,* 308–320.

Kounin, J. (1977). *Discipline and group management in classrooms.* New York: Holt, Rinehart & Winston.

Kratochwill, T. R., Hitchcock, J., Horner, R. H., Levin, J. R., Odom, S. L., Rindskopf, D., & Shadish,

W. R. M. (2010). Single case designs technical documentation. Retrieved from *https://ies.ed.gov/ncee/wwc/Docs/ReferenceResources/wwc_scd.pdf*.

Kusche, C. A., & Greenberg, M. T. (1994). *The PATHS curriculum*. Seattle, WA: Developmental Research and Programs.

Landrum, T. J., Tankersley, M., & Kauffman, J. M. (2003). What is special about special education for students with emotional or behavioral disorders? *Journal of Special Education, 37*, 148–156.

Lane, K. L. (1999). Young students at risk for antisocial behavior: The utility of academic and social skills interventions. *Journal of Emotional and Behavioral Disorders, 7*, 211–223. Lane, K. L. (2002). Primary Prevention Plan: Feedback Form. Retrieved from *www.ci3t.org/measures*.

Lane, K. L. (2004). Academic instruction and tutoring interventions for students with emotional/behavioral disorders: 1990 to present. In R. B. Rutherford, M. M. Quinn, & S. R. Mathur (Eds.), *Handbook of research in emotional and behavioral disorders* (pp. 462–486). New York: Guilford Press.

Lane, K. L. (2007). Identifying and supporting students at risk for emotional and behavioral disorders with multi-level models: Data-driven approaches to conducting secondary interventions with academic emphasis. *Education and Treatment of Children, 30*, 135–164.

Lane, K. L. (2009a). Comprehensive, integrated three-tiered model of prevention: Treatment Integrity Direct Observation Tool (Ci3T TI: DO). Retrieved from *www.ci3t.org/measures*.

Lane, K. L. (2009b). Comprehensive, integrated three-tiered model of prevention: Treatment Integrity Teacher Self-Report Form (Ci3T TI: TSR). Retrieved from *www.ci3t.org/measures*.

Lane, K. L. (2017). Building strong partnerships: Responsible inquiry to learn and grow together TECBD-CCBD keynote address. *Education and Treatment of Children, 40*, 597–617.

Lane, K. L., Barton-Arwood, S. M., Rogers, L., & Robertson, E. J. (2007). Literacy interventions for students with and at risk for emotional or behavioral disorders: 1997 to present. In J. C. Crockett, M. M. Gerber, & T. J. Landrum (Eds.), *Achieving the radical reform of special education: Essays in honor of James M. Kauffman* (pp. 213–241). Mahwah, NJ: Erlbaum.

Lane, K. L., & Beebe-Frankenberger, M. E. (2004). *School-based interventions: The tools you need to succeed*. Boston: Allyn & Bacon.

Lane, K. L., Beebe-Frankenberger, M., Lambros, K. L., & Pierson, M. E. (2001). Designing effective interventions for children at-risk for antisocial behavior: An integrated model of components necessary for making valid inferences. *Psychology in the Schools, 38*, 365–379.

Lane, K. L., Bocian, K. M., MacMillan, D. L., & Gresham, F. M. (2004). Treatment integrity: An essential—but often forgotten—component of school-based interventions. *Preventing School Failure, 48*, 36–43.

Lane, K. L., Bruhn, A. L., Eisner, S. L., & Robertson Kalberg, J. (2010). Score reliability and validity of the Student Risk Screening Scale: A psychometrically sound, feasible tool for use in urban middle schools. *Journal of Emotional and Behavioral Disorders, 18*(4), 211–224.

Lane, K. L., Capizzi, A. M., Fisher, M. H., & Ennis, R. P. (2012). Secondary prevention efforts at the middle school level: An application of the Behavior Education Program. *Education and Treatment of Children, 35*, 51–90.

Lane, K. L., Carter, E., Jenkins, A., Magill, L., & Germer, K. (2015). Supporting comprehensive, integrated, three-tiered models of prevention in schools: Administrators' perspectives. *Journal of Positive Behavior Interventions, 17*, 209–222.

Lane, K. L., Edgecomb, T. B., & Burris, H. (2018, October). *Creating positive, productive classrooms: District-level professional learning for successful low-intensity strategies*. Paper presented at the National PBIS Leadership Forum, Chicago, IL.

Lane, K. L., Givner, C. C., & Pierson, M. R. (2004). Teacher expectations of student behavior: Social skills necessary for success in elementary school classrooms. *Journal of Special Education, 38*, 104–110.

Lane, K. L., Gresham, F. M., & O'Shaughnessy, T. E. (2002). Serving students with or at-risk for emotional and behavior disorders: Future challenges. *Education and Treatment of Children, 25,* 507–521.

Lane, K. L., Harris, K., Graham, S., Driscoll, S. A., Sandmel, K., Morphy, P., . . . Schatschneider, C. (2011). Self-regulated strategy development at tier-2 for second-grade students with writing and behavioral difficulties: A randomized control trial. *Journal of Research on Educational Effectiveness, 4,* 322–353.

Lane, K. L., Harris, K., Graham, S., Weisenbach, J., Brindle, M., & Morphy, P. (2008). The effects of self-regulated strategy development on the writing performance of second grade students with behavioral and writing difficulties. *Journal of Special Education, 41,* 234–253.

Lane, K. L., Kalberg, J. R., Bruhn, A. L., Driscoll, S. A., Wehby, J. H., & Elliott, S. (2009). Assessing social validity of school-wide positive behavior support plans: Evidence for the reliability and structure of the Primary Intervention Rating Scale. *School Psychology Review, 38,* 135–144.

Lane, K. L., Kalberg, J. R., Bruhn, A. L., Mahoney, M. E., & Driscoll, S. A. (2008). Primary prevention programs at the elementary level: Issues of treatment integrity, systematic screening, and reinforcement. *Education and Treatment of Children, 31,* 465–494.

Lane, K. L., Kalberg, J. R., & Edwards, C. (2008). An examination of school-wide interventions with primary level efforts conducted in elementary schools: Implications for school psychologists. In D. H. Molina (Ed.), *School psychology: 21st century issues and challenges* (pp. 253–278). New York: Nova Science.

Lane, K. L., Kalberg, J. R., Lambert, W., Crnobori, M., & Bruhn, A. (2010). A comparison of systematic screening tools for emotional and behavioral disorders: A replication. *Journal of Emotional and Behavioral Disorders, 18,* 100–112.

Lane, K. L., Kalberg, J. R., & Menzies, H. M. (2009). *Developing schoolwide programs to prevent and manage problem behaviors: A step-by-step approach.* New York: Guilford Press.

Lane, K. L., Kalberg, J. R., Menzies, H., Bruhn, A., Eisner, S., & Crnobori, M. (2011). Using systematic screening data to assess risk and identify students for targeted supports: Illustrations across the K–12 continuum. *Remedial and Special Education, 32,* 39–54.

Lane, K. L., Kalberg, J. R., Mofield, E., Wehby, J. H., & Parks, R. J. (2009). Preparing students for college entrance exams: Findings of a secondary intervention conducted within a three-tiered model of support. *Remedial and Special Education, 30,* 3–18.

Lane, K. L., Kalberg, J. R., Parks, R. J., & Carter, E. W. (2008). Student Risk Screening Scale: Initial evidence for score reliability and validity at the high school level. *Journal of Emotional and Behavioral Disorders, 16,* 178–190.

Lane, K. L., Little, M. A., Rhodes, J. R., Phillips, A., & Welsh, M. T. (2007). Outcomes of a teacher-led reading intervention for elementary students at-risk for behavioral disorders. *Exceptional Children, 74,* 47–70.

Lane, K. L., & Menzies, H. M. (2002). The effects of a school-based primary intervention program: Preliminary outcomes. *Preventing School Failure, 47,* 26–32.

Lane, K. L., & Menzies, H. M. (2003). A school-wide intervention with primary and secondary levels of support for elementary students: Outcomes and considerations. *Education and Treatment of Children, 26,* 431–451.

Lane, K. L., & Menzies, H. (2005). Teacher-identified students with and without academic and behavioral concerns: Characteristics and responsiveness to a school-wide intervention. *Behavioral Disorders, 31,* 65–83.

Lane, K. L., & Menzies, H. M. (2009). Student Risk Screening Scale for Early Internalizing and Externalizing Behavior (SRSS-IE). Screening scale. Available from *www.ci3t.org/screening*.

Lane, K. L., Menzies, H., Bruhn, A., & Crnobori, M. (2011). *Managing challenging behaviors in schools: Research-based strategies that work.* New York: Guilford Press.

Lane, K. L., Menzies, H. M., Ennis, R. P., & Bezdek, J. (2013). School-wide systems to promote positive behaviors and facilitate instruction. *Journal of Curriculum and Instruction, 7,* 6–31.

Lane, K. L., Menzies, H. M., Ennis, R. P., & Oakes, W. P. (2015). *Supporting behavior for school success: A step-by-step guide to key strategies.* New York: Guilford Press.

Lane, K. L., Menzies, H. M., Ennis, R. P., & Oakes, W. P. (2018). Effective low-intensity strategies to enhance school success: What every educator needs to know. *Beyond Behavior, 27,* 128–133.

Lane, K. L., Menzies, H. M., Munton, S., Von Duering, R., & English, G. (2005). The effects of a supplemental early literacy program for a student at risk: A case study. *Preventing School Failure, 50,* 21–28.

Lane, K. L., Menzies, H. M., Oakes, W. P., & Kalberg, J. R. (2012). *Systematic screenings of behavior to support instruction: From preschool to high school.* New York: Guilford Press.

Lane, K. L., Menzies, H. M., Oakes, W. P., Zorigian, K., & Germer, K. A. (2014). Professional development in EBD: What is most effective in supporting teachers? In P. Garner, J. M. Kauffman, & M. Elliott (Eds.), *The SAGE handbook of emotional and behavioral difficulties* (2nd ed., pp. 415–425). Los Angeles: SAGE.

Lane, K. L., & Oakes, W. P. (2010). Ci3T Knowledge, Confidence, and Use Survey (Unpublished rating scale). Retrieved from *www.ci3t.org/measures.*

Lane, K. L., Oakes, W. P., Buckman, M. M., & Lane, K. S. (2018). Supporting school success: Engaging lessons to meet students' multiple needs. *Council for Children with Behavior Disorders (CCBD) Newsletter, 33,* 8–9.

Lane, K. L., Oakes, W. P., Cantwell, E. D., Common, E. A., Royer, D. J., Leko, M., . . . Allen, G. E. (2018). Predictive validity of the Student Risk Screening Scale for Internalizing and Externalizing (SRSS-IE) scores in elementary schools. *Journal of Emotional and Behavioral Disorders, 27,* 86–100.

Lane, K. L., Oakes, W. P., Cantwell, E. D., Menzies, H. M., Schatschneider, C., Lambert, W., & Common, E. A. (2017). Psychometric evidence of SRSS-IE scores in middle and high schools. *Journal of Emotional and Behavioral Disorders, 25,* 233–245.

Lane, K. L., Oakes, W. P., Cantwell, E. D., & Royer, D. J. (2016). *Building and installing comprehensive, integrated, three-tiered (Ci3T) models of prevention: A practical guide to supporting school success [Interactive e-book].* Phoenix, AZ: KOI Education.

Lane, K. L., Oakes, W. P., Cantwell, E. D., & Royer, D. J. (2018). *Building and installing comprehensive, integrated, three-tiered (Ci3T) models of prevention: A practical guide to supporting school success V1.2* [Interactive e-book]. Phoenix, AZ: KOI Education.

Lane, K. L., Oakes, W. P., Cantwell, E. D., Schatschneider, C., Menzies, H. M., Crittenden, M., & Messenger, M. (2016). Student Risk Screening Scale for Internalizing and Externalizing behaviors: Preliminary cut scores to support data-informed decision making in middle and high schools. *Behavioral Disorders, 42,* 271–284.

Lane, K. L., Oakes, W. P., Ennis, R. P., Cox, M. L., Schatschneider, C., & Lambert, W. (2013). Additional evidence for the reliability and validity of the Student Risk Screening Scale at the high school level: A replication and extension. *Journal of Emotional and Behavioral Disorders, 21,* 97–115.

Lane, K. L., Oakes, W. P., Ennis, R. P., & Hirsch, S. E. (2014). Identifying students for secondary and tertiary prevention efforts: How do we determine which students have Tier 2 and Tier 3 needs? *Preventing School Failure, 58,* 171–182.

Lane, K. L., Oakes, W. P., Jenkins, A., Menzies, H. M., & Kalberg, J. R. (2014). A team-based process for designing Comprehensive, Integrated, Three-Tiered (Ci3T) Models of Prevention: How does my school-site leadership team design a Ci3T model? *Preventing School Failure, 58,* 129–142.

Lane, K. L., Oakes, W. P., & Magill, L. (2014). Primary prevention efforts: How do we implement and monitor the Tier 1 component of our Comprehensive, Integrated, Three-Tiered (Ci3T) Model? *Preventing School Failure, 58,* 143–158.

Lane, K. L., Oakes, W. P., & Menzies, H. M. (2010). Schoolwide Expectations Survey for Specific Settings (Rating scale). Retrieved from *www.ci3t.org/measures.*

Lane, K. L., Oakes, W. P., & Menzies, H. M. (2014). Comprehensive, Integrated, Three-Tiered Models of Prevention: Why does my school—and district—need an integrated approach to meet students' academic, behavioral, and social needs? *Preventing School Failure: Alternative Education for Children and Youth, 58,* 121–128.

Lane, K. L., Oakes, W. P., Royer, D. J., Cantwell, E. D., Menzies, H. M., & Jenkins, A. (2019). Using the schoolwide expectations survey for specific settings to build expectation matrices. *Remedial and Special Education, 40,* 51–62.

Lane, K. L., Oakes, W. P., Swogger, E. D., Schatschneider, C., Menzies, H. M., & Sanchez, J. (2015). Student Risk Screening Scale for Internalizing and Externalizing behaviors: Preliminary cut scores to support data-informed decision making. *Behavioral Disorders, 40,* 159–170.

Lane, K. L., Parks, R. J., Kalberg, J. R., & Carter, E. W. (2007). Systematic screening at the middle school level: Score reliability and validity of the Student Risk Screening Scale. *Journal of Emotional and Behavioral Disorders, 15,* 209–222.

Lane, K. L., Pierson, M., & Givner, C. C. (2004). Secondary teachers' views on social competence: Skills essential for success. *Journal of Special Education, 38,* 174–186.

Lane, K. L., Robertson, E. J., & Graham-Bailey, M. A. L. (2006). An examination of school-wide interventions with primary level efforts conducted in secondary schools: Methodological considerations. In T. E. Scruggs & M. A. Mastropieri (Eds.), *Applications of research methodology: Advances in learning and behavioral disabilities* (Vol. 19, pp. 157–200). Oxford, UK: Elsevier.

Lane, K. L., Robertson, E. J., Mofield, E., Wehby, J. H., & Parks, R. J. (2009). Preparing students for college entrance exams: Findings of a secondary intervention conducted within a three-tiered model of support. *Remedial and Special Education, 30,* 3–18.

Lane, K. L., Robertson, E. J., Parks, R. J., & Edwards, C. (2006, November). *Strategies for using school-wide data to identify students for secondary interventions: Illustrations at the elementary, middle, and high school levels.* Paper presented at the annual meeting of the Teacher Educators for Children with Behavioral Disorders, Tempe, AZ.

Lane, K. L., Robertson, E. J., & Wehby, J. H. (2002). Primary Intervention Rating Scale. Retrieved from *www.Ci3T.org/measures.*

Lane, K. L., Royer, D. J., Messenger, M. L., Common, E. A., Ennis, R. P., & Swogger, E. D. (2015). Empowering teachers with low-intensity strategies to support academic engagement: Implementation and effects of instructional choice for elementary students in inclusive settings. *Education and Treatment of Children, 38,* 473–504.

Lane, K. L., Royer, D. J., & Oakes, W. P. (in press). Literacy instruction for students with emotional and behavioral disorders: A developing knowledge base. In R. Boon, M. Burke, & L. Bowman-Perrott (Eds.), *Literacy instruction for students with emotional and behavioral disorders (EBD): Research-based interventions for the classroom.* Charlotte, NC: Information Age.

Lane, K. L., Stanton-Chapman, T. L., Roorbach, K. A., & Phillips, A. (2007). Teacher and parent expectations of preschoolers' behavior: Social skills necessary for success. *Topics in Early Childhood, 27,* 86–97.

Lane, K. L., & Walker, H. M. (2015). The connection between assessment and intervention: How does screening lead to better interventions? In B. Bateman, M. Tankersley, & J. Lloyd (Eds.), *Enduring issues in special education: Personal perspectives* (pp. 283–301). New York: Routledge.

Lane, K. L., & Wehby, J. H. (2002). Addressing antisocial behavior in the schools: A call for action. *Academic Exchange Quarterly, 6,* 4–9.

Lane, K. L., Wehby, J. H., & Cooley, C. (2006). Teacher expectations of student's classroom behavior across the grade span: Which social skills are necessary for success? *Exceptional Children, 72,* 153–167.

Lane, K. L., Wehby, J. H., Little, M. A., & Cooley, C. (2005a). Academic, social, and behavioral profiles of students with emotional and behavioral disorders educated in self-contained classrooms and self-contained schools: Part I. Are they more alike than different? *Behavioral Disorders, 30,* 349–361.

Lane, K. L., Wehby, J. H., Little, M. A., & Cooley, C. (2005b). Students educated in self-contained classes and self-contained schools: Part II. How do they progress over time? *Behavioral Disorders, 30,* 363–374.

Lane, K. L., Wehby, J., Menzies, H. M., Doukas, G. L., Munton, S. M., & Gregg, R. W. (2003). Social skills instruction for students at risk for antisocial behavior: The effects of small-group instruction. *Behavioral Disorders, 28,* 229–248.

Lane, K. L., Wehby, J. H., Menzies, H. M., Gregg, R. M., Doukas, G. L., & Munton, S. M. (2002). Early literacy instruction for first-grade students at-risk for antisocial behavior. *Education and Treatment of Children, 25,* 438–458.

Lane, K. L., Wehby, J. H., Robertson, E. J., & Rogers, L. A. (2007). How do different types of high school students respond to schoolwide positive behavior support programs?: Characteristics and responsiveness of teacher-identified students. *Journal of Emotional and Behavioral Disorders, 15,* 3–20.

Lanyon, R. (2006). Mental health screening: Utility of the psychological screening inventory. *Psychological Services, 3,* 170–180.

Lawson, G. M., McKenzie, M. E., Becker, K. D., Selby, L., & Hoover, S. A. (2018, November 16). The core components of evidence-based social emotional learning programs. *Prevention Science.* [Epub ahead of print]

Lee, D. L., Belfiore, P. J., Scheeler, M. C., Hua, Y., & Smith, R. (2004). Behavioral momentum in academics: Using embedded high-p sequences to increase academic productivity. *Psychology in the Schools, 41,* 789–801.

Lee, D. L., & Laspe, A. K. (2003). Using high-probability sequences to increase journal writing. *Journal of Behavioral Education, 12,* 261–273.

Leedy, A., Bates, P., & Safran, S. P. (2004). Bridging the research-to-practice gap: Improving hallway behavior using positive behavior supports. *Behavioral Disorders, 29,* 130–139.

Leerkes, E. M., Paradise, M., O'Brien, M., Calkins, S. D., & Lange, G. (2008). Emotion and cognition processes in preschool children. *Merrill–Palmer Quarterly, 54,* 102–124.

Leff, S. S., Costigan, T., & Power, T. J. (2003). Using participatory research to develop a playground-based prevention program. *Journal of School Psychology, 42,* 3–21.

Lembke, E. S., Hampton, D., & Beyers, S. J. (2012). Response to intervention in mathematics: Critical elements. *Psychology in the Schools, 49,* 257–272.

Lewis, T. J., Colvin, G., & Sugai, G. (2000). The effects of pre-correction and active supervision on the recess behavior of elementary students. *Education and Treatment of Children, 23*(2), 109–121.

Lewis, T. J., Powers, L. S., Kelk, M. J., & Newcomer, L. L. (2002). Reducing problem behaviors on the playground: An investigation of the application of schoolwide positive behavior supports. *Psychology in the Schools, 39,* 181–190.

Lewis, T. J., Sugai, G., & Colvin, G. (1998). Reducing problem behavior through a school-wide system of effective behavioral support: Investigation of a school-wide social skills training program and contextual interventions. *School Psychology Review, 27,* 446–459.

Lohrmann, S., Forman, S., Martin, S., & Palmieri, M. (2008). Understanding school personnel's resistance to adopting schoolwide positive behavior support at a universal level of intervention. *Journal of Positive Interventions, 10,* 256–269.

Lohrmann-O'Rourke, S., Knoster, T., Sabatine, K., Smith, D., Horvath, B., & Llewellyn, G. (2000). School-wide application of PBS in the Bangor area school district. *Journal of Positive Behavior Interventions, 2,* 238–240.

Low, S., Cook, C. R., Smolkowski, K., & Buntain-Ricklefs, J. (2015). Promoting social–emotional competence: An evaluation of the elementary version of Second Step. *Journal of School Psychology, 53,* 463–477.

Luiselli, J. K., Putnam, R. F., & Sunderland, M. (2002). Longitudinal evaluation of behavior support intervention in a public middle school. *Journal of Positive Behavior Interventions, 4,* 182–188.

Lyon, G. R. (1996). Learning disabilities. *The Future of Children, 6,* 54–76.

Mace, C. F., Hock, M. L., Lalli, J. S., West, B. J., Belfiore, P., Pinter, E., & Brown, K. D. (1988). Behavioral momentum in the treatment of noncompliance. *Journal of Applied Behavior Analysis, 21*, 123–141.

MacSuga-Gage, A. S., & Gage, N. A. (2015). Student-level effects of increased teacher-directed opportunities to respond. *Journal of Behavioral Education, 24*, 273–288.

Majeika, C. E., Walder, J. P., Hubbard, J. P., Steeb, K. M., & Ferris, G. J. (2011). Improving on-task behavior using a functional assessment-based intervention in an inclusive high school setting. *Beyond Behavior, 20*, 55–66.

Make time to evaluate your mission, vision statements. (2018). *Nonprofit Communications Report, 16*(9), 4–4.

Malmin, G. (2007). It Is My Choice (Lions Quest) evaluation part 5 of the report: The impact on the behavior of the students (Unpublished evaluation report). Retrieved from *www.lions-quest.org/evaluation-reports*.

Manyema, M., Norris, S., & Richter, L. (2018). Stress begets stress: the association of adverse childhood experiences with psychological distress in the presence of adult life stress. *BMC Public Health, 18*, 1–12.

Marchant, M., & Anderson, D. H. (2012). Improving social and academic outcomes for all learners through the use of teacher praise. *Beyond Behavior, 21*, 22–28.

Marchant, M., Heath, M. A., & Miramontes, N. Y. (2013). Merging empiricism and humanism: Role of social validity in the school-wide positive behavior support model. *Journal of Positive Behavior Interventions, 15*, 221–230.

Maslach, C., Jackson, S. E., & Leiter, M. P. (1996). *Maslach Burnout Inventory manual* (3rd ed.). Mountain View, CA: Consulting Psychology Press.

Mathews, S., McIntosh, K., Frank, J. L., & May, S. L. (2014). Critical features predicting sustained implementation of school-wide positive behavioral interventions and supports. *Journal of Positive Behavior Interventions, 16*, 168–178.

Mattison, R. E., Hooper, S. R., & Glassberg, L. A. (2002). Three-year course of learning disorders in special education students classified as behavioral disorder. *Journal of the American Academy of Child and Adolescent Psychiatry, 41*, 1454–1461.

May, S., Ard, W., Todd, A., Horner, R., Glasgow, A., Sugai, G., & Sprague, J. (2003). *School Wide Information System (SWIS)*. Eugene: University of Oregon, Educational and Community Supports.

Mayer, G. R., Butterworth, T., Nafpaktitis, M., & Sulzer-Azaroff, B. (1983). Preventing school vandalism and improving discipline: A three-year study. *Journal of Applied Behavior Analysis, 16*, 355–369.

McCurdy, B. L., Mannella, M. C., & Eldridge, N. (2003). Positive behavior support in urban schools: Can we prevent the escalation of antisocial behavior? *Journal of Positive Behavior Interventions, 5*, 158–170.

McDougal, J. L., Graney, S. B., Wright, J. A., & Ardoin, S. P. (2010). *RTI in practice: A practical guide to implementing effective evidence-based interventions in your school*. Hoboken, NJ: Wiley.

McIntosh, K., & Goodman, S. (2016). *Integrated multi-tiered systems of support: Blending RTI and PBIS*. New York: Guilford Press.

McIntosh, K., Martinez, R. S., Ty, S. V., & McClain, M. B. (2013). Scientific research in school psychology: Leading researchers weigh in on its past, present, and future. *Journal of School Psychology, 51*, 267–318.

McIntosh, K., Massar, M. M., Algozzine, R. F., George, H. P., Horner, R. H., Lewis, T. J., & Swain-Bradway, J. (2017). Technical adequacy of the SWPBIS tiered fidelity inventory. *Journal of Positive Behavior Interventions, 19*, 3–13.

McIntosh, K., Mercer, S. H., Nese, R. N. T., Strickland-Cohen, M. K., & Hoselton, R. (2016). Predictors of sustained implementation of school-wide positive behavioral interventions and supports. *Journal of Positive Behavior Interventions, 18*, 209–218.

McIntosh, K., Mercer, S. H., Nese, R. N. T., Strickland-Cohen, M. K., Kittelman, A., Hoselton, R., & Horner, R. H. (2018). Factors predicting sustained implementation of a universal behavior support framework. *Educational Researcher, 47*, 307–316.

McIntosh, K., Predy, L. K., Upreti, G., Hume, A. E., Turri, M. G., & Mathews, S. (2014). Perceptions of contextual features related to implementation and sustainability of school-wide positive behavior support. *Journal of Positive Behavior Interventions, 16*, 31–43.

McIntosh, K., Simonsen, B., Horner, R. H., Swain-Bradway, J., George, H., & Lewis, T. (2017). Getting back to school after disruptions: Resources for making your school year safer, more predictable, and more positive. Retrieved from *www.pbis.org/common/cms/files/pbisresources/back%20to%20 school%20after%20disruptions.pdf.*

McKelvey, L. M., McKelvey, N. C., Mesman, G. R., Whiteside-Mansell, L., & Bradley, R. H. (2018). Adverse experiences in infancy and toddlerhood: Relations to adaptive behavior and academic status in middle childhood. *Child Abuse and Neglect, 82*, 168–177.

McKeown, D., Kimball, K., & Ledford, J. (2015). Effects of asynchronous audio feedback on the story revision practices of students with emotional/behavioral disorders. *Education and Treatment of Children, 38*, 541–564.

Mehas, K., Boling, K., Sobieniak, J., Burke, M. D., & Hagan, S. (1998). Finding a safe haven in middle school. *Teaching Exceptional Children, 30*, 20–23.

Menzies, H. M., Lane, K. L., Oakes, W. P., Ruth, K., Cantwell, E. D., & Smith-Menzies, L. (2018). Active supervision: An effective, efficient, low-intensity strategy to support student success. *Beyond Behavior, 27*, 153–159.

Menzies, H. M., Mahdavi, J. N., & Lewis, J. L. (2008). Early intervention in reading: From research to practice. *Remedial and Special Education, 29*, 67–77.

Menzies, H. M., Oakes, W. P., Lane, K. L., Royer, D. J., Cantwell, E. D., Common, E. A., & Buckman, M. (2019). *Elementary teachers' perceptions of comprehensive, integrated, three-tiered models of prevention.* Manuscript submitted for publication.

Merikangas, K. R., He, J., Burstein, M., Swanson, S. A., Avenevoli, S., Cui, L., . . . Swendsen, J. (2010). Lifetime prevalence of mental disorders in U.S. adolescents: Results from the National Comorbidity Survey Replication—Adolescent Supplement (NCS-A). *Journal of the American Academy of Child and Adolescent Psychiatry, 49*, 980–989.

Merritt, E. G. (2016). Time for teacher learning, planning critical for school reform. *Phi Delta Kappan, 98*, 31–36.

Messenger, M., Common, E. A., Lane, K. L., Oakes, W. P., Menzies, H. M., Cantwell, E. D., & Ennis, R. P. (2017). Increasing opportunities to respond for students with internalizing behaviors: The utility of choral and mixed responding. *Behavioral Disorders, 42*, 170–184.

Metzler, C. W., Biglan, A., Rusby, J. C., & Sprague, J. R. (2001). Evaluation of a comprehensive behavior management program to improve school-wide positive behavior support. *Education and Treatment of Children, 24*, 448–480.

Meyer, A. L., Farrell, A. D., Northup, W., Kung, E., & Plybon, L. (2000). *Promoting nonviolence in early adolescence: Responding in peaceful and positive ways.* New York: Kluwer.

Mills, G. E., & Gay, L. R. (2019). *Educational research: Competencies for analysis and applications* (12th ed.). New York: Pearson.

Miramontes, N. Y., Marchant, M., Heath, M. A., & Fischer, L. (2011). Social validity of a positive behavior interventions and support model. *Education and Treatment of Children, 34*, 445–468.

Montalvo, R., Combes, B. H., & Kea, C. D. (2014). Perspectives on culturally and linguistically responsive RtI pedagogics through a cultural and linguistic lens. *Interdisciplinary Journal of Teaching and Learning, 4*(3), 203–219.

National Center for Education Statistics. (2015). *National assessment of educational progress: An overview of NAEP.* Washington, DC: Author.

National Center for Education Statistics. (2018). *National assessment of educational progress: An overview of NAEP.* Washington, DC: Author.

National Center on Intensive Intervention. (2017). Behavior screening rating rubric. Retrieved from *https://intensiveintervention.org/sites/default/files/ncii_bscreening_ratingrubric_july2017.pdf.*

Nelson, J. R. (1996). Designing schools to meet the needs of students who exhibit disruptive behavior. *Journal of Emotional and Behavioral Disorders, 4,* 147–161.

Nelson, J. R., Benner, G. J., Lane, K., & Smith, B. W. (2004). Academic achievement of K–12 students with emotional and behavioral disorders. *Exceptional Children, 71,* 59–73.

Nelson, J. R., Martella, R., & Galand, B. (1998). The effects of teaching school expectations and establishing a consistent consequence on formal office disciplinary actions. *Journal of Emotional and Behavioral Disorders, 6,* 153–161.

Nelson, J. R., Martella, R. M., & Marchand-Martella, N. (2002). Maximizing student learning: The effects of a comprehensive school-based program for preventing problem behaviors. *Journal of Emotional and Behavioral Disorders, 10,* 136–148.

Netzel, D. M., & Eber, L. (2003). Shifting from reactive to proactive discipline in an urban school district: A change of focus through PBIS implementation. *Journal of Positive Behavior Interventions, 5,* 71–79.

Nevin, J. A., Mandell, C., & Atak, J. R. (1983). The analysis of behavioral momentum. *Journal of Experimental Analysis of Behavior, 39,* 49–59.

Newman, L., Wagner, M., Knokey, A., Marder, C., Nagle, K., Shaver, D., & Wei, X. (2011) *The post-high school outcomes of young adults with disabilities up to 8 years after high school: A report from the National Longitudinal Transition Study-2 (NLTS2).* Menlo Park, CA: SRI International.

Noell, G. H., & Gresham, F. M. (1993). Functional outcome analysis: Do the benefits of consultation and prereferral interventions justify the costs? *School Psychology Quarterly, 8,* 200–226.

Oakes, W. P., Lane, K. L., Cantwell, E. D., & Royer, D. J. (2017). Systematic screening for behavior in K–12 settings as regular school practice: Practical considerations and recommendations. *Journal of Applied School Psychology, 33,* 369–393.

Oakes, W. P., Lane, K. L., Cox, M., Magrane, A., Jenkins, A., & Hankins, K. (2012). Tier 2 supports to improve motivation and performance of elementary students with behavioral challenges and poor work completion. *Education and Treatment of Children, 35,* 547–584.

Oakes, W. P., Lane, K. L., Cox, M. L., & Messenger, M. (2014). Logistics of behavior screenings: How and why do we conduct behavior screenings at our school? *Preventing School Failure, 58,* 159–170.

Oakes, W. P., Lane, K. L., & Germer, K. A. (2014). Developing the capacity to implement Tier 2 and Tier 3 supports: How do we support our faculty and staff in preparing for sustainability? *Preventing School Failure, 58,* 183–190.

Oakes, W. P., Lane, K. L., Jenkins, A., & Booker, B. B. (2013). Three-tiered models of prevention: Teacher efficacy and burnout. *Education and Treatment of Children, 36,* 95–126.

Oakes, W. P., Lane, K. L., Lane, K. S., & Buckman, M. M. (2019). Comprehensive, integrated, three-tiered model of prevention: Integrated lesson plan template. Retrieved from *www.ci3t.org.*

Oakes, W. P., Wilder, K., Lane, K. L., Powers, L., Yokoyama, L., O'Hare, M. E., & Jenkins, A. B. (2010). Psychometric properties of the Student Risk Screening Scale: An effective tool for use in diverse urban elementary schools. *Assessment for Effective Intervention, 35,* 231–239.

O'Connor, R. E., Notari-Syverson, A., & Vadasy, P. F. (2005). *Ladders to literacy: A kindergarten activity book.* Baltimore: Brookes.

Odom, S. L., Cox, A. W., Brock, M., & National Professional Development Center on Autism Spectrum Disorder. (2013). Implementation science, professional development, and autism spectrum disorders. *Exceptional Children, 79,* 233–251.

Olweus, D., Limber, S. P., Flerx, V., Mullin, N., Riese, J., & Snyder, M. (2007). *Olweus Bullying Prevention Program: Schoolwide guide.* Center City, MN: Hazelden.

Organisation for Economic Co-operation and Development. (2016). *PISA 2015 results: Vol. 1. Excellence and equity in education.* Paris: OECD.

Page, B. D., & D'Agostino, A. (2005). *Connect with Kids: 2004–2005 study results for Kansas and Missouri.* Durham, NC: Compass Consulting Group.

Pearson Education. (2013). *Scott Foresman Reading Street*. New York: Pearson Education.

Pearson Education. (2015a). *AIMSweb*. San Antonio, TX: Pearson Assessments.

Pearson Education. (2015b). *Q-global® Web-based administration, scoring, and reporting*. New York: Pearson Education.

Peterson, L. D., Homer, A., & Wonderlich, S. (1982). The integrity of independent variables in behavior analysis. *Journal of Applied Behavior Analysis, 15*, 177–192.

Peterson, L. D., Young, K. R., Salzberg, C. L., West, R. P., & Hill, M. (2006). Using self-management procedures to improve classroom social skills in multiple general education settings. *Education and Treatment of Children, 29*, 1–21.

Peterson, R. L., & Skiba, R. (2001). Creating school climates that prevent school violence. *The Clearing House, 94*, 155–163.

Pierce, W. D., & Cheney, C. D. (2017). *Behavior analysis and learning: A biobehavioral approach* (6th ed.). New York: Routledge.

Popham, W. J. (1999). Where large scale educational assessment is heading and why it shouldn't. *Educational Measurement: Issues and Practice, 18*, 13–17.

Purewal Boparai, S., Au, V., Koita, K., Oh, D. L., Briner, S., Burke Harris, N., & Bucci, M. (2018). Ameliorating the biological impacts of childhood adversity: A review of intervention programs. *Child Abuse and Neglect, 81*, 82–105.

Ramsey, M. L., Jolivette, K., Patterson, D. P., & Kennedy, C. (2010). Using choice to increase time on-task, task-completion, and accuracy for students with emotional/behavior disorders in a residential facility. *Education and Treatment of Children, 33*, 1–21.

Reid, R., Gonzalez, J. E., Nordness, P. D., Trout, A., & Epstein, M. H. (2004). A meta-analysis of the academic status of students with emotional/behavioral disturbance. *Journal of Special Education, 38*, 130–143.

Reimers, T. M., Wacker, D. P., & Koeppl, G. (1987). Acceptability of behavioral treatments: A review of the literature. *School Psychology Review, 15*, 212–227.

Reynolds, C. R., & Kamphaus, R. W. (2015). *Behavior Assessment System for Children, Third Edition (BASC-3)*. San Antonio, TX: Pearson Education.

Riggs, N. R., Greenberg, M. T., Kusche, C. A., & Pentz, M. A. (2006). The mediational role of neurocognition in the behavioral outcomes of a social–emotional prevention program in elementary school students: Effects of the PATHS Curriculum. *Prevention Science, 7*, 91–102.

Robertson, E. J., & Lane, K. L. (2007). Supporting middle school students with academic and behavioral concerns within the context of a three-tiered model of support: Findings of a secondary prevention program. *Behavioral Disorders, 33*, 5–22.

Rogers, E. M. (1995). *Diffusion of preventive innovations* (4th ed.). New York: Free Press.

Rogers, E. M. (2002). Diffusion of preventative innovations. *Addictive Behaviors, 27*, 989–993.

Ross, S. W., & Horner, R. H. (2007). Teacher outcomes of school-wide positive behavior support. *Teaching Exceptional Children Plus, 3*(6), Article No. 6.

Ross, S. W., Romer, N., & Horner, R. H. (2011). Teacher well-being and the implementation of school-wide positive behavior interventions and supports. *Journal of Positive Behavior Interventions, 14*, 118–128.

Royer, D. J., Lane, K. L., Cantwell, E. D., & Messenger, M. (2017). A systematic review of the evidence base for instructional choice in K–12 settings. *Behavioral Disorders, 42*, 89–107.

Sadler, R. (1989). Formative assessment and the design of instructional systems. *Instructional Science, 18*, 119–144.

Scott, T. M. (2001). A schoolwide example of positive behavioral support. *Journal of Positive Behavior Interventions, 3*, 88–94.

Scott, T. M., & Barrett, S. B. (2004). Using staff and student time engaged in disciplinary procedures to evaluate the impact of school-wide PBS. *Journal of Positive Behavior Interventions, 6*, 21–27.

Scott, T. M., & Caron, D. B. (2005). Conceptualizing functional behavior assessment as prevention practice within positive behavior support systems. *Preventing School Failure, 50*, 13–20.

Seastrom, M. M. (2002). NCES Statistical Standards. Retrieved from *https://nces.ed.gov/statprog/2002/stdtoc.asp*.

Severson, H. H., & Walker, H. M. (2002). Proactive approaches for identifying children at risk for sociobehavioral problems. In K. L. Lane, F. M. Gresham, & T. E. O'Shaughnessy (Eds.), *Interventions for children with or at risk for emotional and behavioral disorders* (pp. 33–53). Boston: Allyn & Bacon.

Shinn, M. R., Tindal, G. A., & Spira, D. A. (1987). Special education referrals as an index of teacher tolerance: Are teachers imperfect tests? *Exceptional Children, 54,* 32–40.

Simcha-Fagan, O., Langner, T., Gersten, J., & Eisenberg, J. (1975). *Violent and antisocial behavior: A longitudinal study of urban youth* (No. OCD-CB-480). Unpublished report, Office of Child Development, Department of Health, Education, and Welfare, Washington, DC.

Simonsen, B., & Freeman, J. (2015, October). *Positive classroom behavior support: Overview of critical practices and decision-making guide for K–12 classrooms.* Presentation at the National PBIS Leadership Forum, Rosemont, IL. Retrieved from *www.pbis.org/common/cms/files/forum15_presentations/a3_simonsen_freeman.pdf.*

Simonsen, B., Freeman, J., Goodman, S., Mitchell, B., Swain-Bradway, J., Flannery, B., . . . Putman, B. (2015). *Supporting and responding to behavior: Evidence-based classroom strategies for teachers.* Washington, DC: Office of Special Education Programs, U.S. Department of Education.

Skiba, R., & Peterson, R. (2003). Teaching social curriculum: School discipline as instruction. *Preventing School Failure, 47,* 66–73.

Skibbe, L. E., Phillips, B. M., Day, S. L., Brophy-Herb, H. E., & Connor, C. M. (2012). Children's early literacy growth in relation to classmates' self-regulation. *Journal of Educational Psychology, 104,* 541–553.

Special Education Elementary Longitudinal Study. (n.d.). SRI International. Retrieved from *www.sri.com/work/projects/special-education-elementary-longitudinal-study-seels.*

Sprague, J., Walker, H. M., Golly, A., White, K., Myers, D. R., & Shannon, T. (2001). Translating research into effective practice: The effects of a universal staff and student intervention on indicators of discipline and school safety. *Education and Treatment of Children, 24,* 495–511.

Stearns, P. N., & Stearns, C. (2017). American schools and the uses of shame: An ambiguous history. *History of Education, 46,* 58–75.

Stewart, R. M., Martella, R. C., Marchand-Martella, N. E., & Benner, G. J. (2005). Three-tier models of reading and behavior. *Journal of Early and Intensive Behavior Intervention, 2,* 115–124.

Stormont, M., Reinke, W. M., Newcomer, L., Marchese, D., & Lewis, C. (2015). Coaching teachers' use of social behavior interventions to improve children's outcomes: A review of the literature. *Journal of Positive Behavior Interventions, 17,* 69–82.

Stormont, M. A., Smith, S. C., & Lewis, T. J. (2007). Teacher implementation of precorrection and praise statements in Head Start classrooms as a component of a program-wide system of positive behavior support. *Journal of Behavioral Education, 16,* 280–290.

Sugai, G., & Horner, R. (2002). The evolution of discipline practices: School-wide positive behavior supports. *Child and Family Behavior Therapy, 24,* 23–50.

Sugai, G., & Horner, R. H. (2006). A promising approach for expanding and sustaining school-wide positive behavior support. *School Psychology Review, 35,* 245–260.

Sugai, G., & Horner, R. H. (2009). Responsiveness-to-intervention and school-wide positive behavior supports: Integration of multi-tiered system approaches. *Exceptionality, 17,* 223–237.

Sugai, G., Lewis-Palmer, T., Todd, A., & Horner, R. H. (2005). *School-wide Evaluation Tool Version 2.1.* Eugene: University of Oregon.

Sutherland, K. S., & Wehby, J. H. (2001). Exploring the relationship between increased opportunities to respond to academic requests and the academic behavioral outcomes of students with EBD: A review. *Remedial and Special Education, 22,* 113–121.

Sutherland, K. S., Wehby, J. H., & Copeland, S. R. (2000). Effect of varying rates of behavior-specific praise on the on-task behavior of students with EBD. *Journal of Emotional and Behavioral Disorders, 8,* 2–8.

Sutherland, K., & Wright, S. A. (2013). Students with disabilities and academic engagement: Classroom-based interventions. In K. L. Lane, B. G. Cook, & M. Tankersley (Eds.), *Research-based strategies for improving outcomes in behavior* (pp. 34–45). Boston: Pearson.

Swain-Bradway, J., Putman, R., Freeman, J., Simonsen, B., George, H., Goodman, S., . . . Sprague, J. (2017). *PBIS technical guide on classroom data: Using data to support implementation of positive classroom behavior support practices and systems.* Eugene, OR: Positive Behavior Interventions & Support OSEP Technical Assistance Center.

Taylor-Greene, S., Brown, D., Nelson, L., Longton, J., Gassman, T., Cohen, J., . . . Hall, S. (1997). School-wide behavioral support: Starting the year off right. *Journal of Behavioral Education, 7,* 99–112.

Taylor-Greene, S. J., & Kartub, D. T. (2000). Durable implementation of school-wide behavior support. *Journal of Positive Behavior Support, 2,* 233–235.

Thangarajathi, S., & Joel, T. E. (2010). Classroom management: A challenging task for the teachers. *Journal on Educational Psychology, 4,* 11–18.

Todd, A., Haugen, L., Anderson, K., & Spriggs, M. (2002). Teaching recess: Low-cost efforts producing effective results. *Journal of Positive Behavior Interventions, 4,* 46–52.

Torgesen, J. K., & Bryant, B. R. (1994). *Phonological awareness training for reading.* Austin, TX: PRO-ED.

Tschannen-Moran, M., & Woolfolk Hoy, A. (2001). Teacher efficacy: Capturing an elusive construct. *Teaching and Teacher Education, 17,* 783–805.

Ttofi, M. M., & Farrington, D. (2011). Effectiveness of school-based programs to reduce bullying: A systematic and meta-analytic review. *Journal of Experimental Criminology, 7,* 27–56.

Umbreit, J., Ferro, J., Liaupsin, C., & Lane, K. L. (2007). *Functional behavioral assessment and function-based intervention: An effective, practical approach.* Upper Saddle River, NJ: Prentice Hall.

Upshur, C. C., Heyman, M., & Wenz-Gross, M. (2017). Efficacy trial of the Second Step Early Learning (SSEL) curriculum: Preliminary outcomes. *Journal of Applied Developmental Psychology, 50,* 15–25.

U.S. Department of Education, Institute of Education Sciences. (2018). Request for Application: Partnerships and collaborations focused on problems of practice or policy (CFDA Number: 84.324N). Retrieved from *www.grants.gov.*

U.S. Department of Education, Institute of Education Sciences, What Works Clearinghouse. (2016). Children identified with or at risk for an emotional disturbance topic area intervention report: Functional behavioral assessment-based interventions. Retrieved from *http://whatworks. ed.gov.*

Vancel, S. M., Missall, K. N., & Bruhn, A. L. (2016). Teacher ratings of the social validity of schoolwide positive behavior interventions and supports: A comparison of school groups. *Preventing School Failure, 60,* 320–328.

Vannest, K., Reynolds, C. R., & Kamphaus, R. (2015). *BASC-3 Behavioral and Emotional Skill Building Guide.* San Antonio, TX: Pearson Education PsychCorp.

von der Embse, N. P., Sandilos, L. E., Pendergast, L., & Mankin, A. (2016). Teacher stress, teaching-efficacy, and job satisfaction in response to test-based educational accountability policies. *Learning and Individual Differences, 50,* 308–317.

Wagner, M., & Davis, M. (2006). How are we preparing students with emotional disturbances for the transition to young adulthood?: Findings from the National Longitudinal Transition Study–2. *Journal of Emotional and Behavioral Disorders, 14,* 86–98.

Walker, B., Cheney, D., Stage, S., Blum, C., & Horner, R. H. (2005). Schoolwide screening and positive behavior supports: Identifying and supporting students at risk for school failure. *Journal of Positive Behavior Interventions, 7,* 194–204.

Walker, H. M., Block-Pedego, A., Todis, B., & Severson, H. (1991). *School Archival Records Search (SARS): User's guide and technical manual.* Longmont, CO: Sopris West.

Walker, H. M., Colvin, G., & Ramsey, E. (1995). Antisocial behavior in school: Strategies and best practices. *Behavioral Disorders, 21,* 253–255.

Walker, H. M., Forness, S. R., & Lane, K. L. (2014). Design and management of scientific research in applied school settings. In B. Cook, M. Tankersley, & T. Landrum (Eds.), *Advances in learning and behavioral disabilities* (Vol. 27, pp. 141–169). Bingley, UK: Emerald.

Walker, H. M., Hops, H., & Greenwood, C. (1993). *RECESS: A program for reducing negative-aggressive behavior.* Seattle, WA: Educational Achievement Systems.

Walker, H. M., Horner, R. H., Sugai, G., Bullis, M., Sprague, J. R., Bricker, D., & Kaufman, M. J. (1996). Integrated approaches to preventing antisocial behavior patterns among school-age children and youth. *Journal of Emotional and Behavioral Disorders, 4,* 194–209.

Walker, H. M., Irvin, L. K., Noell, J., & Singer, G. H. (1992). A construct score approach to the assessment of social competence: Rationale, technological considerations, and anticipated outcomes. *Behavior Modification, 16,* 448–474.

Walker, H. M., Ramsey, E., & Gresham, F. M. (2004). *Antisocial behavior in school: Evidence-based practices* (2nd ed.). Belmont, CA: Wadsworth.

Walker, H. M., & Rankin, R. J. (1983). Assessing behavioral expectations and demands of less restrictive settings. *School Psychology Review, 12,* 274–284.

Walker, H. M., & Severson, H. (1992). *Systematic Screening for Behavior Disorders: User's guide and technical manual.* Longmont, CO: Sopris West.

Walker, H. M., Severson, H. H., & Feil, E. G. (2014). *Systematic Screening for Behavior Disorders (SSBD) technical manual: Universal screening for PreK–9* (2nd ed.). Eugene, OR: Pacific Northwest.

Walker, H. M., Zeller, R. W., Close, D. W., Webber, J., & Gresham, F. (1999). The present unwrapped: Change and challenge in the field of behavior disorders. *Behavioral Disorders, 24,* 293–304.

Wanzek, J., Stevens, E. A., Williams, K. J., Scammacca, N., Vaughn, S., & Sargent, K. (2018). Current evidence on the effects of intensive early reading interventions. *Journal of Learning Disabilities, 51,* 612–624.

Watson, R. (2015). *Keynote address.* Presented at the annual conference of the Kansas State Department of Education, Kansas City, KS.

Webster-Stratton, C. H., Reid, M. J., & Beauchaine, T. (2011). Combining parent and child training for young children with ADHD. *Journal of Clinical Child and Adolescent Psychology, 40,* 191–203.

Webster-Stratton, C., Reid, M. J., & Stoolmiller, M. (2008). Preventing conduct problems and improving school readiness: An evaluation of the Incredible Years Teacher and Child Training Program in high risk schools. *Journal of Child Psychology and Psychiatry, 49,* 471–488.

Wehby, J. H., Falk, K. B., Barton-Arwood, S., Lane, K. L., & Cooley, C. (2003). Impact of comprehensive reading instruction on the academic and social behavior of students with emotional and behavioral disorders. *Journal of Emotional and Behavioral Disorders, 11,* 225–238.

Wehby, J. H., & Hollahan, S. (2000). Effects of high probability requests on the latency to initiate academic tasks. *Journal of Applied Behavior Analysis, 33,* 259–262.

Weist, M. D., Garbacz, S. A., Lane, K. L., & Kincaid, D. (Eds.). (2017). *Aligning and integrating family engagement in Positive Behavioral Interventions and Supports (PBIS): Concepts and strategies for families and schools in key contexts.* Eugene: University of Oregon Press.

Weist, M. D., Lever, N. A., Bradshaw, C. P., & Owens, S. J. (2014). *Handbook of school mental health: Research, training, practice, and policy.* New York: Springer.

What Works Clearinghouse. (2008). Practice guide: Reducing behavior problems in the elementary school classroom. Retrrieved from *https://ies.ed.gov/ncee/wwc/practice.guide/4.*

What Works Clearinghouse. (2011). Procedures and standards handbook (V 2.1). Retrieved from *http://ies.ed.gov/ncee/wwc/pdf/reference_resources/wwc_procedures_v2_1_standards_handbook.pdf.*

Whitford, D. K., & Addis, A. K. (2017). Caregiver engagement: Advancing academic and behavioral outcomes for culturally and linguistically diverse students in special education. *National Association of Secondary School Principals Bulletin, 101,* 241–255.

Witt, J. C., & Elliott, S. N. (1985). Acceptability of classroom intervention strategies. In T. R. Kratochwill (Ed.), *Advances in school psychology* (Vol. 4, pp. 251–288). Mahwah, NJ: Erlbaum.

Wolf, M. M. (1978). Social validity: The case for subjective measurement or how applied behavior analysis is finding its heart. *Journal of Applied Behavior Analysis, 11,* 203–214.

Wong, H., & Wong, R. (1998). *How to be an effective teacher: The first days of school.* Mountain View, CA: Wong.

Woodcock, R. W., McGrew, K. S., & Mather, N. (2001). *Woodcock–Johnson III Tests of Achievement.* Itasca, IL: Riverside.

Yeaton, W., & Sechrest, L. (1981). Critical dimensions in the choice and maintenance of successful treatments: Strength, integrity, and effectiveness. *Journal of Consulting and Clinical Psychology, 49,* 156–167.

Youth in Mind. (2012). What is the SDQ? Retrieved from *http://sdqinfo.org/a0.html.*

Yudin, M. (2014, October). *PBIS: Providing opportunity. the National PBIS Leadership Forum.* Keynote address presented at the National PBIS Building Capacity and Partnerships to Enhance Educational Reform, Rosemont, IL.

Index

Note. b, f, or *t* following a page number indicates a box, a figure, or a table.